MARTIN BUBER

The Life of Dialogue

MARTIN BUBER

The Life of Dialogue

MAURICE S. FRIEDMAN

The University of Chicago Press
Chicago and London

For Eugenia

The University of Chicago Press, Chicago 60637
The University of Chicago Press, Ltd., London

Copyright © 1960 by Maurice S. Friedman
© 1976 by The University of Chicago
Copyright in the International Copyright Union, 1955
All rights reserved. Published 1955. Phoenix Edition 1976
Printed in the United States of America

ISBN: 0-226-26354-1 (clothbound); 0-226-26356-8 (paperback)
Library of Congress Catalog Card Number: 55-5126

CONTENTS

v

Contents

PREFACE TO THE THIRD EDITION

Among the essays that Martin Buber selected just before his death for preservation in *A Believing Humanism: Gleanings* is a short piece entitled 'In Twenty Years.' This preface might well be entitled 'After Twenty Years,' for it is just twenty years ago that the first edition of *Martin Buber: The Life of Dialogue* was published by Routledge & Kegan Paul in London and the University of Chicago Press in America. At the time of its publication, *The Life of Dialogue* was the first comprehensive and systematic study of Buber's thought in any language; Walter Goldstein's four-volume *Die Botschaft Martin Bubers* was begun earlier than my book but completed later.

When I first encountered Buber in 1944, only two of his works were in English translation, both published only in England: *I and Thou* and an early, inadequate translation of *The Legend of the Baal-Shem*. Today, twenty years after the original publication of *The Life of Dialogue*, well over thirty of Buber's works have been published in English translation, the number in America now exceeding that in England. All of these, with the exception of *Martin Buber and the Theater* and *On the Bible*, have been printed in paperback; *For the Sake of Heaven* in the Atheneum edition was printed, unfortunately, without the important foreword that Buber wrote for the second edition.

In my preface to the original and to the second edition of *The Life of Dialogue* I wrote, "In treating a thinker whom many have criticized before understanding, my aim, first of all, has been to understand." The most important exception to this statement was Hans Kohn's intellectual biography *Martin Buber: Sein Werk und Seine Zeit*, first published in 1930. My remark was particularly aimed, in fact, at the relatively sparse number of commentaries on Buber's thought in English. Since the original publication of *The Life of Dialogue* a spate of books about Buber have been published in England and America—some more scholarly and some more popular, some more concerned with Buber's thought and some with his life, most by a single author but some by many authors, some by Catholics, some by Protestants, and some by Jews. While there has been no lack of misunderstandings of Buber's thought in these commentaries, Buber scholarship in English has reached a new stage of sophistication and insight. In this connection, I should mention in particular Grete Schaeder's masterful work translated into English as *The Hebrew Humanism of Martin Buber*, and a number of less scholarly and impressive, though still praiseworthy, books, such as those by Arthur Cohen, Malcolm Diamond, Aubrey Hodes, Donald J. Moore, Roy Oliver, Paul Pfuetze, Ronald Gregor Smith, and Robert O. Wood. Also worthy of special mention are the thirty or so essays initiated by Paul Arthur Schilpp and edited by me in *The Philosophy of Martin Buber*, a volume in Schilpp's series *The Library of Living Philosophers*, plus the shorter exchanges between thirty-five thinkers and Martin Buber which I conducted, edited, and organized as the first section of Sidney and Beatrice Rome's *Philosophical Interrogations*.

In the words of the distinguished Protestant biblical scholar J. Coert Rylaarsdam, Martin Buber 'is in a unique way the agent through whom, in our day, Judaism and Christianity have met and enriched one another.' If this statement, which I quote in *The Life of Dialogue*, is even more true today than when Professor Rylaarsdam made it, it must be qualified by the recognition that a new stage has been reached in the Jewish-Christian ecumenical dialogue since the earlier periods of Buber's influence. During these early periods, as I show in the chapter 'Buber and Christianity' in *The Life of Dialogue*, Buber's influence on Christian thought was truly revolutionary; yet it was mostly christianized in the process of being taken over, so that many of its salient features were lost. For example, Buber's I-Thou relationship became a Thou-I relationship for many neo-orthodox theologians, who wished to cling to the sundering of God and man through original sin and the total dependency of man on God's grace through faith in Christ. For many, it became a choice *between* I-Thou and I-It, rather than the alternation of the two, as Buber held. For others, only Christ could have an I-Thou relationship with God, whereas ordinary men were largely condemned to I-It. For still others, Christ was the Thou rather than the imageless God to whom Buber points. Finally, far more attention was paid by Christian theologians to the I-Thou relationship between man and God and far less to that between man and man, as a result of which the integral unity of the two in Buber's thought tended to be lost sight of. Even the biblical-sounding language of 'Thou' in Ronald Gregor Smith's beautiful translation of *I and Thou* misled many into thinking of Buber solely in theological terms rather than in the interhuman and anthropological terms which were central for him. In this lies the virtue of Walter Kaufmann's rendering of the *'ich-du Beziehung'* as 'I-You' in his new and far more prosaic translation of *I and Thou*.

If this trend is beginning to be corrected and a new and more authentic Buber renaissance is under way, as the lead article in the London *Times Literary Supplement* for December 28, 1973, suggests may be the case, it is because men like my own former student Father Donald J. Moore, S. J., instead of appropriating Buber for Christianity, have allowed themselves to enter into an open, mutual dialogue with this prophet of the 'narrow ridge' and let their own Christianity be modified by it. These men do not seek to 'baptize' Buber, like the young seminarian who, after talking with me for three hours, plaintively said in parting, 'Buber is so good. How is it that he is not a Christian?' Instead, they recognize, as Father Moore puts it, that 'we who call ourselves Christian would be much more faithful to our task and to our vocation if we could follow, each in his own way, the spirit of Buber.' If this means, as Father Moore also says, that Buber should be called 'a man of universal religion, for he was indeed a man of God,' this universalism itself must be understood as precisely that of the life of dialogue. If Buber did not use his Judaism to shut himself away from persons of other faiths, neither did he have to leave the ground of his Judaism to meet openhearted men and women of other religions. 'I can stand in the doorway of my ancestral house,' Buber wrote, 'and speak into the street. The word that is uttered there will not go astray.'

Many American Jews, including distinguished rabbis, at first greeted Buber's thought with suspicion because of his influence on Christianity, and Protestantism in particular. Today Buber has found a secure place in the thought of American Judaism of all kinds, notwithstanding the fact that he cannot be identified with Reform, Conservative, Reconstructionist, or Orthodox Judaism and that his attitudes toward the Jewish law and toward Arab-Israeli rapprochement make him even now a controversial figure in America and in Israel. There is hardly a single one of the new Jewish theologians—such as Emil Fackenheim, Eugene Borowitz, Arthur Cohen, and Steven Schwarzchild, to name a few—who has not been decisively influenced by his encounter with Buber's thought.

Another way in which the appreciation of Buber has come of age in our day is the recognition that the 'death of God' theologies and above all the impact of Dietrich Bonhoeffer, far from dating Buber, have served to bring into focus the fact that Buber was essentially a 'prophet of religious secularism,' to use the subtitle of Father Moore's book. Religious secularism, to Buber, is that claim for the hallowing of the everyday and the sanctifying of the profane which stands in uncompromising opposition to every tendency to make of religion a separate upper story of spirituality with no binding force in our lives. 'Religion,' Buber once wrote, 'is the great enemy of mankind.' By 'religion' Buber meant the tendency of every organized religion throughout history to promote and sanction a dualism that obscures the face of God and leaves our ordinary lives unhallowed and unhallowable. Buber never attacked organized religion as such, but neither did he support it. It had to submit to the criterion of its place within the dialectic of the movement toward meeting with the eternal Thou and the movement away from it. For Buber, the *mitzvah*, or command of God, can never be divorced from the address of the particular hour and the particular situation and turned into a universally valid prescription or law.

Buber's view of revelation is not one of dialogue without content, as such Orthodox Jewish critics as Eliezer Berkovitz have claimed. But the 'content' is not separable from the form, the address from the unique situation in which the address is heard, and the Torah that is revealed in such situations is not 'law' in the Roman sense of that term but is God's instruction in the dialogue with him. It is not because there is no content but because the content is so irreducibly concrete and so intimately wedded to the uniqueness of the situation and the person's responsibility for it, that Buber could not agree with his friend Franz Rosenzweig on accepting *Halakah* as a universal and then discovering what part of it one can fulfill. Here, as elsewhere in Buber's thought, it is not I-Thou *or* I-It which is the basic choice, but the healthy alternation between I-Thou and I-It. It is this alternation that allows every It to be taken again into the meeting with Thou, every structure to be brought again and again into the meeting between person and person, community and community, people and God, mortal I and 'eternal Thou.'

When *Martin Buber: The Life of Dialogue* was first published, it received widespread recognition and almost universal acclaim in America and England. *Time* had a two-page story on it. The *New York Times Book Review* published a highly commendatory review by the great American theologian Reinhold Niebuhr. Over a hundred reviews of the book appeared in America and England, and Ronald Gregor Smith, the translator of *I and Thou* and *Between Man and Man*, gave an hour presentation about it on the BBC. Martin Buber himself actively sought to arrange for the publication of the book in German, Hebrew, and Japanese. In writing his old friend and long-standing publisher Dr. Lambert Schneider of Heidleberg, Buber characterized *The Life of Dialogue* as 'the classic study of my thought,' and urged him to bring it out as an integral part of a projected many-volume edition of his complete works.

Some of the attention that *The Life of Dialogue* received was due to its being the first study of its kind. Today, twenty years later, when so many studies of Buber have been published in so many languages, including some of great comprehensiveness and authority such as Grete Schaeder's *Hebrew Humanism*, it is quite possible that Martin Buber would call *The Life of Dialogue* a (rather than *the*) 'classic study of my thought.' But that does not mean that *The Life of Dialogue* has been superseded or dated by any of the commentaries that have followed, including my own. For it is still the only systematic study of the development of Buber's philosophy, the dialectic between interpretation and original philosophy, and the application of his philosophy to such fields as theory of knowledge, philosophical anthropology, education, psychotherapy, ethics, social and political philosophy, and the interpretation and philosophy of religion. This is what led Buber himself to write of *The Life of Dialogue*:

> To systematize a wild-grown thought as mine is, without impairing its elementary character seems to me a remarkable achievement. On a rather multifarious work Dr. Friedman has not imposed an artificial unity: he has disclosed a hidden one.

As the only single-volume comprehensive study of Buber's thought, *The Life of Dialogue* can serve both as an introduction to Buber's works for those who have not yet read him and as a commentary and systematic presentation for those who have. The most obvious form in which the unity of Buber's thought expresses itself is his philosophy of dialogue, and much of this book is centered on the developments and implications of that philosophy. But I have also drawn Buber's thoughts together in terms of his attitude toward the nature and redemption of evil. In addition I have attempted to show the significance of Buber's life of dialogue and his attitude toward the redemption of evil for such fields as ethics, social philosophy, psychotherapy, and education.

In systematizing and ordering Buber's thought and evaluating the use that others have made of it, I have had to deal again and again with a special problem—the faithful presentation of the dialogue that existed throughout Buber's creative life between Buber as original thinker and Buber as interpreter of many different religious, literary, and philosophical traditions. Here too one must walk the 'narrow ridge'—between the temptation, which Gershom Scholem, the authority on Jewish mysticism, has fallen into, of considering Buber a thinker who reads his philosophy into his interpretations and that which Carl Jung and W. T. Stace fell into, of considering him a thinker who derives his philosophy almost wholly from his religious tradition.

What is true of Buber's relation to tradition is also true of my relation to Buber. I have not simply read my own thoughts into Buber nor have I merely been a conduit through which Buber's thoughts have flowed unchanged to the readers of my translations, introductions, commentaries, and interpretations of Buber's works. Among the thirty or more works by Buber published in English translation a dozen have been translated and edited by me, in most cases with an introduction, an introductory essay, or even several chapters by me. If through this work, through my editing of the Buber volume of *The Library of Living Philosophers* and the Buber section of *Philosophical Interrogations*, and the many, many courses, lectures, seminars, workshops, and encounter groups I have given or conducted using Buber as principal content or springboard, I have had some share in Buber's becoming so well-known in the English-speaking world in the last twenty years, it is not because I have accepted his thought uncritically or on faith but because I have made it my own. *The Life of Dialogue* was and is a product of my dialogue, first with the works of Martin Buber and later with Martin Buber himself. I brought to that dialogue the existential questions that were real to me, and on the basis of those questions allowed the works to speak to my condition as they would, singling out those passages that called me forth and leaving aside those that did not. In writing *The Life of Dialogue* I found it necessary to stretch my mind, heart, and spirit beyond their usual boundaries to comprehend the meaning and the implications of Buber's thought. In this sense *The Life of Dialogue* is anything but subjective. In order to hear and respond faithfully to the voice that spoke to me through his writings, I had to practice 'inclusion'—to imagine concretely Buber's side of the relationship. By the same token, the comprehensive and systematic character of this book should not mislead the reader into regarding it as some kind of detached, academic exercise. Although the product may not show it, my deepest passion during those years went into plumbing the depths of each of the fields into which Buber had penetrated. Buber, as Carl Friedrichs once said to me, is a seminal thinker. I have tried to nourish these seeds and help them grow into plants—not out of personal loyalty to Buber but out of deep concern for the issues he dealt with. For the same reason, during the quarter of a century in which I have worked on Buber's life and thought, I have also produced a corpus of my own which, while profoundly influenced by my philosophical development of dialogue as a method, a theory of knowledge, and a hermeneutic, is in no sense merely an extension of my Buber work. Three of my books have grown out of a profound concern about the absence of a direction-giving image of the human in our time and the attempts to create such an image to fill the void. *Problematic Rebel* (1963 and 1970) is an intensive study of Melville, Dostoievsky, Kafka, and Camus; *To Deny Our Nothingness* (1967) is an extensive study of contemporary images of man drawing from the writings of thirty philosophers, religious thinkers, literary writers, social thinkers, and psychologists; and *The Hidden Human Image* (1974) is an attempt to apply the conclusions of the first two books on the human image to such fields as science, scientism, and human nature, psychology and psychotherapy, the meeting of literature and religion, anxiety, death, sex, love, and women's liberation, education, encounter groups, and social change. *The Worlds of Existentialism* is an attempt to do justice to the whole range of existentialism by grouping the various thinkers and writers under such foci and issues as phenomenology and ontology, the existential subject, intersubjectivity, atheist, humanist, religious, and theological existentialism, and the meeting of existential philosophy and the theory and practice of psychology and psychotherapy. Finally, *Touchstones of Reality* (1972, 1974) is an autobiographical account of my journey through socialism, pacifism, mysticism, and psychodrama to my present existentialism of dialogue, a report of my own dialogue with the great religions of the world and a discussion of such issues as the limits of the psyche as touchstone of reality, the crisis of values, the partnership of existence, existential trust, and the meaning of trust and openness as opposed to the meaning of theological systems and philosophical world-views.

This last book deserves special mention because in it I have tried to accomplish something that I once saw in the context of a possible revision of *The Life of Dialogue*. About five years after the original publication of *The Life of Dialogue*, I wrote to Martin Buber saying that if I were to write it again I would write a conclusion showing 'existential trust' to be the real heart of Buber's teaching. Buber replied that I was right, that existential trust was indeed the heart of the attitude underlying his life and thought. Since then I have expounded my own understanding of 'basic trust' in *Touchstones of Reality*, the subtitle of which is 'Existential Trust and the Community of Peace.' The essence of *Touchstones* lies in the integral relationship between 'existential trust' and what I call the 'community of otherness.' In *Touchstones*, I show 'existential trust' growing out of the 'partnership of existence' and enabling the modern person to live without the intellectual and creedal securities of earlier theological systems and philosophical world-views. What is more in the chapter on existential trust I consciously replace Tillich's more abstract concept of the 'courage to be' with the more concrete and meaningful concept of the 'courage to address and the courage to respond.'

When I said that none of the later commentaries on Buber's life and thought had superseded *The Life of Dialogue*, I also had in mind my own *Encounter on the Narrow Ridge*, the biography of Buber, the first half of which I finished five years ago and which I hope to publish as a whole by the end of 1976. In this book I allow my dialogue with Buber itself to show and not just the product of that dialogue as in *The Life of Dialogue*. At first I hoped to do this by letting the book 'flow' out of my years of immersion in Buber's thought and life without the paraphernalia of references and footnotes. In point of fact, I have found myself doing more and more complex research for this book than for any I have undertaken in my life—so much so, indeed, that it seems to me futile to attempt to list in the expanded bibliography at the end of this third edition of *The Life of Dialogue* all the sources on which I am drawing for my 'critical biography.' Nonetheless, my goal for this work, which sets it clearly apart from the present book, is to show the encounters themselves —the meetings on the narrow ridge of history and personal life—and the way in which Buber's thought, his image of the human, and his great interpretations grew out of his response to these events and meetings.

'Worte an die Zeit'—'Words to the Time'—Buber entitled two small pamphlets that he wrote in 1919 in response to the crisis of postwar Europe. In the deepest sense of the term, the whole of his works, even his translations of the Hebrew Bible and his retelling of Hasidic tales, may be understood as words addressed to the time: they grow out of situations and speak to situations. To understand the encounters on the narrow ridge in which Buber again and again risked his life-stance and his thought and responded with the resources of his being at that moment is to understand the works themselves as products of that response. This understanding gives the works a dimension of fullness and depth that not even the subtlest and richest intellectual-historical context could give them.

This does not mean that Buber's thought is not of value without the specific events and meetings of his life. In one of his 'Autobiographical Fragments' Buber lamented that he could not do as he ought, go with the worker to whom he was speaking, work beside him in the factory, win his trust in real-life relationship, and show him the way of the creature who accepts the creation. If this was not possible when Buber was alive, it is still less so now that he is dead. He was one of the universal geniuses of our time, a man who ranks with Albert Schweitzer, Albert Einstein, and Mohandas Ghandi, as someone who transcends the bounds of time and place and who speaks and will continue to speak to those whom he did not know and those who come after him. He was the philosopher of dialogue only because in the first instance he lived the life of dialogue. His writings and his thought, as much as his life itself, can only be understood as pointers to a unique reality that cannot be delimited and defined. What made such men as Hermann Hesse and Reinhold Niebuhr speak of Buber as 'one of the few wise men living on the earth today' was not just his eminence as a thinker but also his concern with the 'lived concrete,' the everyday reality which he took up into his imagining and bore as his responsibility. 'More than any other person in the modern world,' said the great Protestant theologian H. Richard Niebuhr at a celebration of Buber's eightieth birthday, 'more even than Kierkegaard, Martin Buber has been for me, and for many of my companions, the prophet of the soul and the witness to the truth which is required of the soul not as solitary, but as companionable being.' In a time in which we are in danger of losing our birthright as human beings, Martin Buber has shown us what it means to live 'the way of man.'

In 1960 I made a number of corrections and additions for the second edition of *The Life of Dialogue*. The two corrections of error that I have made in this third edition are my statements that Buber first used the language of 'I and Thou' as his own in his 1904 essay on the actress Eleanor Duse and that it was Buber's *Daniel* that influenced Rilke's eighth Duino Elegy (actually it was *The Legend of the Baal-Shem*). Beyond this I have made no changes in the text itself. Paperback editions go so quickly into and out of print that it seems pointless to try to bring my many references to Buber's writings into line with the English editions that are available at the time of this writing. The scholar will be able to trace my sources through the information that I have given in the footnotes. Nor have I changed my own rendition of Buber's German to that in the translations published since 1960. One example of this is *'Sein'* and *'Schein'* in 'Elements of the Interhuman,' which I have translated as 'essence' and 'appearance' in contrast to Ronald Gregor Smith's more felicitous rendition of 'being' and 'seeming.' On the other hand, because of my comments in *The Life of Dialogue* on several key terms in his translation of *I and Thou*, in the revised edition published in 1958, Ronald Gregor Smith changed 'reversal' to 'turning' for *Umkehr* and 'salvation' to 'redemption' for *Erlösung*.

All of my quotations from *I and Thou* are from Smith's translation. I have made no attempt in this new edition to bring them into line with Walter Kaufmann's 1970 translation of this classic. Here too the scholar will have no difficulty tracing my sources. The intelligent layman, in my opinion, will be closer to Buber's own meaning if he reads 'turning' instead of Kaufmann's 'return' (*Umkehr*), 'realization' instead of Kaufmann's 'actualization' (*Verwirklichung*), and 'meeting' instead of 'encounter' (*Begegnung*). I cannot help thinking that if Kaufmann had taken part in as many encounter groups as I have, he would never have wished to change 'meeting,' Buber's own preferred rendition, to 'encounter'—this now so overladen term! Neither Smith nor Kaufmann found a way to express in English the difference between the Ich-Du *Beiziehung* and the Ich-Es *Verhältnis*, despite Buber's principle that two different words in German should never be rendered by the same English term. *'Beziehung'* should be 'relationship' and *'Verhältnis,'* 'relation,' or the other way around, but not both the same!

I have deleted some articles, including my own, that no longer seemed essential to the bibliography, but I have left in those that I made use of in writing the book. I have made no attempt to list the many articles that have appeared on Buber's thought in several languages since 1960. The only exceptions here are three central articles by Ernst Simon, Buber's disciple, friend, and literary executor, and forty of the many essays that I myself have written on Buber since the publication of *The Life of Dialogue*. Although the material for one or even several books about Buber is contained in these essays, I cannot imagine that I shall ever try to publish them in book form either as 'collected essays' or revised to fit into some new organic whole. For this reason, I believe it may be of service to Buber scholars to have this listing of my essays about him written over twenty-five years and dealing with almost every phase of his thought. Certainly I shall be able to use very little of them in *Encounter on the Narrow Ridge*, which will be biography foremost and only secondarily interpretation. Finally, with two or three exceptions, I have made no attempt to include the works by and about Buber in Hebrew, even when these exist in no other language, since this book is written in the first instance for the English-speaking reader. I refer the scholar to the comprehensive bibliography published by Moshe Catanè in 1961, which includes all of Buber's Hebrew writings up to that point. I also refer the reader to Hans Kohn's bibliography of essays and books by and about Buber up to 1930, and the more than seven-hundred-item bibliography of Buber's writings in all languages which I compiled for *The Philosophy of Martin Buber* volume of *The Library of Living Philosophers* and which is reprinted in Buber's *Meetings*.

In this last connection a special word of explanation is in order. Paul Arthur Schilpp initiated the series of volumes in *The Library of Living Philosophers* and himself edited all of the volumes. *The Philosophy of Martin Buber* represents a partial exception, in that Professor Schilpp made it clear that he could only undertake to include a Buber volume in this series, as he had been urged by Hugo Bergman, Walter Kaufmann, and others, if I were to do the major work of editing. He himself wrote the letters of invitation and retained final authority as to who would be invited to contribute and on what subjects. He also carried on all the financial matters and the negotiations with the presses in America, England, Germany, and Japan. My own part in the editing was carrying on the correspondence with the contributors and with Martin Buber for a dozen years, editing the essays as they came in, finding translators for the ones not in English, translating myself Buber's autobiographical fragments and his replies to his critics, and preparing an exhaustive bibliography of Buber's philosophically significant writings. Therefore, though I did the chief work of editing, Professor Schilpp remained throughout an active editor of the Buber volume. While I could certainly not be designated 'assistant,' I agreed that his name should appear first and mine second as coeditors of this volume.

I know well all of the new books and articles by Buber that I have listed, but I cannot vouch for all the new books *about* Buber. I include these as an aid to scholars.

I should like to acknowledge my indebtedness to my friends Professor Marvin Fox and the late Professor Abraham J. Heschel for criticism of this book in its early stages. I am deeply grateful to Eugenia Friedman for her invaluable assistance as critic and editor and for working with me for two months compiling the index. I am also greatly indebted to Martin Buber himself, who supplied me with his own writings, even in manuscript form, directed me to significant works about his thought that I did not know, and patiently answered my questions throughout years of correspondence and personal dialogue.

Preface to the Third Edition

Without Buber's help and encouragement, this book could not possibly have achieved its present form. Finally, I acknowledge the kindness of the editors of *Judaism, The Journal of Bible and Religion, The Review of Religion, The Journal of Religion,* and *The Review of Metaphysics* for permission to use materials from articles previously published in those journals.

Maurice S. Friedman

Del Mar, California

PART ONE

INTRODUCTION

CHAPTER ONE

THE NARROW RIDGE

'I HAVE occasionally described my standpoint to my friends as the "narrow ridge," ' writes Buber. 'I wanted by this to express that I did not rest on the broad upland of a system that includes a series of sure statements about the absolute, but on a narrow rocky ridge between the gulfs where there is no sureness of expressible knowledge but the certainty of meeting what remains undisclosed.' [1] Perhaps no other phrase so aptly characterizes the quality and significance of Martin Buber's life and thought as this one of the 'narrow ridge.' It expresses not only the 'holy insecurity' of his existentialist philosophy but also the 'I-Thou,' or dialogical, philosophy which he has formulated as a genuine third alternative to the insistent either-or's of our age. Buber's 'narrow ridge' is no 'happy middle' which ignores the reality of paradox and contradiction in order to escape from the suffering they produce. It is rather a paradoxical unity of what one usually understands only as alternatives—I and Thou, love and justice, dependence and freedom, the love of God and the fear of God, passion and direction, good and evil, unity and duality.

According to the logical conception of truth only one of two contraries can be true, but in the reality of life as one lives it they are inseparable. The person who makes a decision knows that his deciding is no self-delusion; the person who has acted knows that he was and is in the hand of God. The unity of the contraries is the mystery at the innermost core of the dialogue.[2]

In the light of this quality in Buber's thought, it is not surprising that many find his works difficult to understand. Most of us approach a book expecting little other than an extension and application of concepts

---

[1] Martin Buber, *Between Man and Man*, trans. by Ronald Gregor Smith (London: Kegan Paul, 1947), p. 184.
[2] Martin Buber, *Israel and the World, Essays in a Time of Crisis* (New York: Schocken Books, 1948), 'The Faith of Judaism,' p. 17.

which we already possess or at the most a stretching of these concepts through the introduction of new perspectives. We find it painful, therefore, to come up against a thinker like Buber who questions the fundamental channels of our thinking and forces us to think—if we are to follow him at all—in radically other ways.

The German theologian Karl Heim wrote in 1934 that every age has a vital question that particularly belongs to it. To Heim the question for our age is that of the transcendence versus the immanence of God. For others the issue is naturalism versus anti-naturalism or 'humanitarian' religion and ethics versus the 'authoritarian.' Not only in philosophy and theology, but in education, art, politics, economics, and, in fact, every important field of thought, the typical pattern of our age is the increasing division of issues into conflicting and irreconcilable opposites. Thus in education 'objective' classical education battles with education for the individual or education based on 'subjective' interest. Again, science and religion or science and the humanities are set in opposition to each other, or the relation between them is falsified by still another pair of opposites: an objective 'scientific truth' and a subjective 'poetic truth.' In aesthetics art tends to be looked at as imitation of 'objective' reality or as 'subjective' expression. In politics civilization itself is threatened by a growing rift between democracy and communism—with an increasingly ominous insistence that 'peace' is to be obtained through the universalization of one of these points of view and the complete destruction of the other. Those who resort to an analysis of the underlying causes and value presuppositions of modern man's situation in the hope of finding there some clue for his salvation establish the either-or on still another plane: universalism versus exclusivism, knowledge versus will, error versus sin, collectivism versus individualism, environment versus heredity, reason versus emotion, discipline versus permissiveness, security versus freedom—'objectivism' versus 'subjectivism.'

The gravest danger of these either-or's is not the increasing division of men within and between countries into hostile and intolerant groups, nor is it even the conflict and destruction which results and seems likely to result from these divisions. It is the falsification of truth, the falsification of life itself. It is the demand that every man fit his thought and his way of life into one or the other of these hostile camps and the refusal to recognize the possibility of other alternatives which cannot be reduced to one of the two conflicting positions. In the light of this danger and its tremendous implications for our age, I should venture to say that the vital need of our age is to find a way of life and a way of thought which will preserve the truth of human existence in all its concrete complexity and which will recognize that this truth is neither 'subjective' nor 'objective'—neither reducible to individual temperament on the one hand, nor to any type of objective absolute or objective cultural relativism on the other.

In all of Martin Buber's works we find a spiritual tension and seriousness, coupled with a breadth of scope which seeks constantly to relate this intensity to life itself and does not tolerate its limitation to any one field of thought or to thought cut off from life. More remarkable still, Buber has accomplished the rare feat of combining this breadth and intensity into an integral unity of life and thought, and he has done this without sacrificing the concrete complexity and paradoxicality of existence as he sees it. Buber's writings are unusual in their scope and variety, dealing with topics in the fields of religion, mythology, philosophy, sociology, politics, education, psychology, art, and literature. Despite this variety, Buber's philosophy attains a central unity which pervades all of his mature works.

Buber's thought has had a great influence on a large number of prominent writers and thinkers in many different fields, and it seems destined to have a steadily greater influence as its implications become clearer. His influence as a person, what is more, has been almost as great as the influence of his thought. It is this integral combination of greatness as a person and as a thinker which makes Buber one of the rare personalities of our time. The characteristic of both Buber's personality and his work, according to the German educator Karl Wilker, is 'the greatest conceivable consciousness of responsibility.'

The more I have come to know him, not only through his works but also face to face, the more strongly I have felt that his whole personality tolerates no untruthfulness and no unclarity. There is something there that forces one to trace out the last ground of things. . . . He who is thus must have experienced life's deepest essence. . . . He must have lived and suffered . . . and he must have shared with us all our life and suffering. He must have stood his ground face to face with despair. . . . Martin Buber belongs to the most powerful renewal not only of a people but of mankind.[1]

The German Catholic thinkers Eugene Kogon and Karl Thieme speak of Buber in a similar fashion: 'In everything that he writes the undertone reveals that here speaks a man of faith, and, indeed, a man of active faith.' The most astonishing thing that one can say of Buber, they add, is that his person does not give the lie to his works.[2] The socialist thinker, Dr. Heinz-Joachim Heydorn, goes even further in this direction. What makes Buber's life great, he writes, cannot be discovered

---

[1] Karl Wilker, 'Martin Buber,' *Neue Wege*, Zurich, XVII, No. 4 (April 1923), 183 f. (my translation).

[2] Eugene Kogon and Karl Thieme, 'Martin Buber,' *Frankfurter Hefte*, VI, 3 (March 1951), pp. 195-199.

through what he has written in his books or through any sum of his sayings.

Outside of Albert Schweitzer I know no one who has realized in himself a similar great and genuine deep identity of truth and life. . . . This little, old man with the penetrating, incorruptible eyes has already today begun to project into the brokenness of our time like a legendary figure; he is a living proof of what this life is capable of when it wills to fulfill itself fearlessly and only in responsibility. . . . Buber has accomplished what one can only say of a very few: he has reached the limits of his own being . . . and through this has made the universal transparent.[1]

One who has met Buber knows that he is marked above all by simplicity, humour, seriousness, genuine listening, and an unwavering insistence on the concrete. One of the most striking testimonies to Buber as a whole man is that of Hermann Hesse, the famous Swiss novelist and poet:

Martin Buber is in my judgment not only one of the few wise men who live on the earth at the present time, he is also a writer of a very high order, and, more than that, he has enriched world literature with a genuine treasure as has no other living author—the Tales of the Hasidim. . . . Martin Buber . . . is the worthiest spiritual representative of Israel, the people that has had to suffer the most of all people in our time.[2]

Hesse's high estimate of Buber as a literary figure has been forcefully echoed by the noted authority on Greek religion and myth Karl Kerenyi, who impressively asserts Buber's claim to belong to the ranks of 'classical writers' in the fullest and deepest sense of the term. Classical writers, he says, possess the power of calling back to life and inspiriting the past and of recognizing in it a deep level of the soul. 'They are all discoverers and conquerors, reconquerors of what has apparently been lost, and, with every discovery . . . rediscoverers of man.' Buber brings to this task the multiple genius of one of the most gifted of living men, and the sphere of his gift is the universally human. To assess his significance for German and world literature it will be necessary to compare him with his early contemporaries, Hugo von Hofmannsthal and Rainer Maria Rilke, with whom he shared a common atmosphere of style and spirit, but also to go far beyond this atmosphere to the

[1] Heinz-Joachim Heydorn, 'Martin Buber und der Sozialismus,' *Gewerkschaftliche Monatshefte*, Vol. IV, No. 12 (December 1953), pp. 705 f., 709 (my translation).

[2] From a letter of Hesse to a friend explaining his nomination of Buber for a Nobel Prize in literature in 1949. Hermann Hesse, *Briefe*, Vol. VIII of *Gesammelte Werke* (Berlin: Suhrkamp Verlag, 1951), p. 324 ff. (my translation).

world of the Hasidic Jew which Buber *discovered* in the fundamental sense of the term.[1]

From the time of his earliest writings Buber has been generally recognized as a master German stylist. Buber belongs, writes Ludwig Lewisohn, 'to the very thin front ranks of living German masters of prose.' Buber's books, according to the German writer Wilhelm Michel, belong stylistically to the noblest that the essay art of this time has brought forth. His style is a mature one, says Michel, one that has developed with the years and come into its own. It is the speech of an ordered and fully disciplined spirit. 'It is rich with presence and corporeality; it has drunk much of the sensual into itself and has become dense with it. But it has remained full of deep feeling and organic; each of its forms gleams with living meaning. . . . It is the pure devotion to the word of a man simplified for the sake of God.' [2]

In the quarter of a century since Michel wrote the above characterization, the richly sensual quality of Buber's style has tended to decrease in favour of an ever greater simplicity and concreteness on the one hand and a more considered and meditative style on the other. At the same time, even in his scholarly and philosophical works, his writing has never wholly lost that poetic and emotive quality through which he has so remarkably integrated philosophical, religious, and artistic communication into one total address to the reader. In 1954 the German poet Fritz Diettrich said of Buber's style: 'He has made our speech into so choice an instrument of his thought that he has taken his place by the side of Goethe and Schopenhauer as a master stylist.'

I have never yet found a passage in Buber's works where he did not succeed in bringing even very difficult material and philosophical dicta into a framework suitable to them. The cleanness of his thought and of his style are one. From this comes the honesty of his conclusions.[3]

The integral nature of Buber's style defies adequate translation and interpretation. None the less, even the English reader can glimpse in

[1] Karl Kerenyi, 'Martin Buber als Klassiker,' *Neue Schweizer Rundschau*, XX, 2 (June 1952), pp. 89–95, my translation. The poet Rilke wrote with enthusiasm of Buber's *Daniel* (1913) and, according to the English Rilke scholar, B. J. Morse, was influenced by Buber's *Legend of the Baal-Shem* in the writing of the ninth Duino Elegy. The unpublished essay is in the Buber Archives of the Hebrew National and University Library, Jerusalem. See Rainer Maria Rilke, *Briefe an seinen Verleger*, pp. 180, 182.

[2] Ludwig Lewisohn, *Rebirth, A Book of Modern Jewish Thought* (New York: Harper & Brothers, 1935), p. 87; Wilhelm Michel, *Martin Buber, Sein Gang in die Wirklichkeit* (Frankfurt am Main: Rütten & Loening, 1926), pp. 11–14.

[3] Fritz Diettrich, 'Martin Buber. Die Stimme Israels,' an address over the Stuttgart Radio, February 1954, to be published the end of 1954 (my translation).

translation the amazing achievement of condensation, concreteness, and integrality which is found in some of the most recent of his writings: *Images of Good and Evil, Right and Wrong, At the Turning,* and, most especially, 'The Way of Man' in *Hasidism and Modern Man.*

Martin Buber was born in Vienna in 1878 and was brought up until the age of fourteen in the Galician home of his grandfather, Solomon Buber, one of the last great scholars of the *Haskalah* (Jewish enlightenment). He studied philosophy and the history of art at the University of Vienna and the University of Berlin, and in 1904 he received his Ph.D. from the latter university. In his twenties he was the leader of those Zionists who advocated a Jewish cultural renaissance as opposed to purely political Zionism. In 1902 Buber helped found the Jüdischer Verlag, a German-Jewish publishing house, and in 1916 he founded *Der Jude,* a periodical which he edited until 1924 and which became under his guidance the leading organ of German-speaking Jewry. From 1926 to 1930 he published jointly with the Catholic theologian Joseph Wittig and the Protestant doctor and psychotherapist Viktor von Weizsäcker the periodical *Die Kreatur,* devoted to social and pedagogical problems connected with religion. From 1923 to 1933 Buber taught Jewish philosophy of religion and later the history of religions at the University of Frankfurt. In 1938 Buber left Germany to make his home in Palestine, and from that year through 1951 he served as professor of social philosophy at the Hebrew University, Jerusalem. After he became emeritus, the government of the state of Israel asked him to double the size of the Institute for Adult Education that he founded in 1949 and directed until 1953.[1] This Institute trains teachers to go out to the immigration camps to help integrate the vast influx of immigrants into the already established community.

Those who have met Buber or have heard him lecture have discovered the prophetic force of his personality and the tremendous strength and sincerity of his religious conviction. Everywhere he has spoken, the arresting man with the white beard and the penetrating, yet gentle, eyes has shown those present what it means to ask 'real questions' and to give real answers. He has also shown again and again what it means to walk on the narrow ridge not only in one's thinking but in the whole of one's life. One of the foremost Zionist leaders and thinkers, he has also been the leader of those Jews who have worked for Jewish-Arab co-operation and friendship. Pioneer and still the foremost interpreter of Hasidism, he has preserved in his thinking the most positive aspects

---

[1] 'After four years of a very vital existence, the Institute has been closed, following the cessation of mass immigration,' Buber writes. 'There survives a certain activity under the same name, being essentially the merit of my excellent co-worker, Dr. Gideon Freudenberg.' From a letter from Professor Buber to the author of August 8, 1954.

of the Jewish enlightenment, Hasidism's traditional enemy. Translator and interpreter of the Hebrew Bible and spokesman for Judaism before the world, he has been deeply concerned since his youth with Jesus and the New Testament and has carried on a highly significant dialogue with many prominent Christian theologians, Protestant and Catholic alike.

Perhaps the most striking example of how Buber has followed the narrow ridge in his life is his attitude toward the German people after the war. He was the leader of the German Jews in their spiritual battle against Nazism, and he counts himself among 'those who have not got over what happened and will not get over it.' Yet on September 27, 1953, in historic Paulskirche, Frankfurt, Germany, he accepted the award of the Peace Prize of the German Book Trade. In his acceptance speech Buber pointed out that less than a decade before several thousand Germans killed millions of his people and fellow-believers 'in a systematically prepared and executed procedure, the organized cruelty of which cannot be compared with any earlier historical event.'

> With those who took part in this action in any capacity, I, one of the survivors, have only in a formal sense a common humanity. They have so radically removed themselves from the human sphere, so transposed themselves into a sphere of monstrous inhumanity inaccessible to my power of conception, that not even hatred, much less an overcoming of hatred, was able to arise in me. And what am I that I could here presume to 'forgive'!

At the same time Buber pointed to other classes of Germans who knew of these happenings only by hearsay, who heard rumours but did not investigate, and some who underwent martyrdom rather than accept or participate in this murder of a whole people. The inner battle of every people between the forces of humanity and the forces of inhumanity, writes Buber, is the deepest issue in the world today, obscured though it is by the 'cold war' between gigantic camps. It is in the light of this issue that Buber understands both the award of the prize and his duty to accept it:

> Manifestations such as the bestowal of the Hansian Goethe Prize and the Peace Prize of the German Book Trade on a surviving arch-Jew... are moments in the struggle of the human spirit against the demonry of the subhuman and the anti-human. . . . The solidarity of all separate groups in the flaming battle for the becoming of one humanity is, in the present hour, the highest duty on earth. To obey this duty is laid on the Jew chosen as symbol,

even there, indeed just there, where the never-to-be-effaced
memory of what has happened stands in opposition to it.[1]

[1] Martin Buber, *Das echte Gespräch und die Möglichkeiten des Friedens*, speech
made by Buber on occasion of receiving the Friedenspreis des Deutschen Buch-
handels, Frankfurt am Main, Paulskirche, September 27, 1953 (Heidelberg: Lambert
Schneider Verlag, 1953), pp. 5-8. *Das echte Gespräch* is also found as part of *Martin
Buber: Fünf Ansprachen anlässlich der Verleihung des Friedenspreises des Deutschen
Buchhandels* (Frankfurt am Main: Börsenverein Deutscher Verleger- und Buch-
händler-Verbände, 1953), pp. 33-41 (my translation). *Das echte Gespräch* ('Genuine
Conversation and the Possibilities of Peace') was published in English in
Martin Buber, *Pointing the Way, Collected Essays*, ed. and trans. by Maurice S.
Friedman (New York: Harper & Brothers, 1957).

CHAPTER TWO

THE PROBLEM OF EVIL

IN no other area of human experience is it more difficult to preserve the attitude of the 'narrow ridge' than in one's encounter with evil, yet here too the metaphor of the 'narrow ridge' expresses the central quality of Buber's thought. Many in our age who discover the inadequacy of the simple moral opposition between good and evil tend to reduce evil to illusion or objective error, or to absolutize it as something radical, pure, and unredeemable. As a result, most of those who think and write about this problem do so from the standpoint of a choice between that attitude which sees good and evil as part of a higher unity and that which sees them as irreconcilable opposites. Although shadings from the two extremes exist and are recognized, neither side recognizes the independent reality of the position between—the dialectical attitude toward evil which sees it as both real and redeemable. Those philosophers and theologians who have followed Martin Buber in the 'I-Thou' philosophy have usually not seen that this dialectical attitude toward evil is inseparable from it as he understands it.

Evil is one of the deepest and most central problems of human existence—a problem which every individual and every age must face for itself. The problem of evil is significant not primarily because of one's conscious concept of evil but because of the total attitude expressed in the whole of one's life and thought. This attitude, in Buber's words, is 'a mode of seeing and being which dwells in life itself.' It underlies all our valuations, for valuing is nothing other than the decision as to what is good and evil and the attitude which one then takes toward the possibility of avoiding evil or transforming it into good. Valuing lies in turn at the heart of most fields of human thought. This is clearest of all in ethics, which is essentially the study of the relation between the 'is' of human nature and the 'ought' of human possibility. But it is no less important in psychology and the social sciences, for all of these fields are conditioned by the fact that their subject of study is the human being in his relation to other human beings. This implies a recognition not only of the central importance of valuing in human life but also of the way in which the values of the psychologist and the social scientist affect their methods. In literature and the arts valuing affects the relation of the arts to human life and the critical standards by which the intrinsic merit of works of art are judged. This does not mean that all these fields are subject to the censure of some external standard of morality but rather that inherent in the very structure of each are value assumptions. These value assumptions rest upon an implicit and often unconscious attitude toward good and evil.

Buber's system of valuing is so closely connected with the problem of evil that this problem can be used as a unifying centre for his work without doing injustice to the many different fields in which he has written. This is, of course, to use the phrase in a somewhat different and broader sense than is traditional. Traditionally, the problem of evil has been limited to the fields of metaphysics and theology. In our use of it it must be broadened to include other important phases of human life—philosophical anthropology, ethics, psychology, social philosophy, and even politics. This does not mean a change in the problem itself so much as a shift of emphasis and a greater concern with its concrete applications in the modern world.

In theology and philosophy the problem of evil is ordinarily treated under the two headings of natural and moral evil. For the primitive man no such distinction existed, for everything to him was personal. Misfortune was looked on as caused by hostile forces, and these forces were conceived of not as manifestations of one personal God but as many 'moment Gods' or specialized personal deities. The Book of Job, in contrast, rests on faith in one God who transcends the nature which He created. Nature is no longer personal in the old sense, yet God is felt to be responsible for what happens to man through nature, for it is He who directly sustains nature. The Greek view, on the other hand, tends to make God into an impersonal first cause. The development of science and secular civilization since the Renaissance has fortified this view. By the time of Hume, God is no longer considered the direct but only the indirect cause of nature, and nature is not only considered as impersonal but also as mechanical. There is no 'problem of evil' for this mechanistic and deterministic view of the world, for the place of God is finally taken altogether by blind chance, causality, and impersonal law. Yet the reality underlying the problem of evil is present all the time and in intensified form. The consequences of this view are reflected in writers such as Melville, Matthew Arnold, and Thomas Hardy, who picture the universe as a cold, impersonal reality hostile to the very existence of man. 'The heartless voids and immensities of the universe' threaten to annihilate all personality and human values.

Few modern philosophies supply a standpoint from which the problem of evil can be adequately recognized and dealt with. For scientific realism 'evil' is simply technical error. For pragmatism it is ultimately anything which threatens subjective interest by creating deficiencies or preventing their being overcome. For philosophical vitalism evil is the static, anything that stands in the way of vital evolution, while good is vital movement, which it is assumed will ultimately be triumphant, as if there were still another principle of good underlying the whole process. In criticism of this non-dialectical immanentism as it is expressed in the philosophy of Bergson Buber writes:

> The crucial religious experiences of man do not take place in a sphere in which creative energy operates without contradiction, but in a sphere in which evil and good, despair and hope, the power of destruction and the power of rebirth, dwell side by side. The divine force which man actually encounters in life does not hover above the demonic, but penetrates it.[1]

There are four types of evil of which the modern age is particularly aware: the loneliness of modern man before an unfriendly universe and before men whom he associates with but does not meet; the increasing tendency for scientific instruments and techniques to outrun man's ability to integrate those techniques into his life in some meaningful and constructive way; the inner duality of which modern man has become aware through the writings of Dostoievsky and Freud and the development of psychoanalysis; and the deliberate and large-scale degradation of human life within the totalitarian state. What new attitudes toward evil do these typically modern manifestations of evil evoke in the modern man? A greater belief in the reality of evil, certainly, and an impatient rejection of the shallow optimism and naïve faith in progress of preceding ages. For some this has meant a more and more complete determinism and naturalism, for others a return to Gnostic ideas of dualism or early Protestant emphases on original sin. Many have lost the belief in the dignity of man or have tended to move away from life in the world to the certainty of a mystic absolute. Finally, a new attitude original with our age has been the atheistic existentialism which grits its teeth in the face of despair and assigns to man the task of creating for himself a reality where none now exists. A striking example of the way in which the attitude toward evil has been influenced by the horror of recent events is found in a

[1] Martin Buber, *Eclipse of God, Studies in the Relation between Religion and Philosophy* (New York: Harper & Brothers, 1952), 'Religion and Reality,' trans. by Norbert Guterman, p. 31.

statement of Jean-Paul Sartre born out of the experience of the French underground:

> For political realism as for philosophical idealism Evil was not a very serious matter. We have been taught to take it seriously. It is neither our fault nor our merit if we lived in a time when torture has been a daily fact. Chateaubriant, Oradour, the Rue des Saussaies, Tulle, Dachau, and Auschwitz have all demonstrated to us that Evil is not an appearance, that knowing its causes does not dispel it, that it is not opposed to Good as a confused idea is to a clear one, that it is not the effect of passions which might be cured, of a fear which might be overcome, of a passing aberration which might be excused, of an ignorance which might be enlightened, that it can in no way be turned, brought back, reduced, and incorporated into idealistic humanism. . . . We heard whole blocks screaming and we understood that Evil, fruit of a free and sovereign will, is, like Good, absolute. . . . In spite of ourselves, we came to this conclusion, which will seem shocking to lofty souls: Evil cannot be redeemed.[1]

What unites all these attitudes toward evil is their common origin in a deadly serious recognition of the power of evil in the modern world and the intensity with which those who hold them attempt to work out a means of meeting this evil which will enable them to retain their personal integration. But they do not all hold, as does Sartre, that evil is absolute and unredeemable. For those who hold the dialectical attitude toward evil, good cannot exist in solitary splendour, nor is it opposed by a radically separate evil with which it has nothing to do. Evil must exist in this middle position, but it is bound up with good in such a way that both are parts of a larger process, of a greater whole, which is at once origin and goal. Thus evil is in one way or another recognized as having reality, even if only that of a temporary accompaniment of unredeemed creation; but its reality is never permanent, nor is it ever completely divorced from the good. Hence it is capable of redemption by the process of the world spirit, the grace of God, or the redemptive activity of man.

Although many significant changes occur in Buber's thought during the fifty years of his productivity, it is in this middle position between the unreality and the radical reality of evil that we shall always find him. His attitude has changed from a tendency to regard evil in largely negative terms to a tendency to ascribe to it greater and greater emotional and ontological reality. But he has never considered evil an absolute, nor has he lost faith in its possible redemption. Elizabeth

[1] Jean-Paul Sartre, 'Literature in Our Time,' section iv, *Partisan Review*, XV, No. 6 (June 1948), p. 635 ff.

Rotten has quoted Buber as saying, 'One must also love evil . . . even as evil wishes to be loved.' [1] This statement is symbolic of the way in which he has consistently answered this question: good can be maximized not through the rejection or conquest of evil but only through the transformation of evil, the use of its energy and passion in the service of the good.

[1] Elizabeth Rotten, 'Aus den Offenbarungen der Schwester Mechtild von Magdeburg,' *Aus unbekannten Schriften. Festgabe für Martin Buber*, ed. by Franz Rosenzweig and Ludwig Strauss (Berlin: Lambert Schneider Verlag, 1928), p. 65 f.

CHAPTER THREE

HASIDISM

APART from his philosophy of dialogue, Martin Buber is best known for making Hasidism a part of the thought and culture of the western world. Hasidism is the popular mystical movement that swept East European Jewry in the eighteenth and nineteenth centuries. In his essay, *Mein Weg zum Chassidismus* ('My Road to Hasidism'), Buber tells of how his father took him on occasional visits to the Hasidic community of Sadagora in Galicia when he was a child. Although estranged by the conspicuous grandeur of the *zaddik* (the leader of the Hasidic community) and by the wild gestures of the Hasidim in prayer, when he saw the *rebbe* stride through the rows of the waiting he felt that here was a leader, and when he saw the Hasidim dance with the Torah, he felt that here was a community. Later he went through a period of uncreative intellectuality and spiritual confusion, living without centre and substance. Through Zionism he gained new roots in the community, but it was only through Hasidism that the movement which he had joined took on meaning and content. One day on reading a saying by the founder of Hasidism about the fervour and daily inward renewal of the pious man, he recognized in himself the Hasidic soul, and he recognized piety, *hasidut*, as the essence of Judaism. This experience occurred in his twenty-sixth year. As a result of it, he gave up his political and journalistic activity and spent five years in isolation studying Hasidic texts.[1] It was only after he emerged from this isolation into renewed activity that he entered on his real life work as a writer, a speaker, and a teacher.

Of the many different cultural strains that converged in Buber's thought, Hasidism is perhaps the least familiar. The Hebrew word *hasid* means 'pious.' It is derived from the noun *hesed*, meaning lovingkindness, mercy, or grace. The Hasidic movement arose in Poland in the eighteenth century and, despite bitter persecution at the hands of

---

[1] Martin Buber, *Hinweise. Gesammelte Essays* (Zurich: Manesse Verlag, 1953), pp. 179-196; *Hasidism and Modern Man,* Vol. I of *Hasidism and the Way of Man,* ed. and trans. by M. Friedman (N.Y.: Horizon Press, 1958), pp. 47-69.

traditional Rabbinism, spread rapidly among the Jews of eastern Europe until it included almost half of them in its ranks. The founder of Hasidism was Rabbi Israel ben Eliezer (1700-60), who is more commonly known as the Baal-Shem-Tov, the master of the good name of God. Originally a simple teacher, then later a magic healer, he finally gathered about him a group of disciples dedicated to a life of mystic fervour, joy, and love. Reacting against the tendency of traditional Rabbinism toward strict legalism and arid intellectualism, the Baal Shem and his followers exalted simplicity and devotion above mere scholarship.

Despite its excommunication and persecution at the hands of traditional Rabbinism, Hasidism was firmly rooted in the Jewish past and was perhaps more truly an expression of that past than any Jewish movement in modern times. The Hasidic emphasis on piety, on love of God and one's neighbour, and on joy in God's creation goes clearly back to the Prophets, the Psalms, and the school of Hillel. Within the context of post-biblical Judaism Hasidism may be considered as a union of three different currents. One of these is the Jewish law as expressed in the Talmudic *Halakhah*; the second is the Jewish legend and saying as expressed in the Talmudic *Haggadah* and in later Jewish mythology; and the third is the Kabbalah, the Jewish mystical 'tradition.' The central concepts of Hasidism derive from and can only be understood in terms of the theoretical Kabbalah of the Middle Ages and the Lurian Kabbalah of sixteenth-century Safed.

The theoretical Kabbalah (as it is set forth in the *Zohar*, the 'Book of Splendour') is in essence a complex theosophical system which explains creation in terms of ten *sefirot*, aspects or emanations of God. The origin of evil is explained in terms of a disharmony arising within these emanations so that God's quality of judgment became separate from His quality of mercy. To some extent this evil is believed to be prior to man, but to some extent also it is felt to be actualized by the fall of man. The result of this evil is a separation between the *En-Sof*, the hidden nature of God, and the Shekinah, His Glory which is immanent in the world. This separation is expressed in terms of 'the exile of the Shekinah,' and redemption is spoken of in terms of the *yihud*, or the reunification of God and His Glory. This reunification can be initiated and in part brought about through the pious actions of man and through his cleaving to God (*devekuth*); for man is created with free will and with the power to be a co-worker with God in the restoration of the original harmony.

The Lurian Kabbalah is largely based on the *Zohar*, and like it bears marked resemblances to Neo-Platonism and various forms of Gnosticism. It differs from it, however, in a number of new and highly complex concepts which make it of a more theistic nature than the earlier Kabbalah and yet cause it to lay much stronger emphasis on the power of man to bring about the Messianic redemption of Israel and the world. In the *Zohar* the *sefirot* were derived almost directly from the hidden Absolute, passing first through a 'region of pure absolute Being which the mystics call Nothing.' In the Lurian Kabbalah the outgoing movement of creation is thought to have been preceded at every point by a voluntary contraction or self-limitation of God (*tsimtsum*) which makes room for creation and gives man real freedom to do evil as well as good. Thus God is removed from rather than directly present in His creation. However, something of the flavour of divinity remains in the space that God has left, and this flavour is preserved in the various *sefirot* and worlds that then evolve.

Evil here, as in the *Zohar*, is explained as a waste-product of creation and an inevitable result of the limitation, or judgment, that must take place if separate things are to exist at all. But the origin of evil is explained here under a different figure, that of *shevirath ha-kelim*—the breaking of the vessels which contain the divine grace. As the result of the breaking of the vessels, the divine harmony is disrupted, the Shekinah is exiled, and sparks of divinity fall downward into physical creation. In the physical world the sparks are surrounded by hard shells of darkness (*qelipot*), a type of negative evil. This whole process is further confirmed by the fall of man, but it is also within man's power to liberate the divine sparks from their imprisonment in the shells and send them upward again to union with their divine source. Through this liberation the power of darkness is overcome and *tikkun*, the restoration of the original harmony, is effected.

This restoration in itself causes the redemption of man and the world. Though it cannot be completed by man's action, man can start the movement which God will complete by sending down His grace to the world in the form of the Messiah. For this purpose man must not only observe every injunction of the law but he must practise mystical prayer, and he must bring to his actions and prayers special types of mystical intention, or *kavanot*. *Kavanah* represents a deliberate concentration of will, an inner attitude which is far more effective than the particular nature of the action being performed. However, the greatest effectiveness is only secured by the practice of special *kavanot* for each of the different actions. Thus, what was at its best a concern for inward devotion became at its worst an attempt to use magic to bring about the advent of the Messiah.[1]

Hasidism preserved the Messianic fervour of the people, yet it turned that fervour away from the future to the love of God and man in the

[1] Gershom G. Scholem, *Major Trends in Jewish Mysticism* (New York: Schocken Books, 1946), chaps. vi-vii; Ernst Mueller, *History of Jewish Mysticism* (Oxford: East and West Library, 1946), chaps. vi-vii.

present moment. It taught that the present moment is itself the moment of redemption that leads to the ultimate consummation. It infused a new and warm life-feeling into Kabbalistic theory, and it shifted its emphasis away from theosophical speculation to mystical psychology— to a concern with the progress of the individual soul in its efforts to purify itself, to help others, and to cleave to God. Kabbalistic doctrine was replaced by the personality of the *zaddik* in whom the Hasidim found the embodiment of those very virtues which they needed for their redemption and from whom they learned the right way for each of them to travel while in the life of the body. This way varied from Hasid to Hasid, for the Hasidim believed that as God is represented differently by each man, so each must discover his individuality and bring it to ever purer perfection. Not only were individual differences looked on as of value, but it was believed that it was only through them that the perfection of the whole could be reached.[1] This Hasidic individuality is strikingly embodied in a saying of Rabbi Zusya: 'In the coming world, they will not ask me: "Why were you not Moses?" They will ask me: "Why were you not Zusya?" '

The individuality of the Hasidim went hand in hand with a more intimate communal life than had yet been known in the Judaism of the Diaspora, and it is this communal life, centring around the personality of the 'true illuminate,' that Scholem has called Hasidism's greatest originality. Unlike the *rav* of traditional Rabbinism, the *zaddik*, or *rebbe*, was at once a saint, dwelling with God in the solitude of the mountain-tops, and a man of the people, transforming his mysticism into ethos and bringing it to the community in the valley below.[2] The strength of Hasidism lay in the *zaddik*, and the amazing spread of the movement in the first fifty years of its existence is a tribute to the true spiritual charisma of its leaders—'a whole galaxy of saint-mystics,' writes Scholem, 'each of them a startling individuality.' [3]

Unfortunately the strength of the Hasidic movement was also its weakness. The dependence of the Hasidim on the *zaddik* left the way open to a grasping for power which eventually tended to produce a degeneration of the *zaddik* as a spiritual type and the consequent degeneration of the movement. Faith and religious enthusiasm were replaced in many cases by obscurantism and superstition, and the true charismatic was almost obscured by hereditary dynasties of *zaddikim* who lived in oriental luxury and exploited the credulity of the people.[4]

[1] Mueller, *op. cit.*, p. 140 f.; Scholem, *op. cit.*, pp. 338-341; Torsten Ysander, *Studien zum B'estschen Hasidismus in seiner religionsgeschichtlichen Sonderart* (Uppsala: A. B. Lundequistska Bokhandeln, 1933), p. 139; Lazar Gulkowtisch, *Der Hasidismus, religionswissenschaftlich untersucht* (Leipzig: 1927), pp. 31, 56.

[2] Scholem, *op. cit.*, p. 342 ff.; Mueller, *op. cit.*, p. 148.

[3] Scholem, *op. cit.*, p. 337 f.

[4] *Ibid.*, pp. 336 f., 344-348; Mueller, *op. cit.*, p. 145.

Introduction

Hasidism takes over from the Lurian Kabbalah most of its principal concepts in somewhat simplified and popularized form, but it gives these concepts an emotional content that sometimes makes them very different from the original. Thus the idea of *tsimtsum*, or the self-limitation of God, is given a metaphorical rather than a literal interpretation which enables it to coexist with the strongest possible emphasis on the immanence of God, or God's Glory, in all things. The world is in the closest possible connection with God, and nature is in fact nothing but the garment of God. God clothed Himself in the world in order to lead man step by step to the place where he can see God behind the appearances of external things and can cleave to Him in all his actions.

The Hasidic emphasis on the immanence of God is not to be regarded as pantheism, but as panentheism. The godly in the world must be brought through our action to ever greater and purer perfection. Man has a part in the Shekinah which enables him to be a co-worker with God in the perfection of the world toward redemption. Thus the stress of Hasidism is on the actual consummation of religious life—the inward experience of the presence of God and the actualization of that presence in all one's actions.

The attitude of Hasidism toward evil grows out of its concept of God. Since God is embodied in the world, there is no absolute but only relative evil. Evil is the lowest rung or the throne of the good—an appearance, a shell, or a lesser grade of perfection. Evil only seems real because of our imperfect knowledge which causes us to fail to see the deep connections between happenings. Sin correspondingly is self-assertion, not seeing God's immanence in all things. Evil serves the good precisely through its opposition to it, for through evil man comes to know God even as through darkness he comes to know light. Moreover, evil can itself be redeemed and transformed into the good. Not only the sparks of divinity but the *qelipot*, or shell of darkness, may ascend and be purified, and the 'evil impulse' in man, the *yezer ha-ra*, can be redirected and used to serve God.[1]

The fact that Hasidism lays less emphasis upon the knowledge of God's immanence than on the confirmation of that knowledge through dedicated action shows that evil is not for Hasidism, as for the Hindu Vedanta, pure illusion. It has reality, even though this reality is only relative. The sparks must in truth be liberated, the shells must in truth

---

[1] Scholem, *op. cit.*, p. 347 f.; Mueller, *op. cit.*, pp. 141, 143; Chajim Bloch, *Priester der Liebe. Die Welt der Chassidim* (Zurich: Amalthea-Verlag, 1930), p. 22 f.; Simon Dubnow, *Geschichte des Chassidismus* (Berlin: Jüdischer Verlag, 1931), 2 vols., I, 95 f.; Gulkowitsch, *op. cit.*, pp. 48-51, 30 f.; Ysander, *op. cit.*, pp. 134-142, 145 f., 200, 208, 272-276; Paul Levertoff, *Die religiöse Denkweise der Chassidim* (Leipzig: F. C. Hinrischs'sche Buchhandlung, 1918), pp. 10, 38 f.

be transformed, and the 'evil impulse,' which God created and which man made evil through his sin, must be turned once more to the service of God. This turning to God is spoken of by Hasidism as the *teshuvah*— a repentance and purification in which one cleaves to God with all the power with which he formerly did evil. Through the *teshuvah* man not only redeems himself but he liberates the divine sparks in the men and objects around him. The redemption of the individual prepares the way for the ultimate Messianic redemption, but the latter is only brought about through God. The individual redemption is like the ultimate one in that it is a redemption rather than a conquest of evil—a redemption which transforms it into good and realizes the oneness of God in all things. The individual's turning to God is thus the most effective action possible for the *yihud*—the reunification of God with His exiled Shekinah.

For this reason Hasidism transforms the Lurian *kavanah* from a special, magical intention into a general consecration or inner dedication which man brings to all his actions. The Hasidic *kavanah* 'signifies less an effort of the will centred on the attainment of a definite end than the purposeful direction of the whole being in accordance with some feeling springing from the depths of one's nature.'[1] Without *kavanah* no service of God (*abodah*) has any value, for right moral action is dependent on the intensity of inner religious feeling. Thus Hasidism does not recognize any division between religion and ethics—between the direct relation to God and one's relations to one's fellows, nor is its ethics limited to any prescribed and peculiar action. In Hasidism, writes Buber, the Kabbalah became ethos. This meant a true religious revolution in which devotion absorbed and overcame gnosis. The Hasidic movement took from the Kabbalah only what it needed for the theological foundation of an inspired life in responsibility—the responsibility of each individual for the piece of the world entrusted to him.[2]

The Hasidic attitude toward the law, revelation, and the life of the senses is consistent with its concept of *kavanah*. The Torah is a priceless gift of God when it is used to conquer the evil impulse and to transform the inner life of man, but not when it is made an end in itself—a joyless burden or an occasion for intellectual subtlety. Similarly, although Hasidism believes in the historical revelation of God, it regards the feeling and consciousness of God's nearness as equally as important as the acceptance of tradition. The revelation of God to the fathers of Israel must be confirmed and renewed in the inner life of every believer. In the same way Hasidism rejects the Lurian tendency to asceticism for

---

[1] Mueller, *op. cit.*, p. 141 f.
[2] Martin Buber, *The Origin and Meaning of Hasidism*, Vol. II of *Hasidism and the Way of Man*, ed. and trans. by Maurice Friedman (New York: Horizon Press, 1960), IX. 'Supplement: Christ, Hasidism, Gnosis.'

its own sake and emphasizes instead a holy joy in the sensual life which will hallow and sanctify it. The redemption of the individual is twofold: the freeing of the soul from externals which enables it to enter into God and the entrance of God into the world through which the world is purified and uplifted. The life of the senses is, therefore, to be set aside only when the individual becomes attached to it for its own sake so that it becomes a hindrance to his meeting with God.[1]

The real essence of Hasidism is revealed not so much in its concepts as in the three central virtues which derive from these concepts: love, joy, and humility. For Hasidism the world was created out of love and is to be brought to perfection through love. Love is central in God's relation to man and is more important than fear of God, justice, or righteousness. The fear of God is only a door to the love of God—it is the awe which one has before a loving father. God is love, and the capacity to love is man's innermost participation in God. This capacity is never lost but needs only to be purified to be raised to God Himself. Thus love is not only a feeling; it is the godly in existence. Nor can one love God unless he loves his fellow man, for God is immanent in man as in all of His creation. For the same reason the love of God and the love of man is to be for its own sake and not for the sake of any reward.

The Hasidic emphasis on joy also comes from the knowledge of the presence of God in all things. This joy has a double character. It is at once a joyous affirmation of the external world and a joyous penetration into the hidden world behind the externals. In perfect joy the body and the soul are at one: this precludes both extreme asceticism and libertinism. To cultivate joy is one of Hasidism's greatest commandments, for only joy can drive out the 'alien thoughts' and *qelipot* that distract man from the love of God. Conversely, despair is worse than even sin; for it leads one to believe oneself in the power of sin and hence to give in to it.

Humility for Hasidism means a denial of self, but not a self-negation. Man is to overcome the pride which grows out of his feeling of separateness from others and his desire to compare himself with others. But man is at the same time not to forget that he is the son of a king, that he is a part of the godly. Thus Hasidic humility is a putting off of man's false self in order that he may affirm his true self—the self which finds its meaning in being a part and only a part of the whole. Humility, like joy and love, is attained most readily through prayer. Prayer is the most important way to union with God and is the highest means of self-redemption. Hasidic prayer, however, was not always prayer in its most ordinary sense. Sometimes it took the form of traditional prayer, sometimes of mystical meditation in preparation for the prescribed prayers,

[1] Ysander, *op. cit.*, pp. 275 f., 251 f., 256, 178 f., 281, 260-270, 140 ff., 170, 279; Bloch, *op. cit.*, p. 30; Mueller, *op. cit.*, p. 140.

and sometimes of *hitlahabut*, or an ecstatic intuition into the true nature of things.[1] Even the Hasidic singing and dancing might be justifiably conceived, at its highest, as a way of praying.

[1] Ysander, *op. cit.*, pp. 149, 166-171, 176, 335, 137, 279, 189 f., 134 f., 246, 283; Levertoff, *op. cit.*, p. 10; Gulkowitsch, *op. cit.*, pp. 51 f., 57, 59 f., 72; Martin Buber, *For the Sake of Heaven*, trans. by Ludwig Lewisohn (Philadelphia: The Jewish Publication Society, 1945; 2nd Edition, with new Foreword, New York: Harper & Brothers, 1953), p. 7; Dubnow, *op. cit.*, I, 96 f.

PART TWO
BUBER'S EARLY THOUGHT

CHAPTER FOUR

MYSTICISM

THE development of Buber's thought from his earliest essays in 1900 to the statement of his mature philosophy in 1922 can best be understood as a gradual movement from an early period of mysticism through a middle period of existentialism to a final period of developing dialogical philosophy. Most of the ideas which appear in the early periods are not really discarded in the later but are preserved in changed form. Thus Buber's existentialism retains much of his mysticism, and his dialogical philosophy in turn includes important mystical and existential elements.

The revival of mysticism at the turn of the century was in part a reaction against determinism and against the increasing specialization of knowledge. It was also a continuation of the mystical tendencies of the German romantics who could trace their ancestry back through Goethe and Schelling to the Pietists and Jacob Boehme. It was, finally, a result of the growing interest in mythology and in the religions of the Orient. All of these movements exercised a strong influence on Buber's thought. The influence of Hinduism and Buddhism was most important at an early period. That of Taoism came slightly later and has persisted into Buber's mature philosophy. At least as important was the influence of the German mystics from Meister Eckhart to Angelus Silesius. Of these mystics, the two most important for Buber were Meister Eckhart and Jacob Boehme, the former of whom Buber has called 'the greatest thinker of western mysticism.' These mystics provided a bridge for Buber to Jewish mysticism. The German mystical idea of the birth in the soul of the *Urgrund*, or godhead, resembles the Kabbalistic and Hasidic idea of the unification of God and His exiled immanence. The two concepts together led Buber, he says, 'to the thought of the realization of God through man' which he later abandoned for the idea of the meeting of God and man.[1]

[1] Hans Kohn, *Martin Buber, Sein Werk und seine Zeit, Ein Versuch über Religion und Politik* (Hellerau: Jakob Hegner Verlag, 1930), p. 56; *Hasidism, op. cit.*, 'God

One of the basic motivations for Buber's interest in mysticism in this period was his concern with the problem of the relation between the individual and the world. On the one hand, he recognized as prime facts of his experience the division between the 'I' and the world and the duality within man. On the other, he posited the unity of the 'I' and the world in both intellectual and emotional terms. It is this very experience of aloneness and division which may have provided the great attraction of the mystic unity of all things. But it is this experience, too, which probably caused Buber to reject his earlier monistic formulations of an already existing unity which only needs to be discovered for a later emphasis on the necessity of realizing unity in the world through genuine and fulfilled life.

'God is not divided but everywhere whole, and where he reveals himself, there he is wholly present.' This wonderful world-feeling has become wholly our own, writes Buber. We have woven it in our innermost experience. There often comes to us the desire to put our arms around a young tree and feel the same surge of life as in ourselves or to read our own most special mystery in the eyes of a dumb animal. We experience the ripening and fading of far-distant stars as something which happens to us, and there are moments in which our organism is a wholly other piece of nature.[1]

The unity which the ecstatic experiences when he has brought all his former multiplicity into oneness is not a relative unity, bounded by the existence of other individuals. It is the absolute, unlimited oneness which includes all others. The only true accompaniment of such experience is silence, for any attempt at communication places the ecstatic back in the world of multiplicity. Yet when the ecstatic returns to the world, he must by his very nature seek to express his experience. The need of the mystic to communicate is not only weakness and stammering; it is also power and melody. The mystic desires to bring the timeless over into time—he desires to make the unity without multiplicity into the unity of all multiplicity. This desire brings to mind the great myths of the One which becomes the many because it wishes to know and be known, to love and be loved—the myths of the 'I' that

and the Soul,' p. 148; *Between Man and Man, op. cit.,* 'What Is Man?' pp. 184-185. In addition to his many translations and recreations of Hasidic tales and other Jewish legends, Buber edited and wrote introductions to a selection of the parables of Chuang-Tse—*Reden und Gleichnisse des Tschuang-Tse* (Leipzig: Insel-Verlag, 1914), a book of Chinese ghost and love stories—*Chinesischen Geister- und Liebes-geschichten* (Frankfurt am Main: Rütten & Loening, 1911), a book of Celtic sayings —*Die vier Zweige des Mabinogi* (Leipzig: Insel-Verlag, 1914), and a translation of the national epic of Finland—*Kalewala* (Munich: Georg Müller, 1914). Buber's introduction to the *Kalewala* was reprinted under the title 'Das Epos des Zauberers' in *Hinweise, op. cit.,* pp. 84-103.

[1] Martin Buber, 'Ueber Jakob Böhme,' *Wiener Rundschau,* V, No. 12 (June 15, 1901), pp. 251-253.

creates a 'Thou,' of the Godhead that becomes God. Is not the experience of the ecstatic a symbol of the primeval experience of the world spirit?[1] Corresponding to this dialectic between primal unity and the multiplicity of the world is the dialectic between conflict and love. The movement of conflict leads to individuation, that of love to God. Conflict is the bridge in and through which one 'I' reveals itself in its beauty to another 'I.' Love is the bridge through which being unites itself with God. Out of the intermixture of the two comes life, in which things neither exist in rigid separation nor melt into one another but reciprocally condition themselves. This concept finds its completion, writes Buber, in Ludwig Feuerbach's sentence: 'Man with man—the unity of I and Thou—is God.' The most personal lies in the relation to the other. Join a being to all beings and you lure out of it its truest individuality.[2]

God is immanent within the world and is brought to perfection through the world and through the life of man. The world is no being over against one. It is a becoming. We do not have to accept the world as it is; we continually create it. We create the world in that we unknowingly lend our perceptions the concentration and firmness that make them into a reality. But deeper and more inwardly we consciously create the world in that we let our strength flow into the becoming, in that we ourselves enter into world destiny and become an element in the great event.[3]

Human life itself is the bearer and reality of all transcendence. Tao, 'the way,' is unity in change and transformation, and the perfect revelation of Tao is the man who combines the greatest change with the purest unity. Though Tao is the path, order, and unity of everything, it exists in things only potentially until it becomes living and manifest through its contact with the conscious being of the united man. Tao appears in men as the uniting force that overcomes all deviation from the ground of life, as the completing force that heals all that is sundered and broken.[4]

The lived unity of the Tao cannot be attained by knowledge and action as men ordinarily conceive them; for what men call knowledge consists of the sunderance of the senses and mental power, and what men call action consists of the sunderance of intention and deed. Moreover, what men call human love and righteousness has nothing in

---

[1] *Ekstatische Konfessionen* (Jena: Eugen Diedrichs Verlag, 1909), pp. xi-xxvi.

[2] 'Ueber Jakob Böhme,' *op. cit.*, p. 252; Lesser Ury,' p. 45 f. (see below, p. 51, n. 1).

[3] 'Ueber Jacob Böhme,' p. 251.

[4] Martin Buber, *Die Rede, die Lehre, und das Lied* (Leipzig: Insel Verlag, 1920), pp. 40-79. 'Die Lehre von Tao' was originally published as a 'Nachwort' to *Reden und Gleichnisse des Tschuang-Tse*. It was most recently reprinted in *Hinweise, op. cit.*, pp. 44-83, and in *Pointing the Way, op. cit.*, 'The Teaching of the Tao,' pp. 31-58.

common with the love of the perfect man, for it is perverted by being the subject of a command. The true action, the appearance of which is non-action, is a working of the whole being. To interfere with the life of things is to harm both them and oneself. But to rest is to effect, to purify one's own soul is to purify the world, to surrender oneself to Tao is to renew creation. He who performs this action, or non-action, stands in harmony with the essence and destiny of all things.[1]

Thus for Buber's early mystical philosophy, evil is equivalent to inner division and separation from the ground of life, and the redemption of evil is the realization of a lived unity which not only removes the dissension in the individual but makes actual the unity and perfection of the world. Buber does not treat evil as pure illusion but as a negative force interacting with the good in a process leading back to the original unity. For Buber, as for the Baal-Shem, evil is no essence but a lack— the throne of the good, the 'shell' which surrounds and disguises the essence of things. Though negative, evil is real and must be redeemed through the wholeness and purity of man's being.

[1] 'Die Lehre von Tao,' *op. cit.,* pp. 80-94. Cf. Buber's important Foreword to *Pointing the Way,* p. ix-x, in which he states that he has included 'The Teaching of the Tao' in this collection because it belongs to that 'mystical' 'stage that I had to pass through before I could enter into an independent relationship with being.' This experience of the unity of the self is understood by the mystic as the experience of *the* unity, and this leads him to turn away from his existence as a man to a duality of 'higher' hours of ecstasy and 'lower' hours in the world which are regarded as preparation for the higher. 'The great dialogue between I and Thou is silent; nothing else exists than his self, which he experiences as *the* self. That is certainly an exalted form of being untrue, but it is still being untrue.'

CHAPTER FIVE

PHILOSOPHY OF JUDAISM

THE two great movements which revolutionized Judaism in the eighteenth and nineteenth centuries were the *Haskalah*, or enlightenment, and Hasidism. At its outset the rational *Haskalah* turned naturally to western Europe for its inspiration and looked with contempt on the emotional Hasidim. In the same way early Hasidism found in the sceptical and intellectual *Haskalah* an even greater opponent than traditional Rabbinism. It was only in the wave of a new renaissance that these two movements flowed together, and it was in Buber that this synthesis reached both depth and completeness.[1]

Buber's early essays on Judaism set forth with marked clarity the concern for personal wholeness, for the realization of truth in life, and for the joining of spirit and of basic life energies which consistently appears in all of his later writings and determines, as much as any other element of his thought, his attitude toward evil. Almost every important statement which he makes in these early writings about the psychology of the Jewish people (their dynamism, their concern with relation, their inner division, their desire for realization and unity), he later translates into his general philosophy.

The primary task of the Jewish movement, writes Buber, is the removal of the schism between thought and action and the re-establishment of the unified personality who creates out of a single ardour of will. The truly creative person is not the intellectual, nor is he simply the artist. He is the strong and many-sided man in whom human happenings stream together in order to attain new developments in spirit and deed. The redeeming affirmation of a conflict is the essence of all creativity; in the creative person a deep inner division is brought to harmony. To effect this harmony the creative person must have roots in a people through whom he is enriched and fortified. Today faith lies to life and does violence to its surging meanings. But for him who has lost his God the folk can be a first station on his new way. Today Satan tempts the creative man to lose himself in the inessential, to roam about

[1] Kohn, *op. cit.*, pp. 13-15.

31

in the great confusion in which all human clarity and definiteness has ceased. The creative kingdom is there where form and formation thrive, and rootedness is a mighty helper to the individual to remain therein.[1] Man experiences the fullness of his inner actuality and possibility as a living substance which pulls toward opposite poles; he experiences his inner way as a travelling from crossroad to crossroad. In no men was and is this basic duality so central and dominant as in the Jews, and in consequence nowhere has there been such a monstrous and wonderful paradox as the striving of the Jews for unity. For the ancient Jew objective being is unity and Satan a servant of God. It is man's subjective being which is cleaved, fallen, become inadequate and ungodlike. Redemption takes place through the creature's overcoming his own inner duality. The true meaning of the *Galut*, the exile of the Jews, is the falling away from the ancient striving for unity into an unproductive spirituality and intellectuality divorced from life. As a result Judaism split into two antagonistic sides: an official, uncreative side and an underground of Jewish heretics and mystics who carried forward in glowing inwardness the ancient striving for unity.[2]

The spiritual process of Judaism manifests itself in history as the striving after an ever more perfect realization of three interrelated ideas: the idea of unity, the idea of the deed, and the idea of the future. The Jew has always been more concerned with the whole than with the parts, with movement than with the senses, with time than with space. For this reason he has always considered the deed and not faith to be the decisive relation between man and God. These three ideas of unity, the deed, and the future are interrelated through Buber's emphasis on a dynamic realization of the unconditional in the lives of men. Unity is not a static refusal to change, but unity in change. Action is not a reliance on external deeds and formal laws; it is the action of the total being. The future is not the end of time but the fullness of time, not the transcending of the world and mankind but fulfilment through the world and through mankind—it is a fulfilment of the unconditioned will of God in the conditioned lives of men.[3]

Sin is living divided and unfree, and it is the indolence and decisionlessness which makes this possible. Decisionlessness allows one to be conditioned and acted upon, for without decision one's power remains undirected. It is, therefore, just this failure to direct one's inner power which is the inmost essence of evil. In the soul which decides with its

[1] *Die jüdische Bewegung. Gesammelte Aufsätze und Ansprachen*, Vol. I, 1900-14 (Berlin: Jüdischer Verlag, 1916), pp. 12-15, 52, 66-73.

[2] Martin Buber, 'Das Judentum und die Menscheit,' *Drei Reden über das Judentum* (Frankfurt am Main: Rütten & Loening, 1911), pp. 35-56. The essays in *Drei Reden* are also included in a collected edition, *Reden über das Judentum* (Frankfurt am Main: Rütten & Loening, 1923; Berlin: Schocken Verlag, 1932).

[3] 'Die Erneuerung des Judentums,' *Drei Reden, op. cit.*, pp. 75-96.

whole being there is unity of power and direction—the undiminished force of the passionate impulse and the undiverted rectitude of intention. There is no impulse that is evil in itself; man makes it so when he yields to it instead of controlling it. The Mishnah interprets the command 'Thou shalt love the Lord thy God with all thy heart' as loving God with both the 'good' and the 'evil' impulses; this means loving Him with and through the act of decision, so that the ardour of passion is transformed and enters with its whole power into the single deed.

Decision is the realization on earth of divine freedom and unconditionality. Not the material of an action but the strength of the decision which brings it forth and the dedication of the intention which dwells in it determine whether it will flow off into the kingdom of things or press into the All-holy. The name of the act of decision in its last intensity is *teshuvah*, turning. *Teshuvah* means the caesura of a human life, the renewing revolution in the middle of the course of an existence. When in the middle of 'sin,' in decisionlessness, the will awakes to decision, the integument of ordinary life bursts and the primeval force breaks through and storms upward to heaven. When man has raised the conditioned in himself to the unconditioned, his action works on the fate of God. Only for him who lets things happen and cannot decide is God an unknown being who transcends the world. For him who chooses, God is the nearest and most trusted of things. Whether God is 'transcendent' or 'immanent' thus does not depend on God; it depends on men.[1]

Thus in Buber's early philosophy of Judaism good is identified with decision of the whole being, evil with the directionlessness that results from failure to decide. Every important step forward in the development of Buber's philosophy is reflected in his philosophy of Judaism. His existentialism, his philosophy of community, his religious socialism, and his dialogical philosophy all develop within his philosophy of Judaism as well as outside of it. There is, thus, an essential unity of what are in Buber's writings two separate streams of developing thought.

[1] 'Der Geist des Orients und das Judentum' and 'Jüdische Religiosität,' *Reden über das Judentum, op. cit.*, pp. 81-84, 103-113. These essays were originally published together with 'Der Mythos der Juden' in *Vom Geist des Judentums* (Leipzig: Kurt Wolff Verlag, 1916).

CHAPTER SIX

PHILOSOPHY OF REALIZATION

As far as Buber goes beyond transcendental idealism, he still starts with Kant's teaching that we ourselves impose the order of space and time upon experience in order that we may orient ourselves in it. From Kant, Buber says, he gained an inkling 'that being itself was beyond the reach alike of the finitude and the infinity of space and time, since it only appeared in space and time but did not itself enter into this appearance.' But the problem that Buber faced and that he inherited from the age when idealism had begun to break up was that of how man can reach 'reality' without returning to the naïve, pre-Kantian 'objective' view of the universe.[1]

Buber found this reality through perceiving that in addition to man's orienting function he also possesses a 'realizing' function which brings him into real contact with God, with other men, and with nature. The thought of his teacher Wilhelm Dilthey provided an important bridge to this philosophy of 'realization,' for Dilthey based his thought on the radical difference between the way of knowing proper to the '*Geisteswissenschaften*'—the human studies such as philosophy, the social sciences, and psychology—and that proper to the '*Naturwissenschaften*' —the natural sciences. In the former the knower cannot be merely a detached scientific observer but must also himself participate, for it is through his participation that he discovers both the typical and the unique in the aspects of human life that he is studying.[2]

Another important influence on Buber's philosophy of realization, as on his closely related philosophy of Judaism, was the thought of Friedrich Nietzsche. In one of his earliest articles Buber spoke of Nietzsche as 'the first pathfinder of the new culture,' 'the awakener and creator of new life-values and a new world-feeling.' Nietzsche's influence

[1] *Between Man and Man, op. cit.*, 'What Is Man?' pp. 136-137; Kohn, *op. cit.*, pp. 244-245; Hugo Bergmann, 'Begriff und Wirklichkeit. Ein Beitrag zur Philosophie Martin Bubers und J. G. Fichtes,' *Der Jude*, Berlin, X, No. 5 (March 1928), 'Sonderheft zu Martin Bubers fünfzigstem Geburtstag,' pp. 96-97.

[2] H. A. Hodges, *Wilhelm Dilthey, An Introduction* (New York: Oxford University Press, 1944), pp. viii-ix, 12-16.

Philosophy of Realization

may account in part for the dynamism of Buber's philosophy, for its concern with creativity and greatness, for its emphasis on the concrete and actual as opposed to the ideal and abstract, for its idea of the fruitfulness of conflict, and for its emphasis on the value of life impulses and wholeness of being as opposed to detached intellectuality.[1]

Probably the strongest influence on Buber's concept of realization, however, was the existentialist philosophy of Søren Kierkegaard. In Kierkegaard's earlier works are found the germ of some of Buber's most important early and later ideas: the direct relation between the individual and God in which the individual addresses God as 'Thou,' the insecure and exposed state of every individual as an individual, the concept of the 'knight of faith' who cannot take shelter in the universal but must constantly risk all in the concrete uniqueness of each new situation, the necessity of becoming a true person before going out to relation, and the importance of realizing one's belief in one's life. These similarities plus Buber's own treatment of Kierkegaard in his mature works make it clear that Kierkegaard is one of the most important single influences on Buber's thought.[2]

Buber has spoken of Kierkegaard and Dostoievsky together as the two men of the nineteenth century who will, in his opinion, 'remain' in the centuries to come. In Dostoievsky Buber found spiritual intensity, fervour, depth of insight, and an understanding of man's inner cleavage. He also found in him something of that dynamism and concern for realization in life that mark both Nietzsche and Kierkegaard. Finally, he found in him a dialectic very similar to his own intellectual processes and a world-affirming mystic religion of ecstasy, love, and brotherhood which bears a remarkable resemblance to his own thought.

In *Daniel* (1913) we find Buber's concern for unity, realization, and creativity expressed for the first time entirely in its own terms and not as the interpretation of some particular thought or religious or cultural movement. *Daniel* is the first mature and comprehensive expression of Buber's philosophy, and it is at the same time the most creative and organically whole of his books to appear up till that time.

'In each thing,' writes Buber in *Daniel*, 'there opens to you the door

[1] Martin Buber, 'Ein Wort über Nietzsche und die Lebenswerte,' *Kunst und Leben*, Berlin, December 1900; quoted in Kohn, *op. cit.*, p. 36; Kohn, pp. 21-22, 26-27, 227.

[2] Cf. Søren Kierekgaard, *Fear and Trembling*, translated by Walter Lowrie (Princeton: Princeton University Press, 1941), pp. 55-56, 118-120, 189-190. For Buber's treatment of Kierkegaard see Martin Buber, *I and Thou*, translated by Ronald Gregor Smith, 2nd edition, with Postscript by the Author added (New York: Charles Scribner's Sons, 1958), pp. 106-109; *Hasidism and Modern Man, op. cit.*, Book VI, 'Love of God and Love of Neighbor,' pp. 227-233; *Between Man and Man, op. cit.*, 'The Question to the Single One,' pp. 48-82, and 'What Is Man?' pp. 161-163, 171-181; and *Eclipse of God, op. cit.*, 'On the Suspension of the Ethical,' translated by Maurice Friedman, pp. 149-156.

of the One if you bring with you the magic that unlocks it: the perfection of your direction.' But direction is only complete when it is fulfilled with power: the power to experience the whole event. Power alone gives one only the fullness, direction alone only the meaning of the experience—power and direction together allow one to penetrate into its substance, into oneness itself.

The vortex of happenings sweeps over one like a sandstorm which threatens to destroy one. Which type of soul one has is decided by how one withstands it. One type of person thinks only of protection, of the inherited arts of self-defence; he educates his senses to perceive in place of the vortex an ordered world conceived within the framework of basic principles of experience. He no longer meets the world but only his own cause-and-purpose oriented conceptions of it. The other type of person lets stand, to be sure, the ordered world—the world of utility in which he can alone live with other men; he accepts it and learns its laws. But deep within him grows and endures the readiness to go out to meet the naked chaos armed with nothing but the magic of his inborn direction.

Direction is that primeval tension of a human soul which moves it to choose and to realize this and no other out of the infinity of possibilities. In direction the soul does not order reality but opens and delivers itself to it, and not with the senses and understanding alone but with its whole being. Direction is thus a finding of one's own way and a realization of one's inmost being that gives one the strength to withstand in openness the confused stream of outer and inner happenings. But direction is neither individuality, determinism, nor arbitrary self-will. It is the realization of what was already potentially the one true direction of one's personality. Nor does this self-realization exclude fellowship with others. Rather it makes possible true community, from being to being.[1]

There is a twofold relation of men to their experience: the orienting and the realizing. That which man experiences, doing and suffering, creating and enjoying, he can order in the continuity of experience for the sake of his goals or he can comprehend in its power and splendour for its own sake. If man orders it, he works with it according to its forms and laws. And this ordering is not to be despised. How should we not honour the unsurveyable edifice of science and its wonderful development? But everywhere where orienting knowledge rules by itself, it takes place at the cost of the experience of reality.

Realization refers to that enhanced meaning of life which springs from moments of intensified existence and intensified perception. This is what it means to realize: to relate experience to nothing else but itself. And here is the place where the strength of the human spirit

---

[1] Martin Buber, *Daniel, Gespräche von der Verwirklichung* (Leipzig: Insel Verlag, 1913), 'Von der Richtung,' pp. 13, 16-22.

awakens and concentrates and becomes creative. Whereas in the system of experiencing one has only to arrange and order, and living with only one part of one's being can come to terms with the all; in realizing one must bring forth the totality of one's being in order to withstand a single thing or event. But because power thus gives itself to the thing or event, it creates reality in it and through it. For that alone is reality which is so experienced. There is no purely realizing or purely orienting type of man. As in the life of the community attained reality must ever again be placed in the continuity of experience, so in the life of the individual hours of orienting follow hours of realization and must so follow. But the creative man is he who has the most effective power of realization; he is the man in whom the realizing force of the soul has so concentrated into work that it creates reality for all. The creative man possesses the unbroken power of realization, for in his creativity mature orientation is also included as a dependent and serving function.

Realized experience creates the essential form of existence; only here can what we call 'things' and what we call 'I' find their reality. For all experience is a dream of being bound together; orientation divides and sunders it, realization accomplishes and proclaims it. Nothing individual is real in itself, for it is only preparation: all reality is fulfilled binding. In each man there lives, utilized or suppressed, the power to become unified and to enter into reality.

Men of realization are few in our time, which makes up for them with the doers and performers—those who act without being, who give what they do not have, who conquer where they have not fought. The undue predominance of orientation has settled in the blood of our time and has dissolved its reality. Men have objects and know how to attain them. They have a milieu, and they have information about their milieu. They also have spirituality of many kinds, and they talk a great deal. Yet all of this is outside of reality. Men live and do not realize what they live, for their experience is ordered without being comprehended. Their limitations are so closely bound to them that they call them elegant names—culture, religion, progress, tradition, or intellectuality; 'ah, a thousand masks has the unreal!' [1]

All living with the whole being and with unconstrained force means danger; there is no thing, relation, or event in the world that does not reveal an abyss when it is known, and all thinking threatens to shatter the stability of the thinker. He who lives his life in genuine, realizing knowledge must perpetually begin anew, perpetually risk all; and therefore his truth is not a having but a becoming. The orienting man wants security and security once for all: he wants to know his way about, and he wants a solid general truth that will not overturn him. But the man

[1] *Ibid.*, 'Von der Wirklichkeit,' pp. 29-47.

who forgets himself in order to use his power of realization loves the underived truth which he who ventures creates out of the depths. He does not want to know where he is at; for he is not always at the same place, but is ever at the new, at the uttermost, at God. God cannot realize Himself in men otherwise than as the innermost presence of an experience, and the God of this experience is therefore not the same, but always the new, the extreme. Orientation which acts as the all-embracing is thoroughly godless; godless also is the theologian who places his god in causality, a helping formula of orientation, and the spiritualist who knows his way about in the 'true world' and sketches its topography.

The realizing man is unprotected in the world, but he is not abandoned; for there is nothing that can lead him astray. He does not possess the world, yet stands in its love; for he realizes all being in its reality. He has that before which all security appears vain and empty: direction and meaning. When he comes to a crossroads, he makes his choice with immediate decision as out of a deep command. When he acts, he does his deed and no other, and he decides with his being. The deed is not limited for him, as it is for the orienting man, to causality and evolution; he feels himself free and acts as a free man. The orienting man places all happening in formulas, rules, and connections; the realizing man relates each event to nothing but its own intrinsic value. He receives what befalls him as a message; he does what is necessary as a commission and a demonstration. He who descends into the transforming abyss can create unity out of his and out of all duality. Here no 'once for all' is of value; for this is the endless task. This is the kingdom of God: the kingdom of 'holy insecurity.' [1]

All wisdom of the ages has the duality of the world as its subject. However it names the two forces that it makes known—spirit and matter, form and material, being and becoming, reason and will, or positive and negative element—it has in mind the overcoming of their tension, the union of their duality. The longing for unity is the glowing ground of the soul; but the man who is true feels that he would degrade this longing if he surrendered something of the fullness of his experience to please it. He feels that he can only become obedient to it in truth if he strives to fulfil it out of his completeness and preserves his experienced duality undiminished in the force of its distance.

For this reason the faithful man rejects the Absolute of the Vedantic non-dualist as a life-denying unity found apart from the main highroad on which the faithful man must travel. He rejects in like manner the

---

[1] Martin Buber, '*Daniel. Gespräche von der Verwirklichung* (Leipzig: Insel Verlag, 1913), 'Von dem Sinn,' pp. 55-82. 'Today,' writes Buber, 'I would not any more describe the kingdom so extravagantly! (*Daniel* is still too much a book of the "easy word").' From a letter from Professor Buber to the author of August 8, 1954.

Philosophy of Realization

abstract unity of European idealist philosophy and the empty unity of the Taoist who indifferentiates all opposition in himself. True unity is the unity of the world as it is, a unity which excludes nothing and destroys nothing but transforms the stubborn material of life into oneness through the realizing action of men. It is the unity of man and man, of man and the world, of life and death; the unity which is realized by the man who in his own life has direction and meaning. It is the unity which includes all evil, even the kingdom of Satan; for it can accept nothing less than the whole. But just because this is a realized unity, it is one that is never completely attained, one which ever again comes forth as purer and sharper duality. This new duality, in turn, provides the material for an ever higher and more nearly perfect oneness. Each new act of inner unification enables the individual to take unto himself ever greater tensions of world-polarity and bring them to unity.[1]

Hereafter, however Buber may change his philosophy, he never forsakes his belief in a redemption which accepts all the evil of real life and transforms it into the good. Between the extremes of pantheism and an absolute divorced from the world lies the duality of a God who is real in Himself yet must be realized in the world through man's life. In this middle sphere the mystic's demand for a life lived in terms of the highest reality and the existentialist's demand for self-realization and genuine existence may meet in spirit. In *Daniel* this meeting has resulted in a new unity—the philosophy of realization.

[1] *Ibid.*, 'Von der Einheit,' pp. 139-152. Erich Przywara, S.J., identifies the three wrong ways in *Daniel* as the Hindu, the European, and the Chinese, respectively in 'Judentum und Christentum,' *Stimme der Zeit*, CX (1925-26), 87.

CHAPTER SEVEN

DIALECTIC OF RELIGION AND CULTURE

CLOSELY related to Buber's philosophy of realization, and like it an important element in the development of his I-Thou philosophy, is his dialectic of religion and culture. Influenced by Nietzsche, Wilhelm Dilthey, and Georg Simmel,[1] this dialectic combines a theory of religious symbolism with a philosophy of history. Culture and religiousness replace one another in the history of peoples, writes Buber. Culture is the stabilization of the life impulse and life forms between two religious upheavals. Religion is the renewal of the life impulse and life forms between two cultural developments. In the religious upheaval the powers become free. In culture they bind themselves again in new life forms, bind themselves ever faster and tighter, until they lie caught, dull and lifeless, in the forms. Then there comes again a moment when life revolts against the law that has ceased to contain the spirit which created it. In this moment the form is broken and life is summoned to new creation out of the chaos. But this shattering is no simple turning-point. It is much more a fearful crisis that is often decisive not for renewal but for death. And yet there is no other way not only to a new religiousness but also to a new culture. This upheaval can at first find no other expression than the religious, for before man creates new life forms, he creates a new relation to life itself, a new meaning of life. But this renewal must be accompanied by the inner strength to withstand the crisis. Power of the storming spirit to stir up the conflagration, security of the constructing soul to hold itself in the purifying fire: these are the forces which guide a people to rejuvenated life.[2]

This dialectic recognizes a conservative and retaining influence as a necessary accompaniment of the dynamic and creative, if stable life is

[1] Cf. Nietzsche's contrast between the Dionysian and the Apollonian in *The Birth of Tragedy* and *The Will to Power*, Dilthey's contrast between *Geisteswissenschaften* and *Naturwissenschaften*, and Simmel's contrast between 'religiousness' and 'religion' in *Die Religion*, Vol. II of *Die Gesellschaft. Sammlung sozialpsychologischer Monographien*, edited by Martin Buber (Frankfurt am Main: Rütten & Loening, 1906), pp. 7-17. Dilthey and Simmel were both Buber's teachers.

[2] *Die jüdische Bewegung*, Vol. I, *op. cit.*, 'Zwiefache Zukunft' (1912), pp. 216-220.

to result. Yet it also recognizes the process by which the forms encroach on the life that created them until that life must destroy the forms in order to continue its existence. Evil in this scheme is not a separate principle but an undue predominance of one force over the other, especially an imbalance so great that it can no longer be corrected through a religious renewal.

This dialectic is further clarified by Buber's distinction between 'religion' and 'religiousness.' 'Religiousness' is the astonished and worshipful feeling of man that above his conditionality there stands an Unconditioned whose desire is to form a living community with him and whose will he may realize in the world of men. 'Religion' is the sum of customs and teachings in which the religiousness of a certain epoch of a people has been expressed and formed, crystallized in precepts and dogma, and handed down to all future generations as inalterably binding. Religion is true only as long as it is fruitful, and it is fruitful only as long as religiousness is able to fill precept and dogma with new meaning and inwardly transform them to meet the need of each new generation. Religiousness means activity—an elementary setting oneself in relation to the Absolute; religion means passivity—taking upon oneself inherited laws.[1]

Dogmas and precepts are only the changing products of the attempts of the human spirit to fix the working of the Absolute which it experiences in a symbolic order of the knowable and the do-able. The primary reality is the action of the Absolute on the human spirit. Man experiences the Absolute as the great presence that is over against him, as 'Thou' in itself. He grasps the ineffable through the creation of symbols, in signs and speech which reveal God to men for this age. But in the course of ages these symbols are outgrown and new ones bloom in their place until no symbol performs what is needful and life itself in the wonder of its togetherness becomes a symbol.

Religious truth is vital rather than conceptual. It can only be intimated in words and can first be satisfactorily proclaimed only by being confirmed in the life of a man, in the life of a community. The word of the teaching loses its religious character as soon as it is cut loose from its connection with the life of the founder and his disciples and recast into an independently knowable and thoroughly impersonal principle. Each religiously creative age is only a stage of religious truth, for, in distinction from philosophic truth, it is no tenet but a way, no thesis but a process. It is a powerful process of spiritual creation, a creative answer to the Absolute.[2]

Theophany happens to man, and he has his part in it as God has

---

[1] *Reden über das Judentum, op. cit.*, 'Jüdische Religiosität' (1916), pp. 103-105.
[2] *Ibid.*, 'Cheruth. Ein Rede über Jugend und Religion' (1919), pp. 202-209, 217-224.

His. Forms and ideas result from it; but what is revealed in it is not form or idea but God. Religious reality means this, for it is the undiminished relation to God Himself. Man does not possess God; he meets Him.

That through which all religion lives, religious reality, goes in advance of the morphology of the age and exercises a decisive effect upon it; it endures in the essence of the religion which is morphologically determined by culture and its phases, so that this religion stands in a double influence, a cultural, limited one from without and an original and unlimited one from within. This inner reality, from the moment that it is incorporated in religion, no longer works directly, but through religion it affects all spheres of life. Thus theophany begets history.[1]

Religion is thus influenced from the side of religious experience on the one hand and culture on the other. The Absolute enters into the forms of religion and through religion influences culture and history. From this point of view history cannot be understood as a purely immanent development, for it is partially a product of an encounter with a primary reality which transcends culture and gives rise to it. Each of the cultures of history originated in an original relation event, and each must return to such an event before it can find renewal. Similarly, religious forms and symbols arise out of elemental religious experience and must be renewed and transformed by such experience if they are to retain their living reality.

[1] *Reden über das Judentum, op. cit.*, 'Vorwort' (1923), pp. ix-xii (my translation).

CHAPTER EIGHT

COMMUNITY AND RELIGIOUS SOCIALISM

TRUE community, writes Buber, can only be founded on changed relations between men, and these changed relations can only follow the inner change and preparation of the men who lead, work, and sacrifice for the community. Each man has an infinite sphere of responsibility, responsibility before the infinite. But there are men for whom this infinite responsibility exists in a specially active form. These are not the rulers and statesmen who determine the external destiny of great communities and who, in order to be effective, turn from the individual, enormously threatened lives to the general multitude that appears to them unseeing. The really responsible men are rather those who can withstand the thousandfold questioning glance of individual lives, who give true answer to the trembling mouths that time after time demand from them decision.[1]

The principle obstacle to the erection of true community is that dualism which splits life into two independent spheres—one of the truth of the spirit and the other of the reality of life. True human life is life in the face of God, and God is not a Kantian idea but an elementarily present substance—the mystery of immediacy before which only the pious man can stand. God is in all things, but he is realized only when individual beings open to one another, communicate with one another, and help one another—only where immediacy establishes itself between beings. There in between, in the apparently empty space, the eternal substance manifests itself. The true place of realization is the community, and true community is that in which the godly is realized between men.

The prophets, says Buber, demanded a direct godly form of community in contrast to the godless and spiritless state. True to Jewish thought, they did not simply deny the earthly state but insisted that it

[1] *Die Jüdische Bewegung, op. cit.*, Vol. II, 1916-20 (1921), 'Kulturarbeit' (1917), p. 94; *Hasidism and Modern Man*, 'My Way to Hasidism,' p. 67 ff. On Buber's relation to the Christian religious socialist movement, cf. Ephraim Fischoff's Introduction to Buber's *Paths in Utopia* (Boston: Beacon Press, 1958).

must be penetrated by the spirit of true community. It would have been unthinkable to them to have made a compromise with conditions as they were, but it would have been equally unthinkable for them to have fled from those conditions into a sphere of inner life. Never did they decide between the kingdom of God and the kingdom of man. The kingdom of God was to them nothing other than the kingdom of man as it shall become. When they despaired of present fulfilment, they projected the image of their truth into Messianism. Yet here also they meant no opposition to this human world in which we live, but its purification and completion.

Jesus, like the prophets of Israel, wanted to fulfil rather than do away with human society. By the kingdom of God He meant no other-worldly consolation, no vague heavenly blessedness, and also no spiritual or cultic league or church. What He meant was the perfected living together of men, the true community in which God shall have direct rule. Jesus wished to build out of Judaism the temple of true community before the sight of which the walls of the power state must fall to pieces.

But not so did the coming generations understand Him. In the place of the Jewish knowledge of the single world, fallen through confusion but capable of redemption through the struggling human will, came the postulation of a fundamental and unbridgeable duality of human will and God's grace. The will is now regarded as unconditionally bad and elevation through its power is impossible. Not will in all its contrariness and all its possibility is the way to God, but faith and waiting for the contact of grace. Evil is no longer the 'shell' which must be broken through. It is rather the primal force which stands over against the good as the great adversary. The state is no longer the consolidation of a will to community that has gone astray and therefore is penetrable and redeemable by right will. It is either, as for Augustine, the eternally damned kingdom from which the chosen separate themselves or, as for Thomas, the first step and preparation for the true community, which is a spiritual one. The true community is no longer to be realized in the perfect life of men with one another but in the church. It is the community of spirit and grace from which the world and nature are fundamentally separated.[1]

This atmosphere of the dualism of truth and reality, idea and fact, morality and politics is that, writes Buber, in which our present age lives. Corresponding to it is the egoistic nationalism which perverts the goal of community by making it an end itself. It is not power itself which is evil, Buber states, in disagreement with the historian Jacob Burckhardt. Power is intrinsically guiltless and is the precondition for

[1] Martin Buber, *Der heilige Weg* (Frankfurt am Main: Rütten & Loening, 1919), pp. 11-44. Later reprinted in *Reden über das Judentum, op. cit.*, without the introduction, pp. 9-11.

the actions of man. It is the will to power, the greed for more power than others, which is destructive.

A genuine person too likes to affirm himself in the face of the world, but in doing so he also affirms the power with which the world confronts him. This requires constant demarcation of one's own right from the right of others, and such demarcation cannot be made according to rules valid once and for all. Only the secret of hourly acting with a continually repeated sense of responsibility holds the rules for such demarcations. This applies both to the attitude of the individual toward his own life, and to the nation he is a member of.

Not renunciation of power but responsibility in the exercise of power prevents it from becoming evil. This responsibility is lacking in modern nations, for they are constantly in danger of slipping into that power hysteria which disintegrates the ability to draw lines of demarcation. Only in the recognition of an obligation and a task that is more than merely national can the criterion be found which governs the drawing of the distinction between legitimate and arbitrary nationalism.[1]

The mature expression of Buber's concern with realizing the divine through true community is the religious socialism which he developed in the period immediately after the First World War. This development was decisively influenced by the socialism of Buber's friend Gustav Landauer, the social anarchism of Michael Kropotkin, and the distinction between 'community' and 'association' in Ferdinand Tönnies's work, *Gemeinschaft und Gesellschaft* (1887). Community ('Gemeinschaft') Buber defines as an organic unity which has grown out of common possessions, work, morals, or belief. Association ('Gesellschaft') he defines as a mechanical association of isolated self-seeking individuals. It is an ordered division of society into self-seeking individuals held together by force, compromise, convention, and public opinion.

Modern western culture, states Buber, is on the way from 'Gemeinschaft' to 'Gesellschaft.' The mechanical type of social living has replaced the organic. Marxism, the dominant form of modern socialism, desires to overcome the atomization of present-day life and sees itself as the bearer and executor of an evolutionary process. Yet it is nothing other than the process of development from community to association that it is completing. For what today is still left of an autonomy of organic community of wills must, under the working of this tendency, be absorbed into the power of the state. The state will indeed guarantee justice through laws, but the power of the state will be raised to an all-controlling dogma which will make impossible any spontaneous

---

[1] *Israel and the World, op. cit.*, 'Nationalism' (1921), pp. 216-225.

righteousness. Community which once existed universally, and which today exists almost alone in personal life and unnoticed fellowships, will not be able to withstand the all-embracing power of the new socialist state.

In opposition to that socialism which promotes and completes the evolution to 'Gesellschaft' stands another which wills to overcome it. The first movement desires to gain possession of the state and set new institutions in the place of those existing, expecting thereby to transform human relations in their essence. The second knows that the erection of new institutions can only have a genuinely liberating effect when it is accompanied by a transformation of the actual life between man and man. This life between man and man does not take place in the abstraction of the state but rather there where a reality of spatial, functional, emotional, or spiritual togetherness exists—in the village and city community, in the workers' fellowship, in comradeship, in religious union.

In this moment of western culture a great longing for community possesses the souls of men. This longing can only be satisfied by the autonomy of the communal cells which together make up true commonwealth. But this autonomy will never be accorded by the present state, nor by the socialist state which will not renounce its rigid centralization to bring about its own decentralization, nor abandon its mechanical form in favour of an organic one. Hence the renewal of communal cells and the joining of these cells into larger communities and commonwealths must depend on the will of individuals and groups to establish a communal economy. Men must recognize that true participation in community demands no less power of soul than participation in a parliament or state politics and is the only thing that can make the latter effective and legitimate.

The decisive problem of our time, however, is that men do not live in their private lives what they seek to bring to pass in public. Wholly ineffective and illusory is the will for social reality of circles of intellectuals who fight for the transformation of human relations yet remain as indirect and unreal as ever in their personal life with men. The authenticity of the political position of a man is tested and formed in his natural 'unpolitical' sphere. Here is the germinating ground of all genuine communal-effecting force. No lived community is lost, and out of no other element than lived community can the community of the human race be built.[1]

[1] Martin Buber, *Gemeinschaft,* Vol. II of *Worte an die Zeit* (Munich: Dreiländerverlag, 1919), pp. 7-26. On Buber's relation to Landauer see Martin Buber, 'Landauer und die Revolution,' *Masken,* Halbmonatschrift des Duesseldorfer Schauspielhauses, XIV (1918-19), No. 18/19, pp. 282-286; *Hinweise, op. cit.,* 'Erinnerung an einen Tod' (1929), pp. 252-258, and *Pointing the Way, op. cit.,* 'Recollection of a Death,' pp. 115-120; Martin Buber, *Paths in Utopia,* trans. by R. F. C. Hull (London: Routledge, 1949), chap. vi, pp. 46-57; and Kohn,

Community and Religious Socialism

Buber's religious socialism is built on closeness to the land, on the meaningfulness of work and of mutual help, on the leadership of those men who can take responsibility for individual lives, on community built out of direct relationship between men and between groups of men, on the spirit of an eternal yet ever-changing truth, and above all on the reign of God.[1] In this religious socialism Buber's call for the realization of God on earth and his concern for the relations between man and man have merged into one mature whole—the message of true community. This community starts not with facts of economics and history but with the spirit working silently in the depths. Even in 1919 Buber saw the true nature of the socialist power-state which, in the name of compulsory justice and equality, makes impossible spontaneous community and genuine relationship between man and man. True to the 'narrow ridge,' he refused the clamouring either-or of the modern world—the demand that one accept the centralized socialist state because of the defects of capitalism or the capitalist society because of the defects of socialism.

Buber's socialism of this period is religious but it is not 'Utopian,' for it does not base its claims and its hopes on any easily workable scheme or any facile trust in human nature. Rather it demands the thing that is hardest of all, that men live their lives with one another with the same genuineness and integrity as they desire to establish in the pattern of the total community. And it demands it in the face of 'history' and of 'determinism' and by the strength of the power of the spirit to come to man in his deepest need. It does not expect community to be established simply through the grace of God or simply through the will of man, but through the will of man which *in extremis* becomes one with the will of God.

The socialist power-state is not, for Buber, evil in itself any more than the capitalist state. Both are evil in so far as they prevent the springing-up of the good, the socialist state in that it makes impossible even those remnants of true community which exist in the capitalist state, the capitalist state in that the relations between man and man are indirect and perverted, based on desire for exploitation rather than true togetherness. The remedy for these evils is not the immediate establishment of some super-society but simply the strengthening of the forces of good through the will for genuine relationship and true community. The surging tides of inexorable world history are slowly pushed back and reversed by the invisible forces working in the souls of men and in the relations between man and man.

---

op. cit., pp. 29-31. On his relation to Kropotkin see *Paths in Utopia*, chap. v, pp. 38-45. On his relation to Tönnies, see Kohn, *op. cit.*, pp. 195-197, 348.

[1] *Der heilige Weg, op. cit.*, pp. 85-87 (my translation). See also Martin Buber, *Worte an die Zeit*, vol. I, *Grundsätze* (München: Dreiländerverlag, 1919), pp. 5-11.

CHAPTER NINE

THRESHOLD OF DIALOGUE

IN addition to Hasidism, Kierkegaard, and Dilthey, the most important influences on the development of Buber's I-Thou philosophy were Ludwig Feuerbach and Georg Simmel. Buber states in 'What Is Man?' that Feuerbach gave him a decisive impetus in his youth. Unlike Kant, writes Buber, Feuerbach postulates the whole man and not cognition as the beginning of philosophizing, and by man he 'does not mean man as an individual, but man with man—the connection of *I* and *Thou*.'

'The individual man for himself,' runs his manifesto, 'does not have man's being in himself, either as a moral being or a thinking being. Man's being is contained only in community, in the unity of man with man—a unity which rests, however, only on the reality of the difference between I and Thou.' [1]

Simmel, too, is concerned with relation—the relation between man and God, between man and man, and between man and nature. He finds in the concept of the divine the substantial and ideal expression of the relations between men, and he draws an analogy between the relations of man and God and those of man and man which comes quite close to Buber's own I-Thou relation. To 'believe' in God, according to Simmel, means not just a rational belief in His existence but a definite inner relation to Him, a surrender of feeling and direction of life. In the same way to 'believe' in a man means to have a relation of trust to the whole man, a relation which takes precedence over any proof concerning his particular qualities. On the other hand, there is a one-sidedness and absence of mutuality in Simmel's idea of relation which sets it at some distance from that of Buber. The important thing to Simmel is that the individual call up unused potentialities in himself. [2] This emphasis on the psychological and emotional effects of relation is

---

[1] *Between Man and Man, op. cit.*, p. 136 f. Cf. Feuerbach's *Grundsätze der Philosophie der Zukunft* (1843), # 61, 33, 34, 42, 64-66.
[2] Simmel, *Die Religion, op. cit.*, pp. 22 f., 31-5, 39 f., 67 f., 75.

one that is utterly foreign to Buber, for it tends to remove reality away from the relation back into the individual himself.

Particularly illustrative of the gradual development of Buber's dialogical thought is his progressive reinterpretation of the feeling of unity with certain objects of nature. In Buber's essay on Jacob Boehme (1900) this feeling of unity is used to illustrate the idea of man as the microcosm, or little world which contains the whole. In 'Ecstasy and Confession' (1909) it is used to illustrate the oneness in ecstasy of the 'I' and the world. In *Daniel* (1913) it is used to illustrate the unity which is created and realized in the world. And in *Ich und Du* (1922) it is used to illustrate the I-Thou relation, an event which takes place between two beings which none the less remain separate. Two of the specific experiences which Buber mentions in the essay on Boehme— that of kinship with a tree and that of looking into the eyes of a dumb animal—are later used in *I and Thou* as an example not of unity but of the I-Thou relation. Yet the emotional content of the experiences as described in the two works is almost identical! [1]

In *Ereignisse und Begegnungen* ('Events and Meetings') (1917) we find the link between Buber's philosophy of realization and his philosophy of dialogue. What the learned combination of ideas denies, writes Buber in this work, the humble and faithful beholding of any thing confirms. Each thing and being has a twofold nature: the passive, appropriable, comparable, and dissectible and the active, unappropriable, incomparable, and irreducible. He who truly experiences a thing that leaps to meet him of itself has known therein the world. The contact between the inexpressible circle of things and the experiencing powers of our senses is more and other than a vibration of the ether and the nervous system—it is the incarnate spirit. And the reality of the experienced world is so much the more powerful, the more powerfully we experience it, realize it. There is a common reality which suffices for the comparison and ordering of things. But another is the great reality which we can only make into our world if we melt the shell of passivity with our ardour and strength until the active, bestowing side of things leaps up to meet us and embrace us. The world cannot be known otherwise than through things and not otherwise than with the active sense-spirit of the loving man.

The loving man is one who takes up each thing unrelated to other things. For this hour no other lives than this thing which is alone loved in the world, filling it out and indistinguishably coinciding with it. Where the rationalist draws out the general qualities of a thing and places them in categories, the loving man sees what is unique in a thing, its self. This is the active side which the circle of world compre-

---

[1] 'Ueber Jakob Böhme,' *op. cit.*, p. 252 f.; *I and Thou, op. cit.*, pp. 7 f., 96 f.

hensibility misses. In the beloved thing whose self he realizes, the loving man confirms the mysterious countenance of the all.[1]

The 'loving man' of *Events and Meetings* is similar to the realizing man of *Daniel*. But now the twofold nature of life no longer applies to man alone but is inherent in things themselves. The emphasis, moreover, is not on the unity of things, not even the realized unity of *Daniel*, but on the meeting between man and what is over against him, a meeting which never becomes an identity. Because this is an encounter and not a perfect unity and because the encounter takes place not between man and passive objects but between man and the active self of things, man is limited in his ability to form and shape the world and hence to overcome the evil in himself and in the world. But he is also greatly aided, for the active self of things responds to his loving experiencing of them so that the force of the world joins his own force to bring his deed to effectiveness.

Buber says in this book that he is not a mystic, and this statement is supported by the emphasis on the life of the senses in many of its essays.[2] According to Buber's own later testimony, a personal experience played a decisive part in this conversion from the 'mystical' to the everyday. Once after a morning of 'religious enthusiasm' he was visited by a young man. Though friendly and attentive, he was not present in spirit. Later he learned that the young man had come to him for a decision. As we are told that he died not long after, we may imagine that the decision was life or death. The elder man answered the questions that the young man asked, but not the ones he did not ask. He did not meet his despair by 'a presence by means of which we are told that nevertheless there is meaning.' This was, says Buber, an event of judgment.

> Since then I have given up the 'religious' which is nothing but the exception, extraction, exaltation, ecstasy; or it has given me up. I possess nothing but the everyday out of which I am never taken. The mystery is no longer disclosed, it has escaped or it has made its dwelling here where everything happens as it happens. I know no fulness but each mortal hour's fulness of claim and responsibility.[3]

---

[1] Martin Buber, *Ereignisse und Begegnungen* (Leipzig: Insel Verlag, 1917), 'Mit einem Monisten,' pp. 28-35. Reprinted in *Hinweise*, pp. 36-43, and in *Pointing the Way* under the title 'With a Monist,' pp. 25-30.

[2] Cf. 'Der Altar,' 'Bruder Leib,' 'Der Dämon im Traum,' and 'An das Gleichzeitige.' These essays are all reprinted in *Hinweise*, pp. 18-35 and 118-120, and in *Pointing the Way* under the titles 'The Altar,' 'Brother Body,' 'The Demon in the Dream,' and 'To the Contemporary,' pp. 11-25, 59-60.

[3] *Between Man and Man*, 'Dialogue,' p. 13 f. 'It was in the late autumn of 1914, and he died in the war,' wrote Buber to the author on August 8, 1954.

Threshold of Dialogue

Simple immediacy and togetherness, writes Buber, is the most effective form of action. More powerful and more holy than all writing is the presence of a man who is simply and directly there. Productivity is only true existence when it takes root in the immediacy of a lived life. It is the ruling belief of our time that production is the criterion of human worth. But illegitimate production, production without immediacy, is no criterion, for it is not reality but delusion. The overvaluation of productivity is so great in our age that even truly productive men give up the roots of a genuinely lived life and wear themselves out turning all experience to value as public communication. The productivity that is already present in the perception of the artist and the poet is not a will to create but an ability to create. It is the formative element of experience which also accompanies all that befalls the non-artistic man and is given an issue by him as often as he lifts an image out of the stream of perception and inserts it in his memory as something single, limited, and meaningful in itself. But if in perceiving a man already cherishes the intention of utilizing, then he disquiets the experience, deforms its growth, and destroys its meaning. He who meets men with a double glance, an open one which invites fellowship and a secret one which conceals the conscious aim of the observer—he cannot be delivered from his sickness by any talent that he brings to his work, for he has poisoned the springs of his life.[1] This

---

[1] *Ereignisse und Begegnungen,* pp. 66–76. Reprinted in *Hinweisse,* pp. 36–43, and in *Pointing the Way* under the title 'Productivity and Existence,' pp. 5–10. Although it is only with *Ereignisse und Begegnungen* that Buber's thought becomes really dialogical, there are a number of hints of dialogue and explicit uses of the 'I-Thou' terminology in his earlier writing. In his essay on Boehme in 1901 Buber writes that Boehme's dialectic of the reciprocal conditioning of things finds its completion in Ludwig Feuerbach's sentence: 'Man with man—the unity of I and Thou—is God.' (Ueber Jakob Böhme,' p. 252 f.) In 'Lesser Ury' (1903) Buber writes: 'The most personal lies in the relation to the other. Join a being to all beings and you lure out of it its truest individuality.' (*Juedische Kuenstler,* ed. by Martin Buber (Berlin: Juedischer Verlag, 1903), p. 45 f.)
  In the introduction to *Die Legende des Baalschem* (1908) he speaks of legend as 'the myth of I and Thou, the inspired and the inspirer; the finite who enters into the infinite, and the infinite who has need of the finite.' Again in 'Ekstase und Bekenntnis' (1909) he speaks explicitly of the 'I' that creates a 'Thou.' In his later essays of this early period the I-Thou terminology becomes more frequent, especially, as we have seen, in his treatment of community and of theophany. For Buber's own discussion of the development of his dialogical thinking and the circumstances under which he wrote *I and Thou* (including his statement that he did not read Rosenzweig and Ebner's books till later because of a two-year period of 'spiritual askesis') see "Afterword: The History of the Dialogical Principle," in Buber, *Between Man and Man,* tr. Maurice Friedman (New York: Macmillan Paperbacks, 1965). For a far more extensive treatment of the influences on Buber's thought and the development of his early thought than is possible here see the present author's unpublished doctoral dissertation, 'Martin Buber: Mystic, Existentialist, Social

51

double-minded need to exploit life instead of live it makes impossible true life within oneself. It also makes impossible true communication between man and man, for only that man who is simply and directly present can directly communicate with others.

Already in 1916 Buber made his first draft of *I and Thou*, but it was in 1919 that he 'first attained decisive clarity.' In the light of his new understanding he undertakes to explain those parts of his earlier writings which now appear to him inexact or conducive to misunderstanding. Religious reality, he writes, is not what takes place in 'inwardness,' as is generally thought today, but what takes place between man and God in the reality of relation. The statement that whether God is transcendent or immanent does not depend on God but on man is consequently inexact. It depends on the relation between God and man, which, when it is actual, is reciprocal action. Also unsatisfactory is the statement that God arises out of the striving for unity. 'God' cannot arise, only the image of God, the idea of God, and this also cannot arise out of the human but only out of the meeting of the divine and the human. The form in which men recognize God and the conception which men have of Him cannot, to be sure, come into being without the co-operative participation of the creativity of a human person, but what is at work there is no myth-projecting fantasy but man's way of going forth to the meeting. The meeting with God does not rise out of 'experience' and therefore out of detached subjectivity, but out of life. It does not arise out of religious experience, which has to do with a division of the psychic, but out of religious life, that is, out of the whole life of men and of peoples in real intercourse with God and the world.

The concept of the realization of God is not inexact or improper in itself, writes Buber, but it is improperly applied when one speaks of making God out of a truth into a reality. It can thus mislead one to the opinion that God is an 'idea' which only through men becomes 'reality' and further to the hopelessly perverted conception that God is not, but rather becomes—in man or in mankind. This opinion is perverted not because there is no divine becoming in the immanence, but because only through the primal certainty of divine being can we come into contact with the mysterious meaning of divine becoming, the self-division of God in creation and His participation in the destiny of its freedom.

By the same token the summons of our human existence cannot be to overcome the division of being and reality in order to let the divine take seed, grow, and ripen in the perceptible world. We cannot hold with the concept of a reality which is relative and far from God. This

Prophet,' Part I—Introduction, and Part II—The Development of Buber's Thought, The University of Chicago, June 1950. University of Chicago Library, Microfilm T 809.

concept comes from a division between the 'thinking' and the 'feeling' relation of the 'subject' and makes out of this psychological and relative duality of functions an absolute duality of spheres. If we comprehend ourselves in the God-world fullness in which we live, then we recognize that 'to realize God' means to make the world ready to be a place of God's reality. It means, in other, holy words, to make reality one.[1]

Henceforth the emphasis in Buber's thought is not, as heretofore, on the process of realization but on the meeting of God and man and the theophany that illuminates human life and history as the result of that meeting. Only in this development, which has here reached mature expression, has Buber gone decisively beyond the subjectivistic and time-centred vitalism of Nietzsche and Bergson. Only through this final step has he reached the understanding that, though the external form changes, the essence of theophany—the meeting between man and God —remains the same. 'God wills to ripen in men,' Buber has written. Yet it is not God Himself who changes and ripens, but the depth and fullness of man's encounter with God and the ways in which man expresses this meeting and makes it meaningful for his daily life. If God were entirely process, man could not know where that process might lead. There would be no basis then for Buber's belief that the contradiction and ugliness of life can be redeemed through the life of man in the world.

Buber's shift in emphasis to the two-directional meeting of God and man leaves no further room for the concept of an impersonal godhead coming to birth in the soul. God is now, to Buber, the Eternal Thou whom we meet outside as well as within the soul and whom we can never know as impersonal. This does not mean that Buber's new I-Thou philosophy is irreconcilable with the metaphysics of the Kabbalah and Hasidism, but only with his earlier interpretations of that metaphysics. Man's power to reunite God with His Shekinah, Buber writes in a mature work, has its truth in the inwardness of the here and now but in no way means a division of God, a unification which takes place in God, or any diminution of the fullness of His transcendence. 'What turgid and presumptuous talk that is about the "God who becomes"; but we know unshakably in our hearts that there is a becoming of the God that is.'[2]

Buber's new position thus does not exclude a becoming of God in the world but only the concept of God as pure becoming or as ideal which is not yet reality. If creation were not divine, if God were not immanent as well as transcendent, then we would have a gnostic division between God and the world which would leave the world for ever cut off from God and for ever unredeemable.

[1] *Reden, op. cit.,* pp. xi-xix.
[2] *Hasidism and Modern Man, op. cit.,* Book V, 'The Baal-Shem-Tov's Instruction in Intercourse with God,' pp. 215-218; *I and Thou,* p. 82.

PART THREE

DIALOGUE

CHAPTER TEN

ALL REAL LIVING IS MEETING

THE first part of *I and Thou* consists of an extended definition of man's two primary attitudes and relations: 'I-Thou' and 'I-It.' These two attitudes are very similar to the 'realization' and 'orientation' of *Daniel*. The I of man comes into being in the act of speaking one or the other of these primary words. But the two I's are not the same: 'The primary word *I-Thou* can only be spoken with the whole being. The primary word *I-It* can never be spoken with the whole being.' [1]

The real determinant of the primary word in which a man takes his stand is not the object which is over against him but the way in which he relates himself to that object. I-Thou is the primary word of relation. It is characterized by mutuality, directness, presentness, intensity, and ineffability. Although it is only within this relation that personality and the personal really exist, the Thou of I-Thou is not limited to men but may include animals, trees, objects of nature, and God. I-It is the primary word of experiencing and using. It takes place within a man and not between him and the world. Hence it is entirely subjective and lacking in mutuality. Whether in knowing, feeling, or acting it is the typical subject-object relationship. It is always mediate and indirect and hence is comprehensible and orderable, significant only in connection and not itself. The It of I-It may equally well be a he, a she, an animal, a thing, a spirit, or even God, without a change in the primary word. Thus I-Thou and I-It cut across the lines of our ordinary distinctions to focus our attention not upon individual objects and their causal connections but upon the relations between things, the *dazwischen* ('there in-between'). Experiencing is I-It whether it is the experiencing of an object or of a man, whether it is 'inner' or 'outer,' 'open' or 'secret.' One's life of interior feeling is in no way elevated above one's life with the external world, nor is the occultist's knowledge of secret mysteries anything else but the inclusion of the unseen in the world of It. 'O secrecy without a secret! O accumulation of information! It, always It!' [2]

[1] *I and Thou, op. cit.*, p. 3.   [2] *Ibid.*, p. 5.

'The *It* is the eternal chrysalis, the *Thou* the eternal butterfly.' What at one moment was the Thou of an I-Thou relation can become the next moment an It and indeed must continually do so. The It may again become a Thou, but it will not be able to remain one, and it need not become a Thou at all. Man can live continuously and securely in the world of It. If he only lives in this world, however, he is not a man, for 'all real living is meeting.' This meeting with the Thou of man and of nature is also a meeting with God. 'In each process of becoming that is present to us . . ., in each *Thou* we address the eternal *Thou*,' 'the *Thou* in which the parallel lines of relations meet.' This does not mean that one substitutes an abstract concept of 'God in man' for the concrete man before one. On the contrary, it is only when one meets a man as Thou that one really remains concrete. When one faces a human being as one's Thou, he is no longer an object among objects, a nature which can be experienced and described, or a specific point of space and time. 'But with no neighbour, and whole in himself, he is *Thou* and fills the heavens. This does not mean that nothing exists except himself. But all else lives in *his* light.' [1]

In the meeting with the Thou, man is no longer subject to causality and fate, for both of these are handmaidens of the ordered world of continuity and take their meaning from it. It does not even matter if the person to whom the Thou is said is the It for other I's or is himself unaware of the relation. The I-Thou relation interpenetrates the world of It without being determined by it, for meeting is not in space and time but space and time in meeting. 'Only when every means has collapsed does the meeting come about.' Though I-Thou continually becomes I-It, it exists during the moment of meeting as direct and directly present. 'No deception penetrates here; here is the cradle of the Real Life.' [2]

The present of the I-Thou relation is not the abstract point between past and future that indicates something that has just happened but 'the real, filled present.' Like the 'eternal now' of the mystic, it is the present of intensity and wholeness, but it is not found within the soul. It exists only in so far as meeting and relation exist. In contrast, the I of I-It experiences a moment, but his moment has no present content since it is filled with experiencing and using. His actions only have meaning for him when they are completed, for they are always means and never ends in themselves. Similarly, he knows objects only when they are installed in the ordered world of the past, for he has no interest in their uniqueness but only in their relations to other things through which he can use them.[3]

The experiencing of It is planned and purposeful. Yet the man who

[1] *I and Thou, op. cit.*, pp. 17, 11, 6, 8.   [2] *Ibid.*, pp. 12, 9.
[3] *Ibid.*, p. 12 f.

experiences It does not go out of himself to do so, and the It does not respond but passively allows itself to be experienced. The Thou, on the other hand, cannot be sought, for it meets one through grace. Yet the man who knows Thou must go out to meet the Thou and step into direct relation with it, and the Thou responds to the meeting. Man can only enter relation with the whole being; yet it is through the relation, through the speaking of Thou, that concentration and fusion into the whole being takes place. 'As I become *I*, I say *Thou*.' This relation means suffering and action in one, suffering because one must be chosen as well as choose and because in order to act with the whole being one must suspend all partial actions.[1]

Ideas are not outside or above man's twofold attitude of I-Thou and I-It, nor can they take the place of Thou. 'Ideas are no more enthroned above our heads than resident in them.' They are between man and what is over against him. 'The real boundary for the actual man cuts right across the world of ideas as well.' Though many men retire into a world of ideas as a refuge and repose from the experience and use of the world of things, the mankind which they there imagine is no less an It and 'has nothing in common with a living mankind where *Thou* may truly be spoken.' 'The noblest fiction is a fetish, the loftiest fictitious sentiment is depraved.'[2]

Similarly, the act of relation is not emotion or feeling, which remains within the I. Pure relation is love *between* the I and the Thou. Feelings accompany love, but they do not constitute it. 'Feelings dwell in man; but man dwells in his love.' And the Thou dwells in love as well as the I, for love 'does not cling to the *I* in such a way as to have the *Thou* only for its "content," its object.' To the man who loves, people are set free from their qualities as good or evil, wise or foolish and confront him in their singleness as Thou. Hence love is not the enjoyment of a wonderful emotion, not even the ecstasy of a Tristan and Isolde, but the 'responsibility of an *I* for a *Thou*.'[3]

Hate sees only a part of a being. If a man sees a whole being and still hates, he is no longer in relation but in I-It; for to say Thou to a man means to affirm his being. 'Yet the man who straightforwardly hates is nearer to relation than the man without hate and love.'[4] Such a man really has in mind the person whom he hates as distinct from the man whose hatred and love does not mean its object but is void of real intention.[5] The world of the primitive man, even if it was a hell of anguish and cruelty, was preferable to a world without relation because it was real. 'Rather force exercised on being that is really lived than shadowy solicitude for faceless numbers! From the former a way leads

---

[1] *Ibid.*, p. 11.
[2] *Ibid.*, p. 13 f.
[3] *Ibid.*, p. 14 f.
[4] *Ibid.*, p. 16.
[5] I am indebted to Professor Buber for this interpretation.

to God, from the latter only one to nothingness.'[1] Thus though a full I-Thou relationship can only mean love, it is better to hate men than to treat them entirely as objects to be known or made use of.

I-It is not to be regarded as simply evil, however. It is only the reliability of its ordered and surveyable world which sustains man in life. One cannot meet others in it, but only through it can one make oneself 'understood' with others. The I-Thou relation, similarly, is not an unqualified good. In its lack of measure, continuity, and order it threatens to be destructive of life. The moments of the Thou are 'strange lyric and dramatic episodes, seductive and magical, but tearing us away to dangerous extremes, loosening the well-tried context, leaving more questions than satisfaction behind them, shattering security.' Yet the moments of the Thou do what I-It can never do. Though not linked up with one another, each is a sign of the world order and an assurance of solidarity with the world. The Thou comes to bring man out to presentness and reality. If it does not meet one, it vanishes and returns in another form. It is the 'soul of the soul' which stirs within the depths. Yet to remove it into the soul is to annihilate it. You cannot make yourself understood with others concerning it. 'But it teaches you to meet others, and to hold your ground when you meet them. . . . It does not help to sustain you in life, it only helps you to glimpse eternity.'[2]

The child must find for himself his own world, says Buber, through seeing, hearing, touching, and shaping it. This world is not there ready-made. It rises to meet his senses, thus revealing the essential nature of creation as form. In this process the effort to establish relation (with a Teddy-bear, a tea-pot, it does not matter) comes first and is followed by the actual relation, a saying of Thou without words. Only later is the relation split apart into the I and the thing. Hence 'in the beginning is relation,' '*the inborn Thou*' which is realized by the child in the lived relations with what meets it. The fact that he can realize what is over against him as Thou is based on the *a priori* of relation, that is, the potentiality of relation which exists between him and the world. Through this meeting with the Thou he gradually becomes I. Finally, however, he loses his relation with the Thou and perceives it as a separated object, as the It of an I which has itself shrunk to the dimensions of a natural object.[3]

Thus in the silent or spoken dialogue between the I and the Thou both personality and knowledge come into being. Unlike the subject-object knowledge of the I-It relation, the knowing of the I-Thou relation takes place neither in the 'subjective' nor the 'objective,' the emotional nor the rational, but in the 'between'—the reciprocal relationship of whole and active beings. Similarly, personality is neither simply an

[1] *I and Thou, op. cit.*, p. 24. [2] *Ibid.*, p. 33 f.
[3] *Ibid.*, pp. 25-28.

individual matter nor simply a social product, but a function of relationship. Though we are born 'individuals,' in the sense of being different from others, we are not born persons. Our personalities are called into being by those who enter into relation with us. This does not mean either that a person is merely a cell in a social organism. To become a person means to become someone who responds to what happens from a centre of inwardness.

To be fully real the I-Thou relation must be mutual. This mutuality does not mean simple unity or identity, nor is it any form of empathy. Though I-Thou is the word of relation and togetherness, each of the members of the relation really remains himself, and that means really different from the other. Though the Thou is not an It, it is also not 'another I.' He who treats a person as 'another I' does not really see that person but only a projected image of himself. Such a relation, despite the warmest 'personal' feeling, is really I-It.

In the German original the I-It relation is the *Ich-Es Verhältnis,* the I-Thou relation the *Ich-Du Beziehung.* This difference between *Verhältnis* and *Beziehung,* though not carried over in the English translation, is important in indicating the two stages of Buber's insight into man—first, that he is to be understood, in general, in terms of his relationships rather than taken in himself; second, that he is to be understood specifically in terms of that direct, mutual relation that makes him human.[1]

---

[1] Cf. Philip Wheelwright, 'Buber's Philosophical Anthropology,' in Maurice Friedman and Paul Arthur Schilpp, editors, *The Philosophy of Martin Buber,* volume of *The Library of Living Philosophers* (La Salle, Ill.: Open Court Publ. Co., 1963).

CHAPTER ELEVEN

THE WORLD OF *IT*

OUR culture has, more than any other, abdicated before the world of It. This abdication makes impossible a life in the spirit since spirit is a response of man to his Thou. The evil which results takes the form of individual life in which institutions and feelings are separate provinces and of community life in which the state and economy are cut off from the spirit, the will to enter relation. In both cases I-It is not evil in itself but only when it is allowed to have mastery and to shut out all relation. Neither universal causality nor destiny prevent a man from being free if he is able to alternate between I-It and I-Thou. But without the ability to enter relation and cursed with the arbitrary self-will and belief in fate that particularly mark modern man, the individual and the community become sick, and the I of the true person is replaced by the empty I of individuality.

In the history of both the individual and the human race, writes Buber, the proper alternation between I-It and I-Thou is disturbed by a progressive augmentation of the world of It. Each culture tends to take over the world of It from its predecessors or contemporaries. Hence in general the world of objects is more extensive in successive cultures. As a result, there is a progressive development from generation to generation of the individual's ability to use and experience. For the most part this development is an obstacle to life lived in the spirit, for it comes about in the main 'through the decrease of man's power to enter into relation.' [1]

Spirit is not in the I but between I and Thou. To respond to the Thou man must enter into the relation with his whole being, but 'the stronger the response the more strongly does it bind up the *Thou* and banish it to be an object.' Only silence before the Thou leaves it free and unmanifest. But man's greatness lies in the response which binds Thou into the world of It, for it is through this response that knowledge, work, image, and symbol are produced. All of these Thou's which have been changed into It's have it in their nature to change back again into

<hr />

[1] *I and Thou, op. cit.*, p. 37 ff.

presentness. But this fulfilment of their nature is thwarted by the man who has come to terms with the world of It. Instead of freeing, he suppresses; instead of looking, he observes; instead of accepting, he turns to account.[1]

Buber illustrates this statement from the realms of knowledge, art, and action. In knowledge the thing which is seen is exclusively present and exists in itself. Only afterwards is it related to other events or expressed as a general law, i.e. turned into an It so it can enter the structure of knowledge. 'He who frees it from that, and looks on it again in the present moment, fulfils the nature of the act of knowledge to be real and effective *between* men.' But it can be left as It, experienced, used, and appropriated to 'find one's bearings' in the world.[2]

'So too in art; form is disclosed to the artist as he looks at what is over against him. He banishes it to be a "structure".' The nature of this 'structure' is to be freed for a timeless moment by the meeting with the man who lifts the ban and clasps the form. But a man may simply experience art: see it as qualities, analyse how it is made, and place it in the scheme of things. Scientific and aesthetic understanding are not necessary in themselves. They are necessary in order that man 'may do his work with precision and plunge it in the truth of relation, which is above the understanding and gathers it up in itself.' [3]

Finally, in pure effective action without arbitrary self-will man responds to the Thou with his life, and this life is teaching. It 'may have fulfilled the law or broken it; both are continually necessary, that spirit may not die on earth.' The life of such a person teaches those who follow how life is to be lived in the spirit, face to face with the Thou. But they may decline the meeting and instead pin the life down with information as an It, an object among objects.[4]

The man who has come to terms with It has divided his life into two separated provinces: one of institutions—It—and one of feelings—I.

> Institutions are 'outside,' where all sorts of aims are pursued, where a man works, negotiates, bears influence, undertakes, concurs, organizes, conducts business, officiates, preaches. . . . Feelings are 'within,' where life is lived and man recovers from institutions. Here the spectrum of the emotions dances before the interested glance.[5]

Neither institutions nor feelings know man or have access to real life. Institutions know only the specimen; feelings know only the 'object.' That institutions yield no public life is realized by many with increasing distress and is the starting-point of the seeking need of the age. But few

---

[1] *Ibid.*, p. 39 f.   [2] *Ibid.*, p. 40 f.   [3] *Ibid.*, p. 41 f.
[4] *Ibid.*, p. 42.   [5] *Ibid.*, p. 43.

realize that feelings yield no personal life, for feelings seem to be the most personal life of all. Modern man has learned to be wholly concerned with his own feelings, and even despair at their unreality will not instruct him in a better way—'for despair is also an interesting feeling.' [1]

The solution to this lack of real public and personal life is not freedom of feeling, writes Buber. True community arises through people taking their stand in living mutual relation with a living Centre and only then through being in living mutual relation with each other. Community cannot be set up as a goal and directly attained, but can only result from a group of people being united around a common goal, their relation to the Eternal Thou. Similarly, true marriage arises through each partner's revealing the Thou to the other. The erotic literature of the age which is so exclusively concerned with one person's enjoyment of another and the pseudo-psychoanalytical thinking which looks for the solution to the problem of marriage through simply freeing 'inhibitions' both ignore the vital importance of the Thou which must be received in true presentness if human life, either public or personal, is to exist.[2]

In communal life as in the individual it is not I-It but its mastery and predominance which are evil. Communal life cannot dispense with the world of It any more than man himself.

> Man's will to profit and to be powerful have their natural and proper effect so long as they are linked with, and upheld by, his will to enter into relation. There is no evil impulse till the impulse has been separated from the being; the impulse which is bound up with, and defined by, the being is the living stuff of communal life, that which is detached is its disintegration. Economics, the abode of the will to profit, and State, the abode of the will to be powerful, share in life as long as they share in the spirit.[3]

Man's will to profit and to be powerful are impulses which can be given direction by I-Thou in the life of the individual and of the community. I-Thou is not only a direction, it is *the* direction; for it is itself the ultimate meaning and intrinsic value, an end not reached by any means, but directly present. I-Thou is the foundation underlying I-It, the spark of life within it, the spirit hovering over it.

What matters is not that the organization of the state be freer and economics more equitable, though these things are desirable, but that the spirit which says Thou remain by life and reality. To parcel out community life into separate realms one of which is spiritual life 'would mean to give up once and for all to tyranny the provinces that are sunk

---

[1] *I and Thou, op. cit.*, p. 44 f.   [2] *Ibid.*, p. 45 f.   [3] *Ibid.*, p. 48.

64

in the world of *It*, and to rob the spirit completely of reality. For the spirit is never independently effective in life in itself alone, but in relation to the world.' [1] Thus what is good is not pure spirit, any more than what is evil is matter. Good is the interpenetration of spirit into life, and evil is spirit separated from life, life untransformed by spirit.

'Causality has an unlimited reign in the world of *It*' and is 'of fundamental importance for the scientific ordering of nature.' But causality does not weigh heavily on man, who can continually leave the world of It for the world of relation. In relation I and Thou freely confront each other in mutual effect, unconnected with causality. Thus it is in relation that true decision takes place.

Only he who knows relation and knows about the presence of the *Thou* is capable of decision. He who decides is free, for he has approached the Face. . . . Two alternatives are set side by side—the other, the vain idea and the one, the charge laid on me. But now realization begins in me. For it is not decision to do the one and leave the other a lifeless mass, deposited layer upon layer as dross in my soul. But he alone who directs the whole strength of the alternative into the doing of the charge, who lets the abundant passion of what is rejected invade the growth to reality of what is chosen—he alone who 'serves God with the evil impulse' makes decision, decides the event. . . . If there were a devil it would not be one who decided against God, but one who, in eternity, came to no decision.[2]

Direction alone is not enough. To be fulfilled it must be accompanied by all of one's power. If power of impulse is regarded as an evil to be suppressed, then it will accumulate in the soul and turn negative and will frustrate the very fulfilment that direction and the conscious self desire. But if the passion of the temptation is brought into the service of responsibility, then what otherwise appears a mere duty or an external action is transfigured and made radiant by the intention which enters into it.

To use the evil impulse to serve the good is to redeem evil, to bring it into the sanctuary of the good. It is this which is done by the man whose life swings between Thou and It, and it is this which reveals to him the meaning and character of life. 'There, on the threshold, the response, the spirit, is kindled ever anew within him; here, in an unholy and needy country, this spark is to be proved.' [3] Thus man's very freedom to do evil enables him to redeem evil. What is more, it enables him to serve the good not as a cog in a machine but as a free and creative being. Man's creativity is the energy which is given to him to

[1] *Ibid.*, p. 50. [2] *Ibid.*, p. 51 f. [3] *Ibid.*, p. 53.

form and to direct, and the real product of this creativity is not a novel or a work of art, but a life lived in relation, a life in which It is increasingly interpenetrated by Thou.

We make freedom real to ourselves, says Buber, by forgetting all that is caused and making decision out of the depths. When we do this, destiny confronts us as the counterpart of our freedom. It is no longer our boundary but our fulfilment. 'In times of healthy life trust streams from men of the spirit to all people.' But in times of sickness the world of It overpowers the man who has come to terms with it, and causality becomes 'an oppressive, stifling fate.' Every great culture rests on an original response, and it is this response, renewed by succeeding generations, which creates for man a special way of regarding the cosmos, which enables him to feel at home in the world. But when this living and continually renewed relational event is no longer the centre of a culture, then that culture hardens into a world of It. Men become laden with the burden of 'fate that does not know spirit' until the desire for salvation is satisfied by a new event of meeting. The history of cultures is not a meaningless cycle but a spiral ascent to the point 'where there is no advance or retreat, but only utterly new reversal—the break-through.' [1]

Thus there is a limit to the evil which man can bring on himself, a limit to the overrunning mastery of the world of It. Smith's translation of Buber's '*Umkehr*' as 'reversal' does not adequately convey the idea of the Hebrew *teshuvah*, man's wholehearted turning to God, and it is in this sense that Buber has used '*Umkehr*' in earlier works [2] and continues to use it in later ones. It is not merely that man arrives at the last pitch of desperation, the place where he can no longer help himself. When he arrives there he himself performs the one great act which he can perform, the act which calls forth God's grace and establishes new relation. At the very point when man has completely given over his life to the domination of the lifeless mechanism of world process, he can go forth with his whole being to encounter the Thou.

The one thing that can prevent this turning, says Buber, is the belief in fate. It is this belief which threatens to engulf our modern world as a result of the quasi-biological and quasi-historical thought of the age. Survival of the fittest, the law of instincts and habits, social process, dialectical materialism, cultural cycles—all work together to form a more tenacious and oppressive belief in fate than has ever before existed, a fate which leaves man no possibility of liberation but only rebellious or submissive slavery. Even the modern concepts of teleological development and organic growth are at base possession by process—'the abdication of man before the exuberant world of *It*.'

---

[1] *I and Thou, op. cit.*, p. 56. Except here, Smith changes 'reversal' to 'turning' in the 2nd edition.   [2] 'Die Erneuerung des Judentums,' 'Zwiefache Zukunft.' 'Der Geist des Orients und das Judentum,' and *Gemeinschaft*.

All consideration in terms of process is merely an ordering of pure 'having become,' of the separated world-event, of objectivity as though it were history; the presence of the *Thou*, the becoming out of solid connexion, is inaccessible to it.[1]

The free man is he who wills without arbitrary self-will. He knows he must go out to meet his destiny with his whole being, and he sacrifices 'his puny, unfree will, that is controlled by things and instincts, to his grand will, which quits defined for destined being.'

Then he intervenes no more, but at the same time he does not let things merely happen. He listens to what is emerging from himself, to the course of being in the world; not in order to be supported by it, but in order to bring it to reality as it desires, in its need of him, to be brought. . . . The free man has no purpose here and means there, which he fetches for his purpose: he has only the one thing, his repeated decision to approach his destiny.[2]

In the 'free man' of *I and Thou* we meet once again the 'non-action' of the Tao and the *kavanah*, or consecrated action, of the Hasid.

In contrast to the free man stands the self-willed man who, according to Buber, neither believes nor meets. He does not know connection but only the outside world and his desire to use it. He has no destiny, for he is defined by things and instincts which he fulfils with arbitrary self-will. Incapable of sacrifice, he continually intervenes to 'let things happen.' His world is 'a mediated world cluttered with purposes.' His life never attains to a meaning, for it is composed of means which are without significance in themselves. Only I-Thou gives meaning to the world of It, for I-Thou is an end which is not reached in time but is there from the start, originating and carrying-through. The free man's will and the attainment of his goal need not be united by a means, for in I-Thou the means and the end are one.

When Buber speaks of the free man as free of causation, process, and defined being, he does not mean that the free man acts from within himself without connection with what has come to him from the outside. On the contrary, it is only the free man who really acts in response to concrete external events. It is only he who sees what is new and unique in each situation, whereas the unfree man sees only its resemblance to other things. But what comes to the free man from without is only the precondition for his action, it does not determine its nature. This is just as true of those social and psychological conditioning influences which he has internalized in the past as of immediate external events. To the former as to the latter, he responds freely from the depths as a whole and conscious person. The unfree person, on the

---

[1] *I and Thou, op. cit.*, p. 57 f.   [2] *Ibid.*, p. 59 f.

other hand, is so defined by public opinion, social status, or his neurosis that he does not 'respond' spontaneously and openly to what meets him but only 'reacts.' He does not see others as real persons, unique and of value in themselves, but in terms of their status, their usefulness, or their similarity to other individuals with whom he has had relationships in the past.

'Individuality,' the I of I-It, becomes conscious of itself as the subject of experiencing and using. It makes its appearance through being differentiated from other individualities and is conscious of itself as a particular kind of being. It is concerned with its My—my kind, my race, my creation, my genius. It has no reality because it has no sharing and because it appropriates unto itself. 'Person,' on the other hand, the I of I-Thou, makes its appearance by entering into relation with other persons. Through relation the person shares in a reality which neither belongs to him nor merely lies outside him, a reality which cannot be appropriated but only shared. The more direct his contact with the Thou, the fuller his sharing; the fuller his sharing, the more real his I.[1] But the I that steps out of the relational event into consciousness of separation retains reality as a seed within it.

> This is the province of subjectivity in which the *I* is aware with a single awareness of its solidarity of connexion and of its separation. ... Here, too, is the place where the desire is formed and heightened for ever higher, more unconditioned relation, for the full sharing in being. In subjectivity the spiritual substance of the person matures.[2]

No man is pure person and no man pure individuality; no man is entirely free and none, except a psychotic, entirely unfree. But some men are so defined by person that they may be called persons, and some are so defined by individuality that they may be called individuals. 'True history is decided in the field between these two poles.' [3]

When it is not expressed outwardly in relation, the inborn Thou strikes inward. Then man confronts what is over against him within himself, and not as relation or presence but as self-contradiction, an inner *Doppelgänger*. The man who has surrendered to the world of outer and inner division 'directs the best part of his spirituality to averting or at least to veiling his thoughts,' for thinking would only lead him to a realization of his own inner emptiness. Through losing the subjective self in the objective whole or through absorbing the objective whole into the subjective self, he tries to escape the confrontation with the Thou.[4] He hopes to make the world so ordered and

---

[1] *I and Thou, op. cit.*, p. 62 f.   [2] *Ibid.*, p. 63.
[3] *Ibid.*, p. 65.   [4] *Ibid.*, pp. 61, 65-72.

comprehensible that there is no longer a possibility of the dread meeting which he wishes to avoid. And because he dares not meet the Thou in the casual moments of his daily life, he builds for himself a cataclysmic reversal, a way of dread and despair. It is through this way at last that he must go to confront the eternal Thou.

CHAPTER TWELVE

THE ETERNAL THOU

THE inborn Thou is expressed and realized in each relation, writes Buber, but it is consummated only in the direct relation with the Eternal Thou, 'the *Thou* that by its nature cannot become *It*.' This Thou is met by every man who addresses God by whatever name and even by that man who does not believe in God yet addresses 'the *Thou* of his life, as a *Thou* that cannot be limited by another.' 'All God's names are hallowed, for in them He is not merely spoken about, but also spoken to.' Our speaking to God, our meeting Him is not mere waiting and openness for the advent of grace. Man must go forth to the meeting with God, for here too the relation means being chosen and choosing, suffering and action in one. Hence we must be concerned not about God's side—grace—but about our side—will. 'Grace concerns us in so far as we go out to it and persist in its presence; but it is not our object.' [1]

To go out to the meeting with the Eternal Thou, a man must have become a whole being, one who does not intervene in the world and one in whom no separate and partial action stirs. To go out to this meeting he need not lay aside the world of sense as though it were illusory or go beyond sense-experience. Nor need he have recourse to a world of ideas and values. Ideas and values cannot become presentness for us, and every experience, even the most spiritual, can yield us only an It. Only the barrier of separation must be destroyed, and this cannot be done through any formula, precept, or spiritual exercise. 'The one thing that matters' is 'full acceptance of the present.' Of course, the destruction of separateness and the acceptance of the present presuppose that the more separated a man has become, the more difficult will be the venture and the more elemental the turning. But this does not mean giving up the I, as mystical writings usually suppose, for the I is essential to this as to every relation. What must be given up is the self-asserting instinct 'that makes a man flee to the possessing of things before the unreliable, perilous world of relation.' [2]

---

[1] *I and Thou, op. cit.*, p. 75 f.　　　　[2] *Ibid.*, p. 76 ff.

'He who enters the absolute relation is concerned with nothing isolated any more.' He sees all things in the Thou and thus establishes the world on its true basis. God cannot be sought, He can only be met. Of course He is Barth's 'wholly Other' and Otto's *Mysterium Tremendum*, but He is also the wholly Same, 'nearer to me than my *I*.' He cannot be spatially located in the transcendence beyond things or the immanence within things and then sought and found.

If you explore the life of things and of conditioned being you come to the unfathomable, if you deny the life of things and of conditioned being you stand before nothingness, if you hallow this life you meet the living God.[1]

It is foolish to seek God, 'for there is nothing in which He could not be found.' It is hopeless to turn aside from the course of one's life, for with 'all the wisdom of solitude and all the power of concentrated being,' a man would still miss God. Rather one must go one's way and simply wish that it might be *the* way. The meeting with God is 'a finding without seeking, a discovering of the primal, of origin.' The man who thus waits and finds is like the perfected man of the Tao: 'He is composed before all things and makes contact with them which helps them,' and when he has found he does not turn from things but meets them in the one event. Thus the finding 'is not the end, but only the eternal middle, of the way.' Like the Tao, God cannot be inferred in anything, but unlike the Tao, God can be met and addressed. 'God is the Being that is directly, most nearly, and lastingly over against us, that may properly only be addressed, not expressed.' [2]

To make the relation to God into a feeling is to relativize and psychologize it. True relation is a *coincidentia oppositorum*, an absolute which gathers up the poles of feeling into itself. Though one has at times felt oneself simply dependent on God, one has also in this dependence felt oneself really free. And in one's freedom one acts not only as a creature but as co-creator with God, able through one's actions and through one's life to alter the fate of the world and even, according to the Kabbalah, to reunite God with His exiled Shekinah. If God did not need man, if man were simply dependent and nothing else, there would be no meaning to man's life or to the world. 'The world is not divine sport, it is divine destiny.'

You know always in your heart that you need God more than everything; but do you not know too that God needs you—in the fullness of His eternity needs you? . . . You need God, in order to be—and God needs you, for the very meaning of your life.[3]

---

[1] *Ibid.*, p. 78 f.   [2] *Ibid.*, p. 80 f.
[3] *Ibid.*, p. 82.

This primal reality of relation is not contradicted by the experience of the mystics if that experience is rightly understood. There are two kinds of happening in which duality is no longer experienced. The first is the soul's becoming a unity. This takes place within man and it is decisive in fitting him for the work of the spirit. He may then either go out to the meeting with mystery or fall back on the enjoyment and dissipation of his concentrated being. The second takes place not within man but between man and God. It is a moment of ecstasy in which what is felt to be 'union' is actually the dynamic of relation. Here on the brink the meeting is felt so forcibly in its vital unity that the I and the Thou between which it is established are forgotten.

In lived reality, even in 'inner' reality, there is no 'unity of being.' Reality exists only in effective, mutual action, and 'the most powerful and deepest reality exists where everything enters into the effective action, without reserve . . . the united *I* and the boundless *Thou*.' The doctrine of mystical absorption is based on 'the colossal illusion of the human spirit that is bent back on itself, that spirit exists in man.' In renouncing the meaning of spirit as relation, as between man and what is not man, man makes the world and God into functions of the human soul. In actuality, the world is not in man nor is man entirely included within the world. The image of the world is in man but not its reality, and man bears within himself the sense of self, that cannot be included in the world. What matters is how man causes his attitude of soul to grow to real life that acts upon the world.

I know nothing of a 'world' and a 'life in the world' that might separate a man from God. What is thus described is actually life with an alienated world of *It*, which experiences and uses. He who truly goes out to meet the world goes out also to God. Concentration and outgoing are necessary, both in truth, at once the one and the other, which is the One.[1]

The misinterpretation of relation as union has led both eastern and western mystics to make union with God a goal in itself and to turn away from the responsibility of the I for the Thou. To seek consciously to become a saint, or attain 'union,' as is advocated by some modern mystics,[2] is to abandon oneself to the world of It—the world of conscious aims and purposes supported by a collection of means, such as spiritual exercises, abstinence, and recollection. Greater for us than this

[1] *I and Thou, op. cit.*, pp. 85-95.
[2] See for example the writings of Gerald Heard, in particular *The Third Morality* (New York: William Morrow, London: Cassell, 1937), chaps. viii-xi; *Pain, Sex, and Time* (New York: Harper & Brothers, London: Cassell, 1939), chaps. xi-xii, xvi; *A Preface to Prayer* (New York: Harper & Brothers, 1944, London: Cassell, 1945); and *The Eternal Gospel* (New York: Harper & Brothers, 1946, London: Cassell, 1948), chap. xi.

'phenomenon of the brink,' writes Buber, is 'the central reality of the everyday hour on earth, with a streak of sun on a maple twig and the glimpse of the eternal *Thou*.'[1] Reality is to be found not in the pure and lasting but in the whole of man, not in ecstasy beyond the world of the senses but in the hallowing of the everyday.

We may know remoteness from God, but we do not know the absence of God, for 'it is we only who are not always there.' 'Every real relation in the world is consummated in the interchange of actual and potential being, but in pure relation—in the relation of man to God—potential is still actual being. It is only our nature that compels us to draw the Eternal Thou into the world and the talk of It. By virtue of this great privilege of pure relation there exists the unbroken world of Thou which binds up the isolated moments of relation in a life of world solidarity.

> By virtue of this privilege . . . spirit can penetrate and trans-
> form the world of *It*. By virtue of this privilege we are not given
> up to alienation from the world and the loss of reality by the *I*—
> to domination by the ghostly. Turning is the recognition of the
> Centre and the act of turning again to it. In this act of the being
> the buried relational power of man rises again, the wave that
> carries all the sphere of relation swells in living streams to give
> new life to our world.[2]

It is this unbroken world of Thou which assures us that relation can never fall apart into complete duality, that evil can never become radically real and absolute. Without this limit to the reality of evil we would have no assurance that I-It can become I-Thou, that men and cultures can turn back to God in the fundamental act of reversal, the *teshuvah*. Without this limit the world of It would be evil in itself and incapable of being redeemed. Buber describes the relation of the world to what is not the world as a

> double movement, of estrangement from the primal Source, in
> virtue of which the universe is sustained in the process of becoming,
> and of turning toward the primal Source, in virtue of which the
> universe is released in being. . . . Both parts of this movement
> develop, fraught with destiny, in time, and are compassed by grace
> in the timeless creation that is, incomprehensibly, at once emanci-
> pation and preservation, release and binding. Our knowledge of
> twofold nature is silent before the paradox of the primal mystery.[3]

This primal twofold movement underlies three of the most important aspects of Buber's I-Thou philosophy. The first is the alternation between I-Thou and I-It. The second is the alternation between

---

[1] *I and Thou, op. cit.*, p. 87 f.   [2] *Ibid.*, p. 98 ff.
[3] *Ibid.*, p. 100 f.

summons, the approach to the meeting with the eternal Thou, and sending, the going forth from that meeting to the world of men. The third is the alternation between revelation, in which the relational act takes place anew and flows into cultural and religious forms, and the turning, in which man turns from the rigidified forms of religion to the direct meeting with the Eternal Thou. Evil for Buber is the predominance of I-It through a too great estrangement from the primal Source and good the permeation of the world of It by I-Thou through a constant return to the primal Source. As in Buber's Hasidic philosophy the 'evil impulse' can be used to serve God, so I-It, the movement away from the primal Source, can serve as the basis for an ever greater realization of I-Thou in the world of It.

There are three spheres, says Buber, in which the world of relation is built: our life with nature, our life with men, and our life with 'intelligible essences.' Each of these gates leads into the presence of the Word, but when the full meeting takes place they 'are united in one gateway of real life.' Of the three spheres, our life with man 'is the main portal into whose opening the two side-gates leads, and in which they are included.' It is here alone that the moments of relation are bound together by speech, and here alone 'as reality that cannot be lost' are 'knowing and being known, loving and being loved.' The relation with man is thus 'the real simile of the relation with God,' for 'in it true address receives true response.' But in God's response all the universe is made manifest as language.[1]

Solitude is necessary for relation with God. It frees one from experiencing and using, and it purifies one before going out to the great meeting. But the solitude which means absence of relation and the stronghold of isolation, the solitude in which man conducts a dialogue with himself, cannot lead man to God. Similarly, we do not come to God through putting away our 'idols'—our finite goods such as our nation, art, power, knowledge, or money—and allowing the diverted religious act to return to the fitting object. These finite goods always mean using and possessing, and one cannot use or possess God. He who is dominated by an idol has no way to God but the turning, 'which is a change not only of goal but also of the nature of his movement.' [2]

He who has relation with the Eternal Thou also has relation with the Thou of the world. To view the religious man as one who does not need to take his stand in any relation to the world and living beings is falsely to divide life 'between a real relation with God and an unreal relation of *I* and *It* with the world.' No matter how inward he may be, the 'religious' man still lives in the world. Therefore, if he does not have an I-Thou relation with the world, he necessarily makes the world into an It. He treats it as a means for his sustenance or as an object for

[1] *I and Thou, op. cit.,* p. 101 ff.   [2] *Ibid.,* pp. 103-106.

his contemplation. 'You cannot both truly pray to God and profit by the world. He who knows the world as something by which he is to profit knows God also in the same way.'[1]

In the moment of supreme meeting man receives revelation, but this revelation is neither experience nor knowledge. It is 'a presence as power' which transforms him into a different being from what he was when he entered the meeting. This Presence and power include three things: 'the whole fulness of real mutual action,' 'the inexpressible confirmation of meaning,' and the call to confirm this meaning 'in this life and in relation with this world.' But as the meaning cannot be transmitted and made into knowledge, so the confirmation of it cannot be transmitted as 'a valid Ought,' a formula, or a set of prescriptions.

The meaning that has been received can be proved true by each man only in the singleness of his being and the singleness of his life. . . . As we reach the meeting with the simple *Thou* on our lips, so with the *Thou* on our lips we leave it and return to the world.[2]

Man can only succeed in raising relation to constancy if he embodies it 'in the whole stuff of life,' 'if he realizes God anew in the world according to his strength and to the measure of each day.' This is not a question of completely overcoming the relation of It but of so penetrating it with Thou 'that relation wins in it a shining streaming constancy: the moments of supreme meeting are then not flashes in darkness but like the rising moon in a clear starlit night.' Man cannot gain constancy of relation through directly concerning himself with God; for 'reflexion,' bending back towards God, makes Him into an object. It is the man who has been sent forth to whom God remains present.[3]

The mighty revelations at the base of the great religions are the same in being as the quiet ones that happen at all times. Revelation 'does not pour itself into the world through him who receives it as through a funnel; it comes to him and seizes his whole elemental being in all its particular nature and fuses with it.' But there is a qualitative difference in the relation of the various ages of history to God. In some, human spirit is suppressed and buried; in some, it matures in readiness for full relation; in some, the relation takes place and with it fresh expansion of being. Thus in the course of history elemental human stuff is transformed, and 'ever new provinces of the world and the spirit . . . are summoned to divine form.'

The form that is created as a result of this theophany is a fusion of Thou and It. God remains near this form so long as belief and cult are united and purified through true prayer. With degeneration of prayer

[1] *Ibid.*, p. 107. [2] *Ibid.*, pp. 109-114.
[3] *Ibid.*, p. 114 ff.

75

the power to enter into relation is buried under increasing objectification, and 'it becomes increasingly difficult . . . to say *Thou* with the whole undivided being.' In order to be able to say it, man must finally come out of the false security of community into the final solitude of the venture of the infinite.

This course is not circular. It is the way. In each new aeon fate becomes more oppressive, turning more shattering. And the theophany becomes ever *nearer,* increasingly near to the sphere that lies *between beings,* to the Kingdom that is hidden in our midst, there between us. History is a mysterious approach. Every spiral of its way leads us both into profounder perversion and more fundamental turning. But the event that from the side of the world is called turning is called from God's side salvation.[1]

The fundamental beliefs of Buber's I-Thou philosophy are the reality of the I-Thou relation into which no deception can penetrate, the reality of the meeting between God and man which transforms man's being, and the reality of the turning which puts a limit to man's movement away from God. On the basis of these beliefs Buber has defined evil as the predominance of the world of It to the exclusion of relation, and he has conceived of the redemption of evil as taking place in the primal movement of the turning which brings man back to God and back to solidarity of relation with man and the world. Relation is 'good' and alienation 'evil.' Yet the times of alienation may prepare the forces that will be directed, when the turning comes, not only to the earthly forms of relation but to the Eternal Thou.

[1] *I and Thou, op. cit.,* pp. 116-120.

CHAPTER THIRTEEN

WHAT IS MAN?

I

SINCE *I and Thou* Buber had enjoyed thirty years of continuous productivity in an extended range of interests. During this period he has made an unusual translation of the Bible into German in collaboration with Franz Rosenzweig and has written several important works of biblical interpretation. He has also expanded and deepened his interest in Hasidism, Judaism, Zionism, and religious socialism, and he has explored the implications of his I-Thou philosophy for education, community, sociology, psychology, art, and philosophical anthropology.

Though Buber's ideas have validity for the various fields in which he has expressed them, they also retain their nature as integral parts of his philosophy. Buber has himself stressed this unity in his Forewords to *Kampf um Israel* (1933) and *Dialogisches Leben* (1947). In the former he states that all the works which he had published in the last twelve years belong to 'the beginning of a proper expression of my real relation to truth.' In the latter he states that the intention of the essays and talks in the volume, written between 1922 and 1941, is to point to a reality which has been neglected by thought, a reality 'of which I am today, as in the beginning of this work, certain that it is essential for the existence of men, mighty in meaning and in saving power. . . . "I and Thou" stands at the head while all of the others stand in an illustrative and supplementary relation to it.' [1]

It should be recognized at the same time that the supplementary function of Buber's works since *I and Thou* includes not only an elaboration of the I-Thou philosophy and its extension into new fields, but also, as an integral part of this extension, a deepening and solidification. This deepening and solidification has produced several highly

---

[1] Martin Buber, *Kampf um Israel. Reden und Schriften (1921-1932)* (Berlin: Schocken Verlag, 1933), p. vii (my translation); Martin Buber, *Dialogisches Leben. Gesammelte philosophische und pädagogische Schriften* (Zurich: Gregor Muller Verlag, 1947), pp. 9-10 (my translation).

significant developments in Buber's thought: a growing concern with the nature and meaning of evil as opposed to his earlier tendency to treat evil as a negative aspect of something else; a growing concern with freedom and grace, divine and human love, and the dread through which man must pass to reach God; a steady movement toward concern with the simpler and more concrete aspects of everyday life; and an ever greater simplicity and solidity of style.

An especially important and still uncompleted development in Buber's thought is his philosophical anthropology—the study of the problem of man. Buber defines 'philosophical anthropology' as the study of 'the *wholeness* of man,' and he lists the following as among the problems 'which are implicitly set up at the same time by this question':

> man's special place in the cosmos, his connexion with destiny, his relation to the world of things, his understanding of his fellowmen, his existence as a being that knows it must die, his attitude in the ordinary and extraordinary encounters with the mystery with which his life is shot through.[1]

The concern with the wholeness of man rules out the attempt to answer the question of what man is in terms of particular philosophical disciplines:

> Philosophy succeeds in rendering me . . . help in its individual disciplines precisely through each of these disciplines *not* reflecting, and not being able to reflect, on the wholeness of man . . . in every one of these disciplines the possibility of its achieving anything in thought rests precisely on its objectification, on what may be termed its 'de-humanization.'

At the same time Buber disagrees with Heidegger in his belief that philosophical anthropology can provide a foundation for metaphysics or for the individual philosophical sciences. In doing so it would become so general that it would reach a false unity instead of the genuine wholeness of the subject based on 'the contemplation of all its manifold nature.'

> A legitimate philosophical anthropology must know that there is not merely a human species but also peoples, not merely a human soul but also types and characters, not merely a human life but also stages in life; only from the . . . recognition of the dynamic that exerts power within every particular reality and between them, and from the constantly new proof of the one in the many, can it come to see the wholeness of man.

---

[1] *Between Man and Man, op. cit.*, 'What Is Man?', p. 120 f.

What is Man?

Buber proceeds to set up philosophical anthropology as a systematic method which deals with the concrete, existential characteristics of man's life in order to arrive at the wholeness of man:

> Even as it must again and again distinguish within the human race in order to arrive at a solid comprehension, so it must put man in all seriousness into nature, it must compare him with other things, other living creatures, other bearers of consciousness, in order to define his special place reliably for him. Only by this double way of distinction and comparison does it reach the whole, real man.[1]

In defining philosophical anthropology as the problem of finding one essence of man in the constant flux of individuals and cultures, Buber has once again made visible the way of the 'narrow ridge.' For only through this approach can we avoid the abyss of abstract unity on the one hand and that of meaningless relativity on the other. In a further definition of the problem Buber writes: Man's existence is constituted by his participation, at the same time and in the same actions, in finitude and infinity. Related to this definition is his designation of man in 'The Question to the Single One' as the only creature who has potentiality. Even though this wealth of possibility is confined within narrow limits, these limits are only factual and not essential. Man's action is unforeseeable in its nature and extent.[2] It is because of this potentiality that Buber is able to speak in terms of the freedom of man and the reality of evil.

A corollary of Buber's emphasis on the wholeness of man is his rejection of the traditional idea that man is human because of his reason.

> The depth of the anthropological question is first touched when we also recognize as specifically human that which is not reason. Man is not a centaur, he is man through and through. He can be understood only when one knows, on the one hand, that there is something in all that is human, including thought, which belongs to the general nature of living creatures, and is to be grasped from this nature, while knowing, on the other hand, that there is no human quality which belongs fully to the general nature of living creatures and is to be grasped exclusively from it. Even man's hunger is not an animal's hunger. Human reason is to be understood only in connexion with human non-reason. The problem of philosophical anthropology is the problem of a specific totality and of its specific structure.[3]

[1] *Ibid.*, p. 121 ff.   [2] *Ibid.*, p. 77 f.
[3] *Ibid.*, p. 160.

II

Through contrasting man with the rest of nature Buber derives a twofold principle of human life consisting of two basic movements. The first movement he calls 'the primal setting at a distance,' the second 'entering into relation.' The first movement is the presupposition for the second, for we can only enter into relation with being that has been set at a distance from us and thereby has become an independent opposite. Only man can perform this act of setting at a distance because only man has a 'world'—an unbroken continuum which includes not only all that he and other men know and experience but all that is knowable now and in the future. An animal does not have a world but only an environment or realm. An animal selects from his realm those things which he needs, but he does not see it as a separate whole nor, like man, complete what is perceived by what *can* be perceived. This primal distancing is true not only of man's connection with space but of his connection with time. An animal's actions are concerned with its future and that of its young, but only man imagines the future. 'The beaver's dam is extended in a time-*realm*, but the planted tree is rooted in the *world* of time, and he who plants the first tree is he who will expects the Messiah.'

Buber characterizes the act of entering into relation with the world as a 'synthesizing apperception,' the apperception of a being as a whole and as a unity. Only by looking at the world as a world can man grasp being as a wholeness and unity. This is done not simply through 'setting at a distance' but also through entering into relation.

> Only the view of what is over against me in the world in its full presence, with which I have set myself, present in my whole person, in relation—only this view gives me the world truly as whole and one.

Distance makes room for relation, but relation does not necessarily follow. The real history of the spirit begins in the extent of the mutual interaction, reaction, and co-operation of the two movements. They may complete or contend with one another; each may see the other as the means or as the obstacle to its own realization. The great phenomena in history on the side of acts of distance are preponderantly universal while those on the side of acts of relation are preponderantly personal. The first movement shows how man is possible, the second how man is realized. 'Distance provides the human situation, relation provides man's becoming in that situation.'

An animal makes use of a stick as a tool, but only man sets it aside for future use as a specific and persisting It with a known capacity. But it is not enough for man to use and possess things. He also has a great desire to enter into personal relation with things and to imprint on them his relation to them. It is here, in man's relation to things, that we find the origin of art. A work of art is not the impression of natural objectivity nor the expression of spiritual subjectivity. It is the witness of the relation between the human substance and the substance of things.

Art . . . is the realm of 'between' which has become a form. Consider great nude sculptures of the ages: none of them is to be understood properly either from the givenness of the human body or from the will to expression of an inner state, but solely from the relational event which takes place between two entities which have gone apart from one another, the withdrawn 'body' and the withdrawing 'soul.'

In men's relation to one another the twofold principle of human life can be seen still more clearly. An insect society has division of labour, but it allows neither variation nor individual award. In human societies, in contrast, persons confirm each other in a practical way in their personal qualities and capacities. Indeed, a society may be termed human in the measure to which this mutual confirmation takes place. Apart from the tool and the weapon, it is this mutual individual completion and recognition of function which has enabled man to achieve lordship of the earth. An animal cannot see its companions apart from their common life, nor ascribe to the enemy any existence beyond his hostility. Man sets man at a distance and makes him independent. He is therefore able to enter into relation, in his own individual status, with those like himself.

The basis of man's life with man is twofold, and it is one—the wish of every man to be confirmed as what he is, even as what he can become, by men; and the innate capacity in man to confirm his fellow men in this way. That this capacity lies so immeasurably fallow constitutes the real weakness and questionableness of the human race: actual humanity exists only where this capacity unfolds. On the other hand, of course, an empty claim for confirmation, without devotion for being and becoming, again and again mars the truth of life between man and man.

This mutual confirmation is best illustrated by speech. Animals call to one another, but only man speaks to other men as independent and particular others. Man sets his calls or words at a distance like his tools. He gives them independence in order that they may come to life again in genuine conversation. This process is perverted and the reality of speech misused when conversations take place without real dialogue. Genuine conversation, like every genuine fulfilment of relation between men, means acceptance of otherness. This means that although one may desire to influence the other and to lead him to share in one's relation to truth, one accepts and confirms him in his being this particular man made in this particular way. One wishes him to have a different relation to one's own truth in accordance with his individuality. The manipulator of propaganda and suggestion, in contrast, wishes to make use of men. He relates to men not as independently other beings but as to things, things moreover with which he will never enter into relation and which he is eager to rob of their distance.

Thus mutual confirmation of men is most fully realized in what Buber calls 'making present,' an event which happens partially wherever men come together but in its essential structure only rarely. Making the other present means to 'imagine' the real, to imagine quite concretely what another man is wishing, feeling, perceiving, and thinking. In the full making present something of the character of what is imagined is joined to the act of imagining. One to some extent wills what he is willing, thinks what he is thinking, feels what he is feeling. The particular pain which I inflict on another surges up in myself until paradoxically we are embraced in a common situation. It is through this making present that we grasp another as a self, that is as a being whose distance from me cannot be separated from my distance from him and whose particular experience I can make present. This event is not ontologically complete until he knows himself made present by me and until this knowledge induces the process of his inmost self-becoming. 'For the inmost growth of the self is not accomplished, as people like to suppose today, in man's relation to himself, but . . . in the making present of another self and in the knowledge that one is made present in his own self by the other.' An animal does not need confirmation because he is what he is unquestionably. Man, in contrast, needs to have a presence in the being of the other.

> Sent forth from the natural domain of species into the hazard of the solitary category, surrounded by the air of a chaos which came into being with him, secretly and bashfully he watches for a Yes which allows him to be and which can come to him only from one human person to another.[1]

III

It is clear that 'entering into relation' means entering into an I-Thou relation, yet it is equally clear that one cannot identify distance with

---

[1] Martin Buber, 'Distance and Relation,' translated by Ronald Gregor Smith, *The Hibbert Journal*, January 1951, Vol. XLIX, pp. 105-113. 'The connection of the whole work with my writings on dialogical existence . . . is probably clear to the reader,' writes Buber in the 'Vorwort' to the German original, *Urdistanz und Beziehung* (Heidelberg: Verlag Lambert Schneider, 1951).

I-It. When man fails to enter into relation, however, the distance thickens and solidifies, so that instead of being that which makes room for relation it becomes that which obstructs it. This failure to enter into relation corresponds to I-It, and distance thus becomes the presupposition for both I-Thou and I-It. Entering into relation is an act of the whole being—it is in fact *the* act by which we constitute ourselves as human, and it is an act which must be repeated ever again in ever new situations. Distance, in contrast, is not an act and neither is failure to enter into relation: both are states of being.

When Buber speaks in *I and Thou* of I-Thou as preceding I-It in the primitive man and the child, he is speaking of the genesis of these relations. In 'Distance and Relation,' on the other hand, he is speaking ontologically of what constitutes the human being as a human being: he is not here interested in discovering just when, in the life of the race and the individual, man really becomes man but only in discovering what makes up the essence of man once he is man. Even ontologically speaking, however, it might appear that if distance is the presupposition for relationship and I-It is the thickening of distance, then the I-It relation precedes rather than follows the I-Thou. This apparent contradiction rests on a misconception, namely, that the thickening of the distance is closer to the original situation than the entrance into relation. Distance precedes the I-Thou and I-It relations which make up personal existence. This distance given, man is able to enter into relation with other beings or, as we have seen, he is able to enlarge, develop, accentuate, and shape the distance itself. In this shaping of the distance the primary state of things is elaborated as it is not in I-Thou. The I-Thou relation changes nothing in the primary state of things, but the thickening of distance into I-It changes the whole situation of the other being, making it into one's object. Looking at and observing the object, we make it part of an objective world with which we do not enter into relationship. Hence the I-It, or subject-object, relationship is not the primary one but is an elaboration of the given as the I-Thou relationship is not.

In the actual development of the human person, entering into relation precedes the thickening of distance that obstructs relation. The baby does not proceed directly from complete unity with its mother to that primary I-Thou relation which Buber has described in the child. Already in its first days, according to Buber, a child has the fact of distance, that is, the sense of beings as different from and over against him. In entering into relation with its mother the child completes this distance, and it is only later when he ceases to enter into relation that he sees her as an object and falls into the I-It's shaping and elaboration of the distance.[1] This same thing happens later when the child goes

[1] I am indebted to Professor Buber for oral elucidation of these problems.

through that process of emergence of the self which Erich Fromm has described.[1] As consciousness of one's separateness grows, it becomes more and more difficult to overcome the distance through relation; heightened insecurity and need for decision produce an ever greater temptation to accentuate the distance and take refuge in the pseudo-security of the world of It, the world of ordered objectivity and private subjectivity.

In 'Religion and Modern Thought' Buber criticizes Sartre's statement that man 'should affirm himself as the being through whom a world exists.' 'That ordering of known phenomena which we call the world,' writes Buber, 'is, indeed, the composite work of a thousand human generations.' But, he goes on to say, this world has come into existence through our meeting with existing being unknowable to us in its own nature. Though the becoming of a world takes place through us, our social ordering of the world rests, in its turn, on the priority of the meeting with existing being, and this meeting is not our work.[2] Hence here too entering into relation precedes the elaboration of distance, I-Thou precedes I-It.

While I-It can be defined as the enlarging and thickening of distance, it can also be defined as the objectification of the I-Thou relation which sometimes serves as the way back to it and sometimes obstructs the return. The I-Thou relation supplies the form for I-It, the form in which the distance is thickened. The form of the I-Thou relation remains as a means of re-entering relation, of executing anew the essential human act; but this form may block the return to the I-Thou relation through its false appearance of being itself the real thing.

[1] Erich Fromm, *Escape from Freedom* (New York: Rinehart & Co., 1941), chap. ii.
[2] Martin Buber, *Eclipse of God, Studies in the Relation between Religion and Philosophy* (New York: Harper & Brothers, 1952), 'Religion and Philosophy,' translated by Maurice S. Friedman, p. 58 f., 'Religion and Modern Thought,' also my translation, p. 91 f.

CHAPTER FOURTEEN

THE LIFE OF DIALOGUE

THE fundamental fact of human existence, according to Buber's anthropology, is man with man. But the sphere in which man meets man has been ignored because it possesses no smooth continuity. Its experience has been annexed to the soul and to the world, so that what happens to an individual can be distributed between outer and inner impressions. But when two individuals 'happen' to each other, then there is an essential remainder which is common to them, but which reaches out beyond the special sphere of each. That remainder is the basic reality, the 'sphere of between' (*das Zwischenmenschliche*).[1] The participation of both partners is in principle indispensable to this sphere, whether the reciprocity be fully actual or directly capable of being realized through completion or intensification. The unfolding of this sphere Buber calls 'the dialogical.' The psychological, that which happens within the souls of each, is only the secret accompaniment to the dialogue. The meaning of this dialogue is found in neither one nor the other of the partners, nor in both taken together, but in their interchange.

The essential problematic of the sphere of the between, writes Buber, is the duality of being and seeming. We must distinguish between two different types of human existence, one of which proceeds from the essence—from what one really is—the other of which proceeds from an image—from what one wishes to appear to be. Like the I-Thou and the I-It relations, these types are generally mixed with one another since no man lives from pure essence and none from pure appearance. None the less, some men may be basically characterized as 'essence men' (*Wesensmensch*) and some as 'image men' (*Bildmensch*). The essence man looks at the other as one to whom one gives oneself. His glance is spontaneous and unaffected. He is not uninfluenced by the desire to make himself understood, but he has no thought for the conception of himself that he might awaken in the beholder. The image man, in contrast, is primarily concerned with what the other thinks of

[1] *Between Man and Man, op. cit.*, 'What Is Man?', pp. 202-205.

him. With the help of man's ability to allow a certain element of his being to appear in his glance, he produces a look that is meant to affect the other as a spontaneous expression reflecting a personal being of such and such qualities. There is, in addition, a third realm of 'genuine appearance' in which a young person imitates a heroic model and becomes something of what he imitates. Here the mask is a real mask and not a deception. But where the appearance arises from a lie and is permeated by it, the 'sphere of the between' is threatened in its very existence.

Whatever the word 'truth' may mean in other spheres, in the realm between man and man it means that one imparts oneself to the other as what one is. This is not a question of saying to the other everything that occurs to one, but of allowing the person with whom one communicates to partake of one's being. It is a question of the authenticity of what is between men, without which there can be no authentic human existence. The origin of the tendency toward appearance is found in man's need for confirmation. It is no easy thing to be confirmed by the other in one's essence; therefore, one looks to appearance for aid. To give in to this tendency is the real cowardice of man, to withstand it is his real courage. One must pay dearly at times for essential life, but never too dearly. 'I have never met any young man who seemed to me hopelessly bad,' writes Buber. It is only the successive layers of deception that give the illusion of individuals who are 'image men' by their very nature. 'Man is, as man, redeemable.'

True confirmation means that one confirms one's partner as this existing being even while one opposes him. I legitimize him over against me as the one with whom I have to do in real dialogue, and I may then trust him also to act towards me as a partner. To confirm him in this way I need the aid of 'imagining the real.' This is no intuitive perception but a bold swinging into the other which demands the intensest action of my being, even as does all genuine fantasy, only here the realm of my act 'is not the all-possible' but the particular, real person who steps up to meet me, the person whom I seek to make present as just so and not otherwise in all his wholeness, unity, and uniqueness. I can only do this as a partner, standing in a common situation with the other, and even then my address to the other may remain unanswered and the dialogue may die in seed.

If it is the interaction between man and man which makes possible authentic human existence, it follows that the precondition of such authentic existence is that each overcomes the tendency toward appearance, that each means the other in his personal existence and makes him present as such, and that neither attempts to impose his own truth or view on the other. It would be mistaken to speak here of individuation alone. Individuation is only the indispensable personal stamp of all realization of human being. The self as such is not ultimately essential but the created meaning of human existence again and again fulfils itself as self. The help that men give each other in becoming a self leads the life between men to its height. The dynamic glory of the being of man is first bodily present in the relation between two men each of whom in meaning the other also means the highest to which this person is called and serves the fulfilment of this created destiny without wishing to impose anything of his own realization on the other.

In genuine dialogue the experiencing senses and the real fantasy which supplements them work together to make the other present as whole and one. For this dialogue to be real, one must not only mean the other, but also bring oneself, and that means say at times what one really thinks about the matter in question. One must make the contribution of one's spirit without abbreviation and distortion: everything depends here upon the legitimacy of what one has to say. Not holding back is the opposite of letting oneself go, for true speech involves thought as to the way in which one brings to words what one has in mind. A further pre-condition of genuine dialogue is the overcoming of appearance. If, even in an atmosphere of genuine conversation, the thought of one's effect as speaker outweighs the thought of what one has to say, then one inevitably works as a destroyer. One irreparably deforms what one has to say: it enters deformed into the conversation, and the conversation itself is deformed. Because genuine conversation is an ontological sphere which constitutes itself through the authenticity of being, every intrusion of appearance can injure it.

Genuine conversation is most often found in the dialogue between two persons, but it also occurs occasionally in a dialogue of several voices. Not everyone present has to speak for this dialogue to be genuine, but no one can be there as a mere observer. Each must be ready to share with the others, and no one who really takes part can know in advance that he will not have something to say.[1]

Genuine dialogue can thus be either spoken or silent. Its essence lies in the fact that 'each of the participants really has in mind the other or others in their present and particular being and turns to them with the intention of establishing a living mutual relation between himself and them.' The essential element of genuine dialogue, therefore, is 'seeing the other' or 'experiencing the other side.' There is no human situation which is so rotten and God-forsaken that the meeting with otherness cannot take place within it. The ordinary man can, and at times does, break through 'from the status of the dully-tempered dis-agreeableness, obstinacy, and contraryness' in which he lives into an

[1] Martin Buber, 'Elements of the Interhuman,' translated by Ronald Gregor Smith, *Psychiatry*, Vol. XX, No. 2 (May 1957), pp. 105-113.

effective reality. This reality is the simple *quantum satis*, or sufficient amount, 'of that which this man in this hour of his life is able to fulfil and to receive—if he gives himself.'

No factory and no office is so abandoned by creation that a creative glance could not fly up from one working-place to another, from desk to desk, a sober and brotherly glance which guarantees the reality of creation which is happening—*quantum satis*. And nothing is so valuable a service of dialogue between God and man as such an unsentimental and unreserved exchange of glances between two men in an alien place.

It is also possible for a leader of business to fill his business with dialogue by meeting the men with whom he works as persons. Even when he cannot meet them directly, he can be 'inwardly aware, with a latent and disciplined fantasy, of the multitude of these persons,' so that when one of them does step before him as an individual, he can meet him 'not as a number with a human mask but as a person.' [1]

'Experiencing the other side' means to feel an event from the side of the person one meets as well as from one's own side. It is an inclusiveness which realizes the other person in the actuality of his being, but it is not to be identified with 'empathy,' which means transposing oneself into the dynamic structure of an object, hence 'the exclusion of one's own concreteness, the extinguishing of the actual situation of life, the absorption in pure aestheticism of the reality in which one participates.'

Inclusion is the opposite of this. It is the extension of one's own concreteness, the fulfilment of the actual situation of life, the complete presence of the reality in which one participates. Its elements are, first, a relation, of no matter what kind, between two persons, second, an event experienced by them in common, in which at least one of them actively participates, and, third, the fact that this one person, without forfeiting anything of the felt reality of his activity, at the same time lives through the common event from the standpoint of the other.[2]

Experiencing the other side is the essence of all genuine love. The 'eros' of monologue is a display or enjoyment of subjective feelings. The eros of dialogue, on the other hand, means the turning of the lover to the beloved 'in his otherness, his independence, his self-reality,' and 'with all the power of intention' of his own heart. He does not assimilate into his own soul what lives and faces him, but he vows it faithfully to himself and himself to it.

---

[1] *Between Man and Man*, 'Dialogue,' pp. 20-24, 27, 36-39; *Kampf um Israel, op. cit.*, p. 279.

[2] *Ibid.*, 'Education,' p. 96 f.

A man caresses a woman, who lets herself be caressed. Then let us assume that he feels the contact from two sides—with the palm of his hand still, and also with the woman's skin. The twofold nature of the gesture, as one that takes place between two persons, thrills through the depth of enjoyment in his heart and stirs it. If he does not deafen his heart he will have—not to renounce the enjoyment but—to love. . . . The one extreme experience makes the other person present to him for all time. A transfusion has taken place after which a mere elaboration of subjectivity is never again possible or tolerable to him.[1]

The 'inclusion' of the other takes place still more deeply and fully in marriage, which Buber describes as 'the exemplary bond' and 'decisive union.' He who has entered into marriage has been in earnest 'with the fact that the other *is*,' with the fact that he 'cannot legitimately share in the Present Being without sharing in the being of the other.' If this marriage is real it leads to a 'vital acknowledgement of many-faced otherness—even in the contradiction and conflict with it.'[2]

The crises of marriage and the overcoming of them which rises out of the organic depths lead men to recognize in the body politic in general that other persons have not only a different way of thinking, but 'a different perception of the world, a different recognition and order of meaning, a different touch from the regions of existence, a different faith, a different soil.' To affirm this difference in the midst of conflict without relaxing the real seriousness of the conflict is the way in which we can from time to time touch on the other's 'truth' or 'untruth,' 'justice' or 'injustice.'

'Love without dialogic, without real outgoing to the other, reaching to the other, and companying with the other, the love remaining with itself—this is called Lucifer.' This 'love' is evil because it is monological. The monological man is not aware of the 'otherness' of the other, but instead tries to incorporate the other into himself. The basic movement of the life of monologue is not turning away from the other but 'reflexion' (*Rückbiegung*), bending back on oneself. 'Reflexion' is not egotism but the withdrawal from accepting the other person in his particularity in favour of letting him exist only as one's own experience, only as a part of oneself. Through this withdrawal 'the essence of all reality begins to disintegrate.'[3]

Renewed contact with reality cannot be made through the direct attempt to 'remove' or 'deny' the self nor even through despair at one's selfishness, for these entail another and related form of monologue:

[1] *Ibid.*, 'Dialogue,' p. 29 f., 'Education,' p. 96 f.
[2] *Ibid.*, 'The Question to the Single One,' p. 60 f.
[3] *Ibid.*, 'Dialogue,' pp. 21-24.

preoccupation with one's self. The soul does not have its object in itself, nor is its knowing, purifying, and perfecting itself for its own sake 'but for the sake of the work which it is destined to perform upon the world.' One must distinguish here between that awareness which turns one in on oneself and that which enables one to turn to the other. The latter is not only essential to the life of dialogue, but is dialogical in its very nature: it is the awareness of 'the signs' that continually address us in everything that happens. These signs are simply what happens when we enter into relation with occurrences as really having meaning for us. 'Each of us is encased in an armour whose task it is to ward off signs,' for we are afraid that to open ourselves to them means annihilation. We perfect this defence apparatus from generation to generation until we can assure ourselves that the world is there to be experienced and used as we like but that nothing is directed at us, nothing required of us.[1]

In shutting off our awareness of 'the signs' we are shutting off our awareness of the address of God, for He who speaks in the signs is the 'Lord of the Voice,' the eternal Thou. Every man hides, like Adam, to avoid rendering accounts. 'To escape responsibility for his life, he turns existence into a system of hideouts' and 'enmeshes himself more and more deeply in perversity.' The lie displaces 'the undivided seriousness of the human person with himself and all his manifestations' and destroys the good will and reliability on which men's life in common rests. The external conflict between man and man has its roots in the inner contradiction between thought, speech, and action. One's failure to say what one means and do what one says 'confuses and poisons, again and again and in increasing measure,' the situation between oneself and the other man. Unaware that the roots of the conflict are in our inner contradiction, we resist beginning with ourselves and demand that the other change at the same time. 'But just this perspective, in which a man sees himself only as an individual contrasted with other individuals, and not as a genuine person whose transformation helps towards the transformation of the world, contains the fundamental error.'[2]

To begin with one's own soul may seem senseless to one who holds

[1] Martin Buber, *The Way of Man according to the Teachings of Hasidism* (London: Routledge & Kegan Paul, 1950; Chicago: Wilcox & Follett, 1951), pp. 14 f., 36 ff.; *Between Man and Man*, 'Dialogue,' p. 10 f.

[2] *Between Man and Man*, p. 14 f.; *The Way of Man*, pp. 12 f., 30 ff.; Martin Buber, *Right and Wrong*, trans. by Ronald Gregor Smith (London: Student Christian Movement Press, 1952), 'Against the Generation of the Lie' (Psalm 12), pp. 11-16 (also found in Martin Buber, *Good and Evil, Two Interpretations* (New York: Charles Scribner's Sons, 1953), pp. 7-14, which book includes both *Right and Wrong* and *Images of Good and Evil*, trans. by Michael Bullock (London: Routledge & Kegan Paul, 1952); Martin Buber, *Hasidism* (New York: The Philosophical Library, 1948), 'The Beginnings of Hasidism,' pp. 9-12.

himself bankrupt. But one cannot honestly hold oneself bankrupt until one has taken a genuine inventory of one's personality and life, and when one has done so, one usually discovers hitherto unsuspected reserves. 'The man with the divided, complicated, contradictory soul is not helpless: the core of his soul, the divine force in its depths, is capable of . . . binding the conflicting forces together, amalgamating the diverging elements.' This unification of the soul is never final. Again and again temptation overcomes the soul, and 'again and again innate grace arises from out of its depths and promises the utterly incredible: you can become whole and one.' [1] This is no easy promise, however, but one demanding a total effort of the soul for its realization:

It is a cruelly hazardous enterprise, this becoming a whole. . . .
Everything in the nature of inclinations, of indolence, of habits, of fondness for possibilities which has been swashbuckling within us, must be overcome, and overcome, not by elimination, by suppression. . . . Rather must all these mobile or static forces, seized by the soul's rapture, plunge of their own accord, as it were, into the mightiness of decision and dissolve within it.[2]

It is no wonder, writes Buber, that these situations frequently terminate in a persistent state of indecision. Yet even if the effort of unification is not entirely successful, it may still lay the groundwork for future success. 'The unification must be accomplished *before* a man undertakes some unusual work,' but any ordinary work that a man does with a united soul acts in the direction of new and greater unification and leads him, even if by many detours, to a steadier unity than he had before. 'Thus man ultimately reaches a point where he can rely upon his soul, because its unity is now so great that it overcomes contradiction with effortless ease.' In place of his former great efforts all that is now necessary is a relaxed vigilance.[3]

In Hasidism 'the holiest teaching is rejected if it is found in someone only as a content of his thinking.' In religious reality a person becomes a whole. In philosophizing, in contrast, there is a totalization but no wholeness, for thinking overwhelms all the faculties of the person. 'In a great act of philosophizing even the finger-tips think—but they no longer feel.' This contrast must not be understood as one between feeling and thought. The wholeness of the religious person includes thought 'as an autonomous province but one which no longer strives to absolutize its autonomy.' One cannot substitute feeling for this

[1] Martin Buber, 'Erkenntnis tut not,' *Almanach des Schocken Verlags auf das Jahr 5696* (1935-36) (Berlin), pp. 11-14; *The Way of Man*, pp. 12 ff., 25 f., 31; *Images of Good and Evil*, p. 68 f. (*Good and Evil*, p. 127 f.).
[2] *Images*, p. 69 f. (*Good and Evil*, p. 128 f.).
[3] *Ibid.*, p. 70 (p. 129); *The Way of Man*, p. 25 ff.

personal wholeness since feeling at most only indicates that one is about to become whole, and it often merely gives the illusion of wholeness.[1] It is not the dominance of any one faculty but the unity of all faculties within the personality that constitutes the wholeness of man, and it is this that Buber calls 'spirit.'

Spirit is not a late bloom on the tree Man, but what constitutes man. . . . Spirit . . . is man's totality that has become consciousness, the totality which comprises and integrates all his capacities, powers, qualities, and urges. . . . Spiritual life is nothing but the existence of man, in so far as he possesses that true human conscious totality.[2]

Man's wholeness does not exist apart from real relationship to other beings. In *I and Thou*, as we have seen, Buber defines spirit in its human manifestation as 'a response of man to his *Thou*.' These two elements of wholeness and relation are invariably linked together in Buber's mature thought. He defines the relation of trust, for example, as a contact of the entire being with the one in whom one trusts. He posits as the first axiom of the Bible that man is addressed by God in his life and as the second that the life of man is meant by God as a unit. And he couples the recognition that true freedom comes only from personal wholeness with the assertion that freedom is only of value as a springboard for responsibility and communion. The true person is again and again required to detach and shut himself off from others, but this attitude is alien to his innermost being: man wants openness to the world, he wants the company of others.[3] Through relation the whole man shares in an absolute meaning which he cannot know in his life by himself.

Human life touches on absoluteness in virtue of its dialogical character, for in spite of his uniqueness man can never find, when he plunges to the depth of his life, a being that is whole in itself and as such touches on the absolute. . . . This other self may be just as limited and conditioned as he is; in being together the unlimited is experienced.[4]

[1] *Hasidism*, 'The Place of Hasidism in the History of Religion,' p. 192, cf. 'The Foundation Stone,' p. 56 f., 'Spirit and Body of the Hasidic Movement,' pp. 88, 94; *Eclipse of God, op. cit.*, 'Religion and Philosophy,' p. 60 f.; Martin Buber, *Two Types of Faith*, trans. by Norman P. Goldhawk (London: Routledge & Kegan Paul, 1951; New York: The Macmillan Co., 1952), p. 8.

[2] *Israel and the World, op. cit.*, 'The Power of the Spirit,' p. 175.

[3] *I and Thou*, p. 39; *Two Types of Faith*, p. 8; Martin Buber, *At the Turning* (New York: Farrar, Straus & Young, 1952), 'The Dialogue between Heaven and Earth,' p. 53; *Between Man and Man*, 'Education,' p. 90 ff.; Martin Buber, 'Remarks on Goethe's Concept of Humanity,' *Goethe and the Modern Age*, ed. by Arnold Bergstraesser (Chicago: Henry Regnery, 1950), p. 231 ff.

[4] *Between Man and Man*, 'What Is Man?', p. 167 f.

The child knows the Thou before it knows the separated I. 'But on the height of personal existence one must truly be able to say *I* in order to know the mystery of the *Thou* in its whole truth.'[1] Thus partial relation precedes inner wholeness but full relation follows it.

Only the man who has become a Single One, a self, a real person, is able to have a complete relation of his life to the other self, a relation which is not beneath but above the problematic of the relations between man and man, and which comprises, withstands, and overcomes all this problematic situation. A *great* relation exists only between real persons. It can be strong as death, because it is stronger than solitude, because it . . . throws a bridge from self-being to self-being across the abyss of dread of the universe.[2]

'Not before a man can say *I* in perfect reality—that is, finding himself,' writes Buber, 'can he in perfect reality say *Thou*—that is, to God. And even if he does it in a community he can only do it "alone."' Yet the saying of Thou to God must include the saying of Thou to the world and to men.

The real God lets no shorter line reach him than each man's longest, which is the line embracing the world that is accessible to this man. For he, the real God, is the creator, and all beings stand before him in relation to one another in his creation, becoming useful in living with one another for his creative purpose.[3]

The 'Single One' need not hold himself aloof from crowds. 'The Man who is living with the body politic . . . is not bundled, but bound.' He is bound in relation to the destiny of the crowd and does what he can to change the crowd into Single Ones. He takes up into his life the otherness which enshrouds him, but he takes it up 'only in the form of *the* other . . . the other who meets him, who is sought, lifted out of the crowd, the "companion."' The Single One passes his life in the body politic, for the body politic is 'the reservoir of otherness'—'the basic structure of otherness, in many ways uncanny but never quite unholy or incapable of being hallowed, in which I and the others who meet me in my life are inwoven.'[4]

Thus Buber changes Kierkegaard's category of the Single One ('*der Einzelne*') into the man for whom the relation to God includes all other relations without curtailing them. The essence of this new category is responsibility, and responsibility, for Buber, means responding—hearing the unreduced claim of each particular hour in all its crudeness

[1] *Ibid.*, p. 175.
[2] *Ibid.*, 'The Education of Character,' p. 116 f.
[3] *Ibid.*, 'The Question to the Single One,' pp. 43, 50, 52, 'What Is Man?', p. 171 f.
[4] *Ibid.*, 'The Question to the Single One,' pp. 61-65.

and disharmony and answering it out of the depths of one's being. This responsibility does not exclude a man from membership in a group or community, but it means that true membership in a community includes a *boundary* to membership so that no group or person can hinder one's perception of what is spoken or one's answer from the ground of one's being. This perception is not an 'inner light' from God that presents one the answer at the same time as the question. God tenders the situation, but the response comes from the 'conscience'—not the routine, surface, discredited conscience but 'the unknown conscience in the ground of being, which needs to be discovered ever anew.' Something of God's grace enters into this response, to be sure, but man cannot measure the share of grace in the answer. '"Conscience" is human and can be mistaken, it is a thing of "fear and trembling," it can only try to hear.'[1] None the less, if one responds as a whole person, one can have confidence in one's response as one cannot have confidence in any objective knowledge or universal prescriptions of morality. 'What is here called person is the very person who is addressed and who answers.' The 'Hinderer,' or Satan, writes Buber, is the person who prompts one with an answer in such a way as to hinder one's recognizing the situation presented in 'the very ground where hearing passes into being.'[2]

The 'Single One,' then, is the man whose aloneness means not only self-containment but a readiness to respond out of the depths of his being.

I call a great character one who by his actions and attitudes satisfies the claim of situations out of deep readiness to respond with his whole life, and in such a way that the sum of his actions and attitudes expresses at the same time the unity of his being in its willingness to accept responsibility.[3]

This unity of being also means readiness again to become the Single One when I-Thou becomes I-It. The Single One 'must let himself be helped from time to time by an inner-wordly "monastery"' which will not tear him away from relation but will prepare him for new meeting:

Our relations to creatures incessantly threaten to get incapsulated. . . . Every great bond of man . . . defends itself vigorously against continually debouching into the infinite. Here the monastic forms of life in the world, the loneliness in the midst of life into which we turn as into hostelries, help us to prevent the connexion

---

[1] *Between Man and Man*, 'The Question to the Single One,' pp. 54, 65-69. The final quotation is from a letter of August 18, 1952, from Professor Buber to the author.

[2] *Between Man and Man*, 'The Question to the Single One,' p. 68 f.

[3] *Ibid.*, 'The Education of Character,' p. 114.

between the conditioned bonds and the one unconditioned bond from slackening. . . . The loneliness must know the quality of strictness, of a monastery's strictness, in order to do its work. But it must never wish to tear us away from creatures, never refuse to dismiss us to them.[1]

To the extent that the soul achieves unification, it becomes aware of 'direction' and of itself as sent in quest of it. This awareness of direction is ultimately identical with the awareness of one's created uniqueness, the special way to God that is realized in one's relations with the world and men.

The humanly right is ever the service of the single person who realizes the right uniqueness purposed for him in his creation. In decision, taking the direction thus means: taking the direction toward the point of being at which, executing for my part the design which I am, I encounter the divine mystery of my created uniqueness, the mystery waiting for me.[2]

'Decision' is here both the current decision about the immediate situation which confronts one and through this the decision with the whole being for God. 'In the reality of existence all the so diverse decisions are merely variations on a single one, which is continually made afresh in a single direction.' This single direction must itself be understood in a double sense as the direction toward the person purposed for one and the direction toward God. This dual understanding means nothing more than 'a duality of aspects' provided one understands by God something really other than oneself, the author of one's created uniqueness that cannot be derived from within the world. Direction is apprehended through one's inner awareness of what one is meant to be, for it is this that enables one to make a genuine decision. This is a reciprocal process, however, for in transforming and directing one's undirected energies, one comes to recognize ever more clearly what one is meant to be.[3]

One experiences one's uniqueness as a designed or preformed one, intrusted to one for execution, yet everything that affects one participates in this execution. The person who knows direction responds with the whole of his being to each new situation with no other preparation than his presence and his readiness to respond. He is identical, therefore, with the Single One who becomes a whole person and goes out to relation with the Thou. 'Direction is not meeting but going out to meet.' It is not identical with dialogue, but it is, along with personal wholeness, a prerequisite of any genuine dialogue. It is also a product of dialogue

[1] *Ibid.*, 'The Question to the Single One,' p. 54 f.
[2] *Images of Good and Evil*, pp. 68, 82 f. (*Good and Evil*, pp. 127, 142).
[3] *Ibid.*, p. 81 f. (p. 126 f.).

in the sense that the awareness of direction comes into being only in the dialogue itself. One discovers the mystery waiting for one not in oneself but in the encounter with what one meets. Although 'the one direction of the hour towards God . . . changes time and again by concretion,' each moment's new direction is *the* direction if reality is met in lived concreteness.[1]

The goal of creation that we are intended to fulfil is not an unavoidable destiny but something to which we are called and to which we are free to respond or not to respond. Our awareness of this calling is not a sense of what we may become in terms of our position in society nor is it a sense of what type of person we should develop into. 'The purpose of my uniqueness may be felt more or less dimly, it cannot be sensed.'[2] Direction is neither conscious conception nor subconscious fantasy. It is the primal awareness of our unique way to God that lies at the very centre of our awareness of ourself as I. We cannot make direction more rationally comprehensible than this, for it is ultimately a mystery, even as are our freedom and our uniqueness to which it is integrally related.

Closely related to Buber's concept of direction is the Biblical concept of *emunah*, or trust. *Emunah* is the perseverance of man 'in a hidden but self-revealing guidance.' This guidance does not relieve man of taking and directing his own steps, for it is nothing other than God's making known that He is present. *Emunah* is the realization of one's faith in the actual totality of one's relationships to God, to one's appointed sphere in the world, and to oneself. 'By its very nature trust is substantiation of trust in the fulness of life in spite of the course of the world which is experienced.'[3] In this exclusion of a dualism between 'life in the soul' and 'life in the world' *emunah* brings together the wholeness of the Single One, the 'direction' of the man of true decision, and the relation with the concrete of the dialogical man.

> He who lives the life of dialogue knows a lived unity: the unity of *life*, as that which once truly won is no more torn by any changes, not ripped asunder into the everyday creaturely life and the 'deified' exalted hours; the unity of unbroken, raptureless perseverance in concreteness, in which the word is heard and a stammering answer dared.[4]

The lived unity of the life of dialogue, born out of response to the essential mystery of the world, makes this response ever more possible.

[1] *Images of Good and Evil*,' p. 82; Letter of August 18, 1952 (see p. 94, n. 1 above); *Between Man and Man*, 'The Question to the Single One,' p. 78 f.
[2] Letter of August 18, 1952.
[3] *Two Types of Faith*, pp. 40, 170; cf. *Right and Wrong* (*Good and Evil*), 'The Heart Determines, Psalm 73,' 'The Ways, Psalm 1.'
[4] *Between Man and Man*, 'Dialogue,' p. 25.

The Life of Dialogue

The 'sphere of the between,' mutual confirmation, making the other present, overcoming appearance, genuine dialogue, experiencing the other side, personal wholeness, the Single One, responsibility, decision, direction, trust—these are all aspects of the life of dialogue. This life is a part of our birthright as human beings, for only through it can we attain authentic human existence. But this birthright cannot be simply inherited, it must be earned. We must follow Buber in not underestimating the obstacles to the life of dialogue, but we must also follow him in refusing to magnify them into an inexorable fate.

The tendency toward appearance which mars the life of dialogue has its origin not only in the interdependence and need for confirmation that Buber has indicated, but also in the specific social structures that have arisen on this anthropological base: in the ordinary amenities of civilized life which make us habitually pretend toward others what we do not feel; in the institutionalization of social life which makes us tend to relate to others on the basis of our relative positions in these institutions; in the emphasis on prestige and authority which grows out of our social differentiations; in our inner divisions which make us unable to relate to others honestly because we cannot relate as whole persons; in our unawareness of the extent to which our values and attitudes arise, not from a genuine relation to truth, but from the social attitudes of the groups to which we belong.

To emphasize the hold of appearance on our lives is to point out how difficult and also how important it is to become a 'Single One.' This is especially so if one understands by the Single One not Kierkegaard's man, who finds truth by separating himself from the crowd, but Buber's man of the narrow ridge, who lives with others yet never gives up his personal responsibility nor allows his commitment to the group to stand in the way of his direct relationship to the Thou. Another product of the narrow ridge, one equally essential to the life of dialogue, is the realistic trust which recognizes the strength of the tendency toward appearance yet stands ready to deal with the other as a partner and to confirm him in becoming his real self. This open-eyed trust is at base a trust in existence itself despite the difficulties we encounter in making our human share of it authentic. It is the trust, in Buber's words, that 'man is, as man, redeemable.'

PART FOUR
THE NATURE AND REDEMPTION OF EVIL

CHAPTER FIFTEEN

THE NATURE OF EVIL

B UBER'S philosophy of dialogue is the source, ultimately, both for his answer to the question of what man is and to the problem of evil. It is entering into relation that makes man really man; it is the failure to enter into relation that in the last analysis constitutes evil, or non-existence; and it is the re-establishment of relation that leads to the redemption of evil and genuine human existence. Thus at the heart of Buber's philosophy the problem of evil and the problem of man merge into one in the recognition of relation as the fundamental reality of man's life.

> The dynamic of man, that which man as man has to fulfil, is unthinkable without evil. Man first became man through being driven out of Paradise. Good and evil form together the body of the world. If man had simply to live in the good, then there would be no work of man. That work is: to make the broken world whole. Paradise is at the lower end of separateness, but in order that its upper part, the kingdom, the great peace and unification, come, evil is necessary. . . . Evil is the hardness which divides being from being, being from God. The act of decision, of breakthrough . . . that is the act through which man time and again participates in the redemption of the world.[1]

In the Preface to *Images of Good and Evil* Buber writes that he has been preoccupied with the problem of evil since his youth. It was not until the year following the First World War, however, that he approached it independently, and it is only in this, one of the very latest of his books, that he has achieved full maturity and clarity on the subject.[2] The Yehudi in Buber's chronicle-novel reproaches the Seer of

---

[1] Quoted in Kohn, *Martin Buber, op. cit.*, p. 308, from a course on the Tao Te ch'ing which Buber gave at Ascona in the summer of 1924 (my translation).
[2] *Images of Good and Evil*, p. 9.

Lublin for dwelling on Gog, the mythical incarnation of an external, metaphysical evil:

> 'He can exist in the outer world only because he exists within us.'
> He pointed to his own breast. 'The darkness out of which he was hewn needed to be taken from nowhere else than from our slothful and malicious hearts. Our betrayal of God has made Gog to grow so great.' [1]

It is to this speech of the Yehudi's that Buber points in the Preface to *Images of Good and Evil* as the answer to the question of the point of attack for the struggle against evil.[2] This point of attack must not be understood simply as man against what is not man but as what the individual knows from his own inner experience as against what he encounters outside of himself.

> 'I certainly gain no experience of evil when I meet my fellow-man. For in that case I can grasp it only from without, estrangedly or with hatred and contempt, in which case it really does not enter my vision; or else, I overcome it with my love and in that case I have no vision of it either. I experience it when I meet myself.' [3]

Man knows evil when he recognizes the condition in which he finds himself as the 'evil' and knows the condition he has thereby lost and cannot for the time being regain as the good. It is through this inner encounter alone that evil becomes accessible and demonstrable in the world; for 'it exists in the world apart from man only in the form of quite general opposites,' embracing good and ill and good and bad as well as good and evil. The specific opposition good-evil is peculiar to man because it can only be perceived introspectively:

> A man only knows factually what 'evil' is in so far as he knows about himself, everything else to which he gives this name is merely mirrored illusion; . . . self-perception and self-relationship are the peculiarly human, the irruption of a strange element into nature, the inner lot of man.[4]

When the demon is encountered at the inner threshold, there is no longer any room for taking attitudes toward it: 'the struggle must now be fought out.' Despite the real difficulty of this inner struggle, man can overcome temptation and turn back to God. For if evil, in Buber's conception, is rebellion against God with the power He has given man to do evil, good is the turning toward God with this same power. If evil is a lack of direction, good is a finding of direction, of *the* direction toward God. If evil is the predominance of I-It, good is the meeting

---

[1] *For the Sake of Heaven, op. cit.,* p. 54.　　[2] *Images,* p. 11.
[3] *For the Sake of Heaven,* p. 57.　　[4] *Images,* pp. 21 f., 33.

with the Thou, the permeation of I-It by I-Thou. Thus in each case good and evil are bound together as they could not be if evil were an independent substance with an existence of its own.

Good and evil, then, cannot be a pair of opposites like right and left or above and beneath. 'Good' is the movement in the direction of home, 'evil' is the aimless whirl of human potentialities without which nothing can be achieved and by which, if they take no direction but remain trapped in themselves, everything goes awry.[1]

Good and evil are usually thought of as 'two structurally similar qualities situated at opposite poles.' But this is because they are treated as ethical abstractions rather than as existent states of human reality. When one looks at them 'in the factual context of the life of the human person,' one discovers their 'fundamental dissimilarity in nature, structure, and dynamics.' [2]

Evil, for Buber, is both absence of direction and absence of relation, for relation and direction as he uses them are different aspects of the same reality. The man who cannot say Thou with his whole being to God or man may have 'the sublime illusion of detached thought that he is a self-contained self; as man he is lost.' Similarly, the man who does not keep to the One direction as far as he is able may have 'the life of the spirit, in all freedom and fruitfulness, all standing and status—existence there is none for him without it.' [3]

The clearest illustration of the ultimate identity, for Buber, of evil as absence of direction and evil as absence of relation is his treatment of 'conscience.' Conscience, to him, is the voice which calls a man to fulfil the personal intention of being for which he was created. It is 'the individual's awareness of what he "really" is, of what in his unique and non-repeatable created existence he is intended to be.' Hence it implies both dialogue and direction—the dialogue of the person with an 'other' than he now is which gives him an intimation of the direction he is meant to take. This presentiment of purpose is 'inherent in all men though in the most varied strengths and degrees of consciousness and for the most part stifled by them.' When it is not stifled, it compares what one is with what one is called to become and thereby distinguishes and decides between right and wrong. Through this comparison, also one comes to feel guilt.

Each one who knows himself . . . as called to a work which he has not done, each one who has not fulfilled a task which he knows to be his own, each who did not remain faithful to his vocation

[1] *Between Man and Man*, 'The Question to the Single One,' p. 78 f.
[2] *Images*, p. 62 f.
[3] *Between Man and Man*, 'What Is Man?', p. 168; *Images*, p. 83.

which he had become certain of—each such person knows what it means to say that 'his conscience smites him.' [1]

Guilt is the product of not taking the direction toward God. The guilty man is he who shuns the dialogue with God, and this means also he who does not enter into the dialogue with man and the world. 'Original guilt consists in remaining with oneself.' If the being before whom this hour places one is not met with the truth of one's whole life, then one is guilty.

> Heidegger is right to say that . . . we are able to discover a primal guilt. But we are not able to do this by isolating a part of life, the part where the existence is related to itself and to its own being, but by becoming aware of the whole life without reduction, the life in which the individual, in fact, is essentially related to something other than himself.[2]

The fact that one discovers guilt in relation with something other than oneself does not contradict the fact that one discovers evil first of all in the meeting with oneself. This meeting takes place only if one remains aware of the voice of conscience. The man who fails to face the evil within him or affirms it as good is precisely the man who remains with himself and suppresses his awareness of direction, his awareness of the address of God which comes to him from what is 'other' than he.

The specific structure of evil in the human person cannot be explained as a result of the 'moral censorship' of society. 'There can be no question at all here of the psychology of "inhibitions" and "repressions," which operate no less against some social convention or other than when it is a matter of that which is felt to be evil in the full meaning of the word.' One's inner encounter with evil does not presuppose that 'self-analysis' of modern psychology which seeks to penetrate 'behind' the experience, 'to "reduce" it to the real elements assumed to have been "repressed."' What is needed here, rather, is the technique of the philosophical anthropologist who first participates in the experience and then gains the distance indispensable for objective knowledge. 'Our business is to call to mind an occurrence as reliably, concretely and completely remembered as possible, which is entirely unreduced and undissected.' The state of evil is experienced within ourselves in such a way that 'its differentiation from every other state of the soul is unmistakable.' This experience leads us to inquire as to the existence of evil as an ontological reality.[3]

---

[1] *Eclipse of God, op. cit.*, 'Religion and Modern Thinking,' p. 115 f., 'Religion and Ethics,' p. 125 f.

[2] *At the Turning, op. cit.*, p. 56; *Between Man and Man*, 'What Is Man?', p. 165 f.

[3] *Images*, pp. 59, 63 ff.; cf. *Between Man and Man*, 'What Is Man?', pp. 123-126.

If this inquiry is to be successful, says Buber, it must make use of the truth found in the myths of the origin of evil. The experience which has taken place in countless factual encounters with evil has been directly embodied in these myths without passing through any conceptual form. Rightly interpreted, therefore, 'they tell us of the human constitution and movement of evil' and of its relation to good. We can only interpret them rightly, however, if we accord to their account that manner of belief which comes from our personal experience of evil. 'Only out of the conjunction of these two, primordial mythic intuition and directly experienced reality, does the light of the legitimate concept arise for this sphere too, probably the most obscure of all.' The concept which arises from this conjunction serves as an indispensable bridge between myth and reality which enables man to see the two together. Without it man 'listens to the myth of Lucifer and hushes it up in his own life.' [1]

The myths that Buber interprets in *Images of Good and Evil* are the Biblical and the Zoroastrian, for, in his opinion, 'these correspond with two fundamentally different kinds and stages of evil.' He portrays the first of these stages, decisionlessness, through an interpretation of the myths of Adam and Eve, Cain, and the Flood. When Adam and Eve take the fruit, they do not make a decision between good and evil but rather imagine possibilities of action and then act almost without knowing it, sunk in 'a strange, dreamlike kind of contemplation.' Cain, similarly, does not decide to kill Abel—he does not even know what death and killing are. Rather he intensifies and confirms his indecision. 'In the vortex of indecision . . . at the point of greatest provocation and least resistance,' he strikes out. Man grasps at every possibility 'in order to overcome the tension of omnipossibility' and thus makes incarnate a reality which is 'no longer divine but his, his capriciously constructed, indestinate reality.' It is this, in the story of the Flood, which causes God to repent of having made man. The wickedness of man's actions does not derive from a corruption of the soul but from the intervention of the evil 'imagery.' This imagery is a 'play with possibility,' a 'self-temptation, from which ever and again violence springs.' The place of the real, perceived fruit is taken by a possible, devised, fabricated one which *can be* and finally *is* made into the real one. Imagination, or 'imagery,' is not entirely evil, however. It is man's greatest danger and greatest opportunity, a power which can be left undirected or directed to the good. It is in this understanding of imagery that the Talmudic doctrine of the two 'urges' originated. *Yetser*, the Biblical word for 'imagery,' is identical, in fact, with the Talmudic word for the evil and good urges. The 'evil urge' is especially close to the 'imagery of man's heart' which the Bible speaks of as 'evil from his youth,' for it is identical with 'passion, that is, the power peculiar to man, without

[1] *Images*, pp. 57-60, 12.

105

which he can neither beget nor bring forth, but which, left to itself, remains without direction and leads astray.' [1]

Man becomes aware of possibility, writes Buber, 'in a period of evolution which generally coincides with puberty without being tied to it.' This possibility takes the form of possible actions which threaten to submerge him in their swirling chaos. To escape from this dizzy whirl the soul either sets out upon the difficult path of bringing itself toward unity or it clutches at any object past which the vortex happens to carry it and casts its passion upon it. In this latter case, 'it exchanges an undirected possibility for an undirected reality, in which it does what it wills not to do, what is preposterous to it, the alien, the "evil."' It breaks violently out of the state of undirected surging passion 'wherever a breach can be forced' and enters into a pathless maze of pseudo-decision, a 'flight into delusion and ultimately into mania.' Evil, then, is lack of direction and what is done in and out of it: 'the grasping, seizing, devouring, compelling, seducing, exploiting, humiliating, torturing and destroying of what offers itself.' It is not an action, for 'action is only the type of evil happening which makes evil manifest.' The evil itself lies in the intention: 'The project of the sin and the reflecting upon it and not its execution is the real guilt.' [2]

Evil is not the result of a decision, for true decision is not partial but is made with the whole soul. 'Evil cannot be done with the whole soul; good can only be done with the whole soul.' There can be no wholeness 'where downtrodden appetites lurk in the corners' or where the soul's highest forces watch the action, 'pressed back and powerless, but shining in the protest of the spirit.' [3] The absence of personal wholeness is a complement, therefore, to the absence of direction and the absence of relation. If one does not become what one is meant to be, if one does not set out in the direction of God, if one does not bring one's scattered passions under the transforming and unifying guidance of direction, then no wholeness of the person is possible. Conversely, without attaining personal wholeness, one can neither keep to direction nor enter into full relation.

Buber portrays the second stage of evil, the actual decision to evil, through an interpretation of the Zoroastrian myths found in the Avesta and in post-Avestic literature. Here we meet good and evil as primal moving spirits set in real opposition to one another, and here, for the first time, evil assumes a substantial and independent nature. In the hymns of Zoroaster God's primal act is a decision within himself which prepares and makes possible the self-choice of good and evil by which each is first rendered effectual and factual. Created man, similarly, finds

---

[1] *Images*, pp. 13-42.
[2] *Ibid.*, pp. 66-73, 80; *Two Types of Faith, op. cit.*, p. 64 f.
[3] *Images*, p. 70 f.

himself ever again confronted by the necessity of distinguishing deception from truth and deciding between them. The primal spirits stand between God and man and like them choose between good and evil. But in the case of Ahriman, the evil spirit, this choice takes place in pure paradox since in choosing he acknowledges himself precisely as the evil.

This paradox is developed further in the saga of the primeval king Yima, who assumes dominion over the world at the bidding of the highest God, Ahura Mazdah. After a flood similar to the Biblical one, Yima lets loose the demons whom he has hitherto held in check and allows the lie to enter through lauding and blessing himself. Yima's lie is 'the primal lie . . . of humanity as a whole which ascribes the conquest of the power of nature to its own superpower.' It is the existential lie against being in which man sees himself as a self-creator. Man chooses in decisive hours between being-true and being-false, between strengthening, covering, and confirming being at the point of his own existence or weakening, desecrating, and dispossessing it. He who chooses the lie in preference to the truth intervenes directly in the decisions of the world-conflict. 'But this takes effect in the very first instance at just his point of being': by giving himself over to non-being which poses as being, he falls victim to it. Thus Yima falls into the power of the demons whose companion he has become and is destroyed by them.

Corresponding to the myth of Yima's rebellion and of his self-deification and fall are the Old Testament stories of the tower of Babel and of the foolhardy angels, such as Lucifer (Isa. xiv), who imagined themselves godlike and were cast down. Similarly, good and evil appear again and again in the Old Testament, as in the Avesta, as alternative paths before which man stands and which he must choose between as between life and death (Deut. xxx, 19). The human reality corresponding to the myths of Ahriman's choice and Lucifer's downfall, writes Buber, can only be understood through our own observations, supplemented by historical and biographical literature. These give us some insight into the crises of the self which make the person's psychic dynamic secretive and obdurate and lead him into the actual decision to evil.

This second stage of evil as decision follows from the first stage of evil as indecision. The repeated experiences of indecision merge in self-knowledge into 'a course of indecision,' a fixation in it. 'As long as the will to simple self-preservation dominates that to being-able-to-affirm oneself,' this self-knowledge is repressed. But when the will to affirm oneself asserts itself, man calls himself in question. Buber explains the crisis of the self which results from this questioning through a development of his philosophical anthropology. For this anthropology man is the creature of possibility who needs confirmation by others and by himself in order that he may be and become the particular man that he is. 'Again and again the Yes must be spoken to him . . . to liberate him from the dread of abandonment, which is a foretaste of death.' One can in a pinch do without confirmation from others, but not that of oneself. When a person's self-knowledge demands inner rejection, he either falls into a pathologically fragile and intricate relationship to himself, readjusts self-knowledge through that extreme effort of unification called 'conversion,' or displaces his knowledge of himself by an absolute self-affirmation. In this last case, the image of what he is intended to be is totally extinguished, and in its place he wills or chooses himself just as he is, just as he has resolved to intend himself. This self-affirmation in no sense means real personal wholeness but just its opposite—a crystallized inner division. 'They are recognizable, those who dominate their own self-knowledge, by the spastic pressure of the lips, the spastic tension of the muscles of the hand and the spastic tread of the foot.'

The man who thus affirms himself resembles Yima, who proclaims himself his own creator. It is in this light too that we can understand the paradoxical myth of the two spirits, one of whom chose evil precisely as evil. The 'wicked' spirit, in whom evil is already present in a nascent state, has to choose between the affirmation of himself and the affirmation of the order which establishes good and evil. 'If he affirms the order he must himself become "good," and that means he must deny and overcome his present state of being. If he affirms himself he must deny and reverse the order.' The 'good' is now just that which he is, for he can no longer say no to anything that is his. This absolute self-affirmation is the lie against being, for through it truth is no longer what he experiences as truth but what he ordains to be true.[1]

In 'Imitatio Dei,' Buber says that Adam's fall consisted in his wanting to reach the likeness to God intended for him in his creation by other means than that of the imitation of the unknown God. This substitution of self-deification for the 'imitation of God' lies at the heart not only of the fall of Adam but also that of Yima. In Adam's case, however, it is a matter of 'becoming-like-God' through knowing good and evil, whereas in Yima's it is a matter of 'being-like-God' through proclaiming oneself as the creator both of one's existence and of the values by which that existence is judged. The first stage of evil does not yet contain a 'radical evil' since the misdeeds which are committed in it are slid into rather than chosen as such. But in the second stage evil becomes radical because there man wills what he finds in himself. He affirms what he has time and again recognized in the depths of self-awareness as that which should be negated and thereby gives evil 'the substantial character which it did not previously possess.' 'If we may compare the occurrence of the first stage to an eccentric whirling movement, the

[1] *Images*, pp. 43-56, 60 f., 73-79.

process of the freezing of flowing water may serve as a simile to illustrate the second.' [1]

In his interpretation of Psalm 1 in *Right and Wrong*, Buber makes an essential distinction between the 'wicked' man and the 'sinner' corresponding to the two stages of evil which we have discussed. The sinner misses God's way again and again while the wicked opposes it. 'Sinner' describes a condition which from time to time overcomes a man without adhering to him, whereas 'wicked' describes a kind of man, a persistent disposition. 'The sinner *does* evil, the wicked man *is* evil. That is why it is said only of the wicked, and not of the sinners, that their way vanishes . . .' Although the sinner is not confirmed by the human community, he may be able to stand before God, and even entry into the human community is not closed to him if he carries out that turning into God's way which he desires in the depths of his heart. The 'wicked,' in contrast, does not 'stand' in the judgment before God. His way is his own judgment: since he has negated his existence, he ends in nothing. Does this mean that the way of God is closed to the wicked man? 'It is not closed from God's side . . . but it is closed from the side of the wicked themselves. For in distinction to the sinners they do not wish to be able to turn.' Here there arises for us the question of how an evil will can exist when God exists. To this question, says Buber, no human word knows the answer: 'The abyss which is opened by this question advances still more uncannily than the abyss of Job's question into the darkness of the divine mystery.' [2]

Although Buber's distinction between the two stages of evil did not reach its mature form until 1951, a much greater emphasis on the reality of evil is evident in his works since 1940 than in his earlier writings. In *Moses* (1944) we find a new emphasis on the demonic, one which in no way conflicts, however, with the conception of God as the ultimate source of both good and evil. A further step in the direction of radical evil is indicated by the story of Korah's rebellion. Korah's assertion that the people are already holy is the choice of evil, the choice of the people to follow the wrong path of their hearts and reject the way of God. This rebellion of the Korahites seems all the more evil since we are told that it is precisely Moses' humility, his fundamental faith in spontaneity and in freedom, which provokes the 'Korahite' reaction among men of the Korah type. Nor is Moses able to transform this evil into good; he can only extirpate it:

> Since, however, his whole work, the Covenant between God and people, is threatened, he must now doom the rebels to destruction, just as he once ordered Levites to fight against Levites. There is

[1] *Israel and the World, op. cit.*, p. 73; *Images*, pp. 62, 80 f.
[2] *Good and Evil*, 'Right and Wrong,' 'The Ways, Psalm 1,' pp. 51 f., 58 ff.

certainly something sinister underlying the legend of the earth which opened its mouth and swallowed up the rebels.

Although 'here the eternal word is opposed by eternal contradiction,' this is not to be understood as a metaphysical statement implying the absolute and independent reality of evil. It is rather the 'tragedy of Moses,' who cannot redeem the evil of Korah because 'men are as they are.'[1] It is the tragedy of 'the cruel antitheticalness of existence itself,'[2] the tragedy implicit in man's misuse of the freedom which was given him in his creation.

Closely similar to Korah's antinomian revolt in the name of divine freedom is that of the two self-proclaimed Messiahs of the seventeenth and eighteenth centuries, Sabbatai Zevi and Jacob Frank. Buber's distinction between these two men in an essay written between 1940 and 1943 contains the seed of his later distinction between evil as decisionlessness and evil as self-affirmation. Sabbatai Zevi clearly believes in something absolute and in himself in relation to it. When he becomes an apostate to escape martyrdom, 'it is not the belief as such but his belief in himself that does not stand firm.' Frank believes in nothing, not even in himself. He is not a liar but a lie, and 'he can only believe in himself after the manner of the lie by filling the space of the nothing with himself.' As a result he knows no inner restraint, and his very freedom from restraint gives him a magical influence over his followers. When, however, his nihilistic belief in himself is threatened by the crisis of self-reflection, it must draw nourishment from 'the warm flesh and blood of the belief of others in him,' or else it would cease to exist. His group of disciples with its orgies and raptures and its unconditioned self-surrender 'to a leader who leads it into nothing' affords 'an unsurpassable spectacle of disintegration.' 'The abyss has opened,' writes Buber in an historical present that strongly suggests the real present as well. 'It is no more allowed to any man to live as if evil did not exist. One cannot serve God by merely avoiding evil; one must grapple with it.'[3]

There is undoubtedly a close relation between Buber's growing tendency to ascribe reality to evil and the events of the past decades—in particular, the Nazi's persecution of the Jews, the Second World War, and the war in Palestine ('for me the most grievous of the three [wars]'[4]). In the case of Nazism this connection is made explicit in Buber's comparison of Jacob Frank with Hitler. 'It is significant,' writes Buber, 'that it is in our time that the man has arisen in whom the tension

---

[1] Martin Buber, *Moses* (Oxford: East & West Library, 1946), pp. 56-59, 184-190.
[2] *For the Sake of Heaven,* 2nd Edition, *op. cit.,* Foreword, p. x.
[3] *Hasidism, op. cit.,* 'The Beginnings of Hasidism,' pp. 10 ff., 25 f., 29 f.
[4] *Two Types of Faith,* p. 15.

between what one is and what one should be is dissolved—the man without conscience. The secret of Hitler's effectiveness lies, in fact, in his complete and fundamental absence of restraint.' The only person in an earlier age whom Buber can find to compare to Hitler is Jacob Frank, for only these two believed in nothing else than their own power. Such a belief in oneself is ordinarily only possible to one who feels himself in the fullest sense of the term commissioned and empowered by the absolute. Those who do not believe in any absolute cannot believe in this sense in the self, but the absence of restraint is accompanied by the natural ability and perfected readiness to avoid that reflection on oneself that would make one's own emptiness apparent.[1]

Does this new emphasis on a 'radical' and 'substantive' evil mean that we can no longer place Buber in that middle position which regards evil as real but redeemable, thus refusing to ascribe to it an absolute and independent reality? Does Buber's use of the Iranian myths, the most important historical fountainhead of dualism, not only serve to illustrate an anthropological reality but also imply a dualistic metaphysics? *Images of Good and Evil* itself supplies the answer to our question. Buber makes it clear there that it is not man's nature which is evil but only his use of that nature. There are, to be sure, wicked men whose end is non-existence—this accords with the simple facts—but there are no men whom God cuts off as simply evil and therefore by nature hostile to His purpose. If some men bring evil to a 'radical' stage where it possesses a substantial quality, this does not mean that evil is here independent and absolute, nor even ultimately unredeemable, but only that it has crystallized into a settled opposition by the individual to becoming what he is meant to become. 'Good . . . retains the character of direction at both stages,' writes Buber, indicating clearly that there is a good for the second stage even as for the first.[2]

Further evidence that Buber has not left the narrow ridge in his attitude toward evil is his discussion of 'God's will to harden' in *Two Types of Faith* (1950). On the three occasions when the Old Testament speaks of God as 'hardening the heart' of a person or people, it is because of his or their persistent turning away. The hardening comes in an extreme situation as a consequence of perversion 'and . . . dreadfully enough . . . makes the going-astray into a state of having gone-astray from which there is no returning.' 'Sin is not an undertaking which man can break off when the situation becomes critical,' Buber explains, 'but a process started by him, the control of which is withdrawn from him at a fixed moment.'[3]

[1] Martin Buber, *Pointing the Way, op. cit.,* 'People and Leader,' pp. 151-156, 158 ff.
[2] *Images*, pp. 36, 73, 81 ff.
[3] *Two Types of Faith*, pp. 83-90.

The 'special strength to persevere in sin' which God grants the sinner when He 'hardens' his heart is a counterpart, we may surmise, of that absolute self-affirmation with which the 'wicked' closes himself off from God. God will not abridge the freedom which He has given man in creation, and therefore He allows this process of closing off to take place. His 'hardening' is His response to man's decision against Him. It is at once the judgment with which He confirms the wicked in his non-existence and the 'severe grace' with which He points out to him the one road back to real existence.

> Even in the dark hour after he has become guilty against his brother, man is not abandoned to the forces of chaos. God Himself seeks him out, and even when he comes to call him to account, His coming is salvation.[1]

God remains open to man's turning, but for the man whose way has vanished nothing less than a 'conversion'—a turning of the whole being —will suffice.

Despite the importance in Buber's recent thought of such terms as contradiction, tragedy, eclipse of God, and 'radical evil,' he remains essentially different from even the least extreme of the dualists. His affirmation of the oneness of God and the ultimate oneness of God and the world has deepened in its paradoxical quality as he has taken more and more realistic cognizance of the evil of the world, but it has not wavered or weakened. The great significance, indeed, of that second stage of evil which is the newest development in Buber's thought is its concrete base in human existence which makes understandable such extreme phenomena as Hitler and the Nazis without resorting to the dogma of original sin or agreeing with Sartre's assertion that the events of recent years make it necessary to recognize evil as absolute and unredeemable.

---

[1] *At the Turning*, p. 56.

CHAPTER SIXTEEN

THE ECLIPSE OF GOD

THE absolute affirmation of the self in the second stage of evil is an extreme form of man's hiding from the 'signs' which address him. A more common form of cutting oneself off from dialogue is the action of the man who 'musters' each situation or approaches it with a formulated technique or programme. Another is the various types of 'once for all' which make unnecessary the 'ever anew' of real response to the unique situation which confronts one in each hour. This false security prevents us from making our relationships to others real through opening ourselves to them and thereby leads us to 'squander the most precious, irreplaceable and irrecoverable material' of life. It also prevents us from making real our relationship to God, for the meeting with God takes place in the 'lived concrete,' and lived concreteness exists only in so far as the moment retains its true dialogical character of presentness and uniqueness.[1]

The logical and dialectical God of the theologians—the God who can be put into a system, enclosed in an idea, or thought about philosophically as 'a state of being in which all ideas are absorbed'—is not the God who can be met in the lived concrete. The 'once for all' of dogma resists the unforeseeable moment and thereby becomes 'the most exalted form of invulnerability against revelation.' 'Centralization and codification, undertaken in the interests of religion, are a danger to the core of religion, unless there is the strongest life of faith, embodied in the whole existence of the community, and not relaxing in its renewing activity.' [2]

It is only one step from dogma to 'magic,' for a God that can be fixed in dogma can also be possessed and used. 'Always and everywhere

[1] *Between Man and Man*, 'Dialogue,' p. 16, 'What Is Man?', p. 170; *Eclipse of God, op. cit.*, 'Religion and Philosophy,' p. 49.

[2] *Between Man and Man*, 'The Question to the Single One,' p. 57 f.; *Israel and the World, op. cit.*, 'The Love of God and the Idea of Deity,' p. 53; *Kampf um Israel, op. cit.*, p. 203 f.; *Between Man and Man*, 'Dialogue,' p. 18; *The Prophetic Faith, op. cit.*, p. 70.

in the history of religion, the fact that God is identified with success is the greatest obstacle to a steadfast religious life.' Magic operates where-ever one celebrates rites 'without being turned to the Thou and . . . really meaning its Presence.' In magic God becomes a bundle of powers, present at man's command and in the form in which man wishes them.[1]

As a step in one direction leads from dogma to magic, a step in another leads to 'gnosis,' the attempt to raise the veil which divides the revealed from the hidden and to lead forth the divine mystery. Gnosis, like magic, stands as the great threat to dialogical life and to the turning to God. Gnosis attempts to see through the contradiction of existence and free itself from it, rather than endure the contradiction and redeem it. Buber illustrates this contrast through a comparison between Hasidism and the Kabbalah.

> The whole systematic structure of the Kabbalah is determined by a principle of certitude which hardly ever stops short, hardly ever cowers with terror, hardly ever prostrates itself. Hasidic piety, on the other hand, finds its real life just in stopping short, in letting itself be disconcerted, in its deep-seated knowledge of the impotence of all ready-made knowledge, of the incongruity of all acquired truth, in the 'holy insecurity.' [2]

This gnosis is not found in the modern world in theosophies and occult systems alone. 'In many theologies also, unveiling gestures are to be discovered behind the interpreting ones.' Gnosis has even found its way into modern psychotherapy through the teachings of Carl Jung:

> The psychological doctrine which deals with mysteries without knowing the attitude of faith toward mystery is the modern mani-festation of Gnosis. Gnosis is not to be understood as only a historical category, but as a universal one. It—and not atheism, which annihilates God because it must reject the hitherto existing images of God—is the real antagonist of the reality of faith.[3]

Concern with revelation of the future, the attempt to get behind the problematic of life, the desire to possess or use divine power, the

---

[1] *Moses, op. cit.*, pp. 88, 185; *Eclipse of God*, 'God and the Spirit of Man,' trans. by Maurice S. Friedman, p. 161 f.; *Israel and the World*, 'The Faith of Judaism,' pp. 21-24; *Hasidism*, 'Spirit and Body of the Hasidic Movement,' p. 79, 'Symbolical and Sacramental Existence in Judaism,' p. 142 f. Cf. *Moses*, p. 22 f. for Buber's contrast between 'technical magic' and 'magic of spontaneity.'

[2] *Israel and the World*, 'The Faith of Judaism,' pp. 21-24, 'The Two Foci of the Jewish Soul,' p. 31 f.; *Eclipse of God*, 'God and the Spirit of Man,' p. 162; *Hasidism*, 'Symbolical Existence in Judaism,' p. 141 f.

[3] *Eclipse of God*, 'God and the Spirit of Man,' p. 162, 'Reply to C. G. Jung,' p. 175 f.

acceptance of tradition and law as a 'once for all' in which one can take refuge—all these prevent the meeting with God in the lived concrete. Even the belief in immortality may be a threat to the relation of faith, for by making death appear unreal or unserious, it may hinder our recognition of the limits of finitude as the threshold of Eternity.[1] Similarly, the very symbols which man uses to address God often stand in the way of that address.

> The religious reality of the meeting with the Meeter . . . knows only the presence of the Present One. Symbols of Him, whether images or ideas, always exist first when and in so far as Thou becomes He, and that means It.

'God, so we may surmise, does not despise all these similarly and necessarily untrue images, but rather suffers that one look at Him through them.' But there inevitably comes a time when the symbol, instead of enabling men to enter into relation with God, stands in the way of that relation.[2]

The philosopher helps restore the lived concrete to the religious man through destroying the images which no longer do justice to God. But the 'pure idea,' which he raises to the throne of reality in their place, also stands between man and God. Philosophy begins with 'the primary act of abstraction,' that 'inner action in which man lifts himself above the concrete situation into the sphere of precise conceptualization.' The concepts which man develops in this sphere 'no longer serve as a means of apprehending reality, but instead represent as the object of thought Being freed from the limitations of the actual.' From the lived togetherness of I and It, philosophy abstracts the I into a subject which can do nothing but observe and reflect and the It into a passive object of thought. The 'God of the philosophers,' in consequence, is a conceptually comprehensible thing among things, and no longer a living God who can be the object of imagination, wishes, and feelings. Nor is this situation changed by the special place which philosophy gives the absolute as the object from which all other objects are derived, or as 'Speech' (*Logos*), 'the Unlimited,' or simply 'Being.' 'Philosophy is grounded on the presupposition that one sees the absolute in universals.' As a result philosophy must necessarily deny, or at the very least turn away from, the reality on which religion is grounded, 'the covenant of the absolute with the particular, with the concrete.'[3]

---

[1] *For the Sake of Heaven*, *op. cit.*, p. 238 f.; Martin Buber, 'Nach dem Tod,' *Münchener Neuesten Nachrichten*, February 8, 1928.

[2] *Eclipse of God*, 'Religion and Philosophy,' p. 62 f., 'The Love of God and the Idea of Deity,' p. 84.

[3] *Ibid.*, 'Religion and Philosophy,' pp. 44 f., 53-63, 'Religion and Reality,' p. 28.

Both the philosophizing and the religious person wonder at phenomena, says Buber, but 'the one neutralizes his wonder in ideal knowledge, while the other abides in that wonder.' [1] When man has felt at home in the universe, his thought about himself has only been a part of his cosmological thought. But when man has felt himself shut in by a strict and inescapable solitude, his thinking about himself has been deep and fruitful and independent of cosmology. Buber criticizes Aristotle, Aquinas, and Hegel because in their systems of thought man attains to consciousness of himself only in the third person. Man is no longer problematic for himself, and the wonder at man is simply wonder at the universe as a whole. Hegel's theoretical certainty is derived from his incorporation of cosmological rather than actual human time into the groundwork of his image of the universe. 'Cosmological time' is abstract and relativized. In it all the future can appear theoretically present. 'Anthropological time,' in contrast, has reality only in the past. Since the future depends in part on man's consciousness and will, on decisions which have not yet taken place, no certainty of the future is possible within the boundaries of the human world. Marx takes over Hegel's cosmological time to provide the proletariat the security of an assured victory in the future. This security, like Hegel's, is a false one since it ignores man's powers of decisions. 'It depends on the direction and force of this power how far the renewing powers of life as such are able to take effect, and even whether they are not transformed into powers of destruction.' [2]

The submersion of the dialogical life by the 'once for all' of gnosis, theology, philosophy, and social doctrine is only a part of a larger development of civilization. All great civilizations at their early stages are 'life-systems' built up around a supreme principle which pervades the entire existence of the group. This principle is at once a religious and a normative one since it implies a concrete attachment of human life to the Absolute and an attempt to bring order and meaning into earthly existence through the imitation of transcendent Being. All spheres of being are essentially determined by the relationship to this principle. In proportion to the development of its specific forms, however, every civilization strives increasingly to become independent of its principle.

In the great Western civilizations, this manifests itself partly by their individual spheres isolating themselves and each of them establishing its own basis and order, and partly by the principle itself losing its absolute character and validity, so that the holy norm degenerates into a human convention, or by the attachment

---

[1] *Moses*, p. 75.
[2] *Between Man and Man*, pp. 126-129, 131 f., 139-145.

to the absolute being reduced, avowedly or unavowedly, to a mere symbolic-ritual requirement, which may be adequately satisfied in the cultic sphere.[1]

Once the spheres have become independent of the original principle of the civilization, 'religion' no longer means just the whole of one's existence in its relation to the Absolute but a special domain of dogma and cult. 'The original evil of all "religion,"' writes Buber, is 'the separation of "living in God" from "living in the world."' This separated religion is man's greatest danger whether it manifests itself in the form of a cult in which sacramental forms are independent of everyday life or of a soul detached from life in devotional rapture and solitary relation with God. 'The sacrament . . . misleads the faithful into feeling secure in a merely "objective" consummation without any personal participation.' In such a service the real partner of the communion is no longer present. Similarly, when the soul cuts itself off from the world, God is displaced by a figment of the soul itself: the dialogue which the soul thinks it is carrying on 'is only a monologue with divided roles.' [2]

This dualism between the life of the spirit and the life of the world was already present in biblical Judaism, but it gained still greater ground in Christianity because of the latter's surrender of the concept of a 'holy people' for that of personal holiness. 'Those who believed in Christ possessed at every period a twofold being: as individuals in the realm of the person and as participants in the public life of their nations.' Although 'in the history of Christian peoples there has been no lack of men of the spirit afire and ready for martyrdom in the struggle for righteousness,' the norm of realizing the religion in all aspects of social existence can no longer occupy a central place. As a result it is made easy for the secular law to gain ever more ground at the expense of the religious. At the point at which the public sphere encroaches disastrously on the personal, as it does in our time, 'the disparity between the sanctification of the individual and the accepted unholiness of his community' is transferred to an inner contradiction in the redeemed soul.[3]

The apocalyptic element in religion also tends to lead to a dualism between the secular and the religious. The eschatological expectation of the imminent rule of God leads to a desire to do away with law in the name of the divine freedom which is or will be directly present in all creatures without need of law or representation. As soon as this expectation slackens, 'it follows historically that God's rule is restricted

---

[1] *At the Turning, op. cit.,* 'Judaism and Civilization,' pp. 11-15.
[2] *Hasidism,* 'Spinoza,' pp. 104, 99 f., 'Symbolical Existence in Judaism,' p. 132.
[3] *Eclipse of God,* 'Religion and Ethics,' pp. 138-141; *Two Types of Faith, op. cit.,* p. 173.

to the "religious" sphere, everything that is left over is rendered unto Caesar; and the rift which runs through the whole being of the human world receives its sanction.' This dualism enters deeply into Paul's essentially Gnostic view of the world. It is also found in Judaism, where the autochthonous prophetic belief is opposed by an apocalyptic one built up out of elements from Iranian dualism. The one 'promises a consummation of creation,' the other 'its abrogation and supersession by another world completely different in nature.'

> The prophetic allows 'the evil' to find the direction that leads toward God, and to enter into the good; the apocalyptic sees good and evil severed forever at the end of days, the good redeemed, the evil unredeemable for all eternity; the prophetic believes that the earth shall be hallowed, the apocalyptic despairs of an earth which it considers to be hopelessly doomed. . . .[1]

The prophetic and Hasidic belief in the hallowing of the earth also stands in contrast to the pagan world's glorification of the elemental forces and the Christian world's conquest of them. Christianity, through its ascetic emphasis, desanctified the elemental and created a world alien to spirit and a spirit alien to world. 'Even when Christianity includes the natural life in its sacredness, as in the sacrament of marriage, the bodily life is not hallowed, but merely made subservient to holiness.' The result has been a split between the actual and the ideal, between life as it *is* lived and life as it *should* be lived.[2]

All historical religion must fight the tendency of metaphysics, gnosis, magic, and politics to become independent of the religious life of the person, and it must also fight the tendency of myth and cult to aid them in this attempt. What is threatened by these extra-religious elements is the lived concrete—the moment 'in its unforeseeableness and . . . irrecoverableness . . . its undivertible character of happening but once.' The lived concrete is also threatened by those religious elements that destroy the concreteness of the memory of past moments of meeting with God that have been preserved in religious tradition—theology, which makes temporal facts into timeless symbols, and mysticism, which dilutes and weakens the images of memory by proclaiming all experience accessible at once.[3]

In the modern world the moment is expropriated and dispossessed in four different ways. Through the historicizing of the moment it is regarded as a pure product of the past. Through the technicizing of the moment it is treated as purely a means to a goal and hence as existing

---

[1] *Moses*, p. 188; *Israel and the World*, 'The Two Foci of the Jewish Soul,' p. 36.
[2] *Israel and the World*, 'The Power of the Spirit,' pp. 176-179.
[3] *Eclipse of God*, 'Religion and Philosophy,' p. 48 f.; Martin Buber, 'Religion und Philosophie,' *Europäische Revue*, Berlin, V (August 1929), p. 330 f.

only in the future. Through the psychologizing of the moment its total content is reflected upon and reduced to a process or experience of the soul. Through the philosophizing of the moment it is abstracted from its reality. Modern life is divided into levels and aspects. Modern man enjoys erotic, aesthetic, political, and religious experiences independently of one another. As a result, religion is for him only one aspect of his life rather than its totality. The men of the Bible were sinners like us, says Buber, but they did not commit the arch sin of professing God in the synagogue and denying him in the sphere of economics, politics, and the 'self-assertion' of the group. Nor did they believe it possible to be honest and upright in private life and to lie in public for the sake of the commonwealth.[1]

The dualistic character of our age is shown particularly clearly in its relation to work. In times when the relation with the Absolute enters into every sphere of existence men see meaning in their work, but in times like ours when life is divided into separate spheres men experience work as an inescapable compulsion. The nature of work itself is perverted in the modern world by the divorce of technical means from value ends, I-It from I-Thou. The modern industrial worker has to perform meaningless and mechanical work because of an inhuman utilization of human power without regard to the worthiness of the work performed. The modern worker divides his life into hours on a treadmill and hours of freedom from the treadmill, and the hours of freedom cannot compensate for the others for they are conditioned by them. To accept the treadmill and try to reduce working hours is merely to eternalize this condition.[2]

'Man is in a growing measure sociologically determined,' writes Buber. In the technical, economic, and political spheres of his existence he finds himself 'in the grip of incomprehensible powers' which trample again and again on all human purposes. This purposelessness of modern life is also manifested in the worship of freedom for its own sake. Modern vitalism and *Lebensphilosophie* have exchanged a life-drunk spirit for the detached intellect against which they reacted. Progressive education has tended to free the child's creative impulses without helping him to acquire the personal responsibility which should accompany it. This sickness of modern man is manifested most clearly of all, however, in the individualism and nationalism which make power an end in itself. 'Power without faithfulness is life without meaning,' writes

[1] 'Religion und Philosophie,' p. 334; Martin Buber, 'Religion und Gottesherrschaft,' a criticism of Leonhard Ragaz's *Weltreich, Religion und Gottesherrschaft*. *Frankfurter Zeitung*, 'Literaturblatt,' No. 9, April 27, 1923; *Israel and the World*, 'The Man of Today and the Jewish Bible,' p. 90 f., 'And If Not Now, When?' p. 235 f., 'Hebrew Humanism,' p. 246 f.; *Des Baal-Schem-Tow Unterweisung, op. cit.*, p. 116 f.

[2] *Kampf um Israel*, pp. 281, 277.

Buber. If a nation or civilization is not faithful to its basic principle, it can know no real fruitfulness or renewal.[1] The inevitable result of the 'will to power,' whether on the national or individual level, is the tendency to use others as means to one's end. This tendency is found not only in those governed by the 'profit motive' but also in the professional men who give others technical aid without entering into relationship with them. Help without mutuality is presumptuousness, writes Buber; it is an attempt to practise magic. The educator who tries to dominate or enjoy his pupils 'stifles the growth of his blessing,' and it is the same with the doctor and the psychotherapist: 'As soon as the helper is touched by the desire, in however subtle a form, to dominate or to enjoy his patient, or to treat the latter's wish to be dominated or enjoyed by him as other than a wrong condition needing to be cured, the danger of falsification arises, beside which all quackery appears peripheral.' The writer and observer of life who associates with people out of ulterior motives and the 'religious' man who forgets his relation with God in his striving to attain higher and higher spiritual levels are subtler examples still of the will to power.[2]

Yet another product of the dualism of the modern age is the separation of means and ends and the belief that the end justifies the means. The essence of the essays that Buber has written on Zionism over a period of fifty years is the teaching that 'no way leads to any other goal but to that which is like it.' 'It is only the sick understanding of this age that teaches that the goal can be reached through all the ways of the world.' If the means that are used are not consistent with the goal that has been set, then this goal will be altered in the attainment. 'What knowledge could be of greater importance to the men of our age, and to the various communities of our time,' wrote Buber in 1947, than that 'the use of unrighteousness as a means to a righteous end makes the end itself unrighteous?' The person or community which seeks to use evil for the sake of good destroys its own soul in the process.

[1] *Between Man and Man*, 'Dialogue,' p. 39, 'What Is Man?', p. 158; Martin Buber and Franz Rosenzweig, *Die Schrift und ihren Verdeutschung* (Berlin: Schocken Verlag, 1936), 'Der Mensch von heute und die jüdische Bibel,' p. 31 f., from a section of this essay of Buber's which is not included in the translation in *Israel and the World; Between Man and Man*, 'Education,' p. 90 ff., 'What Is Man?', pp. 150-153; Martin Buber, *Die Stunde und die Erkenntnis, Reden und Aufsätze*, 1933-1935 (Berlin: Schocken Verlag, 1936), pp. 16 f., 37 f.; *Israel and the World*, 'Nationalism,' pp. 216, 219 ff., 225; *At the Turning*, 'Judaism and Civilization,' p. 23 f.; *Two Types of Faith*, p. 171; *Israel und Palästina, op. cit.*, pp. 180 f., 12 (my translation).

[2] *Between Man and Man*, 'Education,' p. 94 f.; *For the Sake of Heaven*, pp. 140 f., 216. The sentence on presumptuousness is from a lecture on the belief in rebirth given by Buber at Amersfoort in the summer of 1925 and is quoted by Hans Trüb in 'J. C. Blumhardt über unheimliche Hilfe,' *Aus unbekannten Schriften, op. cit.*, p. 157.

I sometimes hear it said that a generation must sacrifice itself, 'take the sin upon itself,' so that coming generations may be free to live righteously. But it is a self-delusion and folly to think that one can lead a dissolute life and raise one's children to be good and happy; they will usually turn out to be hypocrites or tormented.[1]

The use of evil for the sake of good not only produces inner division and dishonesty, it also betrays it, as Buber shows in his portrayal of the Seer in *For the Sake of Heaven*. If this divided motivation goes far enough, it may even lead to that Gnostic perversion which elevates evil into something holy in itself. The radical Sabbatians believed that they could redeem evil by performing it as if it were not evil, that is by preserving an inner intention of purity in contrast to the deed. 'That is an illusion,' writes Buber, 'for all that man does reacts on his soul, even when he fancies that his soul hovers over the deed.' Buber speaks of this revolt against the distinction between good and evil as 'the lust for overrunning reality.'

> Instead of making reality the starting point of life, full as it is of harsh contradictions, but for this very reason calling forth true greatness, namely the quiet work of overcoming the contradictions, man submits to illusion, becomes intoxicated with it, surrenders his life to it, and in the very measure in which he does this the core of his existence becomes burning and unfruitful, he becomes at once completely stimulated and in his motive power crippled.

This demonic 'lust for overruning reality' is not simply a product of unbelief but a crisis within men's souls, a crisis of temptation, freedom, and dishonesty:

> These are the days in which people still fulfil the commandments, but with a soul squinting away from its own deeds. . . . Behind the demonic mask people fancy to behold the countenance of God's freedom; they do not allow themselves to be deluded by those temptations, but neither do they drive them away. . . . The realms are overthrown, everything encroaches upon everything else, and possibility is more powerful than reality.[2]

---

[1] *Kampf um Israel*, pp. 425 f., 451; *Die Stunde und die Erkenntnis*, p. 126; Martin Buber, 'Drei Sätze eines religiösen Sozialismus,' *Neue Wege*, Zurich, XXII (1928), No. 718, p. 329, reprinted in *Hinweise, op. cit.*, p. 259 ff., and to be published in *Pointing the Way, op. cit.*; Martin Buber, *Zion als Ziel und Aufgabe* (Berlin: Schocken Verlag, 1936), 'Zum Geleit,' p. 5; *For the Sake of Heaven*, pp. 58, 238 f., 256; *Israel and the World*, 'What Are We to Do About the Ten Commandments?', p. 68, 'And If Not Now, When?', p. 238.

[2] *Hasidism*, 'The Foundation Stone,' pp. 39, 49.

The fascination with the demonic in modern literature, the tendency of many to turn psychoanalysis or 'psychodrama' into a cult of self-realization, and the illusory belief that personal fulfilment can come through 'release' of one's deep inward energies all show the peculiarly modern relevance of the 'crisis of temptation and dishonesty' which Buber describes. In Carl Jung's teaching, for example, the integrated soul 'dispenses with the conscience as the court which distinguishes and decides between right and wrong.' The precondition for this integration is the '"liberation from those desires, ambitions, and passions which imprison us in the visible world," through "intelligent fulfilment of instinctive demands."' What this means becomes clear through Jung's statement that it is necessary to succumb 'in part' to evil in order that the unification of good and evil may take place. Jung thus resumes, under the guise of psychotherapy, the Gnostic motif 'of mystically deifying the instincts.'[1]

What lends especial impetus to the various psychological and theosophical cults through which the individual seeks to overrun reality in the modern world is the dualism in the soul of modern man.

> In this man the sphere of the spirit and the sphere of impulse have fallen apart more markedly than ever before. He perceives with apprehension that an unfruitful and powerless remoteness from life is threatening the separated spirit, and he perceives with horror that the repressed and banished impulses are threatening to destroy his soul.[2]

In the philosophical anthropology of Max Scheler, as in the Freudian psychoanalysis from which it in part derives, this division of spirit and impulse is regarded as basic to man's nature. In Buber's opinion this is a mistaken identification of the state of modern man with the state of man in general. The 'central significance of repression and sublimation in Freud's system,' derives from the pathological condition of modern man and is valid in terms of it. Modern man is sick in his very soul, and this sickness springs, in its turn, from his sickness in his relations to others. Freud's categories are of importance precisely because of the decay of organic community, the disappearance of real togetherness in our modern world.

> Where confidence reigns man must often, indeed, adapt his wishes to the commands of his community; but he must not repress them to such an extent that the repression acquires a dominating significance for his life. . . . Only if the organic community disintegrates from within does the repression acquire its dominating

---

[1] *Eclipse of God*, 'Religion and Modern Thinking,' pp. 112-121, 'Reply to C. G. Jung,' p. 176.

[2] *Between Man and Man*, 'What Is Man?', p. 187.

importance. The unaffectedness of wishing is stifled by mistrust, everything around is hostile or can become hostile, agreement between one's own and the other's desire ceases . . . and the dulled wishes creep hopelessly into the recesses of the soul. . . . Now there is no longer a human wholeness with the force and the courage to manifest itself. For spirit to arise the energy of the repressed instincts must mostly first be 'sublimated,' the traces of its origin cling to the spirit and it can mostly assert itself against the instincts only by convulsive alienation. The divorce between spirit and instincts is here, as often, the consequence of the divorce between man and man.[1]

Vital dissociation is the sickness of the peoples of our age, writes Buber, and this sickness is only apparently healed by forcing people together in centralized states and collectivities. The price which the modern world has paid for the liberation of the French Revolution has been the decay of those organic forms of life which enabled men to live in direct relation with one another and which gave men security, connection, and a feeling of being at home in the-world. These organic forms—the family, union in work, and the community in village and town—were based on a vital tradition which has now been lost. Despite the outward preservation of some of the old forms, the inward decay has resulted in an intensification of man's solitude and a destruction of his security. In their place new community forms have arisen which have attempted to bring the individual into relation with others; but these forms, such as the club, the trade union, and the party, 'have not been able to re-establish the security which has been destroyed,' 'since they have no access to the life of society itself and its foundations: production and consumption.'[2]

The corollary of this decay of organic forms is the growing difficulty of genuine conversation, 'and most especially of genuine conversation between men of different kinds and convictions.' 'Direct, open dialogue is becoming ever more difficult and more rare; the abysses between man and man threaten ever more pitilessly to become unbridgeable.' This difficulty of conversation is particularly discernible in the dominance of 'false dialogue,' or 'monologue disguised as dialogue.' In false dialogue the participants do not really have each other in mind, or they have each other in mind only as general and abstracted opponents and not as particular beings. There is no real turning to the other, no real desire to establish mutuality. 'Technical dialogue' too is false dialogue because it 'is prompted solely by the need of objective understanding

[1] *Ibid.*, pp. 185-197.
[2] *Die Stunde und die Erkenntnis*, p. 121 f.; *Between Man and Man*, 'What Is Man?', p. 157 f.; *Paths in Utopia, op. cit.*, p. 139.

and has no real concern with the other person as a person. It belongs, writes Buber in one of his rare notes of sarcasm, 'to the inalienable sterling quality of "modern existence."' It is for monologue that disguises itself as dialogue, however, that Buber reserves his full scorn. Here men have the illusion of getting beyond themselves when actually each speaks only with himself. This type of 'dialogue' is characteristic of our intensely social age in which men are more alone than ever before.

A *debate* in which the thoughts are not expressed in the way in which they existed in the mind but in the speaking are so pointed that they may strike home in the sharpest way, and moreover without the men that are spoken to being regarded in any way present as persons; a *conversation* characterized by the need neither to communicate something, nor to learn something, nor to influence someone, nor to come into connexion with someone, but solely by the desire to have one's own self-reliance confirmed by making the impression that is made, or if it has become unsteady to have it strengthened; a *friendly chat* in which each regards himself as absolute and legitimate and the other as relativized and questionable; a *lovers' talk* in which both partners alike enjoy their own glorious soul and their precious experience—what an underworld of faceless spectres of dialogue! [1]

By far the largest part of what is called conversation today would be more correctly described as talk. In general, people do not really speak to one another. Each turns to the other, to be sure, but he speaks in reality to a fictitious audience which exists only to listen to him. The understanding of true conversation is so rare in our time that one imagines that one can arrange a genuine dialogue before a public of interested spectators with the assistance of proper publicity. But a public debate, on no matter how high a level, can neither be spontaneous, direct, nor unreserved. Such public discussion is unbridgeably separate from genuine dialogue. It is much closer to propaganda, which seeks to win the individual over for a cause. To propaganda the individual as such is always burdensome. Its only concern is more members, more followers, a larger supporting base. Propaganda means mastering the other through depersonalizing him. It is variously combined with coercion, supplementing or replacing it according to need and prospect, but ultimately it is itself nothing other than sublimated coercion, invisibly applied. It sets the soul under a pressure which still allows the illusion of autonomy.

Almost all that one understands in our time as specifically modern

---

[1] Martin Buber, 'Hope for This Hour,' an address translated by me and given by Buber at a tribute for him at Carnegie Hall, New York, April 6, 1952, published in *World Review*, December 1952; *Between Man and Man*, 'Dialogue,' p. 19 f.

stands in opposition to the awareness of one's fellow as a whole, single, and unique person, even if, in most cases, a defectively developed one. In the modern age an analytic, reductive, and derivative glance predominates between man and man. It is analytic, or rather pseudo-analytic, because it treats the whole body-soul being as composite in nature and hence as dissectible—not the so-called unconscious alone, which is susceptible to a relative objectification, but also the psychic stream itself, which can never in reality be adequately grasped as an object. This glance is reductive because it wishes to reduce the manifold person, nourished by the microcosmic fullness of possibility, to a schematically surveyable and generally repetitive structure. And it is derivative because it hopes to grasp what a man has become, and even his becoming itself, in genetic formulas, because it tries to replace the individual dynamic central principle of this becoming by a general concept. Today a radical dissolution of all mystery is aspired to between man and man. Personality, that incessantly near mystery which was once the motive-ground for the stillest inspiration, is levelled out.[1]

Corresponding to the absence of genuine dialogue between men is the absence of real communication between peoples of different situations and points of view. 'The human world,' Buber wrote in 1952, 'is today, as never before, split into two camps, each of which understands the other as the embodiment of falsehood and itself as the embodiment of truth.' Man not only thinks his principle true and the opposing one false, as in earlier epochs, but he now believes 'that he is concerned with the recognition and realization of right, his opponent with the masking of his selfish interest.' The mistrust that reigns between the two camps has been decisively enhanced by the theory of 'ideology' which has become prevalent through the influence of Marx, Nietzsche, and Freud. This theory consists of seeing through and unmasking the other in terms of individual psychology or sociology. One assumes that the other dissembles of necessity and looks for the unconscious motive, 'complex,' or group interest that clothes itself in his seemingly objective judgment. These psychological and sociological theories of 'seeing-through' have again and again fallen into the boundless simplification of reducing man to the newly discovered elements instead of inserting these elements into man's total structure. As a result, the mistrust between man and man has become in a double sense existential.

It is, first of all, no longer only the uprightness, the honesty of the other which is in question, but the inner agreement of his existence itself. Secondly, this mistrust not only destroys trustworthy conversation between opponents but also the immediacy of togetherness of man and man generally.[2]

[1] 'Elements of the Interhuman,' *op. cit.*, sections 2, 4, 5.
[2] 'Hope for This Hour,' *Pointing the Way*, pp. 220-229.

The result of this progressive decline of dialogue and growth of universal mistrust is that man's need for confirmation no longer finds any natural satisfaction. Man seeks confirmation either through himself or through membership in a collective, but both of these confirmations are illusory. He whom no fellow-man confirms must endeavour to restore his self-confirmation 'with ever more convulsive exertions . . . and finally he knows himself as inevitably abandoned.' Confirmation is by its very nature a reciprocal process: the man who does not confirm his fellow-man will not only receive no confirmation from others but will find it increasingly difficult to confirm himself. 'Confirmation through the collective, on the other hand, is pure fiction.' Though the collective employs each of its members in terms of his particular ability and character, it 'cannot recognize anyone in his own being and therefore independently of his usefulness for the collective.' [1]

These two types of illusory confirmation correspond to the false dichotomy which dominates our age, that between individualism and collectivism. Despite their apparent opposition, the individualist and the collectivist are actually alike in that neither knows true personal wholeness or true responsibility. The individualist acts out of arbitrary self-will and in consequence is completely defined and conditioned by circumstances. The collectivist acts in terms of the collectivity and in so doing loses his ability to perceive and to respond from the depths of his being. Neither can attain any genuine relation with others, for one cannot be a genuine person in individualism or collectivism, and 'there is genuine relation only between genuine persons.' [2]

Collectivism is the greater danger to the modern world. Whether in the form of totalitarianism or of self-effacing loyalty to political parties, it represents the desire of this age to fly 'from the demanding "ever anew"' of personal responsibility 'into the protective "once for all"' of membership in a group. 'The last generation's intoxication with freedom has been followed by the present generation's craze for bondage; the untruth of intoxication has been followed by the untruth of hysteria.'

> Today host upon host of men have everywhere sunk into the slavery of collectives, and each collective is the supreme authority for its own slaves; there is no longer, superior to the collectives, any universal sovereignty in idea, faith or spirit.[3]

Collectivism is typical of our age in giving the appearance but not the reality of relation, for in our age the great hopes and dreams of man-

---

[1] 'Hope for This Hour.' Cf. *Images of Good and Evil, op. cit.*, p. 77.
[2] *Between Man and Man*, 'The Question to the Single One,' p. 80 f., 'What Is Man?', p. 200 ff.
[3] *Ibid.*, 'The Question to the Single One,' p. 70, 'The Education of Character,' p. 110.

kind have been fulfilled one after another—'as the caricature of them-selves.' Collectivism imperils 'the immeasurable value which constitutes man,' for it destroys the dialogue between man and God and the living communion between man and man.

> Man in a collective is not man with man. . . . The 'whole,' with its claim on the wholeness of every man, aims logically and success-fully at reducing, neutralizing, devaluating, and desecrating every bond with living beings. That tender surface of personal life which longs for contact with other life is progressively deadened or de-sensitized. Man's isolation is not overcome here, but overpowered and numbed. . . . The actual condition of solitude has its insuper-able effect in the depths, and rises secretly to a cruelty which will become manifest with the scattering of the illusion. Modern collectivism is the last barrier raised by man against a meeting with himself.[1]

'We experience this not only as an hour of the heaviest affliction,' Buber wrote in 1952, 'but also as one that appears to give no essentially different outlook for the future, no prospect of a time of radiant and full living.' [2] With each new crisis in man's image of the universe 'the original contract between the universe and man is dissolved and man finds himself a stranger and solitary in the world.' As a result of this insecurity, man questions not only the universe and his relation to it, but himself. Today, writes Buber, 'the question about man's being faces us as never before in all its grandeur and terror—no longer in philo-sophical attire but in the nakedness of existence.' [3] In other eras of cosmic insecurity there was still 'a *social* certainty' resulting from 'living in real togetherness' in 'a small organic community.' Modern man, in contrast, is homeless both in the universe and in the community. Our modern crisis, as a result, is the most deep-reaching and comprehensive in history.[4] In it the two aspects of social and cosmic insecurity have merged into a loss of confidence in human existence as such:

> The existential mistrust is indeed basically no longer, like the old kind, a mistrust of my fellow-man. It is rather the destruction of confidence in existence in general. That we can no longer carry on a genuine conversation from one camp to the other is the severest symptom of the sickness of present-day man. Existential mistrust is this sickness itself. But the destruction of trust in human existence

[1] *Die Stunde und die Erkenntnis*, p. 126 f.; *Between Man and Man*, 'The Question to the Single One,' p. 80 f., 'What Is Man?', p. 201.
[2] 'Hope for This Hour.'
[3] *Between Man and Man*, 'What Is Man?', pp. 132 f., 145.
[4] *Ibid.*, p. 196 f.

is the inner poisoning of the total human organism from which this sickness stems.[1]

The loss of confidence in human existence also means a loss of trust in God. 'At its core the conflict between mistrust and trust of man conceals the conflict between mistrust and trust of eternity.' In the way leading from one age of solitude to the next, 'each solitude is colder and stricter than the preceding, and salvation from it more difficult.' It is only in our time, however, that man has reached a condition in which 'he can no longer stretch his hands out from his solitude to meet a divine form.' This inability to reach out to God is at the basis of Nietzsche's saying, 'God is dead.' 'Apparently nothing more remains now to the solitary man but to seek an intimate communication with himself.' Modern man is imprisoned in his subjectivity and cannot discern 'the essential difference between all subjectivity and that which transcends it.' [2] This mounting spiral of subjectivism has manifested itself most clearly in the progressive relativizing of all values.

> The conspicuous tendency of our age . . . is not, as is sometimes supposed, directed merely against the sanctioning of . . . norms by religion, but against their universal character and absolute validity . . . their claim to be of a higher order than man and to govern the whole of mankind. In our age values and norms are not permitted to be anything but expressions of the life of a group which translates its own need into the language of objective claims, until at last the group itself . . . is raised to an absolute value. . . . Then this splitting up into groups so pervades the whole of life that it is no longer possible to re-establish a sphere of values common to mankind.[3]

The roots of this relativism lie in part in the philosophy which 'seeks to unmask the spiritual world as a system of deceptions and self-deceptions, of "ideologies" and "sublimations."' Buber traces the development of this philosophy through Feuerbach and Vico to Marx, who made the distinction between good and evil a function of the class struggle, and Nietzsche, who, 'like Marx, saw historical morals as the expression and instruments of the power struggle between ruling and oppressed classes.' [4]

Sartre accepts Nietzsche's cry 'God is dead,' as a valid statement of fact. Recognizing, like Nietzsche, that 'all possibility of discovering

---

[1] 'Hope for This Hour.'
[2] *Ibid., Between Man and Man*, 'What Is Man?', p. 167; *Eclipse of God*, 'Religion and Reality,' p. 33.
[3] *Between Man and Man*, 'The Education of Character,' p. 108 ff., 'The Question to the Single One,' p. 81 f.
[4] *Eclipse of God*, 'Religion and Ethics,' pp. 141-146.

absolute values has disappeared with God,' Sartre adopts as his own Dostoievsky's phrase, 'all is permitted' to man. Since "'life has no meaning *a priori* . . . it is up to you to give it a meaning, and value is nothing else than this meaning which you chöose.'" But, Buber points out, this is just what one cannot do. The very nature of value as that which gives man direction depends on the fact that it is not arbitrarily invented or chosen but is discovered in man's meeting with being.[1] Because value guides man in the process of becoming what he is not, it cannot be derived from what he is. Sartre's concept of the free invention of meaning and value is reminiscent of Buber's second stage of evil in which 'truth' and 'good' arc what the individual ordains as such.

Subjectivism dominates not only the attitude of our age toward values but modern thinking in general. In the progress of its philosophizing the human spirit is ever more inclined to regard the absolute which it contemplates as having been produced by itself, the spirit that thinks it: 'Until, finally, all that is over against us, everything that accosts us and takes possession of us, all partnership of existence, is dissolved in free-floating subjectivity.' In the next age, which is the modern one, the human spirit annihilates conceptually the absoluteness of the absolute. Although the spirit may imagine that it still remains 'as bearer of all things and coiner of all values,' it has annihilated its own absoluteness as well. 'Spirit' is now only a product of human individuals 'which they contain and secrete like mucus and urine.'[2]

In these two stages we can recognize idealism and the various types of modern relativism which have succeeded it—immanentism, psychologism, historicism, naturalism, and materialism. What is in question in this process is not just atheism. The traditional term 'God' is preserved in many cases 'for the sake of its profound overtones.' But this 'God' is utterly unlike the traditional conception of God as an absolute that transcends man. 'Specifically modern thought can no longer endure a God who is not confined to man's subjectivity, who is not merely a "supreme value."' It seeks 'to preserve the idea of the divine as the true concern of religion' and at the same time 'to destroy the reality of the idea of God and thereby also the reality of our relation to Him.' 'This is done in many ways,' writes Buber, 'overtly and covertly, apodictically and hypothetically, in the language of metaphysics and of psychology.'[3]

Even more eloquent than Nietzsche's proclamation that God is dead, writes Buber, are the attempts to fill the now-empty horizon. Heidegger, for example, intimates that after our present imageless era—the era in which 'God is dead'—a new procession of divine images may begin.

[1] *Ibid.*, 'Religion and Modern Thinking,' pp. 88, 93 f. (Cf. Jean Paul Sartre, *L'Existentialisme est un Humanisme*, pp. 33, 89).
[2] *Ibid.*, 'God and the Spirit of Man,' p. 159 ff.
[3] *Ibid.*, 'Religion and Reality,' pp. 28, 32, 26.

But he does not hold, says Buber, that man will again experience and accept his real encounters with the divine as such.[1] What brings about the reappearance of the divine, in Heidegger's view, is human thought about truth; for being, to Heidegger, attains its illumination through the destiny and history of man. 'He whose appearance can be effected or co-effected through such a modern-magical influence,' writes Buber 'clearly has only the name in common with Him whom we men, basically in agreement despite all the differences in our religious teachings, address as God.' Heidegger ends, Buber points out, by allying to his own historical hour this clarification of the thought of being to which he has ascribed the power to make ready for the sunrise of the holy. '"History exists,"' writes Heidegger, '"only when the essence of truth is originally decided."' Yet the hour that he has affirmed as history in this sense is none other than that of Hitler and the Nazis, 'the very same hour whose problematics in its most inhuman manifestation led him astray.' When Heidegger proclaims Hitler as '"the present and future German reality and its law,"' writes Buber, 'history no longer stands, as in all believing times, under divine judgment, but it itself, the unappealable, assigns to the Coming One his way.'[2] Here again we are reminded of the absolute self-affirmation of the second stage of evil!

In modern philosophy of religion the I of the I-It relation steps ever more into the foreground as the 'subject' of 'religious feeling,' the 'profiter from a pragmatist decision to believe.' Even more important than this is the subjectivizing of the act of faith itself, for this latter has penetrated to the innermost depth of the religious life. This subjectivization threatens the spontaneous turning toward the Presence with which the man who prays formerly overcame what distracted his attention. 'The overconsciousness of this man here that he is praying, that he is *praying*, that *he* is praying . . . depossesses the moment, takes away its spontaneity.' His subjectivity enters into the midst of his statement of trust and disturbs his relation with the Absolute.[3]

When he has to interpret his encounters with God as self-encounters, 'man's very structure is destroyed,' writes Buber. 'This is the portent of the present hour.'[4]

In our age the I-It relation, gigantically swollen, has usurped, practically uncontested, the mastery and the rule. The I of this relation, an I that possesses all, makes all, succeeds with all, this I that is unable to say Thou, unable to meet a being essentially, is the lord of the hour. This selfhood that has become omnipotent, with all the It around it, can naturally acknowledge neither God nor

[1] *Eclipse of God*, 'Religion and Reality,' pp. 27-34.
[2] *Ibid.*, 'Religion and Modern Thinking,' pp. 94-97, 99-103.
[3] *Ibid.*, 'God and the Spirit of Man,' p. 162 ff.
[4] *Ibid.*, 'Religion and Reality,' pp. 21, 32 f.

any genuine absolute which manifests itself to men as of non-human origin. It steps in between and shuts off from us the light of heaven.[1]

'Eclipse of the light of heaven, eclipse of God,' this is, as Buber sees it, 'the character of the historical hour through which the world is passing.' This eclipse is not taking place in human subjectivity 'but in Being itself.' It is the human side of 'the silence of God,' of 'God's hiding His face.' [2]

'He who refuses to submit himself to the effective reality of the transcendence,' writes Buber, '. . . contributes to the human responsibility for the eclipse.' This does not mean that man can effect 'the death of God.' Even if there is no longer 'a God of man,' He who is denoted by the name 'lives intact' in the light of His eternity. 'But we, "the slayers," remain dwellers in darkness, consigned to death.' Thus the real meaning of the proclamation that God is 'dead' is 'that man has become incapable of apprehending a reality absolutely independent of himself and of having a relation with it.' Heidegger is right in saying that we can no longer image God, but this is not a lack in man's imagination. 'The great images of God . . . are born not of imagination but of real encounters with real divine power and glory.' Man's power to glimpse God with his being's eye yields no images since God eludes direct contemplation, but it is from it that all images and representations are born. When the I of the I-It relation comes in between man and God, this glance is no longer possible, and, as a result, the image-making power of the human heart declines. 'Man's capacity to apprehend the divine in images is lamed in the same measure as is his capacity to experience a reality absolutely independent of himself.' [3] In all past times men had, stored away in their hearts, images of the Absolute, 'partly pallid, partly crude, altogether false and yet true. . . .' These images helped to protect them from the deception of the voices. This protection no longer exists now that 'God is dead,' now that the 'spiritual pupil' cannot catch a glimpse of the appearance of the Absolute.

False absolutes rule over the soul which is no longer able to put them to flight through the image of the true. . . . In the realm of Moloch honest men lie and compassionate men torture. And they really and truly believe that brother-murder will prepare the way for brotherhood! There appears to be no escape from the most evil of all idolatry.[4]

[1] *Ibid.*, 'God and the Spirit of Man,' p. 165 ff.
[2] *Ibid.*, 'Religion and Reality,' p. 34 f., 'Religion and Modern Thinking,' p. 89 ff.
[3] *Ibid.*, 'Religion and Reality,' pp. 34 f., 22, 'God and the Spirit of Man,' p. 164 f. 'On the Suspension of the Ethical,' p. 154 f.
[4] *Ibid.*, 'On the Suspension of the Ethical,' pp. 149-156.

The most terrible consequence of the eclipse is the silence of God—the loss of the sense of God's nearness. 'It seems senseless to turn to Him who, if He is here, will not trouble Himself about us; it seems hopeless to will to penetrate to Him who may . . . perhaps be the soul of the universe but not our Father.' When history appears to be empty of God, 'with nowhere a beckoning of His finger,' it is difficult for an individual and even more for a people to understand themselves as addressed by God. 'The experience of concrete answerability recedes more and more . . . man unlearns taking the relationship between God and himself seriously in the dialogic sense.' During such times the world seems to be irretrievably abandoned to the forces of tyranny. In the image of Psalm 82, the world is given over by God to judges who 'judge unjustly' and 'lift up the face of the wicked.' This situation is nowhere more clearly described in modern literature than in the novels of Franz Kafka: 'His unexpressed, ever-present theme,' writes Buber, 'is the remoteness of the judge, the remoteness of the lord of the castle, the hiddenness, the eclipse. . . .' Kafka describes the human world as given over to the meaningless government of a slovenly bureaucracy without possibility of appeal: 'From the hopelessly strange Being who gave this world into their impure hands, no message of comfort or promise penetrates to us. He is, but he is not present.' [1]

Not only Kafka, the unredeemed Jew, but even the redeemed Christian soul becomes aware in our day of the eclipse of the light of God, 'of the still unredeemed concreteness of the human world in all its horror.' Nothing in our time has so confirmed Kafka's view or made the silence of God appear so terrifying as the concentration camps of Nazi Germany in which millions of human beings were systematically and scientifically exterminated as if they were insects. Never has the world appeared so forsaken, so engulfed in utter darkness.

How is a life with God still possible in a time in which there is an Oswiecim? The estrangement has become too cruel, the hiddenness too deep. One can still 'believe in the God who allowed these things to happen,' but can one still speak to Him? Can one still hear His word? . . . Dare we recommend to . . . the Job of the gas chambers: 'Call to Him; for He is kind, for His mercy endureth forever'? [2]

[1] *For the Sake of Heaven*, p. 116; *At the Turning*, p. 58 ff.; *Right and Wrong*, 'Judgement on the Judges' (Psalm 82), pp. 30-33; *Two Types of Faith*, pp. 165-168.
[2] *Two Types of Faith*, pp. 162 f., 166 f.; *At the Turning*, p. 61.

CHAPTER SEVENTEEN

THE REDEMPTION OF EVIL

MAN'S turning from evil and taking the direction toward God is the beginning of his own redemption and that of the world. God 'wishes to redeem us—but only by our own acceptance of His redemption with the turning of the whole being.' Our turning is only the beginning, however, for man's action must be answered by God's grace for redemption to be complete. When we go forth to meet God, He comes to meet us, and this meeting is our salvation. 'It is not as though any definite act of man could draw grace down from heaven; yet grace answers deed in unpredictable ways, grace unattainable, yet not self-withholding.' It is senseless, therefore, to try to divide redemption into a part that is dependent on man and a part that is dependent on God. Man must be concerned with his action alone before he brings it about, with God's grace alone after the action is successfully done. 'The one is no less real than the other, and neither is a part-cause ... man's action is enclosed in God's action, but it is still real action.' When man breaks through, he has an immediate experience of his freedom; after his decision has been made, he has an immediate experience that God's hand has carried him.[1] Man's action and God's grace are subsumed under the greater reality of the meeting between God and man.

The decisive turning is not merely an attitude of the soul but something effective in the whole corporeality of life. It is not to be identified with repentance, for repentance is something psychological and purely inward which shows itself outwardly only in its 'consequences' and 'effects.' The turning 'is something which happens in the immediacy of the reality between man and God.' It 'is as little a "psychic" event as is a man's birth or death.' Repentance is at best only an incentive to this turning, and it may even stand in the way of it if a man tortures himself

---

[1] *The Prophetic Faith, op. cit.*, pp. 104, 124; *Hasidism, op. cit.*, 'Spinoza,' pp. 108-111; *Israel and the World, op. cit.*, 'The Faith of Judaism,' p. 18, 'The Two Foci of the Jewish Soul,' p. 32 f.

with the idea that his acts of penance are not sufficient and thereby withholds his best energies from the work of reversal.[1]

The *teshuvah*, or turning to God, is born in the depths of the soul out of 'the despair which shatters the prison of our latent energies' and out of the suffering which purifies the soul. In his darkest hours man feels the hand of God reaching down to him. If he has 'the incredible courage' to take the hand and let it draw him up out of the darkness, he tastes the essence of redemption—the knowledge that his 'redeemer liveth' (Job xix, 18) and wishes to redeem him. But he must accept this redemption with the turning of his whole being, for only thus can he extricate himself from the maze of selfishness where he has always set himself as his goal and find a way to God and to the fulfilment of the particular task for which he is intended.[2]

To turn to God with the whole of one's being means to turn with all of one's passion. Passion is the element without which no deed can succeed, the element which needs only direction in order that out of it the kingdom of God can be built. According to Hasidism, it is the yearning of the divine sparks to be redeemed that brings the 'alien thoughts,' or impure impulses, to man. The alien thoughts of which the Baal-Shem speaks are in our language fantasy, says Buber. The transformation of these impulses, accordingly, can only take place in our imaginative faculty. We must not reject the abundance of this fantasy but transform it and turn it into actuality. 'We must convert the element that seeks to take possession of us into the substance of real life.' The contradictions which distress us exist only that we may discover their intrinsic significance.[3]

The very qualities which make us what we are constitute our special approach to God and our potential use for Him. Each man is created for the fulfilment of a unique purpose. His foremost task, therefore, 'is the actualization of his unique, unprecedented and never-recurring potentialities, and not the repetition of something that another, and be it even the greatest, has already achieved.' We can revere the service of others and learn from it, but we cannot imitate it. Neither ought we envy another's particularity and place nor attempt to impose our own

---

[1] *Two Types of Faith, op. cit.*, p. 26; *Israel and the World*, 'The Faith of Judaism,' p. 20; *The Way of Man, op. cit.*, p. 35 f.

[2] *For the Sake of Heaven, op. cit.*, pp. 113, 116, 202; *Israel and the World*, 'The Man of Today and the Jewish Bible,' p. 101 f.; *The Way of Man*, p. 36.

[3] *Israel and the World*, 'The Faith of Judaism,' p. 17 f.; *Hasidism*, 'The Foundation Stone,' p. 53 f., 'The Beginnings of Hasidism,' p. 30 f.; *Kampf um Israel, op. cit.*, p. 399 f.; Martin Buber, *Ten Rungs, Hasidic Sayings*, trans. by Olga Marx (New York: Schocken Books, 1947), p. 94 f.; Martin Buber, *Tales of the Hasidim, The Early Masters*, trans. by Olga Marx (New York: Schocken Books, 1947), pp. 4, 11-14, 29; *Hasidism and Modern Man*, 'The Baal-Shem-Tor's Instruction in Intercourse with God.'

particular way on him.[1] The way by which a man can reach God is revealed to him only through the knowledge of his essential quality and inclination. Man discovers this essential quality through perceiving his 'central wish,' the strongest feeling which stirs his inmost being. In many cases he knows this central wish only in the form of the particular passion which seeks to lead him astray. To preserve and direct this passion he must divert it from the casual to the essential, from the relative to the absolute. He must prevent it from rushing at the objects which lie across his path, yet he must not turn away from these objects but establish genuine relationship with them. 'Man's task, therefore, is not to extirpate the evil urge, but to reunite it with the good.' If man lends his will to the direction of his passions, he begins the movement of holiness which God completes. In the hallowing which results, 'the total man is accepted, confirmed, and fulfilled. This is the true integration of man.' [2]

The belief in the redemption of evil does not mean any security of salvation. The prophets of Israel, writes Buber, 'always aimed to shatter all security and to proclaim in the opened abyss of the final insecurity the unwished-for God who demands that His human creatures become real . . . and confounds all who imagine that they can take refuge in the certainty that the temple of God is in their midst.' There is no other path for the responsible modern man than this 'holy insecurity.' In an age in which 'God is dead,' the truly religious man sets forth across the God-deprived reality to a new meeting with the nameless God and on his way destroys the images that no longer do justice to God. 'Holy insecurity' is life lived in the Face of God. It is the life in which one learns to speak the truth 'no matter whether a whole people is listening, or only a few individuals,' and learns to speak it quietly and clearly through having been in hell and having returned to the light of day again.[3]

If a man tries to get rid of his insecurity by constructing a defensive armour to protect himself from the world, he has added to the exposedness which is the state of all men the hysteria which makes him run blindly from the thing he fears rather than face and accept it. Conversely, if he accepts his exposed condition and remains open to those things which meet him, he has turned his exposedness into 'holy insecurity.' He has overcome his blind fear and has put in its place the

---

[1] *Tales of the Hasidim, The Early Masters*, p. 29; *The Way of Man*, p. 17 ff.

[2] *For the Sake of Heaven*, p. 117; *The Way of Man*, p. 19 f.; *Images of Good and Evil, op. cit.*, pp. 39–42; *Israel and the World*, 'The Power of the Spirit,' p. 181 f.

[3] *Eclipse of God*, 'Religion and Modern Thinking,' p. 97 f., 'Religion and Philosophy,' p. 63; *Kampf um Israel*, p. 198; Martin Buber, 'Our Reply,' *Towards Union in Palestine, Essays on Zionism and Jewish-Arab Cooperation*, ed. by Martin Buber, Judah L. Magnes, and Ernst Simon (Jerusalem: Ihud Association, September 1945), p. 34.

faith which is born out of the relation with the Thou. The defensive man becomes literally rigid with fear. He sets between himself and the world a rigid religious dogma, a rigid system of philosophy, a rigid political belief and commitment to a group, and a rigid wall of personal values and habits. The open man, on the other hand, accepts his fear and relaxes into it. He substitutes the realism of despair, if need be, for the tension of hysteria. He meets every new situation with quiet and sureness out of the depths of his being, yet he meets it with the fear and trembling of one who has no ready-made answer to life.

The religious essence of every religion, writes Buber, 'is the certainty that the meaning of existence is open and accessible in the actual lived concreteness.' This does not mean that meaning is to be won through any analytical or synthetic reflection upon the lived concrete but through 'living action and suffering itself, in the unreduced immediacy of the moment.' Neither can one aim at experiencing the experience, for one thereby destroys the spontaneity of the mystery and thus misses the meaning. 'Only he reaches the meaning who stands firm, without holding back or reservation, before the whole might of reality and answers it in a living way.' No meeting with God can take place entirely outside of this lived concrete. Even asceticism is essentially a reduction for the sake of preserving the concreteness of the moment when this no longer seems attainable in the fullness of life. Prayer too is not spirituality floating above concrete reality but lived concreteness. Prayer is the very essence of the immediacy between man and God, and praying is, above all words, the action of turning directly to God. In true prayer, no matter what else the individual asks for, he 'ultimately asks for the manifestation of the divine Presence, for this Presence's becoming dialogically perceivable.' The presupposition of a genuine state of prayer is not religious words, pious feelings, or techniques of spiritual concentration but 'the readiness of the whole man for this Presence, simple turned-towardness, unreserved spontaneity.' [1]

All religious reality begins with the acceptance of the concrete situation as given one by the Giver, and it is this which Biblical religion calls the 'fear of God.' The 'fear of God' is the essence of 'holy insecurity,' for 'it comes when our existence becomes incomprehensible and uncanny, when all security is shattered through the mystery.' By 'the mystery' Buber does not mean the as yet undiscovered but the essentially unknowable—'the undefinable and unfathomable,' whose inscrutableness belongs to its very nature. The believing man who passes through this shattering of security returns to the everyday as the henceforth

---

[1] *Eclipse of God*, 'Religion and Philosophy,' pp. 49 f., 52 f., 'God and the Spirit of Man,' p. 163; *Between Man and Man*, 'Dialogue,' p. 15; *Des Baal-Schem-Tow Unterweisung im Umgang mit Gott*, p. 12 f.; *The Way of Man*, p. 21; *Two Types of Faith*, pp. 28, 157, 161.

hallowed place in which he has to live with the mystery. 'He steps forth directed and assigned to the concrete, contextual situations of his existence.' This does not mean that he accepts everything that meets him as 'God-given' in its pure factuality.

> He may, rather, declare the extremest enmity toward this happening and treat its 'givenness' as only intended to draw forth his own opposing force. But he will not remove himself from the concrete situation as it actually is. . . . Whether field of work or field of battle, he accepts the place in which he is placed.[1]

One should not willingly accept evil in one's life but should will to penetrate the impure with the pure. The result may well be an interpenetration of both elements, but it may not be anticipated by saying 'yes' to the evil in advance.[2]

Fear of God is the indispensable gate to the love of God. That love of God which does not comprehend fear is really idolatry, the adoration of a god whom one has constructed oneself. Such a god is easy enough to love, but it is not easy to love 'the real God, who is, to begin with, dreadful and incomprehensible.'[3]

> He who wishes to avoid passing through this gate, he who begins to provide himself with a comprehensible God, constructed thus and not otherwise, runs the risk of having to despair of God in view of the actualities of history and life, or of falling into inner falsehood. Only through the fear of God does man enter so deep into the love of God that he cannot again be cast out of it.[4]

The fear of God is only a gate, however, and not, as some theologians believe, a dwelling in which man can settle down. When man encounters the demonic, he must not rest in it but must penetrate behind it to find the meaning of his meeting with it. The fear of God must flow into the love of God and be comprehended by it before one is ready to endure in the face of God the whole reality of lived life.[5]

Contrary to the teachings of many religious men, the love of God does not mean the submission of one's will in obedience to God. 'When

[1] *Eclipse of God*, 'Religion and Philosophy,' p. 50 ff.
[2] From a conversation between Buber and Max Brod quoted in Max Brod, 'Zur Problematik des Bösen und des Rituals,' *Der Jude*, 'Sonderheft zu Martin Bubers fünfzigstem Geburtstag,' X, 5 (March 1928), ed. by Robert Weltsch, p. 109.
[3] *Eclipse of God*, p. 50 f.; Martin Buber, *Israel and Palestine, The History of an Idea* (London: East & West Library; New York: Farrar, Straus & Young, 1952), p. 89.
[4] *Israel and the World*, 'The Two Foci of the Jewish Soul,' p. 31 f. Cf. *ibid.*, 'Imitatio Dei,' p. 76 f.; *For the Sake of Heaven*, p. 46.
[5] *Israel and the World*, 'The Two Foci of the Jewish Soul,' p. 32; *Eclipse of God*, 'Religion and Philosophy,' p. 50 ff.; *Two Types of Faith*, pp. 137, 154.

and so far as the loving man loves he does not need to bend his will, for he lives in the Divine Will.' God commands that man love Him, but it is not God, but the soul itself, in the original mystery of its spontaneity, that loves Him. Man can be commanded to love God since this means nothing other than the actualization of the existing relationship of faith to Him. 'Love thy neighbour as thyself,' in contrast, does not mean loving feeling but loving action. One cannot command that one *feel* love for a person but only that one deal lovingly with him. *Re-ah*, or 'neighbour,' means, in the Old Testament, anyone with whom one stands in an immediate and reciprocal relationship. '"Love thy *re-ah*" therefore means in our language: be lovingly disposed towards men with whom thou has to do at anytime in the course of thy life.' This lovingkindness will also ultimately come to include the feeling of love, for if a person really loves God, he loves every man whom God loves as he becomes aware that God does love him. To find meaning in existence one must begin oneself and penetrate into it with active love: 'Meet the world with the fullness of your being and you shall meet Him. . . . If you wish to believe, love!' [1]

The love of the Creator and of that which He has created are finally one and the same. '*Imitatio Dei*' does not mean becoming like God as He is in Himself but only the following in His way in relation to justice and love—the divine attributes which are turned toward man. The true meaning of the ethical, writes Buber, is 'to help God by loving His creation in his creatures, by loving it towards Him.' 'People who love each other with holy love bring each other towards the love with which God loves His world.' [2] The true love of man is not a general love for all humanity but a quite concrete, direct, and effective love for particular individuals. Only because one loves specific men can one elevate to love one's relation to man in general.[3] '"Togetherness,"' says David of Lelov in *For the Sake of Heaven*, '"means that each is intimate with the other and each feels lovingkindness for the other."' The Yehudi extends this togetherness even to the sons of Satan, whom God has made us capable of loving:

'Does not redemption primarily mean the redeeming of the evil from the evil ones that make them so? If the world is to be forever-

[1] *Two Types of Faith*, pp. 69 ff., 137; *At the Turning*, pp. 37, 42 ff.

[2] *At the Turning*, p. 37 ff.; *Between Man and Man*, 'The Question to the Single One,' pp. 51 f., 56 f.; *Eclipse of God*, 'Religion and Ethics,' p. 137 f., *Hasidism*, 'God and the Soul,' p. 158.

[3] *Hasidism*, 'Spirit and Body of the Hasidic Movement,' p. 86; Introduction by Buber to Hermann Cohen, *Der Nächste* (Berlin: Schocken Verlag, 1935), p. 6; Martin Buber, 'Kraft und Richtung, Klugheit und Weisheit' (From a letter), *Das werdende Zeitalter*, VII (1928), 97; *Eclipse of God*, 'The Love of God and the Idea of Deity,' p. 77 ff.

more divided between God and Satan, how dare we say that it is God's world? . . . Are we to establish a little realm of the righteous and leave the rest to the Lord? Is it for this that He gave us a mouth which can convey the truth of our heart to an alien heart and a hand which can communicate to the hand of our recalcitrant brother something of the warmth of our very blood?' [1]

In between the self-righteous avoidance of the evil of others and the acceptance and willing of evil lies the difficult path of taking evil upon oneself without being corrupted by it and transforming it into love. This can be done only by the person who has himself reached maturity and quiet of soul. It cannot extend to removing another person's responsibility before God, but it can help him to escape the whirl into which the evil impulse has plunged him.[2]

Through genuine dialogical existence the real person takes part in the unfinished process of creation. 'It is only by way of true intercourse with things and beings that man achieves true life, but also it is by this way only that he can take an active part in the redemption of the world.' Redemption does not take place within the individual soul but in the world through the real meeting of God and man. Everything is waiting to be hallowed by man, for there is nothing so crass or base that it cannot become material for sanctification. 'The profane,' forHasidism, is only a designation for the not yet sanctified. 'Any natural act, if hallowed, leads to God.' The things that happen to one day after day contain one's essential task, for true fulfilled existence depends on our developing a genuine relationship to the people with whom we live and work, the animals that help us, the soil we till, the materials we shape, the tools we use. 'The most formidable power is intrinsically powerlessness unless it maintains a secret covenant with these contacts, both humble and helpful, with strange, and yet near being.' [3]

No renunciation of the object of desire is commanded: it is only necessary that man's relation to the object be hallowed in his life with nature, his work, his friendship, his marriage, and his solidarity with the community. Hence serving God with the 'evil impulse' and 'hallowing the everyday' are essentially the same. 'Hallowing transforms the urges by confronting them with holiness and making them *responsible* toward what is holy.' [4] Transforming the evil passion into good cannot take place inside oneself but only in relation. It is just in his relations

---

[1] *For the Sake of Heaven*, pp. 121, 125.
[2] *Ibid.*, p. 56; *Tales of the Hasidim, The Early Masters*, p. 4 ff.
[3] *The Way of Man*, pp. 21 f., 42-46; *Hasidism*, 'The Foundation Stone,' p. 58, 'Spinoza,' p. 111; *Israel and the World*, 'The Two Foci of the Jewish Soul,' p. 34.
[4] *Hasidism*, 'The Beginnings of Hasidism,' p. 31 f.; *Israel and the World*, 'The Power of the Spirit,' p. 180 f.

with others that man finds it possible to serve God with his fear, anger, love, and sexual desire.

> By no means . . . can it be our true task . . . to turn away from the things and beings that we meet on our way and that attract our hearts; our task is precisely to get in touch, by hallowing our relationship with them, with what manifests itself in them as beauty, pleasure, enjoyment. Hasidism teaches that rejoicing in the world, if we hallow it with our whole being, leads to rejoicing in God.[1]

The sanctification of the profane has nothing to do with pantheism, writes Buber. Pantheism 'destroys or stunts the greatest of all values: the reciprocal relationship between the human and the divine, the reality of the I and the Thou which does not cease at the rim of eternity.' It is because God dwells in the world that the world can be turned into a sacrament. But this does not mean that the world is objectively already a sacrament. It is only capable of becoming one through the redeeming contact with the individual. The foremost meaning of a sacrament is 'that the divine and the human join themselves to each other, without merging themselves in each other, a lived Beyond-transcendence-and-immanence.' This covenant also takes place when two human beings consecrate themselves to each other in marriage or in brotherhood, 'for the consecration does not come by the power of the human partners, but by the power of the eternal wings that overshadow both.' Sacramental existence, like dialogical existence in general, involves a meeting with the other in which the eternal Thou manifests itself. The sacrament 'is stripped of its essential character when it no longer includes an elemental, life-claiming and life-determining experience of the other person, of the otherness, as of something coming to meet and acting hitherwards.'[2]

The essence of the hallowing of the everyday is *kavanah*, or intention. *Kavanah* is identical with the readiness of the Single One to meet all that confronts him. This readiness is an inner preparation, a willingness to remain open and to respond from the depths of one's being, but it is not a preparation of the act itself.

> The substance of the act is ever supplied to us, or rather, it is offered us, by that which happens to us, which meets us—by everything which meets us. Everything desires to be hallowed . . . in the kavanah of redemption in all its worldliness; everything desires to become a sacrament.[3]

---

[1] *The Way of Man*, p. 20.

[2] *Tales of the Hasidim, The Early Masters*, p. 3; *Hasidism*, 'The Foundation Stone,' p. 59, 'Spinoza,' p. 101 ff., 'Symbolical and Sacramental Existence in Judaism,' pp. 117, 130.

[3] *Hasidism*, 'Symbolical and Sacramental Existence,' p. 144.

The sacramental substance cannot be manipulated through special acts or intentions (*kavanot*). It can only be awakened in each object and act 'through the presence of the whole man who wholly gives himself, through sacramental existence.' The essence of *kavanah*, accordingly, is the direction of the whole of one's being and power into each act. It is not the nature of the act but the *kavanah* which determines whether or not it is good or evil, holy or profane, strong or weak in redemptive power.

The great kavanah does not ally itself with any selection of what has been prescribed; everything which is done with that can be the right, the redeeming act. Each act may be the one on which all depends; the determining factor lies in the strength and concentration with which I do the hallowing.[1]

The basis for the Hasidic attitude toward redemption is the belief that redemption, like creation, takes place at every moment. Man's work is enclosed in God's in such a way that each moment of redemption is perfect in itself as well as taking place in the time series of the world. These are not moments of 'a mystical, timeless now.' Each moment is filled with all time, for in it true presentness and the movement of history are united. This union of history and the moment involves a tension and a contradiction, for although redemption takes place at every moment, there is no definite moment in the present or the future in which the redemption of the world could be pronounced as having taken place once for all. 'God's redeeming power is at work everywhere and at all times, but . . . a state of redemption exists nowhere and never.' Historical deed means the surmounting of the suffering inherent in human being, but it also means the piling up of new suffering through the repeated failure of each individual and each people to become what it was meant to be. The right answer to the divine revelation is an entire, undivided human life. 'But splitting up is the historical way of mankind, and the unsplit persons cannot do anything more than raise man to a higher level on which he may thereafter follow his course.'[2]

The core of the Messianic hope does not belong to eschatology and the margin of history where it vanishes into the timeless but to 'the centre, the ever-changing centre . . . to the experienced hour and its possibility.' The Messiah, the righteous one, must rise out of the historic loam of man, out of the dramatic mystery of the One facing the other. Redemption is not dependent upon Messianic calculations or any apocalyptic event, but on the unpremeditated turning of our whole world-life to God. This turning is open to the whole of mankind and to

---

[1] *Ibid.*, p. 134, 'Spirit and Body of the Hasidic Movement,' p. 72 f., 'The Beginnings of Hasidism,' p. 28.
[2] *Ibid.*, 'Spinoza,' p. 111; *Moses, op. cit.*, pp. 88, 199.

all ages, for all are face to face with redemption and all action for God's sake is Messianic action. As every sinner can find forgiveness, so every civilization can be hallowed, writes Buber, and this hallowing can take place without primitivizing or curtailment.[1]

The Jewish belief in redemption is not first of all *pistis*, faith in the proposition that redemption will come at some future date, but *emunah*, trust in God whose oneness also implies the ultimate oneness of God and the world. This trust in the ultimate oneness of God and the world is a faith in the power of the spirit to penetrate and transform all impulses and desires, to uplift and sanctify everything material. It is the faith 'that there is really only One Power which, while at times it may permit the sham powers of the world to accomplish something in opposition to it, never permits such accomplishment to stand.' But this trust in God does not imply any illusions about the present state of the world. 'The unredeemed soul refuses to give up the evidence of the unredeemed world from which it suffers, to exchange it for the soul's own salvation.' The Jew experiences the world's lack of redemption perhaps more intensely than any other group, writes Buber. He feels it against his skin, tastes it on his tongue.

> He always discovers only that mysterious intimacy of light out of darkness which is at work everywhere and at all times; no redemption which is different in kind, none which by its nature would be unique, which would be conclusive for future ages, and which had but to be consummated.[2]

Judaism does not neglect spiritual inwardness, as Simone Weil believed, but neither is it content with it. It demands that inward truth become real life if it is to remain truth: 'A drop of Messianic consummation must be mingled with every hour; otherwise the hour is godless, despite all piety and devoutness.' The corollary of this demand for the redemption of the world and not just of the individual soul is the refusal to accept the Gnostic rejection of creation—the division between the kingdom of this world and the kingdom of God which leaves the evil of the world forever unredeemable. 'The world is reality, and it is reality created not to be overcome but to be hallowed.' Judaism cannot accept a redemption in which half of the world will be eternally damned

---

[1] Martin Buber, *The Prophetic Faith*, trans. by Canon Witton Davies (New York: The Macmillan Co., 1949), pp. 137, 142, 144; *Hasidism*, 'Spirit of the Hasidic Movement,' pp. 70, 74 ff., 'Spinoza,' pp. 112, 116; *Israel and the World*, 'The Faith of Judaism,' p. 21; *Between Man and Man*, 'What Is Man?', p. 142; *At the Turning*, pp. 21 ff., 50 f.; *Two Types of Faith*, p. 170 f.; cf. *Images of Good and Evil*, p. 26.

[2] *Two Types of Faith*, p. 168 f.; *Israel and the World*, 'The Power of the Spirit,' p. 180 ff., 'And If Not Now, When?', p. 237 f., 'The Two Foci of the Jewish Soul,' p. 34 f.

or cut off from God: 'There can be no eternity in which *everything* will not be accepted into God's atonement.' [1]

What saved Judaism is not, as the Marcionites imagine, the fact that it failed to experience 'the tragedy,' the contradiction in the world's process, deeply enough; but rather that it experienced the *contradiction as theophany*. This very world, this very contradiction, unabridged, unmitigated, unsmoothed, unsimplified, unreduced, this world shall be—not overcome—but consummated. . . . It is a redemption not from the evil, but of the evil, as the power which God created for his service and for the performance of his work.[2]

This universal at-onement finds expression in the Jewish concept of *yihud*, or unification. *Yihud* is the proclamation of the oneness of God— not the passive acknowledgment of this oneness, a statement of a subject about an object, but an act of meeting, 'the dynamic form of the divine unity itself.' It does not take place through creedal profession or magic manipulation, but through the concrete meeting of I and Thou by which the profane is sanctified and the mundane hallowed. It is 'the continually renewed confirmation of the unity of the Divine in the manifold nature of His manifestations.' This confirmation must be understood in a quite practical way: it is brought about through man's remaining true 'in the face of the monstrous contradictions of life, and especially in the face of . . . the duality of good and evil.' The unification which thus takes place 'is brought about not to spite these contradictions, but in a spirit of love and reconciliation.' [3]

The 'national universalism' of the prophets, writes Buber, looks to each people to contribute to redemption in its own particular way. This national universalism, in Buber's opinion, is the only answer to the present conflict between national sovereignty and the need for international co-operation: 'A new humanity capable of standing up to the problems of our time can come only from the co-operation of national particularities, not from their being levelled out of existence.' The full response to God's address to mankind must be made not only as individuals but as peoples, and not as peoples taken as ends in themselves but as 'holy peoples' working toward redemption through establishing the kingship of God. To become a 'holy people' means, for Israel and for all peoples, to realize God's attribute of justice in the indirect relations of the people with one another and His attribute of love in their direct relations. It means the fulfilment of God's truth and

---

[1] *At the Turning*, pp. 34-40; *Israel and the World*, 'The Faith of Judaism,' p. 25 ff., 'The Two Foci of the Jewish Soul,' p. 34 ff., 'The Man of Today and the Jewish Bible,' p. 101, 'The Spirit of Israel and the World of Today,' p. 191 f.

[2] *Israel and the World*, 'The Faith of Judaism,' p. 26.

[3] *Ibid.*, p. 15; *Hasidism*, 'Spirit of the Hasidic Movement,' p. 78.

justice on earth. 'To drive the plowshare of the normative principle into the hard sod of political fact' is 'a tremendously difficult undertaking,' writes Buber, 'but the right to lift a historical moment into the light of superhistory can be bought no cheaper.' [1]

This fulfilment can only take place if the synthesis of people, land, and work results in the coming to be of a true community, for only in true community can justice and love be realized and the people hallowed. 'All holiness means union between being and thing, between being and being; the highest rung of world-holiness, however, is the unity of the human community in the sight of God.' Only a true community can demonstrate the Absolute and point the way to the kingdom of God: 'Though something of righteousness may become evident in the life of the individual, righteousness itself can only become wholly visible in the structures of the life of a people.' The righteousness of a people, in turn, must be based upon real communities, composed of real families, real neighbourhoods, and real settlements, and upon 'the relationships of a fruitful and creative peace with its neighbours.' The peacemaker 'is God's fellow-worker,' but we make peace not by conciliatory words and humane projects but through making peace 'wherever we are destined and summoned to do so: in the active life of our own community and in that aspect of it which can actively help determine its relationship to another community.' [2]

The decisive test of brotherhood is not within the community but at the boundary between community and community, people and people, church and church, for this is the place where diversity of kind and mind is felt most strongly. 'Every time we stand this test a new step is taken toward a true humanity, gathered in the name of God.' One of the central emphases of Buber's Zionism, correspondingly, has been his insistence that the Jews live *with* the Arabs and not just *next* to them. [3] For many years one of the leaders of *Ihud* (Unity) and of the League for Jewish-Arab Rapprochement and Co-operation, Buber wrote in 1939 in an open letter to Gandhi:

> I belong to a group of people who from the time Britain conquered Palestine have not ceased to strive for the conclusion of a genuine peace between Jew and Arab. By a genuine peace we inferred and still infer that both peoples together should develop

[1] *Israel and Palestine*, pp. 118, 136; *At the Turning*, pp. 37 f., 24.

[2] Martin Buber, 'Der Chaluz und seine Welt' (Aus einer Rede), *Almanach des Schocken Verlag auf das Jahr 5697* (1936-37), p. 89 f.; *Kampf um Israel*, pp. 25 f. (my translation), 253, 268 f., 273; *Israel and the World*, 'The Spirit of Israel and the World of Today,' pp. 186 f., 193, 'The Gods of the Nations and God,' p. 210, 'And If Not Now, When?', p. 239.

[3] The first two sentences are from an unpublished address by Buber on 'Fraternity' to the World Brotherhood Association in California in 1952; *Kampf um Israel*, p. 451.

the land without the one imposing its will on the other. In view of the international usages of our generation, this appeared to us to be very difficult but not impossible.[1]

Whether Buber speaks of the establishment of community or religious redemption, his goal is 'the goal of the ages,' and the way to that goal is through the fulfilment and redemption of individual human beings in direct and upright relation with one another.

'Never will a work of man have a good issue if we do not think of the souls whom it is given us to help, and of the life between soul and soul, and of our life with them and of their lives with each other. We cannot help the coming of redemption if life does not redeem life.'[2]

Although in the final analysis the only thing that can help is what is true and right, in an emergency this is not always possible. Living entails doing injustice: the fact that we cannot breathe and eat without destroying organic life has symbolic meaning for our human existence. But the humanity of our existence begins there where we say: We shall do no more injustice than we must to live. Only then do we become responsible to this life, and this responsibility cannot be laid down according to any set principle but must be ever again recognized in the depths of the soul according to the demands of each concrete situation.

In order to preserve the community of men, we are often compelled to accept wrongs in decisions concerning the community. But what matters is that in every hour of decision we are aware of our responsibility and summon our conscience to weigh exactly how much is necessary to preserve the community, and accept just so much and no more; . . . that we . . . struggle with destiny in fear and trembling lest it burden us with greater guilt than we are compelled to assume.[3]

---

[1] *Towards Union in Palestine, op. cit.*, p. 120; *Israel and the World*, 'The Land and Its Possessors' (From an Open Letter to Gandhi), p. 231 f. Cf. Martin Buber and J. L. Magnes, *Two Letters to Gandhi* (Jerusalem: Reuben Mass, 1939), pp. 10-20.
[2] *For the Sake of Heaven*, p. 256.
[3] *Israel and the World*, 'Hebrew Humanism,' p. 246 ff., *Kampf um Israel*, p. 438 f. Cf. 'Our Reply,' *op. cit.*, p. 34 f. In his open letter to Gandhi, Buber wrote: 'We have not proclaimed . . . the teaching of non-violence, because we believe that a man must sometimes use force to save himself or even more his children. But . . . we have taught and we have learnt that peace is the aim of all the world and that justice is the way to attain it. . . . No one who counts himself in the ranks of Israel can desire to use force.' Page 19 f. 'I am forced to withstand the evil in the world just as the evil within myself. I can only strive not to have to do so by force. . . . But if there is no other way of preventing the evil destroying the good, I trust I shall use force and give myself up to God's hands.' Page 20 f.

True community is the link between the social Utopia of modern man and the direct theocracy of the Bible. This does not mean, writes Buber, that religious socialism and the kingdom of God are to be identified. The one is man's action while the other cannot be completed without God's grace. But neither can they be separated, for man's action and God's grace are intimately bound together. The essence of Buber's religious socialism is his belief that the centre of community must be the relation of the individual members of the community to God. Though the Single One 'cannot win to a legitimate relation with God without a legitimate relation to the body politic,' the prior relation is that with God, for this is 'the defining force.' The importance of Hasidism does not lie in its teaching, writes Buber, but in its 'm~de of life which shapes a community.' Yet Hasidic life is characterized first of all by its wholly personal mode of faith, and it is only through the action of this faith that a community is formed.[1]

True community cannot be built on the basis of either new institutions, on the one hand, or individual good-will, on the other, so long as the relations between men remain fundamentally unchanged. The absence of directness in the relations between men in the modern world can only be overcome by men who respond to the concrete situations which confront them with openness and with all of their power, by men who mean community in their innermost heart and establish it in their natural sphere of relations. Such men do not proceed out of community; they prove themselves ready for community by living genuinely with other men. Genuine education for community is identical, therefore, with genuine education of character—the education of real persons who deny no answer to life and the world but are ready to respond out of a living unity to everything essential that they meet.[2]

To establish true community man must rise in rebellion against the illusion of modern collectivism: he must rescue his real personal self from the domination of the collective. The first step in this rebellion must be to smash the false alternative of our epoch—that of individualism and collectivism. In its place he must put the vital, living knowledge that 'the fundamental fact of human existence is man with man.' This knowledge can only be attained through man's personal engagement, through his entering with his whole being into dialogue. The central question for the fate of mankind, accordingly, the question on the

[1] Martin Buber, *Königtum Gottes*, Vol. I of *Das Kommende. Untersuchungen zur Entstehungsgeschichte des Messianischen Glaubens* (Berlin: Schocken Verlag, 1932), p. 144; *Kampf um Israel*, p. 260 f.; Martin Buber, 'Drei Sätze eines religiösen Sozialismus,' *Neue Wege*, Zurich, XXII (1928), No. 7/8, 328; *Between Man and Man*, 'The Question to the Single One,' p. 76; *Hasidism*, 'The Beginnings of Hasidism,' p. 1 f.

[2] *Kampf um Israel*, pp. 268 f., 273, 291 f.; *Between Man and Man*, 'The Education of Character,' p. 116.

answer to which the future of man as man depends, is the rebirth of dialogue. This means, above all, the overcoming of the massive existential mistrust in ourselves and others, for it is this that stands in the way of genuine relation between man and man.[1]

The will to overcoming this existential mistrust must begin with a 'criticism of criticism' which will assign proper boundary lines to those newly discovered elements by means of which the sociological and psychological theorists have attempted to unmask and 'see through' the motivations of individuals and groups of men. Man is not to be 'seen through' but 'to be perceived ever more completely in his openness and his hiddenness and in the relation of the two to each other.' This is a clearsighted trust of man which perceives his manifoldness and wholeness without any preconceptions about his background and which accepts, accredits, and confirms him to the extent that this perception will allow. Only those who can in this way overcome the mistrust in themselves and recognize the other in the reality of his being can contribute to the re-establishment of genuine dialogue between men.[2]

Only through this renewal of immediacy between man and man can we again experience immediacy in the dialogue with God. 'When the man who has become solitary can no longer say "Thou" to the "dead" known God, everything depends on whether he can still say it to the living unknown God by saying "thou" with all his being to another living and known man.' If after long silence and stammering we genuinely say Thou to men who are unlike ourselves and whom we recognize in all their otherness, then we shall have addressed our eternal Thou anew.[3] Before we can genuinely address the Thou, however, we must escape from that modern idolatry which leads us to sacrifice 'the ethical' on the altar of our particular causes. A new conscience must arise in men which will summon them to guard with the innermost power of their souls against the confusion of the relative with the Absolute.

> To penetrate again and again into the false absolute with an incorruptible, probing glance until one has discovered its limits, its limitedness—there is today perhaps no other way to reawaken the power of the pupil to glimpse the never-vanishing appearance of the Absolute.[4]

We have to deal with the meaningless till the last moment, writes Buber in a comment on Franz Kafka, but in the very act of suffering its contradiction we experience an inner meaning. This meaning is not at

---

[1] *Between Man and Man*, 'What Is Man?', p. 201 ff.; 'Hope for This Hour,' *op. cit.*
[2] 'Hope for This Hour.'
[3] *Ibid.; Between Man and Man*, 'What Is Man?', p. 168.
[4] *Eclipse of God*, 'On the Suspension of the Ethical,' p. 155 f.

all agreeable to us yet it is turned toward us, and it 'pushes straight through all the foulness to the chambers of our hearts.' Kafka depicted the course of the world in gloomier colours than ever before, yet he also proclaimed *emunah* anew, 'with a still deepened "in spite of all this," quite soft and shy, but unambiguous.' 'So must Emunah change in a time of God's eclipse in order to preserve steadfast to God, without disowning reality.' The eclipse of the light of God is no extinction. Although the I-Thou relation has gone into the catacombs, something is taking place in the depths that even tomorrow may bring it forth with new power. Until this happens it is worthier not to explain the eclipse 'in sensational and incompetent sayings, such as that of the "death" of God, but to endure it as it is and at the same time to move existentially toward a new happening . . . in which the word between heaven and earth will again be heard.' [1] The cry of the Job of the Bible and the Job of the gas chambers must become our own. We too must contend with God.

We do not put up with earthly being, we struggle for its redemption, and struggling we appeal to the help of our Lord, Who is again and still a hiding one. In such a state we await His voice, whether it come out of the storm or out of the stillness which follows it. Though His coming appearance resemble no earlier one, we shall recognize again our cruel and merciful Lord.[2]

[1] *Kampf um Israel*, 'Ein Wort über Franz Kafka,' p. 213; *Two Types of Faith*, p. 168 f.; *Eclipse of God*, 'God and the Spirit of Man,' p. 167, 'Religion and Modern Thinking,' p. 91.
[2] *At the Turning*, p. 61 f.

CHAPTER EIGHTEEN

FOR THE SAKE OF HEAVEN

IT is Buber's chronicle-novel *Gog und Magog* (*For the Sake of Heaven*) which, in Karl Kerenyi's opinion, has won for Buber a secure place among the ranks of classical writers. This work is breath-taking even more for its insights into the phenomena of the spirit than for its perfection of style, writes Kerenyi. It belongs to the heights of prose epicry next to such master works as Thomas Mann's *Erwählten* and Per Lagerqvist's *Barrabbas*. The great achievement of this chronicle is its evocation of fighters of the spirit who are without comparison in the whole of epic world literature in the ardour and exclusiveness of the unfolding of their religious powers.

Martin Buber has also accomplished this great feat: he has allowed the good *and* the evil, the holy *and* the dangerous to appear in his own and his most beloved sphere. His chronicle rises above conditions of time and people as does every work which is a 'classic.' [1]

In *For the Sake of Heaven* Buber has given a vivid and dramatic embodiment to his attitude toward evil and its redemption. This does not mean, as Buber points out, that he wrote this chronicle in order to give a definitive expression to his teaching. He wrote it rather to point to a reality, a reality which is so real in the actual events that occurred that he needed only supply the connecting links in the spirit of the existing facts and sayings in order to make it complete. 'He who expects from me a teaching which is anything other than a pointing of this kind will always be disappointed,' writes Buber. While there is no doubt that Buber's sympathies lie mainly with one side of the conflict he portrays, he did not write the book until he felt that he had penetrated to the essence of the happenings on both sides. He could not give himself to the service of one of the two sides and still do this. Therefore, the only acceptable standpoint was that of tragedy. By this Buber does not mean tragedy in the classical Aristotelian sense of the downfall of a hero, but

[1] Kerenyi, *op. cit.*, pp. 96-99.

149

rather tragedy in a profounder sense of two men living in opposition to each other, each just as that which he is. The opposition here is not one between a 'good' and an 'evil' will, but the cruel opposition of existence itself. Buber writes that for twenty-five years he was unable to write this novel as it should be written. But as a result of the Second World War, with its atmosphere of a tellurian crisis, the frightful waging of power, and the signs here and there of a false Messianic, the novel wrote itself.[1]

In its external form *For the Sake of Heaven* is a historical novel built around the conflicts of two Hasidic communities during the Napoleonic wars. The main characters of the novel were actually famous *zaddikim* of the late eighteenth and early nineteenth centuries, and the relations between them which Buber describes are based on actual Hasidic manuscripts and legends. The two main characters are Jaacob Yitzhak, the Seer of Lublin, and his disciple, Jaacob Yitzhak, called 'the holy Yehudi,' or simply 'the Yehudi,' who founded the congregation of Pshysha. Buber says of the Seer in his Introduction to *The Tales of the Hasidim, The Early Masters:*

> He was filled with ceaseless waiting for the hour of redemption and finally initiated and played the chief part in the secret rites which he and certain other zaddikim . . . performed with the purpose of converting the Napoleonic wars into the pre-Messianic final battle of Gog and Magog. The three leaders in this mystic procedure all died in the course of the following year. They had 'forced the end,' they died at its coming. The magic, which the Baal Shem had held in check, broke loose and did its work of destruction.

Of the Yehudi, Buber says in *Tales of the Hasidim, The Later Masters:*

> The Yehudi kept on the other side of the realm of magic which the Seer and his friends entered at that time in an attempt to reach the Messianic sphere by affecting current events; he did not wish to hasten the end, but to prepare man for the end.[2]

We can best get at the heart of *For the Sake of Heaven* by extracting from it those parts that deal with the character of the Seer and the Yehudi and with the encounters between them. We are told that when the Seer was born he 'saw' from one end of the world to the other, but that he 'was so dismayed by the flood of evil which he beheld engulfing the earth,' that he begged that his vision be limited. Yet he was passion-

---

[1] *For the Sake of Heaven*, 2nd Edition, *op. cit.*, 'Preface'; *Gog und Magog, op. cit.*, 'Nachwort,' pp. 401-408.
[2] *Tales of the Hasidim, The Early Masters, op. cit.*, p. 33; Martin Buber, *Tales of the Hasidim, The Later Masters* (New York: Schocken Books, 1948), p. 35.

ately concerned with sinners and preferred the evil-doer who knew that he was evil to the just man who knew that he was just. He was greatly interested in the evil impulse, 'seeing that without it there is no manner of fruitfulness, whether of the body or the spirit.' Yet he pointed out 'that fruitfulness alone does not suffice; the test is the quality of the fruit brought forth.' Despite his advice to avoid melancholy with all one's might because it promotes the feeling that one is a slave to sin, the Seer found himself troubled by the fact that he lightened the heart of others yet himself remained heavy of heart. This may have been because the power of his eyes was not equalled by the greatness of his heart. Buber describes him in another work as at once humble and proud and as too wrapped up in his personal world of spiritual urges to have a real relation with those outside him.[1]

The Yehudi is pictured as a younger man of great strength and sincerity who is unusual in his combination of deep study and fervent ecstatic prayer. He is spoken of as a man who does not know anger, yet he angers many of his contemporary Hasidim because of the irregularity of his hours of prayer and his insistence on inward spiritual preparation before praying. He is marked by an intense concern for the truth as something to live and fight for and by the unusual suffering which arises out of his identification with the sufferings of the exiled Shekinah.

The Yehudi comes to Lublin because he hears that the Seer 'consorts with good and evil,' and it is with good and evil that the Seer's first sermon after his arrival deals. The two first human beings knew good and evil, it relates, in terms of what things were forbidden and what were not. But the serpent clearly referred to a different type of knowing when he said that they had to become as God to know good and evil. They would know good and evil as one who creates both, i.e. not as something to do or not to do, but as two contradictory forms of being. But God knows good and evil as clearly opposed whereas the '"first human beings, so soon as they had eaten of the fruit of the tree, knew good and evil as blended and confused."' Through God's self-limitation (*tsimtsum*) He has given genuine power to every human being with which he may rebel against God. The good consists of man's turning to God with the whole of this power to do evil. God really tempts man, moreover, and demands that he give up everything and go through the extremity of danger and the gate of dread before he can receive the grace which enables him to love God '"in the manner in which only He can be loved."' But the serpent '"tainted the truth of temptation with a lie"' because he prevented man from standing veraciously face to face with whatever impels him to act in contradiction to God's word.

---

[1] *For the Sake of Heaven*, pp. 4–7; *Tales of the Hasidim, The Later Masters*, p. 34.

Nevertheless, even the primeval darkness serves God's purpose, for where it weighs most heavily it causes a seed of light to awaken. And even though, fearful of the coming of light, it swells and extends beyond the boundary assigned to it, "'it never succeeds in smothering the seed of light.'" The hidden power of the light grows although "'it is full of soreness and sorrow'" until the final conflict in which the flame of the black fire will roll over the peoples of the world and "'challenge God Himself to combat.'" Thus will arise Gog of the land of Magog who will lead the final battle of the darkness against the light and will be struck down by the Messiah Himself.

Thus the redemption of God waxes in secret and through the very evil which tries to destroy it; for even the power of destruction derives originally from God. The *yod*, or dot, in *Shaddai*, the name of God, "'is the primeval originating point of creation which, prior to any creative act, stood above the radiance of God.'"

'It is by virtue of this dot that the awful power of God, which at any moment could utterly devastate and annihilate the world, brings about the world's redemption instead. . . . We come to learn about the darkness when we enter into the gate of fear, and we come to learn about the light, when we issue forth from that gate; but we come to learn about that dot only when we reach love.' [1]

It is after this sermon that the Yehudi has his first important encounter with the Seer. Unlike the Seer he views the power of Gog not as a primeval, metaphysical evil but as the power of evil within us, and it is precisely this inner evil which troubles him. One helps others by meeting their evil lovingly. Otherwise than lovingly one cannot help them. Hatred and condemnation of the evil-doer will make him evil himself and not just in his actions, for it will cause him to cut himself off and imprison himself in the world of his actions. But what am I to do with the evil within me, asks the Yehudi, "'where no element of strangeness has divisive force and no love has redeeming force'"? It is there that one directly experiences an evil which would compel one to use the powers of one's own soul to betray God.

To the Yehudi's question of how 'to prevent the evil from using the good in order to crush it,' the Seer responds that God Himself uses evil. The Yehudi's answer to this statement reveals clearly his fundamental opposition to the Seer. The Seer believes that the *zaddik* may use evil for the purpose of the good because the effect of one's actions depends on God alone. The Yehudi, on the other hand, believes that mortal good which seeks to make use of evil drowns and dissolves in that evil so that it no longer exists. At the same time, he believes that what God

---

[1] *For the Sake of Heaven*, pp. 42-48, 58.

demands of him is to learn to endure the evil which He endures. To endure evil is to meet the temptation which confronts one, but it does not mean to allow oneself to be compelled by it. 'Freedom dwells with God,' and human beings have a share in this very freedom which prevents them from being compelled.[1]

Later when the Seer develops the implications of his sermon on Gog and Magog into the statement that the Hasidim must strive to intensify the conflict on earth so that it may hasten the coming of the Messiah, the Yehudi tells the Rabbi that he does not believe in miraculous happenings which contradict the course of nature, but regards the miraculous and the natural as two aspects of the same thing—as God's pointing finger, or revelation, and God's creative hand, or creation. The miracle is 'our receptivity to the eternal revelation' and therefore does not take place through magic and incantations but through openness to God. Similarly the coming of redemption depends not upon our power or on the practice of magic incantation over mysterious forces, but on our repentance and our return to God.

> So long as man still deems that there is a counsel for him by virtue of which he can liberate himself, so long he is still far from liberation . . . for so long does the Lord still hide His countenance from him. Not until man despairs of himself and turns to God with the entire force of that despair . . . will help be given him.[2]

At the Seer's suggestion the Yehudi leaves him and founds a congregation of his own. He remains a loyal disciple of the Seer's, however, despite the latter's growing hatred and distrust of him. By this time the lines of the conflict are clearly drawn: The Seer trusts in magic, the Yehudi in grace, the Seer tries to 'hasten the end' while the Yehudi concerns himself with hallowing the everyday and with the turning of the individual to God; the Seer is concerned with keeping the light pure and building the power of darkness while the Yehudi is concerned with helping the light pierce the darkness. It is not surprising, therefore, that the Yehudi's congregation should develop along lines radically different from those of the Seer's. Through his own emphasis on the divine power of the *zaddik* and through the awe of his disciples, the Seer holds the place of an oriental potentate in his congregation. The Yehudi, on the other hand, preserves an informal and democratic relation with his disciples. He sits among them on a temporary seat, 'so that, despite the deep seriousness of his leadership, the picture presented was one of an uncomplicated and familiar comradeship.' The Seer uses the spiritual power of his disciples as a magic force to hasten the coming of redemption, while the Yehudi helps his disciples find the path that 'they seek

[1] *Ibid.*, pp. 58-61.
[2] *Ibid.*, pp. 37-38, 62, 99 f., 108-113.

to pursue of themselves and for their own sake.' It is this very path which the individual must take for the sake of the Shekinah.[1]

The Yehudi founds his congregation on a positive and coherent body of teaching, and it is in this teaching that we can most clearly find Buber's own wisdom and belief. Lowly as man is, the Yehudi tells a disciple, he contains within him the image of God and is in relation to Him. Nor is man wholly without power in this relationship. He cannot exercise a magic influence upon God through conscious striving, and such striving is itself a proof of his failure. But when he seeks to effect nothing and turns himself to God, then he is not without effect. Man's turning is not for the sake of individual redemption alone. It is also for the sake of the Shekinah. For the sake of the Shekinah we must set free good from evil wherever we meet them blended together, and we must do this first of all within ourselves.[2]

Immeasurable possibilities of redemption lie in individual souls and in the relations between these souls, the Yehudi teaches. But redemption of the individual cannot take place in isolation. He must find his realization in community. A communal life of justice, love, and consecration such as Pshysha embodied is itself the greatest force for redemption, for redemption depends simply upon our return to the good, and it is in community that the relation to God and man can take its most positive form. The Yehudi teaches that redemption is at hand and cannot wait until future lives, and at the same time he teaches that it depends on our turning to the good.[3] He thus transforms the apocalyptic tension which accompanied the expectation of the Messiah into the 'hallowing of the everyday,' and he loses none of the force of this tension in so doing. On the contrary, his single-mindedness results in a heightening of spiritual tension, for he concentrates his being in what he is doing at the moment rather than using that moment as a means to some future end.

A statement of the Yehudi's in regard to his enemies shows particularly clearly the basis of his faith in the ultimate redemption of evil:

> "'You are not to think that those who persecute me do so out of an evil heart. The heart of man is not evil; only its 'imagination,' is so; that is to say what it produces and devises aribitrarily, separating itself from the goodness of creation, that is the thing called evil. Even so it is with those; the fundamental motive of their persecution of me is to serve Heaven.'"

On the other hand, the Yehudi does not believe that the redemption of evil is something that can take place quickly and easily or without great

---

[1] *For the Sake of Heaven*, pp. 145 f., 223 f., 230, 249.
[2] *Ibid.*, pp. 35, 115-121, 185, 213 f., 249, 255.
[3] *Ibid.*, pp. 230 f., 246, 256, 265.

suffering. To redeem evil is to reunite God with His Shekinah, and this is the ultimate task to which all the ages of men must consecrate their lives. This task can only be fulfilled if men return to the good, and the return to the good is born out of suffering and despair. Only in the depths of suffering and despair do men come to know grace.[1] When the Yehudi first arrives in Lublin, the exile of the Shekinah is already his greatest concern. Required to tell a story to the disciples, he tells of a wagoner who demanded his help to lift a wagon and then told him after he had lifted it that it was upset in order that he might help. He interprets this story in terms of the exile of the Shekinah:

'The road of the world . . . is the road upon which we all fare onward to meet the death of the body. And the places in which we meet the *Shechinah* are those in which good and evil are blended, whether without us or within us. In the anguish of the exile which it suffers, the *Shechinah* looks at us and its glance beseeches us to set free good from evil. If it be but the tiniest fragment of pure good, which is brought to light, the *Shechinah* is helped thereby.[2]

The Yehudi at one point ascribes his inability to be a good husband or father to the fact that he suffers in himself the exile of the Shekinah. But later in his life he has a vision which suggests that his service to the Shekinah is impaired by his inadequacy in his relation to the created being.

The Yehudi beheld a woman swathed from her head to her ankles in a black veil. Only her feet were naked and through the shallow water in which they stood it could be seen that dust, as from long wayfaring on an open road, covered them. But they also bore bleeding wounds.

The woman spoke: 'I am weary unto death, for ye have hunted me down. I am sick unto death, for ye have tormented me. I am shamed, for ye have denied me. Ye are the tyrants, who keep me in exile.

'When ye are hostile to each other, ye hunt me down. When ye plot evil against each other, ye torment me. When ye slander each other, ye deny me. Each of you exiles his comrades and so together ye exile me.

'And thou thyself, Jaacob Yitzhak, dost thou mind how thou meantest to follow me and estrangedst thyself from me the more? One cannot love me and abandon the created being. I am in truth with you. Dream not that my forehead radiates heavenly beams. The glory has remained above. My face is that of the created being.'

She raised the veil from her face and he recognized the face.[3]

---

[1] *Ibid.*, pp. 278, 202, 282.   [2] *Ibid.*, pp. 32-35.   [3] *Ibid.*, pp. 228-230.

The face that the Yehudi recognizes is probably that of his first wife, whom he had abandoned for the sake of God. The naked feet refer to an early experience of the Yehudi's—the experience of being tempted one night by the entrance into his room of a woman in a nightgown and with bare feet.[1] The Yehudi jumps out of the window to avoid being compelled by her beauty and by his burning compassion for her humanity. The reference to this incident in the dream might suggest that the Yehudi's denial of the Shekinah lay in his having fled from his 'evil impulses' rather than having used them creatively in his relations with others.

The Yehudi did not have an opportunity to complete his work. He died before he was fifty, in the fullness of his strength. 'The story of his death is enveloped in more mystery than that of any other *zaddik*,' writes Buber in *Tales of the Hasidim, The Later Masters*. Buber relates there several different legends concerning the Yehudi's death. From these he has chosen for his chronicle the one which is at once the strangest and the most characteristic of the relations between the Seer and the Yehudi as he has described them in the rest of the chronicle. According to this version, the Seer asks the Yehudi to die 'so that through the Yehudi the Seer might learn from the upper world what next step to take in the great Messianic enterprise.'[2]

Despite the unusual nature of this request, the reader is not unprepared either for the request or its fulfilment. The Seer has continued to ask the Yehudi to co-operate in his enterprises even after the latter removed to Pshysha, and the Yehudi has co-operated in so far as he could conscientiously do so. Moreover, the Yehudi's loyalty to the Seer has remained unwavering despite the latter's hatred and suspicion. The Yehudi's disciple Benjamin pleads with him not to obey the Seer. To this the Yehudi replies that to be a Hasid means that one will not refuse to give his life. But Benjamin asks him how he can bring a message to the Seer when he is opposed to all his goings-on.

> "'How foolishly you speak, Benjamin,'" he replied and smiled; yes, truly, he smiled. "If one is permitted to bring a message from the world of truth, it is bound to be a message of truth!'"

Shortly before his death, the Yehudi reveals once again his insight that external evil has its roots in the inner evil of the human heart. He speaks to Rabbi Bunam of "'the three hours of speechless horror after the tumult of the wars of Gog and Magog and before the coming of the Messiah.'" These hours "'will be much more difficult to endure than all the tumult and thunder, and . . . only he who endures them will see the Messiah.'"

[1] I am indebted to Professor Buber for these interpretations.
[2] *Tales of the Hasidim, The Later Masters*, p. 35.

'But all the conflicts of Gog and Magog arise out of those evil forces which have not been overcome in the conflict against the Gogs and Magogs who dwell in human hearts. And those three hours mirror what each one of us must endure after all the conflicts in the solitariness of his soul.'

The Yehudi speaks these words in a whisper in the midst of a great ecstasy of prayer such as he has experienced from his youth on, not without danger of death. Shortly thereafter he falls into a new and final state of ecstasy which brings him thirty-six hours later to his death. The moments before his death are given up entirely to the thought of the Shekinah, God's exiled Glory, for whom he has suffered and endeavoured during his life.

Toward the dawn of the third day of beseeching penitence, Yerachmiel, who was watching beside him, heard him whispering the words of the prayers: 'She is like the palm tree. She who is slain for Thy sake. And considered as a sheep on the butcher's block. Scattered among those who wound her. Clinging and cleaving to Thee. Laden with Thy yoke. The only one to declare Thy oneness. Dragged into exile. Stricken on the cheek. Given over unto stripes. Suffering Thy pain.' [1]

At the very moment of his death, the Yehudi repeats the phrase, 'The only one to declare Thy oneness.' These words are symbolic of the Yehudi's life and are the most fitting for its close; for of all of the characters in this novel, deeply religious though they are, it is only he who has declared God's oneness, only he who has refused to work for redemption with external means and who has refused to accept a division of the world between God and the devil or a redemption that is anything less than the redemption of all evil and the recognition of God as the only power in the universe.

Buber's portrayal of the tragic conflict between the Yehudi and the Seer clearly shows that his concept of the redemption of evil does not mean any easy overcoming of the contradictions of life. Instead it includes those contradictions and the tragedy arising from them as an integral part of the redemption. We can gain a deeper understanding of the tragedy inherent in the relations between the Yehudi and the Seer from the fact that the Seer consistently identifies himself with Korah and the Yehudi, by implication, with Moses. According to the Seer, Korah's intention had been a good one, except for the fact that he had arrogantly emphasized his freedom from sin as against Moses and Aaron who had incurred sin. The Seer has shared Korah's pride, whereas the Yehudi has approached the meekness of Moses. More important

[1] *For the Sake of Heaven*, pp. 280, 284 f.

157

still, the Seer has resembled Korah in his demand for immediate redemption. The Yehudi, in contrast, is like Moses in his recognition that the people *are* not holy but must *become* so. The Seer shortly before his death gains some insight into the true nature of his relationship with the Yehudi, and he expresses this in terms of the conflict between Moses and Korah. The soul of Moses and the soul of Korah return in every generation, he says. Korah will be redeemed, he adds, on the day that the soul of Korah will willingly subject itself to the soul of Moses. This realization comes too late, however, for the Yehudi is already dead. Although the Seer feels horror at the thought that he has been among the rebels against God, the contradiction is overcome, if at all, only at the moment of his death when his eyes open wide 'as in immense astonishment.' [1]

That the Yehudi actually carries on the task of Moses in a different situation is clear from Buber's identification of the Yehudi with Deutero-Isaiah's 'suffering servant of the Lord.' [2] The servant, in Buber's interpretation, is neither Israel as a whole nor Christ, but a single figure embodied in different men at different times. The servant takes on himself the afflictions and iniquities of Israel and the nations, and through his sufferings he carries forward the covenant between God and Israel, the covenant to hallow the whole of community life, which Israel has not fulfilled. In so far as they have borne their sufferings willingly, writes Buber, the scattering of the Jews in the Diaspora can be understood as a continuation of the 'suffering servant.' [3] The Yehudi, then, stands in the succession of servants who voluntarily accept the sufferings of the exile, both the exile of the Jews from Palestine and the exile of the Shekinah from God. Understood in this way, the tragic conflict between the Yehudi and the Seer is a part of that redemptive process whereby this very world with all its contradictions is hallowed and the kingdom of man transformed into the kingdom of God.

[1] *For the Sake of Heaven*, p. 299, 308; Martin Buber, *Moses* (Oxford: East and West Library, 1946), p. 189 f.

[2] *For the Sake of Heaven*, 2nd Edition, 'Preface'; *Gog und Magog*, 'Nachwort,' p. 407.

[3] *The Prophetic Faith, op. cit.*, pp. 217-235.

PART FIVE
BETWEEN MAN AND MAN

CHAPTER NINETEEN

BUBER'S THEORY OF KNOWLEDGE

I

'I HAVE no inclination to systematizing,' Buber has said, 'but I am of course and by necessity a philosophizing man.'[1] The real opposition for Buber is not between philosophy and religion, as it at first appears to be, but between that philosophy which sees the absolute in universals and hence removes reality into the systematic and the abstract and that which means the bond of the absolute with the particular and hence points man back to the reality of the lived concrete—to the immediacy of real meeting with the beings over against one.[2] Human truth is participation in Being, writes Buber, not conformity between a proposition and that to which the proposition refers. It cannot claim universal validity yet it can be exemplified and symbolized in actual life.

Any genuine human life-relationship to Divine Being—i.e. any such relationship effected with a man's whole being—is a human truth, and man has no other truth. The ultimate truth is one, but it is given to man only as it enters, reflected as in a prism, into the true life-relationships of the human person.[3]

In existential thinking man vouches for his word with his life and stakes his life in his thought. 'Only through personal responsibility can man find faith in the truth as independent of him and enter into a real relation with it.' The man who thinks 'existentially' brings the unconditioned nature of man into his relation with the world. He pledges himself to the truth and verifies it by being true himself.[4]

Many who see the importance of Buber's thought for such realms as

---

[1] From a letter from Professor Buber to me of August 11, 1951.

[2] Cf. *Eclipse of God, op. cit.,* 'Religion and Philosophy,' pp. 44 ff., 49 f., 53-63.

[3] Martin Buber, 'Remarks on Goethe's Concept of Humanity,' *Goethe and the Modern Age,* ed. by Arnold Bergstraesser (Chicago: Henry Regnery Co., 1950), p. 232 f.

[4] *Between Man and Man,* 'The Question to the Single One,' p. 81 f.; *Images of Good and Evil,* p. 55 f.

ethics and religion fail to see its radical significance for epistemology, or theory of knowledge, and many criticize it on the basis of other, incompatible epistemologies without knowing that they are doing so. The significance of Buber's theory of knowledge lies in the fact that it expresses and answers the felt need of many in this age to break through to a more humanly realistic account of the way in which we know. The independent springing up of other writers who have sought to answer this need in a similar way is as much a testimony to the significance of the general trend of Buber's thought as is the rapidly increasing number of thinkers who have been directly or indirectly influenced by him.[1]

[1] Among those who have been particularly influenced by Buber in their epistemology are Gaston Bachelard, John Baillie, Ludwig Binswanger, Emil Brunner, Friedrich Gogarten, Karl Heim, Hermann von Keyserling, and, in part, Nicholas Berdyaev and Dorothy Emmet. (Cf. John Baillie, *Our Knowledge of God* (New York: Scribners, 1939), pp. 161, 201-216; Gaston Bachelard, 'Preface' to *Je et Tu*, trans. from *Ich und Du* by Geneviève Bianquis, pp. 7-15; Ludwig Binswanger, *Grundformen und Erkenntnis menschlichen Daseins* (Zurich: Max Niehans Verlag, 1942); Emil Brunner, *Christianity and Civilisation*, Gifford Lectures of 1947, First Part: *Foundations* (London: Nisbet & Co., 1948), chap. iii—'The Problem of Truth'; Emil Brunner, *Wahrheit als Begegnung*; Friedrich Gogarten, *Ich glaube an den dreieinigen Gott;* Karl Heim, *Glaube und Denken* and *God Transcendent;* Graf Hermann Keyserling, *Das Buch vom Ursprung*, chaps. 'Das Zwischenreich' and 'Instinkt und Intuition'; Nicholas Berdyaev, *Solitude and Society*, trans. by George Reavey (London: Geoffrey Bles, 1938), 'Third Meditation, The Ego, Solitude and Society,' especially pp. 67-85; Dorothy M. Emmet, *The Nature of Metaphysical Thinking* (London: Macmillan & Co. Ltd., 1949), chaps. iii, ix, x, especially pp. 207-215. See also Leslie Allen Paul, *The Meaning of Human Existence* (Philadelphia & New York: J. P. Lippincott Co., 1950), chaps. iv and v. Where facts of publication are not given above, see Bibliography section—'Works other than Buber's on Dialogue and the I-Thou Relation.'

Those who have arrived at a dialogical or I-Thou philosophy independently of Buber and without influencing him include Ferdinand Ebner, Eberhard Grisebach, Karl Jaspers, Gabriel Marcel, Eugene Rosenstock-Huessy, Franz Rosenzweig, and Max Scheler. The thought of Marcel, the French Catholic existentialist, bears remarkable resemblance to Buber's even in its terminology, but, according to Marcel's own statement to Buber when they met in Paris in 1950, he was not influenced by Buber's *Ich und Du* in writing his *Journal Métaphysique*. On the other hand, it is incomprehensible that I. M. Bochenski speaks of Marcel's use of the I-Thou philosophy as 'eigenartig'—peculiar to Marcel—and does not even mention Buber or Ferdinand Ebner, both of whom wrote in German several years before Marcel's earliest writing on 'je et toi.' (Cf. Innocentius M. Bochenski, *Europäische Philosophie der Gegenwart* (Bern: A. Francke Verlag, 1947), pp. 178-185, in particular p. 184. Bochenski mentions Buber in the 2nd edition, but inadequately.) The merging of Marcel's and Buber's influence can be seen in Maurice Nédoncelle, *La Réciprocité des Consciences* (Paris: Aubier, Éditions Montaignes, 1942). Aubier, Éditions Montaigne also published Marcel's *Être et Avoir* (1935) and *Homo Viator* (1944) and *Je et Tu*, the French translation of Buber's *I and Thou* (1938). (Cf. Ferdinand Ebner, *Das Wort und die geistigen Realitäten*; Gabriel Marcel, *Journal Métaphysique*, 2nd Part; Marcel, *Being and Having*, pp. 104-111, 149-168, 233-239; Paul Ricœur, *Gabriel Marcel et Karl Jaspers*, pp. 157-185, and especially Part II, chap. ii, 'Le "toi" et la "communication"';

Buber's Theory of Knowledge

In its traditional form epistemology has always rested on the exclusive reality of the subject-object relationship. If one asks how the subject knows the object, one has in brief form the essence of theory of knowledge from Plato to Bergson; the differences between the many schools of philosophy can all be understood as variations on this theme. There are, first of all, differences in emphasis as to whether the subject or the object is the more real—as in rationalism and empiricism, idealism and materialism, personalism and logical positivism. There are differences, secondly, as to the nature of the subject, which is variously regarded as pure consciousness, will to life, will to power, the scientific observer, or the intuitive knower. There are differences, thirdly, as to the nature of the object—whether it is material reality, thought in the mind of God or man, pantheistic spiritual substance, absolute and eternal mystical Being, or simply something which we cannot know in itself but upon which we project our ordered thought-categories of space, time, and causation. There are differences, finally, as to the relation between subject and object: whether the object is known through dialectical or analytical reasoning, scientific method, phenomenological insight into essence, or some form of direct intuition.

Buber's 'I-Thou' philosophy cuts underneath all of these distinctions to establish the 'I-Thou' relation as an entirely other way of knowing, yet one from which the I-It, or subject-object, relation is derived. Buber agrees with Kant that we cannot know any object in itself apart from its relation to a knowing subject. At the same time, through the present-ness and concreteness of the meeting with the 'other,' Buber avoids the pitfalls of the idealist who removes reality into the knowing subject, of Descartes who abstracts the subject into isolated consciousness, and of

Eberhard Grisebach, *Gegenwart. Eine kritische Ethik*; Karl Jaspers, *Philosophie II, Existenzerhellung*; Jaspers, *The Perennial Scope of Philosophy*, trans. by Ralph Manheim (London: Routledge & Kegan Paul, 1950); Eugen Rosenstock-Huessy, *Angewandte Seelenkunde*; Franz Rosenzweig, *Der Stern der Erlösung*.) For facts of publication not given see Bibliography, Section—'Works other than Buber's on Dialogue and the I-Thou Relation.'
For resumés, discussions, and attempted syntheses of the general trend in the direction of a dialogical theory of knowing, cf. Rosenstock-Huessy, *Der Atem des Geistes*, Part I, 'Eine neue Wissenschaft,' esp. chap. i and Bibliography; Rosenzweig, 'Das neue Denken'; Baillie ,*Our Knowledge of God*, chap. v, ╪ 17, 'The World of Others'; John Cullberg, *Das Du und die Wirklichkeit* (Uppsala: Uppsala Universitets, 1933, Vol. I), Part I, 'Historisch-Kritischer Teil,' chaps. i-iv; Hermann Levin-Goldschmidt, *Philosophie als Dialogik*, first half and Bibliography; Simon Maringer, *Martin Bubers Metaphysik der Dialogik im Zusammenhang neuerer philosophischer und theologischer Strömungen* (Köln: Buchdruckerei Steiner, Ulrichgasse, 1936); and Buber's 'Nachwort' to *Die Schriften über das Dialogische Prinzip, op. cit.* This 'Nachwort' is Buber's only historical treatment of the movement and his place in it. His critique of Jaspers and Grisebach is of especial importance.

Kant who asserts that we cannot know reality but only the categories of our thought.

Although the I-Thou relation was independently discovered by others, some even before Buber, it is he who gave it its classical form, and it is he also who clarified the difference between the I-Thou and the I-It relations and worked out the implications of this distinction in a systematic and thorough-going fashion. The German theologian Karl Heim has spoken of this distinction between I-Thou and I-It as 'one of the decisive discoveries of our time'—'the Copernican revolution' of modern thought. When this new conception has reached fuller clarity, it must lead, writes Heim, 'to a second new beginning of European thought pointing beyond the Cartesian contribution to modern philosophy.' [1]

Buber's I-Thou philosophy implies a different view of our knowledge of our selves, other selves, and the external world than any of the traditional subject-object theories. From Buber's basic premise, 'As I become I, I say Thou,' it follows that our belief in the reality of the external world comes from our relation to other selves. This view is also held by Friedrich Heinrich Jacobi, Ludwig Feuerbach, Ferdinand Ebner, Gabriel Marcel, Max Scheler, Karl Löwith, and many others.[2] This social conception of knowledge is of fundamental significance because it means a complete reversal of the former direction of thought which derived the relation between persons from the relation of the knowing subject to the external world. According to this earlier and still popular way of thinking, we know the external world of the senses directly and other selves only mediately and by analogy. Thus it is thought that the child has direct knowledge of material things through his senses and that through the smiles and gestures of other persons (originally associated with his desire to make use of them) he arrives at a knowledge of them as persons. These theories overlook the fact that the I is not an I, the self not a self, except through its meeting with the Thou. The feral child brought up by the wolves has a human body and originally a human brain, but it is not human: it does not have that distance from the world and other selves which is a necessary pre-supposition for its entering into relation with a Thou and becoming an I. The child who does come to know others as persons does so through his meeting with persons and through the innate potentiality of becoming a person through meeting (this is what Buber means by speaking

[1] Heim, *Glaube und Denken*, 1st ed., p. 405 ff.; Heim, *Ontologie und Theologie*, Zeitschrift für Theologie und Kirche, neue Folge XI (1930), p. 333.

[2] Ludwig Feuerbach, *Grundsätze der Philosophie der Zukunft* (1843), # 64-66; Karl Löwith, *Das Individuum in der Rolle der Mitmenschen, Ein Beitrag zur anthropologischen Grundlegung der ethischen Probleme* (Munich: Drei Masken Verlag, 1928). On Jacobi see Buber's 'Nachwort' to *Die Schriften über das dialogische Prinzip*, p. 287 f. See p. 162, n. 1, above.

of the 'inborn' and 'a priori' Thou). It is only because the meeting of the I and the Thou precedes the child's awareness of himself as I that he is able to infer the meaning of the actions of others.[1] On the basis of his relationship with others, the child then comes to a knowledge of the external world, that is, through his social relationships he receives those categories that enable him to see the world as an ordered continuum of knowable and passive objects. This is the process which Buber has described as the movement of the child from the I-Thou to an I-It relation with people and things. The child establishes what is 'objective' reality for him through the constant comparison of his perceptions with those of others. This dialogue with others is often a purely technical one and hence itself belongs to the world of I-It, but the compelling conviction of reality which it produces is entirely dependent upon the prior (if forgotten) reality of the meeting with the Thou.

In pointing to the prior reality of I-Thou knowing, Buber is not setting forth a dualism such as is implied by Nicholas Berdyaev's rejection of the world of social objectification in favour of existential subjectivity or Ferdinand Ebner's relegation of mathematical thinking to the province of the pure isolated I ('*Icheinsamkeit*').[2] To Buber I-Thou and I-It alternate with each other in integral relation. It is important, on the other hand, not to lose sight of the fact that though the world of It is a social world which is derived from the world of Thou, it often sets itself up as the final reality. Its sociality, as a result, becomes largely 'technical dialogue' with the social understood either as an organic, objective whole or as the mere communication and interaction between human beings who may in fact relate to each other largely as Its. Here is where Buber's terminology shows itself as clearer than Heidegger's '*Dasein ist Mitsein*' (existence is togetherness) and Marcel's understanding of knowledge as the third-personal object of the dialogue between a first and a second person. Both of these thinkers tend to confuse the social nature of I-Thou with the social nature of I-It, the reality of true dialogue with the indirect togetherness of ordinary social relations.[3]

The I-Thou relation is a direct knowing which gives one neither

[1] *I and Thou*, p. 27; Baillie, *op. cit.*, pp. 207-218; Herbert H. Farmer, *The World and God* (London: Nisbet & Co., 1935), pp. 13-19; Heim, *Glaube und Denken*, pp. 252-269, *God Transcendent*, pp. 91-101; Paul, *The Meaning of Human Existence*, pp. 130-140.
[2] Cf. Berdyaev, *Solitude and Society* and *Slavery and Freedom*; Ebner, *Das Wort und die geistigen Realitäten*, p. 16 and chap. xii—'Das mathematische Denken und das Ich.'
[3] Marcel, *Journal Métaphysique*, pp. 136-144; Löwith, *op. cit.*, Sec. II—'Strukturanalyse des Miteinanderseins'; Cullberg, *Das Du und die Wirklichkeit*, chaps. iv, vii-x; Heim, *Glaube und Denken*, pp. 342-349. The attempts of Löwith, Heim, Cullberg and others to combine Heidegger's ontology with the I-Thou relation are

165

knowledge about the Thou over against one nor about oneself as an objective entity apart from this relationship. It is 'the genuinely reciprocal meeting in the fullness of life between one active existence and another.' [1] Although this dialogical knowing is direct, it is not entirely unmediated. The directness of the relationship is established not only through the mediation of the senses, e.g. the concrete meeting of real living persons, but also through the mediation of the 'word,' i.e. the mediation of those technical means and those fields of symbolic communication, such as language, music, art, and ritual, which enable men ever again to enter into relation with that which is over against them. The 'word' may be identified with subject-object, or I-It, knowledge while it remains indirect and symbolic, but it is itself the channel and expression of I-Thou knowing when it is taken up into real dialogue.

Subject-object, or I-It, knowledge is ultimately nothing other than the socially objectivized and elaborated product of the real meeting which takes place between man and his Thou in the realms of nature, social relations, and art. As such, it provides those ordered categories of thought which are, together with dialogue, primal necessities of human existence. But as such also, it may be, like the indirect and objective 'word,' the symbol of true dialogue. It is only when the symbolical character of subject-object knowledge is forgotten or remains undiscovered (as is often the case) that this 'knowledge' ceases to point back toward the reality of direct dialogical knowing and becomes instead an obstruction to it. When I-It blocks the return to I-Thou, it poses as reality itself: it asserts that reality is ultimately of the nature of abstract reason or objective category and that it can be understood as something external, clearly defined, and entirely 'objective.'

When this has taken place, the true nature of knowledge as communication—as the 'word' which results from the relation of two separate existing beings—is forgotten. 'Words' are taken to be entities independent of the dialogue between man and man and the meeting between man and nature, and they are either understood as expressions of universal ideas existing in themselves or as nominative designations for entirely objective empirical reality. The latter way of seeing words attempts to separate the object from the knowing subject, to reduce words to sheer denotation, and to relegate all 'connotations' and all that is not 'empirically verifiable' to subjective emotion or 'poetic truth.' The former retains the true symbolic character of the 'word' as

essentially vitiated by the basic difference between this ontology and that underlying a thoroughgoing dialogical philosophy. This has become increasingly clear as Buber has developed and made explicit his own ontology in 'What Is Man?' (*Between Man and Man*) and 'Distance and Relation.' See Buber's critique of Heidegger in 'What Is Man?' (*Between Man and Man*, pp. 163-181) and 'Religion and Modern Thinking' (*Eclipse of God*, pp. 94-104).

[1] *Eclipse of God*, 'Religion and Philosophy,' p. 46.

something more than a conventional sign and as something which does refer to a true order of being, but it misunderstands the nature of the symbol as giving indirect knowledge of an object rather than as communicating the relation between one existing being and another. Metaphysical analogies, as Dorothy Emmet has shown, are analogies between relationships rather than between one object which is familiar and known as it is in itself and one which is either abstract or unknown.[1] A symbol is not a concrete medium for the knowledge of some universal, if not directly knowable reality—though this is the way in which most writers on symbolism from Plato and Plotinus to Urban, Coomaraswamy, and Jung have treated it.[2] It is instead a mythical or conceptual representation of a concrete reality. It is first of all the product of the real meeting in the actual present of two separate beings; only when it becomes abstract and universalized is that meeting forgotten.

The difference between Buber's understanding of the symbol and that of the modern logical positivist, who also rejects Platonic universals, can be seen most clearly in Buber's use of the term 'signs.' Buber, as we have seen, portrays the total moral action in terms of 'becoming aware' of the 'signs' and responding to them. The 'signs' are just everything which we meet, but seen as something really addressing us, rather than as objective phenomena. A 'sign' is ordinarily defined as a conventional or arbitrary symbol whereby everybody may derive the same meaning from a thing, and this is the meaning which the logical positivist gives to 'symbol.' This would apply equally to red lights, algebraic symbols, and the prediction of future events on the basis of tea leaves or the stars. What Buber means by 'sign' in contrast, is something which does not speak to everybody but just to the one who sees that it 'says' something to him. Moreover, the same thing may 'say' different things to different people, and to a man who rests content to be an 'observer' it will say nothing at all. This 'saying' is thus nothing other than the 'I-Thou' relation whether it be the full, reciprocal I-Thou relation between men or the less complete and non-reciprocal relation with nature or in artistic creation and appreciation. Our inherited mechanisms of defence protect us from seeing the signs as really addressing us. 'Becoming aware' is the openness which puts aside this perfected shell in favour of

---

[1] Emmet, *The Nature of Metaphysical Thinking*, chaps. v, ix. On 'the Word' see Emmet, pp. 224-227; Ebner, *op. cit.*, chaps. ii-viii, x-xiv; Rosenstock-Huessy, *Angewandte Seelenkunde* and *Das Atem der Geistes*; Romano Guardini, *Welt und Person* (Würzburg; Wekbund-Verlag, 1950), pp. 107-111; Löwith, *op. cit.*, 2. Abschnitt, 'Miteinandersein als Miteinander Sprechen,' ⧧ 24-32.
[2] Cf. Wilbur Marshal Urban, *Language and Reality* (New York: Macmillan Co., 1939); Ananda K. Coomaraswamy, *Hinduism and Buddhism*; Carl G. Jung, *Modern Man in Search of a Soul* (1932), *Psychology and Religion* (1938), *The Integration of the Personality* (1940), and *The Secret of the Golden Flower* (with Richard Wilhelm) (1931).

true presentness, that is, of being willing to see each new event as something which is, despite all resemblance to what has gone before, unique and unexpected.[1]

One must understand the full significance of this presentness if one is to understand the symbolic function and the dependent and mediate reality of the I-It relation.[2] What takes place in the present is ordered through the abstracting function of I-It into the world of categories—of space and time, cause and effect. We usually think of these categories as reality itself, but they are actually merely the symbolic representation of what has become. Even our predictions of the future actually belong to the world of the past, for they are generalizations based on the assumptions of unity, continuity, cause and effect, and the resemblance of the future to the past. Nor does the partial success of these predictions show that we have real knowledge of the future, for we do not know this 'future' until it is already past, that is, until it has been registered in the categories of our knowledge-world.

It is the presentness of the I-Thou relation which shows most clearly the logical impossibility of criticizing I-Thou knowing on the basis of any system of I-It. Although psychology, for example, may show that many human relations which are thought genuine are actually neurotic projections from the past and hence I-It, it cannot question the fundamental reality of the I-Thou relation nor establish any external, 'objectively' valid criteria as to which relations are I-Thou and which I-It. The reason it cannot do this is that it is itself an ordered system of knowledge. As such, it observes its phenomena after they have already taken their place in the categories of human knowing. Also, in so far as it is scientific, it excludes the really direct and present knowing of I-Thou. This knowing, when it reaches its full development in 'seeing the other,' or making the other present (which surely happens again and again in really effective psychotherapy), is itself the ultimate criterion for the reality of the I-Thou relation.

[1] *Between Man and Man*, 'Dialogue,' pp. 10-13, 'The Education of Character,' p. 113 f.

[2] Karl Heim has made Buber's distinction between the presentness of the I-Thou relation and the pastness of I-It the basis for his whole philosophy of dimensions and hence in turn of his theology. He has shown the way in which the present flows into the past and from this the way in which what has become past may again become present reality. He has misunderstood the full significance of Buber's distinction, however, when he identifies the present with the I and the past with the It—and an important part of his epistemology is based on this identification. (*Glaube und Denken*, 1st ed., chap. iii, pp. 200-278; *God Transcendent*, chaps. iv-v.) Real presentness cannot be identified with the I, for the I does not exist in itself, but only in relation to a Thou or an It. Presentness exists, moreover, not *in* the I but *between* the I and the Thou. I-It, on the other hand, is always past, always 'already become,' and this means that the I of the I-It relation is as much a part of the past as the 'object' which it knows.

Buber's Theory of Knowledge

The presentness of the I-Thou relation is also fatal to the attempt of logical positivism to relegate ethics, religion, and poetry to subjective emotion without real knowledge value. Seen in the light of Buber's dialogical philosophy, this is nothing other than the attempt of subject-object, or I-It, knowledge to dismiss the ontological reality of the I-Thou knowing from which it derives its own existence. This means that it judges the present entirely by the past as if there were no present reality until that reality had become past and therefore capable of being dealt with in our thought categories. It also means that it abstracts the knowing subject from his existence as a person in relation to other persons and then attempts to establish an 'objective' impersonal knowledge abstracted from even that knowing subject.

Still another illustration of the importance of the distinction between the presentness of true becoming and the pastness of having become is the tendency of many thinkers to identify the inheritance of tradition with the forms into which tradition has cast itself.[1] On the basis of a misleading biological analogy, they think of society, the family, the church, or the law as a living organism and of the individuals of the past, present, and future as cells in this organism. This way of thinking is a distortion of the true way in which tradition is actually inherited, namely through each individual's making that part of the tradition his own which comes alive for him as Thou. What is more, the fact that it is a distortion is hidden by the false appearance of presentness and dynamism which the biological analogy lends. This analogy, like all social application of evolutionism, is actually entirely a matter of the past and of static categories of cause and effect—in other words of the I-It, or subject-object, way of knowing.

The contrast between the presentness of I-Thou and the pastness of I-It also provides us with a key to the most misunderstood and most often criticized part of Buber's I-Thou philosophy—his assertion of the reality of the I-Thou relation with nature.[2] What Buber's critics on this point overlook is that the reason that objects are It to us and not Thou is that they have already been enregistered in the subject-object world of the past. We think that we know the 'real' objects although usually we know them only indirectly and conceptually through the

[1] See, for example, T. S. Eliot, *Notes Towards the Definition of Culture* (New York: Harcourt Brace, 1951).

[2] John Cullberg has cited this part of Buber's thought as proof that he still posits a mystical or aesthetic unity which in fact negates the true 'otherness' of the Thou. Hermann Levin-Goldschmidt has used it to prove that although Buber talks of dialogue, he has not in fact left the mystical monologue which projects a Thou on to things which obviously cannot be a Thou. (Cullberg, *op. cit.*, pp. 39-46, 162-167; Hermann Levin-Goldschmidt, *Hermann Cohen und Martin Buber, Ein Jahrhundert Ringen um jüdische Wirklichkeit*, Geneva: Editions Migdal, 1946, pp. 72-76.)

categories of I-It. Consequently, we find it difficult to understand Buber's meaning when he says in 'Dialogue' that all things 'say' something to us. Similarly, because we tend to associate 'person' with the human body-mind individual abstracted from his relation to the Thou, we forget that he is only a 'person' when he is actually or potentially in such a relation and that the term 'personal' applies as much to the relationship itself as to the members of the relation. As a result, we cannot help suspecting Buber of 'animism' or mystical 'projection' when he speaks of an I-Thou relation with non-human existing beings: we can only imagine such a relation as possible with things that have minds and bodies similar to ours and in addition possess the consciousness of being an I.

In the presentness of meeting, however, are included all those things which we see in their uniqueness and for their own selves, and not as already filtered through our mental categories for purposes of knowledge or use. In this presentness it is no longer true (as it obviously is in the 'having become' world of active subject and passive object) that the existing beings over against us cannot in some sense move to meet us as we them. Because these existing beings are real, we can feel the impact of their active reality even though we cannot know them as they are in themselves or describe that impact apart from our relation to it. This 'impact' is not that which can be objectively observed by any subject, for in objective observation the activity of the object is actually thought of as part of a causal order in which nothing is really active of itself. It is rather the 'impact' of the relation in the present moment between the human I and that non-human existing being which has become real for him as 'Thou'. This impact makes manifest the only true uniqueness, for that inexhaustible difference between objects which we sometimes loosely call 'uniqueness' is really nothing other than a product of our comparison of one object with another and is nothing that exists in the object in itself.

Though natural things may 'say' something to us and in that sense have 'personal' relations with us, they do not have the continuity, the independence, or the living consciousness and consciousness of self which make up the person. A tree can 'say' something to me and become my Thou, but I cannot be a Thou for it. This same impossibility of reciprocity is found in the work of literature and art which becomes Thou for us, and this suggests by analogy that as the poem is the 'word' of the poet, so the tree may be the 'word' of Being over against us, Being which is more than human yet not less than personal.[1] This does not mean, however, any monistic or mystical presupposition of unity between subject and object. Quite to the contrary, this view alone allows to non-human existing beings their true 'otherness' as something

[1] Cf. *Between Man and Man*, 'Dialogue,' p. 14 f.

more than the passive objects of our thought categories and the passive tools of our will to use.

Artistic creation and appreciation, like the I-Thou relation with nature, are modified forms of dialogue which by their very nature cannot be reciprocal. The artist, or 'onlooker' as Buber calls him, is not intent on analysing and noting traits, as is the observer, but instead sees the object freely 'and undisturbed awaits what will be presented to him.' He perceives an existence instead of a sum of traits, and he makes a genuine response to this existence. This response manifests itself as creation of form rather than as an answering with one's personal existence of that which addresses one. Yet it retains the betweenness, the presentness, and the uniqueness which characterize the true I-Thou relation as distinct from I-It.[1]

In his latest writing Buber has laid greater emphasis than ever before on the difference between our knowledge of other persons and our knowledge of things. We have in common with every thing the ability to become an object of observation, but it is the privilege of man, through the hidden action of his being, to be able to impose an insurmountable limit to his objectification. Only as a partner can man be perceived as an existing wholeness. To become aware of a thing or being means, in general, to experience it, in all concreteness, as a whole, yet without abridging abstractions. But man is categorically different from all things and from all non-human beings. Though he is perceivable as a being among beings and even as a thing among things, he cannot really be grasped except from the standpoint of the gift of spirit which is his alone among all things and beings. This spirit cannot be understood in isolation, however, but only as decisively joined in the personal existence of this living being—the person-defining spirit. To become aware of a man, therefore, means in particular to perceive his wholeness as person defined by spirit: to perceive the dynamic centre which stamps on all his utterances, actions, and attitudes the tangible sign of oneness. Such an awareness is impossible if and so long as the other is for me the detached object of my contemplation or observation, for he will not thus yield his wholeness and its centre. It is only possible when I step into elemental relationship with the other, when he becomes present for me. For this reason, Buber describes awareness in this sense as *personale Vergegenwärtigung*, making present the person of the other.[2]

II

A recognition of the implications of the I-Thou relation for epistemology would not mean a rejection of those essential and eminently

[1] *Ibid.*, pp. 8 ff., 25.
[2] 'Elements of the Interhuman,' *op. cit.*, p. 109 f.

useful objective techniques which the social sciences have developed. These sciences cannot dispense with objectification since science as such deals only with objects. However, they can recognize that the discoveries of science are themselves products of true scientific 'intuition,' or rather 'confrontation.' Objectification necessarily follows this discovery, but it cannot take its place.[1] What is necessary, therefore, is that we overcome the tendency to regard the subject-object relation as itself the primary reality. When this false objectification is done away with, the human studies will be in a position to integrate the I-Thou and the subject-object types of knowing. This implies the recognition that subject-object knowledge fulfils its true function only in so far as it retains its symbolic quality of pointing back to the dialogical knowing from which it derives. The way toward this integration has been indicated by Buber himself in his treatment of philosophical anthropology, psychology, education, ethics, social philosophy, myth, and history.

Walter Blumenfeld, in a book based on Buber's 'What Is Man?', suggests that in order to be accepted as valid Buber's anthropology would have to be grounded on empirical psychology and an objective and scientific hierarchy of values, in other words, on pure subject-object epistemology.[2] In so doing he fails to see the integral relation between Buber's anthropology and his I-Thou epistemology. Although philosophical anthropology cannot replace the specific disciplines dealing with the study of man, neither can those disciplines be entirely separated from it. If the basic purpose of the study of man is defined by the image of man as the creature who becomes what only he can become through confronting reality with his whole being, then the specific branches of that study must also include an understanding of man in this way, and this means not only as an object, but also, to begin with, as a Thou.

It may be objected that Buber's concern for man's wholeness prejudges the conclusions to be reached or that it is not a 'value-free' method. These objections are likely to be reinforced in the minds of those who make them by the qualifications which Buber sets for the philosophical anthropologist: that he must be an individual to whom man's existence as man has become questionable, that he must have experienced the tension of solitude, and that he must discover the essence of man not as a scientific observer, removed in so far as possible from the object that he observes, but as a participant who only after-

---

[1] From a letter from Professor Buber to the writer, December 4, 1952.

[2] Walter Blumenfeld, *La Antropología Filosófica de Martín Buber y la Filosofía Antropológica*, Un Ensayo, Vol. VI of Colección *Plena Luz, Pleno Ser* (Lima: Sociedad Peruana de Filosofía, Universidad Nacional Mayor de San Marcos, Publicaciones del Cuarto Centenario, 1951), pp. 18-25, 97-102, 108-113, 120-126, 138, 141-150.

wards gains the distance from his subject matter which will enable him to formulate the insights he has attained.[1]

The tremendous prestige of the scientific method has led many to forget that science investigates man not as a whole but in selective aspects and as part of the natural world. Scientific method is man's most highly perfected development of the I-It, or subject-object, way of knowing. Its methods of abstracting from the concrete actuality and of largely ignoring the inevitable difference between observers reduce the I in so far as possible to the abstract knowing subject and the It in so far as possible to the passive and abstract object of thought. Just for these reasons scientific method is not qualified to find the wholeness of man. It can compare men with each other and man with animals, but from such comparison and contrast there can only emerge an expanding and contracting scale of similarities and differences. This scale, consequently, can be of aid in categorizing men and animals as differing objects in a world of objects but not in discovering the uniqueness of man as man.

The objections to Buber's method of knowing what man is stem for the most part from the belief that there is no other way of knowing than the subject-object, or I-It, and hence that any knowing into which the whole man enters must be a poor combination of 'objectivity' and 'subjectivity' in which subjective emotion corrupts the otherwise objective power of reason. It is, in fact, only the knowing of the I-Thou relation which makes possible the conception of the wholeness of man. Only I-Thou sees this wholeness as the whole person in unreserved relation with what is over against him rather than as a sum of parts, some of which are labelled objective and hence oriented around the thing known and some subjective and hence oriented around the knower. A great novelist and great psychological observer such as Proust still does not give us the insight into the essence of man that we find in the novels of Dostoievsky and the poetry of Blake. Proust's world was preponderantly made up of subjective emotions and objective observations, whereas Dostoievsky and Blake first participated fully in what they experienced and only later attained the distance which enabled them to enter into an artistic relationship with it and give it symbolic and artistic expression.

The observation of the social sphere as a whole, the determination of the categories which rule within it, the knowledge of its relations to other spheres of life, and the understanding of the *meaning* of social existence and happening are and remain philosophical tasks, writes Buber. Philosophy does not exist, however, without the readiness of the philosophizing man to make decisions, on the basis of known truth, as to whether a thought is right or wrong, an action good or bad. Thus

Between Man and Man, 'What Is Man?', pp. 124 f., 132 f., 180 f., 199 f.

173

philosophical treatment of social conditions and events includes valuation—criticism and demand. Living social thinking only comes to a person when he really lives with men, when he does not remain a stranger to its group structures or entirely outside its mass movements. Without genuine social binding there is no genuine social experience, and without genuine social experience there is no genuine social thought.

Knowledge, for all this, remains an *ascetic* act. The knower, to be sure, must enter with his whole being into what he knows; he must bring unabridged into the act of knowing the experience which his binding with the situation presents him. But he must make himself as free from the influence of this binding as he is able through the strongest concentration of spiritual power. If this has taken place, he need not concern himself with the extent to which his knowledge is influenced against his will by his membership in a group. On the basis of knowledge won in this way, the social thinker values and decides, censures and demands, without violating the laws of his science.[1]

The participation of the knower in the situation which he knows must not be confused with Bergson's concept of an absolute intuition which gives man a sympathetic knowledge of the world without any separation from it. Bergson no longer abstracts the subjective consciousness from the full human person nor static concepts from the dynamic stream of time, as did the earlier metaphysicians whom he criticizes, but he fails to see the real difference or distance between the I and the Thou. Metaphysical knowledge, according to him, is obtained through an inward turning: the thinker by discerning the process of duration within himself is able to intuit the absolute reality in other things.[2]

Intuition does not set aside the duality between the beholder and that which is beheld, writes Buber. The beholder places himself in the position of the beheld and experiences his especial life, his feelings and drives, from within. That he can do so is explicable through a deep community between the two, but the fact of duality is not thereby weakened. On the contrary, it is just this division of the original community that lays the foundation for the act of intuition. The intuition which enables us to place ourselves within another person may lessen the difference, but it cannot overcome the tension between our image of the person and the factual existing person. Just as in conversation the tension between the meaning which the word I use has for me and that which it has for my partner can prove itself fruitful and lead to a deeper personal understanding, so out of the tension between the image

---

[1] Martin Buber, *Pointing the Way,* 'The Demand of the Spirit and Historical Reality,' p. 181.

[2] Henri Bergson, *An Introduction to Metaphysics,* trans. by T. E. Hulme (New York: The Liberal Arts Press, 1949).

of a person and the existing person a genuine understanding can arise. The fruitful meeting between two men issues in a breakthrough from image to being. The Thou whom I thus meet is no longer a sum of conceptions, nor object of knowledge, but a substance experienced in giving and receiving.

Intellect operates where we know in order to act with some purpose; instinct operates where we act purposefully without needing knowledge; intuition where our whole being becomes one in the act of knowing. Intellect holds us apart from the world which it helps us use; instinct joins us with the world but not as persons; intuition binds us as persons to the world which is over against us without being able to make us one with it. The vision which intuition gives us is, like all our perceptions, a limited one, yet it affords us an intimate glimpse into hidden depths.[1]

[1] *Pointing the Way*, 'Bergson's Concept of Intuition' (1943), pp. 81-86. After this book was in proof, I received from Professor Buber 'Der Mensch und sein Gebild,' a new lecture on the anthropology of art. The fourth section represents so significant a development in Buber's epistemology that I feel it should be paraphrased here: Our relation to nature is founded on numberless connections between movements to something and perceptions of something. Even the images of fantasy, dreams, delirium, draw their material from this foundation; our speech and our thinking are rooted in it and cannot withdraw from it without losing their tie with life; even mathematics must concretize itself ever again in the relationship with it. That to which we move and which we perceive is always sensible. Even when I myself am the object of my perceiving movement and moving perception, I must to some extent make use of my corporeality in my perception. The same holds for every other I in genuine communication with me: as my partner, my Thou, he can be comprehended by me in his full independence without his sensible existence being curtailed. It is not so, however, with all that is treated as an object to which I can ascribe no I. I can present all this in its independence only by freeing it from its sensible representation. What remains, is divested of all the properties which it possessed in my meeting with it. It exists, but not as something that may be represented. We know of it only that it is and that it meets us. Yet in all the sense world there is not *one* trait that does not stem from this meeting. The sense world itself arises out of the intercourse of being with being. ('Der Mensch und sein Gebild,' which will be a part of Buber's forthcoming book on philosophical anthropology, was published by Verlag Lambert Schneider, Heidelberg, 1955.)

CHAPTER TWENTY

EDUCATION

EDUCATION, to Buber, means a conscious and willed 'selection by man of the effective world.' The teacher makes himself the living selection of the world, which comes in his person to meet, draw out, and form the pupil. In this meeting the teacher puts aside the will to dominate and enjoy the pupil, for this will more than anything else threatens to stifle the growth of his blessings. 'It must be one or the other,' writes Buber: 'Either he takes on himself the tragedy of the person, and offers an unblemished daily sacrifice, or the fire enters his work and consumes it.' The greatness of the educator, in Buber's opinion, lies in the fact that his situation is unerotic. He cannot choose who will be before him, but finds him there already.

He sees them crouching at the desks, indiscriminately flung together, the misshapen and the well-proportioned, animal faces, empty faces, and noble faces in indiscriminate confusion, like the presence of the created universe; the glance of the educator accepts and receives them all.[1]

The teacher is able to educate the pupils that he finds before him only if he is able to build real mutuality between himself and them. This mutuality can only come into existence if the child trusts the teacher and knows that he is really there for him. The teacher does not have to be continually concerned with the child, but he must have gathered him into his life in such a way 'that steady potential presence of the one to the other is established and endures.' 'Trust, trust in the world, because this human being exists—that is the most inward achievement of the relation in education.' But this means that the teacher must be really there facing the child, not merely there in spirit. 'In order to be and to remain truly present to the child he must have gathered the child's presence into his own store as one of the bearers of his communion with the world, one of the focuses of his responsibilities for the world.' [2]

[1] *Between Man and Man*, 'Education,' pp. 89 f., 83-96, quotation from p. 94.
[2] *Ibid.*, p. 98.

What is most essential in the teacher's meeting with the pupil is that he experience the pupil from the other side. If this experiencing is quite real and concrete, it removes the danger that the teacher's will to educate will degenerate into arbitrariness. This 'inclusiveness' is of the essence of the dialogical relation, for the teacher sees the position of the other in his concrete actuality yet does not lose sight of his own. Unlike friendship, however, this inclusiveness must be largely one-sided: the pupil cannot equally well see the teacher's point of view without the teaching relationship being destroyed. Inclusiveness must return again and again in the teaching situation, for it not only regulates but constitutes it. Through discovering the 'otherness' of the pupil the teacher discovers his own real limits, but also through this discovery he recognizes the forces of the world which the child needs to grow and he draws those forces into himself. Thus, through his concern with the child, the teacher educates himself.[1]

In his essays on education Buber points to a genuine third alternative to the either-or's of conflicting modern educational philosophies. The two attitudes of the 'old' and the 'new' educators which Buber cited in 1926 are still dominant in educational theory and practice today. On the one hand, there are those who emphasize the importance of 'objective' education to be obtained through the teaching of Great Books, classical tradition, or technical knowledge. On the other, there are those who emphasize the subjective side of knowledge and look on education as the development of creative powers or as the ingestion of the environment in accordance with subjective need or interest. Like idealism and materialism, these two types of educational theory represent partial aspects of the whole. Looking at education in terms of the exclusive dominance of the subject-object relationship, they either picture it as the passive reception of tradition poured in from above—in Buber's terms, the 'funnel'—or as drawing forth the powers of the self—the 'pump.'[2] Only the philosophy of dialogue makes possible an adequate picture of what does in fact take place: the pupil grows through his encounter with the person of the teacher and the Thou of the writer. In this encounter the reality which the teacher and writer present to him comes alive for him: it is transformed from the potential, the abstract, and the unrelated to the actual, concrete, and present immediacy of a personal and even, in a sense, a reciprocal relationship. This means that no real learning takes place unless the pupil participates, but it also means that the pupil must encounter something really 'other' than himself before he can learn.

The old, authoritarian theory of education does not understand the need for freedom and spontaneity. But the new, freedom-centred educational theory misunderstands the meaning of freedom, which is

---

[1] *Ibid.*, pp. 96-101.   [2] *Ibid.*, p. 89.

indispensable but not in itself sufficient for true education. The opposite of compulsion is not freedom but communion, says Buber, and this communion comes about through the child's first being free to venture on his own and then encountering the real values of the teacher. The teacher presents these values in the form of a lifted finger or subtle hint rather than as an imposition of the 'right,' and the pupil learns from this encounter because he has first experimented himself. The doing of the teacher proceeds, moreover, out of a concentration which has the appearance of rest. The teacher who interferes divides the soul into an obedient and a rebellious part, but the teacher who has integrity integrates the pupil through his actions and attitudes. The teacher must be 'wholly alive and able to communicate himself directly to his fellow beings,' but he must do this, in so far as possible, with no thought of affecting them. He is most effective when he 'is simply there' without any arbitrariness or conscious striving for effectiveness, for then what he is in himself is communicated to his pupils.[1] Intellectual instruction is by no means unimportant, but it is only really important when it arises as an expression of a real human existence. As Marjorie Reeves has shown in her application of Buber's I-Thou philosophy to education, the whole concept of the 'objectivity' of education is called in question by the fact that our knowledge of things is for the most part mediated through the minds of others and by the fact that real growth takes place 'through the impact of person on person.'[2]

Two well-known English thinkers, one a leading educator, and the other a prominent poet and writer, each make Buber's essay on 'Education' the centre of a book on that subject. One of these writers obviously proceeds from the side of the older education with its emphasis on absolute values, the other from the side of the newer education with its emphasis on freedom and relativity of values; yet they are in virtually complete agreement in their acceptance of Buber's thought about education.

Sir Fred Clarke states in *Freedom in the Educative Society* that while the popular educational theory in England is that of 'development,' the popular practice is that of an imposed code. Following Buber, he redefines education as the creative conquest of freedom through tension and responsibility. Freedom is the goal and discipline is the strategy. This does not mean imposing from above or converting persons into instruments but the recognition that education is releasing of instinct *plus* encounter. Educational discipline, Clarke says, is just that selection of the effective world by the teacher which Buber has outlined. The

---

[1] *Between Man and Man*, 'Education,' pp. 83-90, 'The Education of Character,' p. 105.
[2] Marjorie Reeves, *Growing up in a Modern Society* (London: University of London Press, 1946), pp. 9-12; cf. pp. 34-38.

teacher concentrates and presents in himself a construct of the world, and this must be understood as a practical artistic activity, not as a technique. The teacher is disinterested, yet he is very much a self, for he is a living embodiment of a world rather than an abstract social code or system of morality.[1]

Buber's doctrine offers to contribute to English thought on education a balancing force of which it stands in grave need. . . . For he places educational authority on a ground which is not merely consistent with freedom, but is also the necessary condition for the achievement of such freedom as a wise education can guarantee. Moreover, he appears to find the secret in a peculiar and paradoxical blend of self-suppression and self-assertion in the teacher.[2]

Clarke stresses that Buber's secret lies not in any science of teaching or philosophy of education but in the supreme *artistry* that teaching demands in practice. He is joined in this emphasis by Sir Herbert Read, who reports in *Education Through Art* that his visits to the art classes in a great many schools have shown that good results depend on right atmosphere and that right atmosphere is the creation of the teacher. The creation of this atmosphere, according to Read, depends above all upon the gift of 'enveloping' the pupil which Buber has defined. Here Read is referring not only to the teacher's selective embodiment of the world but also to his experiencing the teaching process from the pupil's as well as from his own side. He agrees with Buber and Clarke that it is not the free exercise of instinct that matters but the opposition that it encounters, and he states further that the whole structure of education envisaged in his book depends on a conception of the teacher similar to that of Buber. According to Read, Buber's conception completes the psychological analyses of the child made by such psychologists as Trigant Burrows, Ian Suttie, and Jean Piaget. It avoids the taboo on tenderness on the one hand and undue pampering on the other. It can thus play a part in the 'psychic weaning' of the child, for it gives us a new, more constructive conception of tenderness.[3]

Read loses sight of Buber's concept of dialogue, however, when he suggests that Buber's teaching shows how to replace the inter-individual tensions of the classroom by 'an organic mode of adaptation to the social organism as a whole' and when he reinterprets the teacher's concentration of an effective world as a selective screen in which what

[1] Sir Fred Clarke, *Freedom in the Educative Society, Educational Issues of Today*, ed. by W. R. Niblett (London: University of London Press, 1946), pp. 53-67.
[2] *Ibid.*, p. 67 f.
[3] *Ibid.*, p. 68; Sir Herbert Read, *Education Through Art* (New York: Pantheon Books, 1945), 2nd Ed., pp. 279-289.

is kept in and what is left out is determined by the organic social pattern through the medium of the teacher's 'sense of a total organism's feeling-behaviour.' [1] Buber does indeed point a way out of both isolated individualism and the 'oppositeness' between the pupil and the teacher. He does so, however, not through any attempt to recapture organic wholeness in the classroom nor through any positing of organic wholeness in society, but through the dialogical relation in which the I and the Thou remain separate and really 'other' beings.

The task of the educator, writes Buber, is to bring the individual face to face with God through making him responsible for himself rather than dependent for his decisions upon any organic or collective unity. Education worthy of the name is essentially education of character. The concern of the educator is always with the person as a whole both in his present actuality and his future possibilities. The teacher's only access to the wholeness of the pupil is through winning his confidence, and this is done through his direct and ingenuous participation in the lives of his pupils and through his acceptance of responsibility for this participation. Feeling that the teacher accepts him before desiring to influence him, the pupil learns to *ask*. This confidence does not imply agreement, however, and it is in conflict with the pupil that the teacher meets his supreme test. He may not hold back his own insights, yet he must stand ready to comfort the pupil if he is conquered or, if he cannot conquer him, to bridge the difficult situation with a word of love. Thus the 'oppositeness' between teacher and pupil need not cease, but it is enclosed in relation and so does not degenerate into a battle of wills. Everything that passes between such a teacher and a pupil may be educative, for 'it is not the educational intention but . . . the meeting which is educationally fruitful.' [2]

There are two basic ways by which one may influence the formation of the minds and lives of others, writes Buber. In the first, one imposes one's opinion and attitude on the other in such a way that his psychic action is really one's own. In the second, one discovers and nourishes in the soul of the other what one has recognized in oneself as the right. Because it is the right, it must also be living in the other as a possibility among possibilities, a potentiality which only needs to be unlocked—unlocked not through instruction but through meeting, through the existential communication between one who has found direction and one who is finding it.

The first way is most highly developed in propaganda, the second in education. The propagandist is not really concerned with the person whom he wishes to influence. Some of this person's individual properties are of importance to the propagandist, but only in so far as they can

---

[1] *Education Through Art*, p. 287 ff.
[2] *Between Man and Man*, 'The Education of Character,' pp. 103-108.

be exploited for his purposes. The educator, in contrast, recognizes each of his pupils as a single, unique person, the bearer of a special task of being which can be fulfilled through him and through him alone. He has learned to understand himself as the helper of each in the inner battle between the actualizing forces and those which oppose them. But he cannot desire to impose on the other the product of his own struggle for actualization, for he believes that the right must be realized in each man in a unique personal way. The propagandist does not trust his cause to take effect out of its own power without the aid of the loudspeaker, the spotlight, and the television screen. The true educator, in contrast, believes in the power which is scattered in all human beings in order to grow in each to a special form. He has confidence that all that this growth needs is the help which he is at times called to give through his meeting with this person who is entrusted to his care.[1]

The significance for education of Buber's distinction between propaganda and legitimate influence can hardly be overestimated. The ordinary approaches to this problem have tended to be anxious and unfruitful. One of these is the desire to safeguard the student by demanding of the teacher an illusory objectivity, as if the teacher had no commitment to a certain field of knowledge, to a method of approaching this field, and to a set of attitudes and value assumptions which are embodied in the questions which he raises. It is also impossible to safeguard the student by any distinctions in content, such as what is 'progressive' and what is 'reactionary,' what is 'patriotic' and what is 'subversive,' what is in the spirit of science and what is not. These are in essence distinctions between the propaganda of which one approves and the propaganda of which one disapproves. They betray a lack of real faith in the student as a person who must develop his own unique relation to the truth. The true alternative to false objectivity and to standards set from the outside is not, of course, that subjectivity which imprisons the teacher within his own attachments or the absence of any value standards. It is the teacher's selection of the effective world and the act of inclusion, or experiencing the other side, to which Buber has pointed.

The real choice, then, does not lie between a teacher's having values and not having them, but between his imposing those values on the student and his allowing them to come to flower in the student in a way which is appropriate to the student's personality. One of the most difficult problems which any modern teacher encounters is that of cultural relativism. The mark of our time, writes Buber, is the denial that values are anything other than the subjective needs of groups. This denial is not a product of reason but of the sickness of our age; hence it is futile to meet it with arguments. All that the teacher can do is to

---

[1] 'Elements of the Interhuman,' *op. cit.*, p. 110 f.

help keep awake in the pupil the pain which he suffers through his distorted relation to his own self and thus awaken his desire to become a real and whole person. The teacher can do this best of all when he recognizes that his real goal is the education of great character. Character cannot be understood in Kerschensteiner's terms as an organization of self-control by means of the accumulation of maxims nor in Dewey's terms as a system of interpenetrating habits. The great character acts from the whole of his substance and reacts in accordance with the uniqueness of every situation. He responds to the new face which each situation wears despite all similarity to others. The situation 'demands nothing of what is past. It demands presence, responsibility; it demands you.' [1] The teacher is not faced with a choice between educating the occasional great character and the many who will not be great. It is precisely through his insight into the structure of the great character that he finds the way by which alone he can influence the victims of collectivism. He can awaken in them the desire to shoulder responsibility again by bringing before them 'the image of a great character who denies no answer to life and the world, but accepts responsibility for everything essential that he meets.' [2]

Just what this attitude toward the education of character means in practice is best shown by Buber's own application of it to adult education. He conceives of adult education not as an extension of the professional training of the universities but as a means of creating a certain type of man demanded by a certain historical situation. The great need in the state of Israel today is the integration into one whole of the peoples of very different backgrounds and levels of culture who have immigrated there. To meet this need Buber has set up and directed an institute for adult education which devotes itself solely to the training of teachers to go out into the immigration camps and live with the people there. To produce the right kind of teacher the institute has developed a method of teaching based on personal contact and on living together in community. Instruction is not carried on in general classes but individually in accordance with what each person needs. [3] The education of these future teachers toward the task which lies ahead of them would be impossible if the teacher were not in a position to get to know the students individually and to establish contact with every one of them. 'What is sought is a truly reciprocal conversation in which both sides are full partners.' The teacher leads and directs this conversa-

[1] *Between Man and Man*, 'The Education of Character,' pp. 108-116.
[2] *Ibid.*, pp. 113-116.
[3] From an informal address by Professor Buber on 'Adult Education in Israel,' edited by me from a transcript of the recording and published in *Torch*, the Magazine of the National Federation of Jewish Men's Clubs of the United Synagogue of America, June 1952.

tion, and enters it without any restraint. The teacher should ask genuine questions to which he does not know the full answer himself, and the student in turn should give the teacher information concerning his experiences and opinions. Conversely, when the teacher is asked a question by the student, his reply should proceed from the depths of his own personal experience.[1]

In order to be able to teach in an immigration camp, the student has to learn to live with people in all situations of their lives, and for this reason the teachers at the institute are prepared to deal with the personal lives of the students. This concern with the students' personal lives does not mean that the students do not learn the classics, Jewish and otherwise, but they do so in order that they may become whole persons able to influence others and not for the knowledge itself. 'Adult education is concerned with character,' says Buber, 'and character is not above situation, but is attached to the cruel, hard demand of this hour.'[2]

[1] Martin Buber, 'A New Venture in Adult Education,' *The Hebrew University of Jerusalem*, Semi-Jubilee Volume (Jerusalem: The Hebrew University, April 1950), p. 117 f.

[2] 'Adult Education in Israel,' *op. cit.*

CHAPTER TWENTY-ONE

PSYCHOTHERAPY

BECAUSE Buber's dialogical philosophy does not imply any dualistic rejection of the ordered world of I-It but only an inter-penetration of that world by I-Thou, it does not exclude the findings of the more scientifically or mechanistically oriented schools of psychology, such as behaviourism, associationism, or Freudian psycho-analysis. To the extent, however, that these schools of psychology are given over to pure subject-object knowledge of the nature of man, the philosophy of dialogue must limit their competence to judge the essence of man as a whole in relation to other men. The attempt of behaviour-istic psychology, for example, to externalize reality into pure action-response not only denies the reality of the participating subjective consciousness but, equally important, the reality of personality as a more or less integral whole and the reality of the relations between persons as that which calls the personality into existence.[1]

If psychology and psychoanalysis are to be successful in their en-deavour to understand and to heal men, they must be grounded in a realistic conception of what man is. This conception must not only be able to deal with the individual in isolation and in terms of individual complexes and aspects of his personality but also as a whole person in relation to other persons and to society. It is just here—in the concep-tion of what makes up a person and how he relates to other individuals and to society—that the different schools of psychology part company. This divergence is as much a matter of method as of final aim, for both are affected by the underlying conception of what man is.

One who understands the essence of man in terms of the dialogical relation between men must walk a narrow ridge between the indivi-dualistic psychology which places all reality within the isolated in-dividual and the social psychology which places all reality in the organic group and in the interaction of social forces. An American psycho-analyst who comes remarkably close to this narrow ridge is Erich Fromm. Fromm criticizes Freud for picturing all interpersonal relations

---

[1] Cf. Paul, *The Meaning of Existence, op. cit.*, chap. iii, 'The Crisis for Psychology.'

as the use of the other to satisfy biologically given drives and hence as a means to one's ends. He redefines the key problem of psychology as 'that of the specific kind of relatedness of the individual towards the world and not that of the satisfaction or frustration of this or that instinctual need per se.' Fromm, like Buber, holds that man's nature is a social product and also holds that man is genuinely free and responsible. He takes over Harry Stack Sullivan's concept of psychology as fundamentally social psychology, or 'psychology of interpersonal relationships.' At the same time, he rejects those theories, 'more or less tinged with behaviouristic psychology,' which assume 'that human nature has no dynamism of its own and that psychological changes are to be understood in terms of the development of new "habits" as an adaptation to new cultural patterns.'[1]

The psychological significance of the I-Thou relation was recognized, independently of Buber, in Ferdinand Ebner's *Das Wort und die geistigen Realitäten*. Insanity, writes Ebner, is the end product of *'Icheinsamkeit'* and *'Dulosigkeit'*—the complete closedness of the I to the Thou. It is a spiritual condition in which neither the word nor love is any longer able to reach the individual. The irrationality of the insane man lies in the fact that he talks past men and is unable to speak to a concrete Thou. The world has become for him the projection of his I, not just theoretically, as in idealism, but practically, and for this reason he can only speak to a fictitious Thou.[2]

This type of psychosis is explained by Buber in poetic terms in *I and Thou*. 'If a man does not represent the *a priori* of relation in his living with the world,' writes Buber, 'if he does not work out and realize the inborn *Thou* on what meets it, then it strikes inwards.' As a result, confrontation of what is over against one takes place in oneself, and this means self-contradiction—the horror of an inner double. 'Here is the verge of life, flight of an unfulfilled life to the senseless semblance of fulfilment, and its groping in a maze and losing itself ever more profoundly.'[3]

Ebner's and Buber's intuitions of the origin of insanity have been confirmed by Viktor von Weizsäcker, a doctor and psychiatrist who has made an important contribution to the field of psychosomatic medicine. Buber unquestionably exercised an important influence on von Weizsäcker since it was during the years in which the two men associated as co-editors of the periodical *Die Kreatur* that von Weizsäcker began

[1] Erich Fromm, *Escape from Freedom* (New York: Rinehart & Co., 1941), chaps. i, ii, and Appendix, see especially pp. 9-15, 26, 289-294, 298 f.; Erich Fromm, *Man for Himself, An Inquiry into the Psychology of Ethics* (New York: Rinehart & Co., 1947), pp. 20-24. It is probable that Buber exercised some direct influence on Fromm's thought since as a young man Fromm belonged to the Frankfurt circle of students of the Bible and Judaism led by Franz Rosenzweig and Martin Buber.
[2] Ebner, *op. cit.*, pp. 47 f., 81, 155.   [3] *I and Thou*, p. 69 f.

his application of dialogical philosophy to medicine and psychotherapy. What makes us mistrustful of many psychotics, writes von Weizsäcker, is that their self-deification and self-degradation lack all moderation. The cause of this overvaluation of the self is the isolation of the psychotic, the fact that he has no Thou for his I. The result of this absence of a Thou is just such an inner double as Buber pointed to in *I and Thou*. This illusion of the double is unavoidable after a man has lost his connection with a Thou, writes von Weizsäcker, for the state of aloneness that he has reached then is unbearable. 'The splitting of the I represents—for an instant—the now unattainable relation of the I to the Thou.' [1]

Von Weizsäcker has pointed out the implications of the I-Thou philosophy not only for psychotherapy but for medicine in general. He sets forth a 'medical anthropology' which begins with the recognition of the difference between the objective understanding of some*thing* and the 'transjective' understanding of some*one*. The patient, like the doctor, is a subject who cannot become an object. The doctor can, none the less, understand him if he begins not with objective knowledge but with questions. Only through the real contact of the doctor and the patient does objective science have a part in the history of the latter's illness. As soon as this contact is lacking, all information about functions, drives, properties, and capacities is falsified. This too is a doctrine of experience, writes von Weizsäcker, a doctrine of the comradeship of doctor and patient along the way of the illness and its cure. This comradeship takes place not despite technique and rationalization but through and with them. The smooth functioning of the objective practitioner lasts just as long as there is a self-understood relation between doctor and patient, unnoticed because unthreatened. But if the *de facto* assent to this relation falls away, then the objectivity is doubtful and no longer of use. [2]

Von Weizsäcker expands this relationship of doctor and patient into an all-embracing distinction between objective and 'inclusive' (*'umfassender'*) therapy. He uses 'inclusive' here in the same sense as that in which Buber uses 'inclusion' (*'Umfassung'*) in his discussion of education, that is, as experiencing the other side. The most important characteristic of an inclusive therapy, in von Weizsäcker's opinion, is that the doctor allows himself to be changed by the patient, that he allows all the impulses that proceed from the person of the patient to

---

[1] Viktor von Weizsäcker, *Fälle und Probleme. Anthropologische Vorlesungen in der medizinischen Klinik* (Stuttgart: Ferdinand Enke Verlag, 1947), p. 187 ff. (my translation).

[2] Viktor von Weizsäcker, *Arzt und Kranker*, Vol. I, 3rd Ed. (Stuttgart: K. F. Koehler Verlag, 1949), 'Stücke einer medizinischen Anthropologie' (first appeared in *Die Kreatur*, Vol. II, 1927), pp. 79-88, 136-147, 'Kranker und Arzt' (1928), p. 166 ff.

Psychotherapy

affect him, that he is receptive, not only with the objective sense of sight but also with hearing, which brings the I and the Thou more effectively together. Only through this ever-new insertion of his personality can the doctor bring his capacities to full realization in his relation with his patient.[1]

A number of European psychologists and psychoanalysts in addition to von Weizsäcker have recognized the importance of Buber's I-Thou philosophy for psychology and have made contributions to the understanding of the relationship between the two. One of the most important of these contributions is Ludwig Binswanger's voluminous *Grundformen und Erkenntnis menschlichen Daseins*, in which Binswanger reorients his psychology entirely around the I-Thou relation and relies heavily on Buber's concept of 'meeting.' Binswanger sees particularly clearly that the loving meeting of I and Thou can in no sense be equated with Heidegger's 'Mitsein' (togetherness) or 'Fürsorge' (solicitude), and he also follows Buber in his recognition that the I-Thou relation is an ontological reality which cannot be reduced to what takes place within each of the members of the relationship.[2]

Another application of Buber's thought to psychology is that of the psychoanalyst Arie Sborowitz. Sborowitz compares the teachings of Buber and C. G. Jung and suggests an approach that would combine the essential elements of both. He shows how Buber stresses the positive —the elements of true relationship—and Jung the negative—the obstacles to relationship, such as 'introjection,' 'projection,' and 'identification,' and he suggests that the one is necessarily the ground for the reality of the other. Jung has given important emphasis to destiny, Buber to relationship, and these two, in Sborowitz's opinion, may go together to make up an adequate conception of psychology. This conception must include both the individual's relations to others and his relation to his own self, both grace and freedom, responsibility and destiny, oneness with the world and oneness in oneself.[3]

The emphases of Buber and Jung are not so compatible as Sborowitz

[1] *Ibid.*, pp. 169-179. Cf. *Between Man and Man, op. cit.*, 'Education,' pp. 98-101; *Dialogisches Leben, op. cit.*, 'Über das Erzieherische,' pp. 281-285. Cf. Viktor von Weizsäcker, *Diesseits und jenseits der Medizin, Artz und Kranker*, new series (Stuttgart: K. F. Koehler Verlag, 1950), 'Grundfragen Medizinischer Anthropologie' (1947), pp. 143-147, 'Nach Freud' (1948), p. 258. See also: Viktor von Weizsäcker, *Anonyma* (Bern: Verlag A. Francke, 1946), 'Es-Bildung,' p. 24 ff., 'Begegnung der Monaden,' p. 27 f.

[2] Binswanger, *op. cit.*, pp. 16 ff., 21, 29-34, 46 f., 57, 82 ff., 85 f., 97 ff., 105 f., 130-133, 163, 166 f., 210-215, 234 f., 264 f. For a more comprehensive discussion of Binswanger's *Grundformen*, see Edith Weigert 'Existentialism and Psychotherapy,' *Psychiatry*, XII (1949), 399-412.

[3] Arie Sborowitz, 'Beziehung und Bestimmung, Die Lehren von Martin Buber und C. G. Jung in ihrem Verhältnis zueinander,' *Psyche, Eine Zeitschrift für Tiefenpsychologie und Menschenkunde in Forschung und Praxis*, II (1948), 9-56.

thinks. Buber sees reality as between selves, Jung as within the self, and their concepts of relationship to others and of personal vocation correspond to those basic views. To Jung destiny is something that takes place within the soul or self whereas to Buber destiny, or vocation (*Bestimmung*), is the response of the self to that outside it which addresses it. To Buber every man has something unique to contribute, but he is *called* to fulfil this potentiality, not *destined*. The integration of the personality, correspondingly, is not an end in itself to Buber, as it is to Jung: one becomes whole in order to be able to respond to what addresses one. Jung ignores the fact that the essential life of the individual soul 'consists of real meetings with other realities,' writes Buber. Although he speaks of the self as including both the I and the 'others,' the 'others' are clearly included not in their actual 'otherness,' but 'only as contents of the individual soul that shall, just as an individual soul, attain its perfection through individuation.' Both God and man are incorporated by Jung in 'the self,' and this means that they are included not as Thou but as It. It is not surprising, therefore, that Jung speaks of the integrated self as 'indistinguishable from a divine image' and of self-realization as 'the incarnation of God.' The fact that this process of self-deification takes place through the 'collective unconscious' does not give it the universality that it at first appears to, for Jung makes it clear that 'even the collective unconscious . . . can enter ever again into experience only through the individual psyche.' [1]

Sborowitz also fails to see the difference between Jung's system with its universally valid conceptions and Buber's anti-systematic emphasis on the concrete, the unique, and the unexpected. Jung's system, like that of most schools of psychoanalysis, is based on the reality of the typical, the general, the past—what has already become and is already enregistered in our categories of thought. As such it cannot possibly understand the real uniqueness of each person nor the reality of the healing which takes place in the relationship *between* analyst and patient. The analyst-patient relationship may, in fact, be an I-Thou relationship similar to that between the teacher and the pupil, and it is probable that in practice the success of any analytic cure is due quite as much to whether or not such a relationship exists as to the technical competence of the doctor.[2] Particularly important in this relationship is what Buber has variously called 'seeing the other,' 'experiencing the other side,' 'inclusion,' and 'making the other present.' This 'seeing the other' is not, as we have seen, a matter of 'identification' or 'empathy,' but of a concrete imagining of the other side which does not at the same

---

[1] *Eclipse of God, op. cit.,* 'Religion and Modern Thinking,' pp. 104-121, 'Supplement: Reply to C. G. Jung,' pp. 171-176; *I and Thou,* p. 86. Cf. Jung, *The Integration of the Personality, op. cit.*
[2] Cf. *The Meaning of Human Existence,* pp. 85-93.

time lose sight of one's own. The analyst may tend, however, to reduce the patient's history and present happenings to general categories, and the patient may tend to lose his own sense of being a whole person engaged in present meetings. Analysis helps the patient to avoid the neurotic identifications and projections which he has carried over from the past, but it may hinder his responding to the unique and unexpected in the real present. Analysis may tend to turn the patient back in on himself, and it may lead him to regard true as well as pseudo-relationships as internal events within separate individuals.

Buber has himself made several important distinctions between the philosophy of dialogue and the theory of psychoanalysis. He points out that serving God with the 'evil urge' is like psychoanalytic 'sublimation' in that it makes creative use of basic energies rather than suppressing them. He speaks of the evil urge in connection with 'the uplifting of sexuality,' and he identifies alien thoughts and the evil urge with imagination and fantasy. But he also shows that serving God with the evil urge differs from sublimation, as it is conceived by Freud, in that it takes place as a by-product of the I-Thou relationship rather than as an essentially individual event in which the individual uses his relationship with other things for his own self-realization. '"Sublimation" takes place within the man himself, the "raising of the spark" takes place between man and the world.' It is 'a real encounter with real elements of Being, which are outside ourselves.' [1]

Hasidic teaching is like psychoanalysis, writes Buber, in that it refers one from the problematic of external life to that of the inner life, and it shows the need of beginning with oneself rather than demanding that both parties to a relationship change together. It differs from psychoanalytic theory, however, in that it does not proceed from the investigation of individual psychological complications but rather from the whole man. Pulling out separate parts and processes always hinders the grasping of the whole, and only the understanding of wholeness as wholeness can lead to the real transformation and healing of the individual and of his relations with his fellow-men. This does not mean that the phenomena of the soul are not to be observed, but none of them is to be placed in the centre of observation as if all the rest were derived from it. One must rather begin with all points, and not in isolation but just in their vital connection. Finally, and most important of all according to Buber, the person is not treated here as an object of investigation but is summoned 'to set himself to rights,' to bring his inner being to unity so that he may respond to the address of Being over against him. [2]

---

[1] *Tales of the Hasidim, The Early Masters, op. cit.,* p. 21; *Hasidism, op. cit.,* 'The Beginnings of Hasidism,' p. 31 f., 'The Foundation Stone,' pp. 50 f., 54 f.
[2] *The Way of Man, op. cit.,* p. 29 f.

Buber gives us the fullest insight into the implications of dialogue for psychotherapy in his discussion of the way in which the great *zaddikim* healed those who came to them for help. To obtain a right perspective we must remember, he says, 'that the relation of a soul to its organic life depends on the degree of wholeness and unity attained by the soul.'

The more dissociated the soul is, so much the more is it at the mercy of the organic life; the more unified it is in itself, so much the more is it the master of its physical ailments and attacks; not as if it vanquished the body, but because through its unity it ever saves and guards the unity of the body.

This process of healing can best be effected, writes Buber, 'through the psycho-synthetic appearance of a whole, unified soul, which lays hold of the shattered soul, agitates it on all sides, and hastens the event of crystallization.' Here the term 'psycho-synthetic' is clearly used in conscious contrast with 'psychoanalytic' to suggest the procedure from wholeness as contrasted with the procedure from isolated parts and complexes. The unified soul shapes a centre in the soul which is calling to her and at the same time takes care that this soul does not remain dependent upon her. The helper does not place his own image in the soul that he helps. Instead 'he lets her see through him, as through a glass, the essence of all things.' He then lets her uncover that essence in herself and appropriate it as the core of her own living unity.[1]

That Buber does not feel that such a way of healing is closed to the professional psychotherapist is shown by his preface to Hans Trüb's posthumous book, *Heilung aus der Begegnung* ('Healing Out of Meeting'). In this preface he treats of the paradox of the analyst's profession. The doctor analyses the psychic phenomena which the patient brings before him according to the theory of his school, and he does so in general with the co-operation of the patient, whom the tranquilizing and to some extent orienting and integrating procedure tends to please. But in some cases the presentiment comes over him that something entirely other is demanded of him, something incompatible with the economics of the calling and threatening to its regulated procedures. What is demanded of him is that he draw the case out of the correct methodological objectification and himself step forth out of his protected professional superiority into the elementary situation between one who asks and one who is asked. The abyss in the patient calls to the abyss, the real, unprotected self, in the doctor and not to his confidently functioning security of action.[2]

---

[1] *Hasidism*, 'Spirit and Body of the Hasidic Movement,' p. 87 f.

[2] Martin Buber, 'Heilung aus der Begegnung,' *Neue Schweizer Rundschau*, XIX, Heft 6 (October 1951), pp. 382-386. This is the preface to Hans Trüb, *Heilung aus der Begegnung. Eine Auseinandersetzung mit der Psychologie C. G. Jungs*, edited by Ernst Michel and Arie Sborowitz (Stuttgart: Ernst Klett Verlag, 1952).

The analyst returns from this paradox into the methodic, but he does so as a changed person returning into a changed method, namely as one for whom the necessity has opened of a genuine personal meeting between the one in need of help and the helper. In this new methodic the unexpected, that which contradicts the prevailing theories and demands his personal participation, finds place.

He has left in a decisive hour . . . the closed room of psychological treatment in which the analyst rules by means of his systematic and methodological superiority and has gone forth with his patient into the air of the world where selfhood is opposed to selfhood. There in the closed room, where one probed and treated the isolated psyche according to the inclination of the self-encapsulated patient, the patient was referred to ever-deeper levels of his inwardness as to his proper world; here outside, in the immediacy of human standing over against each other, the encapsulation must and can be broken through, and a transformed, healed relationship must and can be opened to the sick person in his relations to otherness—to the world of the other which he cannot remove into his soul. A soul is never sick alone, but always through a betweenness, a situation between it and another existing being. The psychotherapist who has passed through the crisis may now dare to touch on this.[1]

A significant confirmation of Buber's attitude toward psychotherapy is found in the recent developments in the 'client-centred' therapy of Dr. Carl R. Rogers and the University of Chicago Counseling Center. In *Client-Centered Therapy* (1951) Dr. Rogers states that the role of the counsellor in 'nondirective' therapy is not, as is often thought, a merely passive *laissez faire* policy, but an active acceptance of the client as a person of worth for whom the counsellor has real respect. Client-centred therapy stresses above all the counsellor's assuming the internal frame of reference of the client and perceiving both the world and the client through the client's own eyes.[2]

The striking parallel between this conception and Buber's concepts of 'seeing the other,' 'experiencing the other side,' and 'making the other present' is strengthened by Roger's descriptions of what seeing through the client's eyes actually means. For Rogers as for Buber it is important in the process of the person's becoming that he know himself to be understood and accepted, or in Buber's terms made present and confirmed, by the therapist. For both men this means 'an active experiencing with the client of the feelings to which he gives expression,'

[1] *Ibid.*, p. 384 f. (my translation).
[2] Carl R. Rogers, *Client-Centered Therapy, Its Current Practice, Implications, and Theory* (Boston: Houghton Mifflin Co., 1951), pp. 20-29.

191

a trying 'to get *within* and to live the attitudes expressed instead of observing them.' For both this implies at the same time a certain distance and absence of emotional involvement—an experiencing of the feelings from the side of the client without an emotional identification that would cause the counsellor to experience these feelings himself, as counsellor. Finally, it implies for both a laying aside of the preoccupation with professional analysis, diagnosis, and evaluation in favour of an acceptance and understanding of the client based on true attitudes of respect which are deeply and genuinely felt by the therapist.[1] Rogers is willing to extend this respect and trust even to a patient in danger of committing suicide or one who has been institutionalized. He explains this attitude in a statement remarkably close to Buber's spirit:

> To enter deeply with this man into his confused struggle for self-hood is perhaps the best implementation we now know for indicating the meaning of our basic hypothesis that the individual represents a process which is deeply worthy of respect, both as he is and with regard to his potentialities.[2]

A corollary of client-centred therapy is the recognition that good interpersonal relationships depend upon the understanding and acceptance of the other as a separate person, 'operating in terms of his own meanings, based on his own perceptual field.' Here too Rogers is like Buber, and like him also he sees the recognition of the separateness of others as made possible through a relationship in which the person is himself confirmed in his own being. A person comes to accept others, in Rogers's opinion, through his acceptance of himself, and this in turn takes place through the acceptance of the child by the parent or of the client by the therapist.[3] In this same connection Rogers discusses the possibility that the real essence of therapy is not so much the client's memory of the past, his explorations of problems, or his admission of experiences into awareness as his direct experiencing in the therapy relationship.

> The process of therapy is, by these hypotheses, seen as being synonymous with the experiential relationship between client and therapist. Therapy consists in experiencing the self in a wide range of ways in an emotionally meaningful relationship with the therapist.[4]

Although this new concern with the experiential relationship between client and therapist was 'still in an infant and groping stage' in 1951,

---

[1] Carl R. Rogers, *Client-Centered Therapy, op. cit.*, pp. 29-45, 55.
[2] *Ibid.*, pp. 43-49, quotation from p. 45.
[3] *Ibid.*, p. 520 ff.
[4] *Ibid.*, pp. 158-172, quotation from p. 172.

there are indications that Rogers himself, if not the counselling group as a whole, has moved somewhat further in this direction since then. In a recent paper Rogers defines a person as a fluid process and potentiality 'in rather sharp contrast to the relatively fixed, measurable, diagnosable, predictable concept of the person which is accepted by psychologists and other social scientists to judge by their writings and working operations.' The person as process is most deeply revealed, he writes, in a relationship of the most ultimate and complete acceptance, and he himself describes this relation as 'a real I-Thou relationship, not an I-It relationship.' Like Buber, too, he sees the person as moving in a positive direction toward unique goals that the person himself can but dimly define.[1]

More significant parallels still are found in a recent description by Rogers of the role of the therapist. The therapist, he writes, 'enters the relationship not as a scientist, not as a physician who can accurately diagnose and cure, but as a person, entering into a personal relationship.' Like Buber in the Preface to *Heilung aus der Begegnung*, Rogers recognizes that the therapist must really risk himself in the therapeutic relationship. He must risk the client's repudiation of him and the relationship, and the consequent loss of a part of himself. The therapist conducts the therapy without conscious plan and responds to the other person with his whole being, 'his total organismic sensitivity.' In describing the results of this total personal response, Rogers again makes use of Buber's concept of the I-Thou relation:

> When there is this complete unity, singleness, fullness of experiencing in the relationship, then it acquires the 'out-of-this-world' quality which therapists have remarked upon, a sort of trance-like feeling in the relationship from which both client and therapist emerge at the end of the hour, as if from a deep well or tunnel. In these moments there is, to borrow Buber's phrase, a real "I-Thou" relationship, a timeless living in the experience which is *between* client and therapist. It is at the opposite pole from seeing the client, or oneself, as an object.[2]

Through his willingness to risk himself and his confidence in the client, the therapist makes it easier for the client to take the plunge into the stream of experiencing. This process of becoming opens up a new way of living in which the client 'feels more unique and hence more alone' but at the same time is able, like Buber's 'Single One,' to enter into

[1] From an unpublished paper of Professor Rogers entitled 'Some Personal Formulations,' written in 1952 and quoted with the permission of the author.

[2] From an unpublished paper of Professor Rogers entitled 'Persons or Science?— A Philosophical Question,' written in 1952 and quoted with the permission of the author.

relations with others that are deeper and more satisfying and that 'draw more of the realness of the other person into the relationship.' [1]

In his preface to Hans Trüb's book Buber points primarily to the trail which Trüb himself broke as a practising psychoanalyst who saw the concrete implications of Buber's thought for psychotherapy. Trüb, like Sborowitz, was deeply influenced by both Buber and Jung, but he has shown more clearly than Sborowitz the limitations of Jung's thought. He describes how he went through a decade-long crisis in which he broke with his personal and doctrinal dependence on Jung in favour of the new insights that his relationship with Buber gave him. What had the greatest influence on Trüb was not Buber's doctrine but the meeting with him as person to person, and it is from this meeting that the revolutionary changes in Trüb's method of psychotherapy proceeded. Trüb writes that he found himself fully disarmed in time by the fact that in conversation Buber was not concerned about the ideas of his partner but about the partner himself. It became ever clearer to Trüb that in such unreserved interchange it is simply not possible to bring any hidden intention with one and to pursue it. In this dialogic one individuality did not triumph over the other, for each remained continually the same. Yet Trüb emerged from this meeting '"renewed for all time," with my knowledge of the reality of things brought one step nearer to the truth.' 'What gives Buber his imperishable greatness and makes his life into symbolic existence,' writes Trüb, 'is that he steps forth as this single man and talks directly to men.' [2]

Martin Buber is for me the symbol of *continually renewed decision.* He does not shut the mystery away in his individuality, but rather from out of the basic ground of the mystery itself he seeks binding with other men. He lets a soft tone sound and swell in himself and listens for the echo from the other side. Thus he receives the direction to the other and thus in dialogue he finds the other as his partner. And in this meeting he consciously allows all of his individuality to enter . . . for the sake of the need and the meaning of the world.[3]

Trüb describes how in his work with his patients he became aware of the invariable tendency of the primary consciousness to become mono-

[1] From an unpublished paper of Professor Rogers entitled 'Persons or Science?— A Philosophical Question,' written in 1952 and quoted with the permission of the author. The last two sentences have been slightly altered from the original under instructions from Professor Rogers in a letter to me of December 12, 1952.

[2] Hans Trüb, 'Individuation, Schuld und Entscheidung. Über die Grenzen der Psychologie,' in *Die kulturelle Bedeutung der Komplexen Psychologie,* ed. by Psychologischen Club Zürich (Berlin: Julius Springer Verlag, 1935), pp. 529-542, 553, quotations from pp. 542, 553 (my translation). This essay will be found in whole or in part in Trüb, *Heilung aus der Begegnung* (see p. 190, n. 2, above).

[3] *Ibid.,* p. 554 (my translation).

logical and self-defeating. He also tells how this closed circle of the self was again and again forced outward toward relationship through those times when, despite his will, he found himself confronting his patient not as an analyst but as human being to human being. From these experiences he came to understand the full meaning of the analyst's responsibility.[1] The analyst takes responsibility for lost and forgotten things, and with the aid of his psychology he helps to bring them to light. But he knows in the depths of his self that the secret meaning of these things that have been brought to consciousness first reveals itself *in the outgoing to the other.*

> *Psychology* as science *and psychology* as function know about the soul of man as about something in the third person. . . . They look down from above into the world of inner things, into the inner world of the individual. And they deal with its contents as with their 'objects,' giving names and creating classifications. . . . But the psychotherapist in his work with the ill is *essentially a human being.* . . . Therefore he seeks and loves the human being in his patients and allows it . . . to come to him ever again.[2]

The personal experience which caused Trüb to break through from the security of Jung's system to the insecurity of Buber's meeting and relationship was an overwhelming sense of guilt. This guilt was no longer such as could be explained away or removed, for it was subjectively experienced as the guilt of a person who had stepped out of real relationship to the world and tried to live in a spiritual world above reality.[3] Both Trüb and Buber show that guilt is an essential factor in the person's relations to others and that it performs the necessary function of leading him to desire to set these relations to rights. It is just here, in the real guilt of the person who has not responded to the legitimate claim and address of the world, that the possibility of transformation and healing lies.[4]

Buber's and Trüb's understanding of guilt as a primal reality sets them in marked contrast to the predominant modern trend toward explaining it away as the product of social and psychological conditioning. True guilt, of course, is not the neurotic, tormented self-preoccupation which so often goes by that name. 'There is a sterile kind of heart-searching,' writes Buber, 'which leads to nothing but self-torture, despair and still deeper enmeshment.' This latter is not a true awareness of the voice, but 'reflexion,' a turning back on oneself which

[1] *Ibid.*, pp. 543-550.
[2] *Ibid.*, p. 550 f. (my translation). Cf. Hans Trüb, *Aus einem Winkel meines Sprechzimmers* (Berlin: Verlag Lambert Schneider, 1930), also to be found in whole or in part in *Heilung aus der Begegnung.*
[3] 'Individuation, Schuld und Entscheidung,' pp. 531-539.
[4] Martin Buber, 'Heilung aus der Begegnung,' *op. cit.*

uses up the energies that one could spend in turning to the Thou. True guilt, in contrast, takes place *between* man and man. It has an ontic, superpersonal character of which the feeling of guilt is only the subjective and psychological counterpart. 'Guilt does not reside in the human person. On the contrary, he stands in the most realistic sense in the guilt which envelops him.' Similarly, the repression of guilt and the neuroses which result from this repression are not merely psychological phenomena but real events between men.[1]

Real guilt is the beginning of *ethos*, or responsibility, writes Trüb, but before the patient can become aware of it, he must be helped by the analyst to become aware of himself in general. This the analyst does through playing the part both of confidante and big brother. He gives the neurotic the understanding which the world has denied him and makes it more and more possible for him to step out of his self-imprisonment into a genuine relation with the analyst. In doing this, says Trüb, the analyst must avoid the intimacy of a private I-Thou relationship with the patient, on the one hand, and the temptation of dealing with the patient as an object, on the other.[2] This means, in effect, that he must have just that dialogical relationship of concrete but one-sided inclusion which Buber has designated as that proper for the teacher.[3] It cannot become the mutual inclusion of friendship without destroying the therapeutic possibilities of the relationship. But neither can it make the patient into an It. The analyst must be able to risk himself and to participate in the process of individuation.[4]

The analyst must see the illness of the patient as an illness of his relations with the world, writes Trüb. The roots of the neurosis lie both in the patient's closing himself off from the world and in the pattern of society itself and its rejection and non-confirmation of the patient. Consequently, the analyst must change at some point from the consoler who takes the part of the patient against the world to the person who puts before the patient the claim of the world. This change is necessary to complete the second part of the cure—that establishment of real relationship with the world which can only take place in the world itself. 'On the analyst falls the task of preparing the way for the resumption in direct meeting of the interrupted dialogical relationship between the individual and the community.' The psychotherapist must test the patient's finding of himself by the criterion of whether his self-realization can be the starting-point for a new personal meeting with the world. The patient must go forth whole in himself, but he must also recognize

---

[1] *The Way of Man*, pp. 14, 36; Buber, 'Heilung aus der Begegnung,' *op. cit.*

[2] Trüb, 'Individuation, Schuld und Entscheidung,' p. 533 f.; Hans Trüb, 'Vom Selbst zur Welt,' *Psyche* I (1947), 41-45.

[3] *Between Man and Man*, 'Education,' pp. 97-101.

[4] Trüb, 'Vom Selbst zur Welt,' p. 55 f.

that it is not his own self but the world with which he must be concerned. This does not mean, however, that the patient is simply integrated with or adjusted to the world. He does not cease to be a real person, responsible for himself, but at the same time he enters into responsible relationship with his community.[1]

'This way of frightened pause, of unfrightened deliberation, of personal participation, of rejection of security, of unsparing stepping into relationship, of the bursting of psychologism—this way of vision and of risk is that which Hans Trüb went,' writes Buber. 'Surely other psychotherapists will find the trail that Trüb broke and carry it still further.' [2]

[1] *Ibid.*, pp. 48-67, quotation from p. 44 (my translation).

[2] Buber, 'Heilung aus der Begegnung,' *op. cit.*

SUPPLEMENTARY NOTE (1959): 'Heilung aus der Begegnung' now appears in English translation in *Pointing the Way*, 'Healing through Meeting,' pp. 93-97. In 'Guilt and Guilt Feelings,' trans. by Maurice Friedman, *Psychiatry*, Vol. XX, No. 2 (May 1957), pp. 114-129, Buber distinguishes between 'groundless' neurotic guilt and 'existential guilt.' 'Existential guilt occurs when someone injures an order of the human world whose foundations he knows and recognizes as those of his own existence and of all common human existence.' In a chapter in his forthcoming philosophical anthropology Prof. Buber sets forth a theory of the unconscious as existing prior to the split between the physical and the psychic and therefore as not identifiable with the psyche. In his important Postscript to the second edition of *I and Thou* Buber stresses the need of a one-sided 'inclusion' in the relationship between therapist and patient which is, nonetheless, an I-Thou relation founded on mutuality, trust, and partnership in a common situation.

Carl Jung in *The Undiscovered Self* (Boston: Little, Brown, 1958) emphasizes the psychotherapist's concern with the particular, unique individual before him and his concrete problems. 'Today, over the whole field of medicine, it is recognized that the task of the doctor consists in treating the sick patient, not an abstract illness,' (p. 12) A large sample of Ludwig Binswanger's thought is now available in English in Rollo May, Ernest Angel, Henri F. Ellenberger, editors, *Existence, A New Dimension in Psychiatry and Psychology* (New York: Basic Books, 1958), Chaps. VII-IX, pp. 191-364. (Cf. also pp. 80-86, 119-124.) One may question whether by adding the I-Thou relation as one further existential category to those Heidegger has provided us, Binswanger has succeeded in the synthesis of Heidegger's ontology and Buber's dialogue that forms the core of his existential analysis. (Cf. my article, 'Shame, Existential Psychotherapy, and the Image of Man,' *Commentary*, fall or winter 1959.) Carl R. Rogers's essay, 'Persons or Science? A Philosophic Question,' appears in *American Psychologist*, X (1955), pp. 267-278. The *differences between Rogers and Buber* became particularly clear in a dialogue that I moderated between them at the University of Michigan on April 18, 1957. Rogers emphasizes subjective becoming, Buber the 'between.' Rogers emphasizes unqualified acceptance of the client by the therapist whereas Buber emphasizes a confirmation which begins with acceptance but goes on to helping the other in the struggle against himself for the sake of what he is meant to become. (Cf. Rogers's articles on 'Becoming a Person' in *Pastoral Psychology*, Vol. VII, January and February 1956). Cf. items by Farber & Friedman in supplementary bibliography.

CHAPTER TWENTY-TWO

ETHICS

BUBER defines the ethical as the affirmation or denial of the conduct and actions possible to one 'not according to their use or harmfulness for individuals and society, but according to their intrinsic value and disvalue.'

> We find the ethical in its purity only there where the human person confronts himself with his own potentiality and distinguishes and decides in this confrontation without asking anything other than what is right and what is wrong in this his own situation. ... One may call the distinction and decision which rises from these depths the action of the *preconscience*.

He goes on to explain that the criterion by which the distinction and decision are made may be a traditional one or one perceived by the individual himself. What really matters 'is that the critical flame shoots up ever again out of the depths' and the truest source for this critical flame is 'the individual's awareness of what he "really" is, of what in his unique and nonrepeatable created existence he is intended to be.' [1]

It is clear that one foundation of Buber's definition of ethics is his philosophy of dialogue with its emphasis on wholeness, decision, presentness, and uniqueness. Another is his philosophical anthropology with its emphasis on the potentiality which only man has and on the direction which each man must take to become what only he can become. It might seem, however, that this emphasis on an inner awareness which gives one the power of distinguishing and deciding between right and wrong is a type of moral autonomy which contradicts the dialogical nature of the rest of Buber's philosophy. Buber makes it clear, however, that he is talking about neither 'moral autonomy' nor 'moral heteronomy,' neither self-created morality nor morality imposed from without.[2] Pure moral autonomy is a freedom that is simply 'freedom from' without any 'freedom for.' Pure moral heteronomy is a 'respon-

---

[1] *Eclipse of God, op. cit.*, p. 125 f.　　　　[2] *Ibid.*, p. 129 f.

sibility' that is simply imposed moral duty without any genuine freedom or spontaneity. The narrow ridge between the two is a freedom that means freedom *to* respond, and a responsibility that means both address from without and free response from within.

Thorough-going moral autonomy destroys all concept of morality because it destroys all notion of value. Buber criticizes, for this reason, Sartre's definition of value as the meaning of life which the individual chooses:

> One can believe in and accept a meaning or value . . . if one has discovered it, not if one has invented it. It can be for me an illuminating meaning, a direction-giving value, only if it has been revealed to me in my meeting with being, not if I have freely chosen it for myself from among the existing possibilities and perhaps have in addition decided with a few fellow creatures: This shall be valid from now on.[1]

Kant's 'moral autonomy' is not thorough-going in this same sense, for its self-legislation does not refer to the self as the final judge of value but rather to universal reason and to the kingdom of ends to which one belongs by virtue of being a rational being.

> Looking back now on all previous attempts to discover the principle of morality, we need not wonder why they all failed. It was seen that man was bound to laws by duty, but it was not observed that the laws to which he is subject are *only those of his own giving*, though at the same time they are *universal*, and that he is only bound to act in conformity with his own will—a will, however, which is designed by nature to give universal laws. . . . I will therefore call this the principle of *Autonomy* of the will, in contrast with every other which I accordingly reckon as Heteronomy.[2]

Kant's categorical imperatives, 'Act always on such a maxim as thou canst at the same time will to be a universal law' and 'So act as to treat humanity, whether in thine own person or in that of any other, in every case as an end withal, never as means only,' are actually in one sense imposed from without. In order to follow Kant one must suppress one's existential subjectivity in favour of a rational objectivity in which one participates only by virtue of having previously defined the essence of value as one's rational nature. It is, in fact, a clear example of the 'objective' masquerading as the 'subjective,' and nothing makes this clearer than Kant's suspicion of all empirical actions as probably in fact

---

[1] *Ibid.*, 'Religion and Modern Thinking,' p. 93.
[2] Immanuel Kant, *Fundamental Principles of the Metaphysic of Morals*, trans. by Thomas K. Abbott, with an Introduction by Marvin Fox (New York: The Liberal Arts Press, 1949), p. 49 f.

tainted by some non-moral motive. Nothing is good for Kant except a 'good will,' nor does he ever seriously envisage the possibility of turning to the good with the 'evil impulse' in such a way as to unify impulse and will.[1] It is just such a split as this that Buber avoids, and it is for this reason that he can speak of 'intrinsic value and disvalue' in a more genuine sense than either Kant or Sartre.

Buber's concept of the responsibility of an I to a Thou is closely similar to Kant's second formulation of the categorical imperative: Never treat one's fellow as a means only but always also as an end of value in himself. But even here, where Kant's and Buber's ethics seem to join, there is an essential difference. Kant's sentence grows out of an 'ought' based on the idea of human dignity. Buber's related concepts of making the other present and not imposing one's own truth on him are based on the ontological reality of the life between man and man.[2] To Kant the respect for the dignity of others grows out of one's own dignity as a rational being bound to act according to universal laws. For Buber the concern for the other as an end in himself grows out of one's direct relation to this other and to that higher end which he serves through the fulfilment of his created uniqueness. Thus Kant's imperative is essentially subjective (the isolated individual) and objective (universal reason) whereas Buber's is dialogical. In Kant the 'ought' of reason is separated from the 'is' of impulse. In Buber 'is' and 'ought' join without losing their tension in the precondition of authentic human existence—making real the life between man and man.

The dominant ethical debate in our age, that between moral absolutism and moral relativism, is carried on exclusively in terms of the subject-object relationship. The 'objectivists' posit the absolute nature of values and tend to ignore the fact that a value is always a value for a person rather than something with an absolute, independent existence. They speak, like Wolfgang Köhler, of the 'objective requiredness' of values, and, like Eliseo Vivas, they describe the relation to these values as the relation of a subject to an independent object to which man simply responds.[3] Wishing to rescue ethics from the identification of the 'ought' and the 'is' which is characteristic of the interest theories of ethics and of cultural relativism, objectivists tend to fall into a dualism

---

[1] Immanuel Kant, *Fundamental Principles of the Metaphysic of Morals*, trans. by Thomas K. Abbott, with an Introduction by Marvin Fox (New York: The Liberal Arts Press, 1949), pp. 11, 16-25, 31, 38, 45 f. 'The inclinations themselves, being sources of want, are so far from having an absolute worth for which they should be desired that, on the contrary, it must be the universal wish of every rational being to be wholly free from them' (p. 45).

[2] Buber, 'Elemente des Zwischenmenschlichen,' *op. cit.*, section 4.

[3] Wolfgang Köhler, *The Place of Values in a World of Facts* (New York: Liveright Publishing Corp., 1938); Vivas, *The Moral Life and the Ethical Life*, *op. cit.*, pp. 187, 190, 215-219, 237-246.

which radically sunders man's nature and his moral norms. Vivas, for example, posits the 'objectivity of evil' as the only alternative to its being merely subjective and defines morality in terms of the opposition between objective duty and subjective inclination:

> The search for the right alternative forces on one a distinction between obedience to something objective and obedience to what one desires, obedience to self. . . . The ideal, of course, of moral education is that the distinction be totally erased. But only a weak, sentimental, shallow, Pelagian attitude toward human nature would conceive of the ideal as within the reach of men. The City of God is not the City of Man; man cannot hope to rear a perfect city. Normally, therefore, the distinction between what we desire and what is right is very sharp, and the two terms of the distinction are apprehended as more or less exclusive.[1]

The 'subjectivists,' on the other hand, reduce all value to the subjective interest of individuals or cultural groups. This type of objective description of subjective phenomena tends to make the 'is' equal to the 'ought': it implies that one 'ought' to accept the values of his cultural group just because they are those values, or that one 'ought' to follow subjective interest just because one has this interest. This subjective-objective confusion destroys the essence of moral philosophy because it cannot in fact establish any distinction between sheer objective description of what takes place and the discovery of the 'normative,' that is, of the values which determine what man ought to do.[2]

The fact that different groups have different values is usually immensely oversimplified in popular thought. 'Groups' are regarded as static, distinct, and homogeneous units rather than as dynamic and interacting ones. The individuals in these groups, moreover, are regarded as cells of an organic whole rather than as persons interacting with each other in relations some of which are of a more and some of a less determined nature. As a result, the cultural relativist tends to lose sight of his concrete existence in the overwhelming preponderance of the collectivity. Insecure as an individual, he tends to project his forgotten 'I' on the group and to absolutize the group and its values.

Here we see the clear path that is taken in our day from the denial of all values to their false absolutization. It is no accident, in my opinion, that the most important historical application of Nietzsche's philosophy of the superman was not in the direction of individualism but of collectivism. Both nihilism and cultural relativism leave the individual apparently free to do as he pleases without referring to moral values but actually in terrible insecurity until he can find something

[1] Vivas, *The Moral Life*, p. 239.
[2] Cf. *Ibid.*, Part I—'Animadversions upon Naturalistic Moral Philosophies.'

more than himself that is of value. The superman and totalitarianism offer this something more than oneself, and both are characterized by the fact that they do in fact remove all intrinsic value from the individual and make him simply a means to a greater goal in which he can symbiotically participate. Hence, both in the end mean the denial of freedom, personal integrity, and personal responsibility in the name of a value which turns out to be more tyrannically absolute than any that preceded it.

Thus whether the I or the It, the subjective or the objective is stressed, the failure to see moral problems in terms of the relation of I and Thou ends in the submission of the I to the world of It. Buber, through his dialogical philosophy, avoids not only the 'objectivism' of the moral absolutists but also the 'subjectivism' of the cultural relativists. If values do not exist for him apart from persons, neither can they be reduced to subjective feeling or 'interest.' The value lies in the *between*—in the relation of the I to a Thou which is not an It yet is really other than the I.

Here we find the crucial distinction between Buber's dialogical philosophy and pragmatism, which resembles it in a number of other ways. As Paul Pfeutze has pointed out, both the dialogical philosophy and pragmatism emphasize the concrete and the dynamic, both reject starting with metaphysical abstractions in favour of starting with human experience, both insist upon 'the unity of theory and practice, inner idea and outer deed,' and both insist on the element of faith and venture.[1] Despite these resemblances, the ethics of pragmatism differs from that of Buber's dialogical philosophy in two central points. First, pragmatism is entirely based upon the subject-object relationship, and this means that, contrary to its claims, it is actually given over to the abstract and static world of the past rather than the concrete and dynamic present. This is shown clearly in the appeal to scientific empiricism as the test of values rather than to the direct and concrete experience of the I-Thou relation. Second, pragmatism, like all interest theories of ethics, has no way of escaping the subjectivism which grounds all value ultimately on subjective feeling, nor is this any less the case because of the objective methods that pragmatism supports

[1] Paul E. Pfuetze, *The Social Self* (in the thought of George Herbert Mead and Martin Buber), New York: Bookman Associates, 1954, pp. 274, 295 n. 131. William James writes in 'The Will to Believe': 'The more perfect and more eternal aspect of the universe is represented in our religions as having personal form. The universe is no longer a mere *It* to us, but a *Thou*, if we are religious; and any relation that may be possible from person to person might be possible here. . . . We feel, too, as if the appeal of religion to us were made to our own active goodwill, as if evidence might be forever withheld from us unless we met the hypothesis half-way.' William James, *Essays in Pragmatism*, ed. by Alburey Castell (New York: Hafner Publishing Co., 1949), p. 106 f.

for the judgment of whether our actions will in fact produce the values that we think they will.[1]

It is the domination of subjective-objective thinking that has produced the traditional but false dichotomy between 'selfishness' and 'unselfishness,' egoism and altruism. There can be no such thing as pure 'self'ishness since no self originates or exists in isolation from others and even the most subjective interest is still of a social nature. On the other hand, since in every action we enter into relations with others which involve *both* ourselves and them, there can be no such thing as pure 'unself'ishness. Karl Löwith suggests that the real meaning of egoism versus altruism is the question of whether we relate to others for our sakes or for theirs. The situation is better described, in my opinion, by Erich Fromm's suggestion that true love of others does not mean denial of self nor true self-love denial of love for others.[2]

One cannot divide up a relationship into two separate parts one of which is 'mine' and one of which is 'thine' and then choose between them. One can only choose by one's actions and attitudes to move in the direction of relationship and reciprocity—I-Thou—or separateness and mutual exploitation—I-It. One's giving to the other may indeed be at the expense of something that one wants and needs oneself for the best of reasons. But this does not mean that one is sacrificing one's self in the giving. One is rather affirming one's self through a response that takes one out of the realm of domination and enjoyment into the realm of real personal existence. Up to a certain point, this applies even in a relationship in which the other person treats one strictly as It, for the other must be a Thou for us unconditionally and not dependent on how he treats us. No I-Thou relationship can be complete without reciprocity, however, and our ability to treat the other person as Thou is, in fact, limited by the extent to which he does or does not treat us as a Thou. True giving is giving in relationship, whether it be the gift of material support or the gift of a caress or a word. It is only possible to give in a very limited degree to one who remains resolutely closed to relationship.

Buber's philosophy of dialogue not only finds the narrow ridge between the subjectivist identification and the objectivist sundering of the 'is' and the 'ought,' but it also radically shifts the whole ground of ethical discussion by moving from the universal to the concrete and

---

[1] Cf. Marvin Fox, 'Discussion on the Diversity of Methods in Dewey's Ethics Theory,' *Philosophy and Phenomenological Research*, Vol. XII, No. 1 (September 1951), pp. 123-129.

[2] Löwith, *Das Individuum in der Rolle des Mitmenschen, op. cit.*, pp. 71-76; Fromm, *Man for Himself, op. cit.*, pp. 119-141. On the implications of dialogue for egoism and altruism cf. also Karl Barth, *Die kirchliche Dogmatik*, Vol. III—*Die Lehre von der Schöpfung*, Zweiter Teil (Part 2 of third volume published separately) (Zurich: Evangelischer Verlag, A. G. Zollikon, 1948), p. 312 ff.

from the past to the present—in other words, from I-It to I-Thou. Buber does not start from some external, absolutely valid ethical code which man is bound to apply as best as possible to each new situation. Instead he starts with the situation itself.

> The idea of responsibility is to be brought back from the province of specialized ethics, of an 'ought' that swings free in the air, into that of lived life. Genuine responsibility exists only where there is real responding.[1]

Most of the traditional ethical values—not killing, stealing, committing adultery, lying, cheating, and so forth—are in fact implied in the I-Thou relation, but not as an absolute code. Rather these traditional ethical values must be understood as the symbolic expression of what takes place when people stand in true dialogical relation to each other. It is unlikely in most cases, for example, that one could truly express one's responsibility to a Thou by killing him. The traditional values are useful and suggestive, but one may not for all that proceed from them to the situation. Rather one must move from the concrete situation to the decision as to what is the right direction in this instance.

> No responsible person remains a stranger to norms. But the command inherent in a genuine norm never becomes a maxim and the fulfilment of it never a habit. Any command that a great character takes to himself in the course of his development does not act in him as part of his consciousness or as material for building up his exercises, but remains latent in a basic layer of his substance until it reveals itself to him in a concrete way. What it has to tell him is revealed whenever a situation arises which demands of him a solution of which till then he had perhaps no idea. Even the most universal norm will at times be recognized only in a very special situation. . . . There is a direction, a 'yes,' a command, hidden even in a prohibition, which is revealed to us in moments like these. In moments like these the command addresses us really in the second person, and the Thou in it is no one else but one's own self. Maxims command only the third person, the each and the none.[2]

The responsible quality of one's decision will be determined by the degree to which one really 'sees the other' and makes him present to one. It is here, in experiencing the relationship from the side of the other, that we find the most important key to the ethical implications of Buber's dialogue—an implication that none of the other thinkers who have written on the I-Thou relationship has understood in its full significance. Only through 'seeing the other' can the I-Thou relationship

---

[1] *Between Man and Man*, 'Dialogue,' p. 16.
[2] *Ibid.*, 'The Education of Character,' p. 114.

become fully real, for only through it can one be sure that one is really helping the other person. To deal lovingly with thy neighbour means to recognize that he is not just another I but a Thou, and that means a really 'other' person. Only if we see a man in his concrete otherness is there any possibility of our confirming him in his individuality as that which he must become. 'Seeing the other' is for this reason of central significance, not only for ethical action, but for love, friendship, teaching, and psychotherapy.

To see through the eyes of the other does not mean, as we have seen, that one ceases to see through one's own. The Thou 'teaches you to meet others,' but it also teaches you 'to hold your ground when you meet them.' [1] Ethical action is not altruism and self-denial. Nor is it an impartial objectivity which adjudicates conflicting interests as if from the standpoint of a third person. It is the binding of decision and action in the relation of I and Thou. The best example of what this means in practice is Buber's reply to a public statement of Gandhi about Zionism and the Nazi persecution of the Jews. Gandhi, in December 1938, suggested that the Jews in Germany use *satyagraha*, or soul-force, as the most effective reply to Nazi atrocities. The Jews, said Gandhi, should refuse to be expelled or submit to discriminating treatment but should, if necessary, accept death voluntarily. 'If the Jewish mind could be prepared for voluntary suffering, even a massacre could be turned into a day of thanksgiving and joy that Jehovah had wrought deliverance of the race even at the hands of the tyrant. For to the God-fearing, death has no terror.' In his reply Buber pointed out that Gandhi both misunderstood the nature of the Nazi regime and ignored the importance of the existence of India in his own successful work with the Hindus of South Africa.

No Jew in Germany could have spoken as did Gandhi in South Africa without being killed immediately . . . the martyrdom to which German Jews were subjected in concentration camps and dungeon-cells had no witnesses and, being unnoticed and unknown, could not affect public opinion or modify public policy. Gandhi, as the leader of 150,000 Hindus in South Africa, knew that Mother India with its hundreds of millions would ultimately stand in back of him. This knowledge . . . gave him and his followers the courage to live, to suffer, to resist, and to fight stubbornly—though non-violently—for their rights.[2]

What Buber was essentially pointing out to Gandhi was that each one must have his own ground in order to deal justly with the other, that

---

[1] *I and Thou*, p. 33.
[2] Quoted in Solomon Liptzin, *Germany's Stepchildren* (Philadelphia: The Jewish Publication Society, 1944), pp. 264-267.

pure spirituality divorced from the concrete is futile and ineffective: 'Would the Mahatma,' he wrote, 'who advises the Jews that Palestine is not a geographic district but an ideal within their hearts, accept the doctrine that India was not a subcontinent but merely an ideal wholly divorced from any soil? Is it not rather an ideal because it exists in reality?'[1] The Jews cannot be responsible without experiencing from the side of the Arabs what it means for the Jews to have settled in Palestine, but neither can they give up their own claim.

We considered it a fundamental point that in this case two vital claims are opposed to each other, two claims of a different nature and a different origin which cannot objectively be pitted against one another and between which no objective decision can be made as to which is just, which unjust. We . . . consider it our duty to understand and to honour the claim which is opposed to ours and to endeavour to reconcile both claims. . . . Where there is faith and love, a solution may be found even to what appears to be a tragic opposition.[2]

One can only be 'responsible' if one is responsible to someone. Since the human Thou must constantly become an It, one is ultimately responsible to the Eternal Thou who never becomes an It. But it is just in the concrete that we meet the Eternal Thou, and it is this which prevents dialogue from degenerating into 'responsibility' to an abstract moral code or universal idea. The choice, therefore, is not between religion and morality but between a religion and morality wedded to the universal and a religion and morality wedded to the concrete.

Only out of a personal relationship with the Absolute can the absoluteness of the ethical co-ordinates arise without which there is no complete awareness of self. Even when the individual calls an absolute criterion handed down by religious tradition his own, it must be reforged in the fire of the truth of his personal essential relation to the Absolute if it is to win true validity. But always it is the religious which bestows, the ethical which receives.[3]

The reason why it is always the religious which bestows and the ethical which receives is to be found in the nature of good as Buber understands it. The good for Buber is not an objective state of affairs nor an inner feeling, but a type of relationship—the dialogue between

---

[1] Quoted in Solomon Liptzin, *Germany's Stepchildren* (Philadelphia: The Jewish Publication Society, 1944), p. 267 f.

[2] *Israel and the World, op. cit.*, 'The Land and Its Possessors' (from an open letter to Gandhi, 1939), p. 231 f. For the complete text of Gandhi's statement and of Buber's reply to Gandhi see Martin Buber and Judah Magnes, *Two Letters to Gandhi* (Jerusalem: Reuben Mass, 1939), pp. 39-44 and 5-21 respectively.

[3] *Eclipse of God*, 'Religion and Ethics,' p. 129.

man and màn and between man and God. This means that the good cannot be referred back to any Platonic universals or impersonal order of the cosmos, nor can it be founded in any general system of utility or justice. It grows instead out of that which is most particular and concrete, not the pseudo-concreteness of the 'empirically verifiable' but the actual present concreteness of the unique direction toward God which one apprehends and realizes in the meeting with the everyday.

Good conceived thus cannot be located within any system of ethical co-ordination, for all those we know came into being on its account and existed or exist by virtue of it. Every ethos has its origin in a revelation, whether or not it is still aware of and obedient to it; and every revelation is revelation of human service to the goal of creation, in which service man authenticates himself.[1]

[1] *Images of Good and Evil*, p. 83. For a further study of Buber's ethics and its relation to his philosophical anthropology and his philosophy of religion and the problems of the person and trust, cf. my essay 'The Bases of Buber's Values' in Friedman and Schilpp, eds., *The Philosophy of Martin Buber, loc. cit.*

CHAPTER TWENTY-THREE

SOCIAL PHILOSOPHY

I

MODERN man is insecure and repressed—isolated from his fellows yet desperately clinging to the collectivity which he trusts to protect him from the might of other collectivities. Divided within himself into instincts and spirit, repressions and sublimations, he finds himself incapable of direct relation with his fellows either as individuals in the body-politic or as fellow members of a community. The tremendous collective power with which he allies himself gives him neither relationship nor freedom from fear but makes his life a sterile alternation between universal war and armed peace. The modern crisis is thus a crisis both of the individual and of society at large.

Though many social reformers of the last century have recognized the double character of this crisis, few of them have really faced the problem in both of its aspects. Some have argued that it is necessary to change society first and that this change will in itself produce a change in the individual. Others have said that we must start with the individual and that change in individuals will inevitably result in changed social relationships and a new pattern of society. Martin Buber has refused to fall into this dilemma as he has refused the either-or of individualism and collectivism. In both cases he has resolved the tension between the two poles through a creative third alternative—the relation between man and man. This relation takes place not only in the I-Thou of direct meeting but also in the We of community. Similarly, it must be based not only on the personal wholeness of the individual but also on a social restructuring of society. Relation is the true starting-point for personal integration and wholeness and for the transformation of society, and these in turn make possible ever greater relation.

Both moral and social philosophy are basically determined by whether one believes the individual, the organic group, or the dialogue between man and man to be of basic reality and value. For the radical individualist, both interpersonal relations and society can be nothing but the sum of separate individuals. For those who make society the basic reality, on the other hand, the individual is only a derivative reality and value. For these latter, also, the relations between individuals are essentially indirect, mediated through their common relationship to society. For the dialogical philosopher, however, both the individual and society exist as reality and value but they are derived from the basic reality of the meeting between man and man. Thus for him the 'individual' and 'society' are abstractions which must not be taken for reality itself.

The individual is a fact of existence in so far as he steps into a living relation with other individuals. The aggregate is a fact of existence in so far as it is built up of living units of relation.[1]

Buber designates a category of 'the essential *We*' to correspond on the level of the relation to a host of men to the 'essential *Thou* on the level of self-being.' As the primitive Thou precedes the consciousness of individual separateness whereas the essential Thou follows and grows out of this consciousness, so the primitive We precedes true individuality and independence whereas the essential We only comes about when independent people have come together in essential relation and directness. The essential We includes the Thou potentially, for 'only men who are capable of truly saying *Thou* to one another can truly say *We* with one another.' Through this essential We and only through it can man escape from the impersonal 'one' of the nameless, faceless crowd. 'A man is truly saved from the "one" not by separation but only by being bound up in genuine communion.' [2]

There is, of course, a reality of society which is something more than a complex pattern of dialogical relationships. Buber himself warns against blurring the distinction between the 'social' in general and the togetherness of true dialogue. In 1905 Buber used the term 'das Zwischenmenschliche' (a now familiar expression which he was the first to employ) as the social-psychological in general, 'the life of men together in all its forms and actions,' 'the social seen as a psychological process.' Half a century later he restricted the use of the term to that in human life which provides the basis for direct dialogical relations. In distinction to it he now set the sphere of the 'social' in which many individual existences are bound into a group with common experiences and reactions but without any personal relation necessarily existing between one person and another within the group. There are contacts, especially within the life of smaller groups, which frequently favour personal relationships, and not seldom, also, make them more difficult. But in no case does membership in the group already involve an essential relation between one member and another. What is more, the direction of groups in general, at least in the later periods of human

[1] *Between Man and Man*, 'What Is Man?', p. 202 f.   [2] *Ibid.*, p. 175 ff.

history, has been toward the suppression of the elements of personal relation in favour of the elements of pure collectivity.[1]

The structure of modern society makes true dialogue difficult, and the tremendous force of social and psychological conditioning often brings society close to that deterministic and organic social structure that many accept as reality. But it is precisely here that the ethical question enters in most forcefully. If the basic reality and value is the organic group, then there is nothing to be done about this condition, and what is is what ought to be. If, on the other hand, the basic reality and value is the concrete dialogical relations between men, then there is a vital necessity for a restructuring of society that will enable the relations between men to be of a more genuinely dialogical nature. For this reason Buber has called for a socialist restructuring of society into a community of communities, and for this reason also he has stressed the danger of the confusion between the 'social' and the 'political' principles and the need for transforming the political, in so far as possible, into the social sphere.

II

The 'social principle,' for Buber, means the dialogical while the 'political' means the necessary and ordered realm of the world of It. The former means free fellowship and association, the latter compulsion and domination.[2] A social restructuring of society is necessary, in Buber's opinion, because capitalism is inherently poor in organic community and is becoming poorer every day. Marxist socialism cannot remedy this poverty of structure because its means—unity and centralization—are entirely unlike and cannot possibly lead to its ultimate ends—multiplicity and freedom. Both the Marxist movement and the Soviet regime have constantly subordinated the evolution of a new social form to political action. They have oscillated in practice between radical centralization and tolerance of relative decentralization (in the form of producer Soviets and compulsory co-operatives when these served a political purpose), but they have never put the social principle above the political nor attempted to realize Marx's dictum that the new society will be gestated in the womb of the old. True socialism, in contrast, summons the reality of community from out of the depths of a people where it lies hidden and undeveloped underneath the incrusta-

---

[1] Introduction by Martin Buber to the first edition of Werner Sombart's *Das Proletariat* (Frankfurt am Main: Rütten & Loening, 1906), the first volume of *Die Gesellschaft*, a collection of forty social-psychological monographs edited by Martin Buber from 1906 to 1912. Quoted in Kohn, *Martin Buber, op. cit.*, pp. 310-313 (Footnote 2 to p. 89); 'Elements of the Interhuman,' *op. cit.*, section 1, 'The Social and the Interhuman.'

[2] Martin Buber, 'Society and the State,' *World Review*, May 1951, New Series 27, p. 5.

tions of the state. Communal living grows most easily out of closeness of people in mode of life, language, tradition, and common memories. There is, for this reason, a legitimate connection between the nation and socialism which supports rather than obstructs the international character of socialism as a force for world unity and peace. Socialism based on the political principle starts from the top with an abstract and uniform political order. Socialism based on the social principle starts at the bottom and discovers those elements of genuine community which are capable of development. 'True socialism is real community between men, direct life-relations between I and Thou, just society and fellowship.'[1]

The social restructuring of society cannot take place as a result of the blind working of economic forces or success in production. It demands a consciousness and will—setting a goal and demanding extraordinary efforts in order to reach that goal. This goal is based on the longing for 'rightness'—the vision of perfection that in religious expectation takes the form of Messianism—perfection in time—and in social expectation the form of Utopia—perfection in space. The Utopian systems that grow out of this longing for social rightness are by no means essentially the same, for they tend to two opposite forms. One is 'schematic fiction' which starts from a theory of the nature of man and deduces a social order which shall employ all man's capacities and satisfy all his needs. The other undertakes to transform contemporary man and his conditions on the basis of an impartial and undogmatic understanding of both. This latter form is aware of the diversity and contrariety of the trends of the age and tries to discover which of these trends are aiming at an order in which the contradictions of existing society will truly be overcome.[2]

This latter, according to Buber, is genuine 'Utopian' socialism. If it does not expect blind providence to save man through technical and material change, neither does it trust to a 'free-ranging human intellect which contrives systems of absolute validity.' True community can only be built if it satisfies a situation and not an abstraction. For this reason the movement to community must be 'topical,' that is, growing out of the needs of a given situation and realizing itself to the greatest possible degree here and now. At the same time this local and topical realization must be nothing but a point of departure for the larger goal of organic cells unified in a restructured society.[3]

The reconstruction of society can only begin, writes Buber, with 'a radical alteration of the relationship between the social and the political

[1] *Paths in Utopia, op. cit.*, pp. 13 f., 48 f., 56, 98 f., 118, 124 f.; *Kampf um Israel, op. cit.*, p. 291.
[2] *Paths in Utopia*, pp. 11 f., 26, 58 f.
[3] *Ibid.*, pp. 26, 81, 134.

order.' The state must cease to be a *machina machinarum* which 'strangles the individuality of small associations' and must become instead a *communitas communitatum*—a union of communities within which the proper autonomous life of each community can unfold. In this latter form of state the compulsive order that persisted would not be based on the exploitation of human conflicts but would represent the stage of development which had been reached. There is a degree of legitimate compulsion, writes Buber, and this is determined by the degree of incapacity for voluntary right order. In practice, however, the state always greatly exceeds this degree of legitimate compulsion because accumulated power does not abdicate except under necessity. Only the vigorous pressure of those groups that have increased their capacity for voluntary order can force the state to relinquish some measure of its power.[1]

The essential point is to decide on the fundamentals: a restructuring of society as a League of Leagues, and a reduction of the State to its proper function, which is to maintain unity; or a devouring of an amorphous society by the omnipotent State. . . . The right proportion, tested anew every day according to changing conditions, between group-freedom and collective order; or absolute order imposed indefinitely for the sake of an era of freedom alleged to follow 'of its own accord.' [2]

The essential thing which enabled man to emerge from Nature and to assert himself, writes Buber, is, more than his technical efficiency, the fact that he banded together with others in a social life which was at once mutually dependent and independent. The line of human progress up till now has been 'the forming and re-forming of communities on the basis of growing personal independence'—'functional autonomy, mutual recognition and mutual responsibility.' Buber calls this mutual dependence of increasingly free and independent individuals the 'decentralistic social principle.' This principle has been subordinated in the modern world to the 'centralistic political principle,' and modern industrial development and economy have aided this process through creating a struggle of all against all for markets and raw materials. Struggles between whole societies have replaced the old struggles between States. The resulting emphasis on the organization of power has caused democratic forms of society no less than totalitarian forms to make complete submission to centralized power their guiding principle.[3]

'The social vitality of a nation,' writes Buber, 'and its cultural unity and independence as well, depend very largely upon the degree of social spontaneity to be found there.' This social spontaneity is continually threatened and diminished by the fact that the political principle is

---

[1] *Paths in Utopia*, pp. 27, 39 f., 47.   [2] *Ibid.*, p. 148.   [3] *Ibid.*, pp. 129-132.

always stronger in relation to the social principle than the given conditions require.[1] This difference between the strength of the political and the social principles is called the 'political surplus' by Buber and is explained in terms of the difference in nature between 'Administration' and 'Government.'

By Administration we mean a capacity for making dispositions which is limited by the available technical facilities and recognized in theory and practice within those limits; when it oversteps its limits, it seals its own doom. By Government we understand a non-technical, but 'constitutionally' limited body; this signifies that, in the event of certain changes in the situation, the limits are extended and even, at times, wiped out altogether.[2]

The excess in the capacity for making dispositions beyond that required by given conditions is what we understand by political power, and the measure of this excess, the 'political surplus,' represents the difference between Administration and Government. This political surplus cannot be determined exactly, nor can it be done away with entirely, for it depends upon the latent state of crisis between nations and within every nation. As long as this latent crisis exists, the state must have that excess of decision which will make possible special powers in the event that the crisis becomes active. Nevertheless, even in this situation a movement toward righting the balance in the direction of the social principle is possible. 'Efforts must be renewed again and again to determine in what spheres it is possible to alter the ratio between governmental and administrative control in favour of the latter.' The change in the apportionment of power in the direction of decentralization must be accompanied by a continuous change in the nature of power, and political Government transformed into social Administration as far as the particular conditions permit.[3]

The continued supremacy of the centralistic political principle, however, is in general assured by the negative nature of the present peace and the preparation for new war. The unifying power of the state rests primarily on this general instability and not on the punitive and propagandistic facilties at the state's disposal. It is necessary, therefore, that we begin the social restructuring of society with the establishment of a true, positive, and creative peace between peoples. This peace cannot be attained through political organization, writes Buber, but through 'the resolute will of all peoples to cultivate the territories and raw materials of our planet and govern its inhabitants, together.'[4]

If, instead of the prevailing anarchical relationships among nations, there were co-operation in the control of raw materials,

[1] 'Society and the State,' p. 11 f.   [2] *Ibid.*
[3] *Ibid.*, p. 12.   [4] *Ibid.*, p. 11; *Paths in Utopia*, p. 132.

agreement on methods of manufacture of such materials, and regulation of the world market, Society would be in a position, for the first time, to constitute itself as such.[1]

The great danger in such planetary production is that it will result in 'a gigantic centralization of power' which will devour all free community. If international co-operation is to lead to true world peace, it must rest on the base of a confederation of commonwealths all of which are in turn based on 'the actual and communal life of big and little groups living and working together.' [2]

Everything depends on whether the collectivity into whose hands the control of the means of production passes will facilitate and promote in its very structure and in all its institutions the genuine common life of the various groups composing it . . . on whether centralist representation only goes as far as the new order of things absolutely demands.[3]

This is not a question of either-or, but of an unwearying scrutiny which will draw ever anew the right line of demarcation between those spheres which must be centralized and those which can be reserved to the autonomous regulation of the individual communities. The larger the measure of autonomy granted to local, regional, and functional groups, the more room will be left for the free unfolding of social energies.[4]

The excess power of the state cannot be destroyed by revolution, for it is the result of a relationship between men which makes the coercive order necessary and, in particular, the weakness of those communal groups which could force the state to yield this excess power. The creation and renewal of a real organic structure itself destroys the state and replaces superfluous compulsion. 'Any action . . . beyond this would be illegitimate and bound to miscarry because . . . it would lack the constructive spirit necessary for further advance.' Revolutions are tragically destined to produce the opposite of their positive goal so long as this goal has not taken shape in society before the revolution.

In the social as opposed to the political sphere, revolution is not so much a creative as a delivering force whose function is to set free and authenticate . . . it can only perfect, set free, and lend the stamp of authority to something that has already been foreshadowed in the womb of the pre-revolutionary society.[5]

The real way for society to prepare the ground for improving the relations between itself and the political principle, according to Buber,

[1] 'Society and the State,' p. 11. [2] *Paths in Utopia*, p. 132 f.
[3] *Ibid.*, p. 133 f. [4] *Ibid.*, p. 134; 'Society and the State,' p. 12.
[5] *Paths in Utopia*, pp. 44–48.

Social Philosophy

is 'social education.' Social education seeks to arouse and develop the spontaneity of fellowship which is 'innate in all unravaged souls' and which is entirely harmonious with the development of personal existence and personal thought. This can only be accomplished, however, by the complete overthrow of the political trend which nowadays dominates education. True education for citizenship in a state is not education for politics but 'education for the effectuation of Society.' [1] Politics does not change social conditions. It only registers and sanctions changes that have taken place.[2]

III

'"Utopian" socialism regards the various forms of Co-operative Society as being the most important cells for social re-structure,' writes Buber. This does not mean that consumer and producer co-operatives in their present form can serve that purpose, for the co-operative movement has not developed in the direction of an organic alliance of production and consumption in a comprehensive communal form or a true federation of local societies. Instead the consumer co-operatives have tended to become large-scale, capitalistic bureaucracies, and the producers co-operatives have become specialized and impersonal or have succumbed to the temptation of getting others to work for them. Consumer co-operatives are least suited to act as cells for social reconstruction because common purchasing 'brings people together with only a minimal and highly impersonal part of their being.' Buber finds the remedy for these deficiencies in what he calls the 'Full Co-operative' (*Vollgenossenschaft*). The Full Co-operative at its best combines production and consumption, industry and agriculture in a co-operative community centring around commonly-held land. Although less widespread and successful than the consumer and producer co-operatives, these Full Co-operatives have existed in many places as an outgrowth of consumer or producer co-operatives or as separate communal experiments.[3]

Full Co-operatives have usually been unsuccessful, writes Buber, fo they have often been built on the flimsy base of sentiment or the in flexible base of dogma. Common sentiment is not enough to hold community together, and dogma results in the paralysis, isolation, c fragmentation of a community. Moreover, unlike consumer co-oper tives which grew out of local needs, they have often taken their point departure from an abstract idea or theory without reference to giv localities and their demands. For this reason they have lacked the ba for federation which the consumer co-operatives possessed through t

---

[1] 'Society and the State,' p. 12.
[2] *Israel and Palestine, op. cit.*, p. 140.
[3] *Paths in Utopia*, pp. 61-67, 78 f., 81.

215

identity of local problems in different places. A third reason for the
failure of these communal experiments, or 'Colonial' Full Co-operatives
is their isolation from society and from each other. This isolation can
be remedied by federation of the communities with each other, for
federation makes up for the smallness of communal groups by enabling
members to pass from one settlement to another and by allowing the
groups to complement and help each other. Furthermore, because of
the need for markets for their surplus production, the refusal of youth
to be cut off from the outside world, and the need to influence the
surrounding world, it is important that these communities maintain
some real, if variable, relation with society at large.[1]

The most powerful effort in the direction of Full Co-operatives, in
Buber's opinion, has been the Village Communes which have taken the
form of an organic union of agriculture, industry, and the handicrafts
and of communal production and consumption. The modern communal village possesses a latent pervasive force which could spread to
the towns if further technological developments facilitate and actually
require the decentralization of industry. Already many countries show
significant beginnings in the direction of organically transforming the
town and turning it into an aggregate composed of smaller units.

The most promising experiment in the Village Commune, according
to Buber, has been that of the Jewish communes in Palestine. These
have been based on the needs of given local situation rather than on
abstract ideas and theories. At the same time they have not been limited
to the purely topical but have combined it with ideal motives inspired
by socialistic and Biblical teachings on social justice. The members of
these communes have combined a rare willingness to experiment and
critical self-awareness with an 'amazingly positive relationship—
amounting to a regular faith— . . . to the inmost being of their
Commune.' The communes themselves, moreover, have worked together in close co-operation and at the same time have left complete
freedom for the constant branching off of new forms and different types
of social structure, the most famous of which are the *kvuza* and the
kibbuz. 'Nowhere, as far as I see, in the history of the Socialist movement,' writes Buber, 'were men so deeply involved in the process of
differentiation and yet so intent on preserving the principle of integration.' [2]

The rapid influx of Jewish refugees into Palestine has resulted in many
cases in the rise of a quasi-elite who have not been able to provide true
leadership for the communes and have come into conflict with the
genuine *chaluzim.* The failure of the quasi-*chaluzim* lies not in their
relationship to the idea, to the community, or to their work, but in
their relationship to their fellows. This is not a question of intimacy

[1] *Paths in Utopia*, pp. 71-74, 79.   [2] *Ibid.*, pp. 140-148.

such as exists in the small *kvuza* and is lost in the big. It is rather a question of openness.

A real community need not consist of people who are perpetually together; but it must consist of people who, precisely because they are comrades, have mutual access to one another and are ready for one another. . . . The internal questions of a community are thus in reality questions relating to its own genuineness, hence to its inner strength and stability.[1]

Despite an inadequate development of neighbourly relationship between the communes, Buber feels that the Jewish communes are of central significance in the struggle for a structurally new society in which individual groups will be given the greatest possible autonomy and yet will enjoy the greatest possible interrelationship with each other. This picture of the socialist restructuring of society is based on the awareness of an underlying trend toward social renewal—a trend which is not at present dominant but has the potentiality of becoming so. This trend 'is thoroughly topical and constructive,' Buber writes. The changes at which it aims are feasible in the given circumstances and with the means at its disposal. Of equal importance, it is based on an eternal human need: 'the need of man to feel his own house as a room in some greater, all-embracing structure in which he is at home, to feel that the other inhabitants of it with whom he lives and works are all acknowledging and confirming his individual existence.'[2] The decision between the centralistic socialism of political power and the spontaneous socialism of genuine social change is, for this reason, the most important decision of the next generation. 'The coming state of humanity in the great crisis,' said Buber in 1952, 'depends very much on whether another type of socialism can be set up against Moscow, and I venture even today to call it Jerusalem.'[3]

IV

Commenting on Buber's social philosophy, Paul Pfuetze writes:

It seems to be a remedy which . . . cannot be taken by the patient until he is already well. Communities incorporating the I-Thou attitude and the Utopian socialism of Buber cannot be manufactured to order—except perhaps in a small new land like modern Israel, or at certain plastic points within the established order, there to work as yeast in the lump.[4]

---

[1] *Ibid.*, p. 143 ff.   [2] *Ibid.*, p. 139 f.
[3] From an address on Israel given by Professor Buber at the Jewish Theological Seminary of America in New York City, April 1, 1952.
[4] *The Social Self, op. cit.*, p. 347 f.

Pfuetze's comment is not so much a criticism of Buber's social philosophy as a reminder of the difficulties which would attend the attempt to apply it in any large-scale industrial society, difficulties Buber himself would be the first to recognize. Buber is not advocating a simple substitution of one social structure for another but a direction of movement, a 'restructuring.' He is not advocating simple decentralization, but the greatest measure of decentralization compatible with the need of the state to maintain unity. Nor does he suggest that this social restructuring will come about through any revolution or merely political change, but through social education—'the education of a generation with a truly social outlook and a truly social will.' [1] In this connection, as we have seen, Buber redefines education for citizenship as education for the effectuation of society, or the social principle. This redefinition of true citizenship is of particular significance at the present time when 'citizenship' is almost universally regarded as a purely political virtue. Not only the blind loyalty of the totalitarian conception of citizenship and the compulsory conformity of the democracies, but even the exclusive emphasis of the liberal on the citizenship of political organization and votes serves to increase the power of the centralized state and to strengthen the political principle at the expense of the social. This diminution of social spontaneity has grown to such a degree in our time that education throughout the world is dominated by the political trend and society is generally politicized.

> The crucial thing here was not that the State, particularly in its more or less totalitarian forms, weakened and gradually displaced the free associations, but that the political principle with all its centralistic features percolated into the associations themselves, modifying their structure and their whole inner life, and thus politicized society to an ever-increasing extent.[2]

It is this domination of the political principle that stands in the way of recognizing the realistic significance of Buber's social philosophy. That a genuine social revolution can only take place from below will first become convincingly clear, writes Heinz-Joachim Heydorn, when we are able to free ourselves from the predominance of a purely political thought that does not understand the long-term problems of our modern life.

Buber's inquiries represent, in my opinion, the most important contribution that has been made in many years to the question of socialism. Here the basic question of all renewal is posed once again: the question about man. But this question remains closely

---

[1] 'Society and the State,' p. 12.
[2] *Ibid.*, p. 11 f.; *Paths in Utopia*, p. 131.

bound to reality; it is concerned with man in his present-day form, with man in our time. The reality in which this man lives, the reality of his technical greatness, has barred him in growing measure from the true road to himself. We shall not be able to re-open this road for him if we wish to redeem him through purely political means without restoring to him the immediacy of his existence.[1]

A significant confirmation of Buber's social philosophy is contained in Kurt Riezler's article, 'What Is Public Opinion?' Riezler defines public opinion as the concern of an I and a You about 'what They, the others, taken collectively, are thinking and saying,' and he defines society itself as a growing and changing group based on the mutual response of I and Thou. 'I and Thou,' he writes, 'are the eternal cell of any living body social.' He uses the term 'response' as including genuine responsibility, listening as well as speaking, and an element of possible surprise—all in clear contrast to 'the general interest in salesmanship, the worship of efficiency for its own sake,' and 'the emphasis of psychological schools on stimuli, conditioned responses and the manipulation of emotions.' These emphases 'conjoin in inflating the concept of propaganda and allow the simple fact of Adam's and Eve's mutual response . . . to fall into scholarly oblivion.' This mutual response is the real cohesive force of society, for when a crisis comes it is this which is tested: 'Only a response of honesty to honesty can re-establish the common ground, face the facts, revise the assumptions, and keep the society flexible enough to withstand the storm.'[2]

This flexibility is endangered by the formation of large social groups which receive their opinions ready made and cease to communicate with one another. Such cleavages are the inevitable result of the mass society of our age. If they grow and 'split the society on a nationwide scale into parts that no longer understand one another's language, the free society faces its doom.' This is just what took place in Germany, Riezler points out, years before Hitler captured the machinery of the state.[3] He concludes:

> Only if and in so far as the mass society of the industrial age can be and remain a universe of mutual response, in which responsive and responsible people respond to one another in matters of common concern, will this mass society remain a society . . . mutual response must exist in an understandable form between those who know and those who do not know; the former must call for and listen to the latter's response.[4]

[1] Heydorn, 'Martin Buber und der Sozialismus,' *op. cit.*, p. 709 (my translation).
[2] Kurt Riezler, 'What Is Public Opinion?', *Social Research*, XI (1944), pp. 398-415.
[3] *Ibid.*, p. 418 ff.   [4] *Ibid.*, p. 426.

The conclusion to be drawn from Riezler's treatment of public opinion is that true community must be re-established in mass society if that society is to remain a free one which serves the people. Thus Buber's restructuring of society into genuine communities, however 'impractical' it may seem, is a necessity toward which we must work. This does not mean any optimism about the ease with which Buber's social philosophy can be applied. On the contrary, to turn one's face in the right direction is to see how far we have to go. The dominance of the social principle over the political cannot be achieved through any rearrangement of existing relations but only through really changed relations within and between communities.

Here not only the present mass structure of individual nations stands in the way but also the relations between nations. Faith in dialogue is perhaps the one antidote to the fear which makes us see a country with an ideology different from our own as the alien, the 'other,' which has to be destroyed in order that we can live in a truly 'human' world, that is, a world dominated solely by our own 'world-view' or ego-perspective. Yet no faith in dialogue can be genuinely founded unless it includes the whole man, with all of his irrationality and 'evil impulses,' as the bearer of this dialogue. Nor can it be genuinely founded if it thinks in terms of the 'dialogue' between states rather than between peoples, between the representatives of states rather than between the responsible and tested leaders of genuine communities. What is more, as Buber has pointed out, the resumption of true dialogue between peoples will only be possible when the existential mistrust which divides the world into two hostile camps is overcome. Commenting on Robert Maynard Hutchins' call for a Civilization of the Dialogue which can be attained when we induce the other party to talk through 'exhibiting an interest in and a comprehension of what he might say if he were willing to speak,' [1] Buber writes:

> Nothing stands so much in the way of the rise of a Civilization of Dialogue as the demonic power which rules our world, the demonry of basic mistrust. What does it help to induce the other to speak if basically one puts no faith in what he says? The meeting with him already takes place under the perspective of his untrustworthiness. And this perspective is not incorrect, for his meeting with me takes place under a corresponding perspective.[2]

'The factual life of factual men,' writes Buber, 'is smeared and crusted over with the varnish of political fiction.' Some of the reproaches which

---

[1] Robert Maynard Hutchins, 'Goethe and the Unity of Mankind,' *Goethe and the Modern Age*, ed. by Arnold Bergstraesser (Chicago: Henry Regnery, 1950) p. 399 f.

[2] 'Hope for This Hour,' *op. cit.*

the one side hurls at the other are realistic enough, he adds, but in order for this reality to be regarded concretely it must first be freed from its incrustation of catchwords. In the closed sphere of the exclusively political there is no way to penetrate to the factual nor to relieve the present situation. 'Its "natural end" is the technically perfect suicide of the human race.' It is just this powerlessness of politics which must be recognized today before it is too late, and it must be recognized by men who will come together out of the camps and will talk with one another, despite their criticism of the opposing system and their loyalty to their own. If these men will begin to speak with one another not as pawns on a chessboard but as they themselves in the chamber of human reality, a tiny seed of change will have been started which could lead to a transformation of the whole situation.

I mean especially just those who are basically convinced of the rightness of the idea from which their government ultimately stems and know, just for that reason, that the catastrophe which would flow from the victory of the regime would mean the collapse of the idea.[1]

If men such as these arise, they will have behind them an unorganized group for whom they speak. Although they will be 'independent persons with no other authority than that of the spirit,' they may yet be effective in the time that approaches as no merely political representatives can be. Unlike the latter, they will not be bound by the aims of the hour and hence will be able to distinguish between the true and the exaggerated needs of their own and other people. When they have sifted out of the alleged amount of antagonisms the real conflicts between genuine needs, they will be ready to move toward a settlement of those conflicts on the base of the fundamental question: What does every man need in order to live as man? 'If the globe is not to burst asunder,' writes Buber, those who stand in the authority of the spirit must come to one another out of the camps and dare to deal with this question in terms of the whole planet. There is one front of such men, writes Buber, the representatives of a true humanity who fight together even without knowing it, each in his own place. Only through genuine dialogue between them in which each of the partners, even when he stands in opposition to the other, attends to, affirms, and confirms him as this existing other, 'can the opposition, certainly not be removed from the world, but be humanly arbitrated and led toward its overcoming.'[2]

[1] Martin Buber, 'Abstrakt und Konkret,' *Hinweise, op. cit.*, p. 327 ff., an additional note to 'Hoffnung für diese Stunde,' the German original of 'Hope for This Hour.' 'Hoffnung für diese Stunde' was published in *Hinweise*, pp. 313-326.

[2] *Pointing the Way*, 'Genuine Dialogue and the Possibilities of Peace,' 'Hope for This Hour,' 'Validity and Limitation of the Political Principle (1953).

Social Philosophy

SUPPLEMENTARY NOTE (1959): For an important statement by Buber on the problem of Jewish-Arab co-operation in the Near East see his essay, 'Israel and the Command of the Spirit,' trans. by Maurice Friedman, *Congress Weekly*, XXV, No. 14 (Sept. 8, 1958), p. 10 ff. On international relations in general see Buber's statement in the 'Hydrogen Cobalt Bomb' special issue of *Pulpit Digest*, XXXIV, No. 194 (June 1954), p. 36, and Irwin Ross's interview with Buber in the New York *Post*, Vol. 156, No. 300 (November 7, 1957), M2, 'Voice of the Sages,' Article II. In an address at Cambridge University on June 5, 1958 Dag Hammarskjold, the Secretary General of the United Nations, echoes Buber's call for renewed 'contact and communications across geographical and political boundaries.' Hammarskjold quotes at length from Buber's statement on unmasking in *Pointing the Way*, 'Hope for This Hour,' p. 223 f., referring to Buber as 'one of the influential thinkers of our time whose personal history and national experience have given him a vantage point of significance.' (United Nations Press Release SG/684, June 5, 1958.) In a recent press conference Secretary General Hammarskjold announced his intention of translating into Swedish some of the essays from the 'Politics, Community, and Peace' section of *Pointing the Way*. 'I think that Martin Buber has made a major contribution' in these essays, said Hammarskjold, 'and I would like to make that more broadly known.' (Note to Correspondents # 1934, February 5, 1959, p. 5.)

Although Reinhold Niebuhr considers Buber the greatest living Jewish Philosopher, he is, in contrast to Hammarskjold, highly critical of Buber's social philosophy. In his review of *Pointing the Way* Niebuhr suggests that Buber's thought becomes utopian when its illuminating insights into personal life are applied to the relations of the 'we' and 'they' of organized groups or nations. (*New York Times Book Review*, April 13, 1958.) In a letter to me of June 22, 1956, Niebuhr writes: 'Personal relations exist in transcendence over the basic structure of society, which is partly organic and partly an artifact . . . insofar as the justice, particularly in modern technical society, depends upon artfully constructed equilibria of power.' To this Buber replied in two letters to me: 'There is indeed a norm of justice. . . . But man tends to accept and to realise this norm only in general and abstract laws . . . and without justice in personal relations justice becomes poisonous.' (July 1956.) 'What Niebuhr calls the basic structure of society is . . . based on personal relations, and where it subdues them it becomes wrong. As to modern technical society, of course it depends upon "artfully constructed equilibria of power," but what depends on them is its order and not its justice. . . . I cannot see the God-willed reality of justice anywhere other than in "being just," and this means of course: being just as far as it is possible here and now, under the "artful" conditions of actual society. . . . Sometimes, striving to be just, I go on in the dark, till my head meets the wall and aches, and then I know: Here is the wall, and I cannot go further. But I could not know it beforehand, nor otherwise.' (November 29. 1956.) The political order embodies justice in the sense of making it possible and of putting limits on the practice of injustice. But real justice does not exist until men actually make use of the foundation and material provided by this impersonal political order to build just relationships in concrete situations. (This correspondence between Buber and Niebuhr will be published in Maurice Friedman, ed., 'Martin Buber' section, *Interrogations of Contemporary Philosophers*, ed. by Sidney C. Rome. New Haven: Yale Univ. Press. 1960.)

PART SIX
BETWEEN MAN AND GOD

CHAPTER TWENTY-FOUR

SYMBOL, MYTH, AND HISTORY

THE ETERNAL THOU AS RELIGIOUS SYMBOL

ONE of the aspects of Buber's thought on God which is most difficult to understand is his characterization of God as an 'Absolute Person,' as Being which becomes Person in order to know and be known, to love and be loved by man. This concept decisively sets Buber off from those mystics who look at the ground of being as impersonal Godhead and regard God as only the personal manifestation of this ground. It seems to the impersonalist and the mystic that Buber is limiting God, for they think of personality as limitation and the Eternal Thou as a designation for God as He is in Himself. What Buber really means is made unmistakably clear in 'Religion and Philosophy,' in which he speaks of Buddha's relation to the 'Unborn, Unoriginated, Uncreated' as an I-Thou relation because Buddha stands essentially related to it with his whole being.

> The personal manifestation of the divine is not decisive for the genuineness of religion. What is decisive is that I relate myself to the divine as to Being which is over against me, though *not* over against me *alone*.[1]

Thus the 'Eternal Thou' is not a symbol of God but of our relation with God. What is more, no real symbol of God is possible for we do not know Him as He is in Himself!

It is indeed legitimate to speak of the person of God within the religious relation and in its language; but in so doing we are making no essential statement about the Absolute which reduces it to the personal. We are rather saying that it enters into the relationship as the Absolute Person whom we call God. One may understand the personality of God as His act—it is, indeed, even permissible for

---

[1] *Eclipse of God, op. cit.,* p. 39 f.

225

the believer to believe that God became a person for love of him, because in our human mode of existence the only reciprocal relation with us that exists is a personal one.[1]

Some critics, on the other hand, point to just such statements as the above to assert that Buber is really still a mystic postulating an impersonal, monistic ground of being.[2] That they do so is, in my opinion, because they misunderstand the meaning of personality to the extent of thinking of it as an objective description of a being taken for himself rather than as something that exists in relation and pre-eminently in the relation between God and man. Because, at least in part, they think of personality as objective, they hope to safeguard God's personality, or His personal relations with man, by limiting His nature to the personal alone. The Biblical God, on whom they base this limitation, is actually the imageless God, the God who manifests Himself in nature and in history but cannot be limited to any of these manifestations.

It is not necessary to know something about God in order really to believe in Him: many true believers know how to talk *to* God but not *about* Him. If one dares to turn toward the unknown God, to go to meet Him, to call to Him, Reality is present.[3]

Thus Buber walks the narrow ridge between the mystic and the non-mystic, between one who asserts unity with the ground of being and the other who either removes God into the transcendence beyond direct relation or limits Him to objective 'personal' existence.

To the metaphysician, and particularly to the Whiteheadian metaphysician, it cannot be comprehensible that Buber speaks of God as an Absolute Person, for a person is in relation and therefore is limited and in that sense relative. Yet it is precisely on this paradox that Buber rests his thought. To speak of God as the Eternal Thou, as Being in relation to Becoming, is to express the same paradox. Whitehead is similar to Buber in his emphasis upon the concrete meeting between God and the world as opposed to the valuation of the abstract unity of God. Like Buber, too, he conceives of the redemption of evil as taking place through the relation and mutual love of God and the world. He differs from Buber, however, in that he is less concerned with *our* relation to God than with the generic relation of God to creatures; relation in the end is for him an objective matter—I-It rather than I-Thou. Moreover, Whitehead does not emphasize, as does Buber, that God is transcendent as well as immanent, absolute as well as in relation. Though God and

---

[1] *Eclipse of God*, 'Religion and Ethics,' p. 126 f.

[2] Cf. E. La B. Cherbonnier, 'The Theology of the Word of God,' *Journal of Religion*, XXXIII, No. 1 (January 1953), 28 f.

[3] *Eclipse of God*, 'Religion and Philosophy,' p. 40.

the world are, for Whitehead, opposites, they complete one another through a flowing dialectical interaction which lacks the marked polar tension of Buber's 'meeting' or 'over-againstness.'[1] Buber thus stands at a half-way point between Whitehead and Kierkegaard, having greater tension and paradox than Whitehead but less tension and more direct relation than Kierkegaard. He agrees with Kierkegaard in his rejection of the religion of immanence, but he does not consider the subjective relation to the transcendent a paradox or absurdity, as does Kierkegaard in the *Concluding Unscientific Postscript*, for his I-Thou category includes both inwardness and relation.[2]

This problem of the immanence and transcendence of God is an especially vexatious one, and here too Buber walks the narrow ridge. That not many others walk with him on this ridge is suggested by the fact that Karl Heim and Melville Channing-Pearce make use of Buber's thought to point to the unqualified transcendence of God, while J. B. Coates writes, 'I find the experience of Buber's "I-Thou" world a convincing demonstration of divine immanence'! Gogarten stresses the 'otherness' of the divine Thou, Marcel and Nédoncelle the togetherness, making the I-Thou relation into a 'we.'[3] Buber himself denies that God is either merely immanent or merely transcendent.

> Of course God is the 'wholly Other'; but He is also the wholly Same, the wholly Present. Of course He is the *Mysterium Tremendum* that appears and overthrows; but He is also the mystery of the self-evident, nearer to me than my I.[4]

Romano Guardini, very possibly under Buber's influence, makes use of this same terminology of God as at once 'the other' and 'the same,' other than man but not hostile or alien, the same as man but not

---

[1] Alfred North Whitehead, *Religion in the Making* (New York: The Macmillan Co., 1946), pp. 90-100, 150-160; Whitehead, *Process and Reality, An Essay in Cosmology* (New York: The Macmillan Co., 1929), pp. 521-532. For a further comparison of Buber and Whitehead cf. Hugo Bergmann, 'Der Physiker Whitehead,' *Die Kreatur*, Berlin, Vol. II (1927-28), pp. 356-362, especially p. 361 ff., and Maurice Friedman, *Martin Buber: Mystic, Existentialist, Social Prophet. op. cit.*, pp. 326-331, 428. Cf. Charles Hartshorne, 'Buber's Metaphysics,' *The Philosophy of Martin Buber, loc. cit.*

[2] For an extended comparison between Buber and Kierkegaard's *Concluding Unscientific Postscript* see again my dissertation, *Martin Buber, op. cit.*, Appendix.

[3] Note A, pp. 539-543. Cf. also Maringer, p. 122, 'Anmerkungen 12.' VI. Heim, *Glaube und Denken* and *God Transcendent;* Nicodemus, *Renascence;* Coates, *The Crisis of the Human Person, op. cit.*, p. 244 f.; Gogarten, *Ich glaube an den dreieinigen Gott;* Marcel, *Journal Métaphysique, op. cit.*, Part II. especially pp. 170, 293 f.; Nédoncelle, *La Reciprocité des Consciences, op. cit.*, especially Part I—'La Communion des Consciences' and chap. iii—'La Découverte de l'Absolu Divin.' [4] *I and Thou*, p. 79.

identical.[1] J. E. Fison, under Buber's influence, also shows a clear grasp of the narrow ridge between transcendence and immanence:

> The antithesis of either God objective and apart from us or else God subjective and a part of us needs to be overcome in the higher and deeper synthesis towards which Professor Buber points with his emphasis on the I-Thou relationship of meeting.[2]

In the light of Buber's clear statement of this middle position, it is strange to find John Baillie criticizing him for making God 'Wholly Other' and too simply Thou and not I.[3] Baillie's criticism is perhaps based on the confusion of Buber's Eternal Thou with a symbol of God as He is in Himself. Even though God is within us as well as outside us, we must still relate to him as Thou. His Thou-ness by no means implies simple transcendence, for if God were simply transcendent we could have no relation to Him at all. He would then be merely a hostile and terrifying 'Other' or some Gnostic divinity entirely cut off from our world and our life.

This same misunderstanding has been expressed in connection with the problem of whether the reciprocity of man and God in the I-Thou relationship must necessarily imply an equality that denies man's creatureliness and discourages the humility which man should have before God. Guardini, Maurice Nédoncelle, and H. H. Farmer have convincingly shown that reciprocity does not imply equality, as has Buber himself. Gogarten and Cullberg have taken the contrary view and have sought to protect the distance between man and God by positing God as the subject and man the object, God as always the I and man as always the Thou. This denial of reciprocity and this equation of the Thou with the object both constitute a fundamental distortion of the I-Thou relationship which takes from it much of its meaning. For Buber, in contrast, the mystery of creation implies that God gives man the independent existence and real spontaneity that enable him to recognize himself as an I and to say Thou to God. A genuinely reciprocal relationship demands that man regard himself not as an object of God's thought but as a really free person—a partner in dialogue.[4]

Our relation to the Eternal Thou is perhaps best understood from the nature of the demand which one person makes on another if the two of them really meet. The demand is not, as Gogarten would say, that the I

---

[1] Guardini, *Welt und Person, op. cit.*, chap. iii—'Gott und "der Andere",' pp. 23-29.

[2] Fison, *The Blessing of the Holy Spirit, op. cit.*, p. 23.

[3] Baillie, *Our Knowledge of God, op. cit.*, pp. 233-239.

[4] Guardini, *Welt und Person*, pp. 23-29, 111-114; Nédoncelle, pp. 86-109; Herbert H. Farmer, *The World and God, op. cit.*, pp. 23-31, 60-66, 97 f., 201 f.; *Eclipse of God*, 'Religion and Ethics,' p. 138. Cf. my review of Abraham J. Heschel's *Man Is Not Alone* in the *Journal of Religion*, October 1951.

choose between the I and the Thou and give up his own self for the other. Rather it is the demand of the relationship itself—the demand that if you are to meet me, you must become as much of a person as I am. God places on man an unconditional demand. In order to remain open to God, he must change in his whole being. This demand makes more comprehensible God's double aspect of love and justice: judgment is the individual's judgment of himself when he cuts himself off from relationship with God. This 'judgment of his non-existence,' as Buber calls it, does not mean that God ceases to love him.

This emphasis on reciprocity in no way jeopardizes true humility before God, but an undue emphasis on humility does jeopardize reciprocity. True humility means that one sees oneself as addressed with one's very life and one's life task as that of responding to this address. False humility goes beyond this and denies the reality of the address and the response by denying the reality of the self and of man's freedom to answer or remain silent. For this reason, an undue emphasis on humility actually becomes a form of not responding to God. It allows a man the illusion that he is escaping from the burden of freedom and responsibility, and it thus destroys true personal relationship. In the end these two must go together—genuine reciprocity and utter humility. On the narrow ridge of their togetherness the man of faith walks, avoiding the abyss of self-affirmation on the one hand and self-denial on the other.

Everyone must have two pockets, so that he can reach into the one or the other, according to his needs. In his right pocket are to be the words: 'For my sake was the world created,' and in his left: 'I am dust and ashes.' [1]

THE SYMBOL AND THE CONCRETE

Buber's I-Thou philosophy implies a radical reversal of the idealist and mystical attitude toward symbolism which sees the symbol as the concrete manifestation of some universal if not directly knowable reality. For Buber the meaning of the symbol is found not in its universality but in the fact that it points to a concrete event which witnesses just as it is, in all its concreteness, transitoriness, and uniqueness, to the relation with the Absolute. The symbol does, of course, become abstract when it is detached from a concrete event. But this is a metamorphosis of the central content of the symbol, a metamorphosis which deprives the symbol of its real meaning just by giving it the all-meaning of the 'universal' and the 'spiritual.' This all-meaning is always only a substitute for the meaning apprehended in the concrete. It never really means

---

[1] A Hasidic saying from *Ten Rungs, op. cit.*, p. 106.

a particular time, a particular place, and a particular event happening to individuals in all their uniqueness. Symbolic events are instead regarded as merely manifestations of the universal and hence as not having meaning in themselves but only to the extent that they have lost their particularity.

Here we have again the distinction between the I-It relation which leads back to the reality of I-Thou and that which obstructs the entrance into I-Thou, the distinction between religion which sees meaning as the bond between the Absolute and the concrete and philosophy which sees it as the bond between the Absolute and the universal. The true symbol, as Buber understands it, is that which derives from and points back to the concrete relationship.

> It does not belong to the nature of symbols to hover timelessly over concrete actualities. Whenever the symbol appears, it owes its appearance always to the unforeseen, unique, occasion, to its having appeared the first time. The symbol derives its enduring character from a transitory event. . . . For the image of the un-broken meaning . . . serves always in the first instance our born, mortal body—everything else is only repetition, simplification, imitation. . . . The covenant which the Absolute enters into with the concrete, not heeding the general, the 'idea,' . . . chooses movements made by the human figure. . . . And this sign endures. It may lose in immediate validity, in 'evidential value,' but it may also renew itself out of later human existence, which accomplishes anew.[1]

Because the symbol means the covenant between the Absolute and the concrete, its meaning is not independent of lived human life in all its concreteness. Not only does this lived concreteness originally produce the symbol, but only this can renew its meaning for those who have inherited it and save it from becoming merely spiritual and not truly existential.

> All symbols are ever in danger of becoming spiritual, and not binding images, instead of remaining real signs sent into life; all sacraments are ever in danger of becoming plain experiences, levelled down to the 'religious' plane, instead of remaining the incarnate connection between what is above and what is below. Only through the man who devotes himself is the original power saved for further present existence.[2]

The highest manifestation of the symbol is, in fact, a human life lived in relation to the Absolute. The prophets were symbols in that sense, for

---

[1] *Hasidism, op. cit.,* 'Symbolical and Sacramental Existence in Judaism,' p. 117 f.
[2] *Ibid.,* p. 118.

God does not merely speak through their mouths, as through the Greek oracle or prophet, but *the whole human being* is for Him a mouth. Passivity and activity, possession and speech, go together here in 'one single, inclusive function, and the undivided person is necessary to establish the indivisible function.'[1]

MYTH

The most concrete and dramatic form of the symbol is the myth. To such writers as C. G. Jung and Ananda K. Coomaraswamy the myth is an embodiment in different forms and cultures of a perennial reality, the spiritual process whereby the one becomes the many and the many returns unto the one or the psychological process whereby integration of the personality is achieved and the divine Self realized within the unconscious.[2] In his early thinking Buber also thought of myth as a particular manifestation of a universal mystical reality. Yet by 1907 he was already developing in a different direction by distinguishing between the 'pure myth' in which there is variety without differentiation and the 'legend' in which the subject is divided and God and the hero or saint stand opposed to one another as I and Thou.[3] In 1921 he expanded and developed this concept into a distinction between myth, saga, and legend. Myth is the expression of a world in which the divine and the human live next to and in one another; saga is the expression of a world in which they are no longer intertwined and man already begins to sense with a shudder what is over against him; legend expresses a world in which the separation is completed, but now a dialogue and interchange takes place from sphere to sphere and it is of this that the myth tells.[4]

Since *Ich und Du* (1923) Buber's dialogical understanding of myth has become increasingly clear. 'Real myth,' he wrote in 1950, 'is the expression, not of an imaginative state of mind or of mere feeling, but of a real meeting of two Realities.'[5] Myth is not a human narrative of a one-sided divine manifestation, as Buber once thought, but a 'mythization' of the memory of the meeting between God and man. Some myths contain within themselves the nexus of a concrete historical event

[1] *Ibid.*, pp. 118-123; *The Prophetic Faith, op. cit.*, p. 112 f.
[2] Cf. Jung, *Modern Man in Search of a Soul* (1933), *Psychology and Religion* (1938), *The Integration of the Personality* (1940); Ananda K. Coomaraswamy, *Hinduism and Buddhism*.
[3] Foreword to *Die Legende des Baalschem, op. cit.*
[4] *Der grosse Maggid und seine Nachfolge, op. cit.*, 'Vorwort,' p. v f.
[5] Introductory note by Buber, written in 1950, to Martin Buber, 'Myth in Judaism,' trans. by Ralph Manheim, *Commentary*, Vol. IX (June 1950), p. 565 f. For the original of this essay see 'Der Mythos der Juden,' in *Vom Geist des Judentums, op. cit.*, also reprinted in *Reden über das Judentum, op. cit.*

experienced by a group or by an individual while many have lost their historical character and contain only the symbolic expression of a universal experience of man. To this latter class belong the Jewish and Zoroastrian myths of the origin of evil which Buber uses to illustrate his anthropological treatment of good and evil. He writes concerning them: 'We are dealing here, as Plato already knew, with truths such as can be communicated adequately to the generality of mankind only in the form of myths.' [1] It is important to recognize, however, that even here countless concrete meetings of I and Thou have attained symbolic expression in the relatively abstract form. It is just this in fact which gives these myths their universality and profundity. Because these myths are products of actual human experience, they tell us something of the structure of human reality which nothing else can tell us.[2]

Buber's characterization of myth as a product of the I-Thou relation finds significant support in the thought of two important modern writers on myth, Ernst Cassirer and Henri Frankfort. Buber's distinction between the I-It and the I-Thou relations is closely similar to Cassirer's distinction between 'discursive' and 'mythical' thinking. Discursive thinking, writes Cassirer, denotes what has already been noticed. It classifies into groups and synthesizes parts into a whole. It does not contemplate a particular case but instead gives it a fixed intellectual 'meaning' and definite character through linking it with other cases into a general framework of knowledge. The particular is never important in itself but only in terms of its relation to this framework. Mythical thought, on the contrary, is not concerned with relating data but with a sudden intuition, an immediate experience in which it comes to rest. 'The immediate content . . . so fills his consciousness that nothing else can exist beside and apart from it.' This content 'is not merely viewed and contemplated, but overcomes a man in sheer immediacy.' [3]

This similarity between mythical thinking and the I-Thou relation is made explicit through Professor (and Mrs.) Frankfort's use of Buber's distinction between I-It and I-Thou, their identification of myth with the dynamically reciprocal I-Thou relation in which every faculty of man is involved, and their recognition of the unique and unpredictable character of the Thou—'a presence known only in so far as it reveals itself.'

'Thou' is not contemplated with intellectual detachment; it is experienced as life confronting life. . . . The whole man confronts

---

[1] *Moses, op. cit.*, p. 17; *Israel and the World, op. cit.*, 'Biblical Leadership,' p. 119 f.; *Images of Good and Evil, op. cit.*, p. 12.

[2] *Images of Good and Evil*, pp. 57-60.

[3] Ernst Cassirer, *Language and Myth*, trans. by Suzanne Langer (New York: Harper & Brothers, 1946), pp. 11, 18, 27.

a living 'Thou' in nature; and the whole man—emotional and imaginative as well as intellectual—gives expression to the experience.[1]

HISTORY

Buber goes significantly beyond Cassirer and even Frankfort, however, in his understanding of the relation between history and myth. Identifying history with discursive thinking, Cassirer speaks of the historical fact as meaningful only as a member of a course of events or a teleological nexus and not in its particularity and uniqueness. Frankfort recognizes that myth arises not only in connection with man's relation to nature, the cosmos, and the change of the seasons, but also in his relation to a transcendent God in the course of history. But when he speaks of the will of God, the chosen people, and the Kingdom of God as 'myths,' he tends to remove from history that concreteness which is of its very essence.

The doctrine of a single, unconditioned, transcendent God . . . postulated a metaphysical significance for history and for man's actions. . . . In transcending the Near Eastern myths of immanent godhead, they [the Hebrews] created . . . the new myth of the will of God. It remained for the Greeks, with their peculiar *intellectual* courage, to discover a form of speculative thought in which myth was entirely overcome.[2]

Thus myth to Frankfort is primarily important as a form of thought rather than as an embodiment of concrete events. For Buber, as we have seen, the emphasis is the other way around. For this reason the meeting with God in history is even more important to him than the meeting with God in nature. True history, in consequence, must include just that concreteness and uniqueness which Cassirer attributes to mythical thinking. Much of history is, of course, universal and abstract; yet real history also contains at its core the memory of the concrete and particular meeting between I and Thou. 'I hold myth to be indispensable,' writes Buber, 'but I do not hold it to be central. . . . Myth must verify itself in man and not man in myth. . . . What is wrong is not the mythization of reality which brings the inexpressible to speech, but the gnosticizing of myth which tears it out of the ground of history and biography in which it took root.'[3]

---

[1] H. and H. A. Frankfort, et. al., *The Intellectual Adventure of Ancient Man, An Essay on Speculative Thought in the Ancient Near East* (Chicago: The University of Chicago Press, 1946), p. 4 ff.

[2] *Ibid.*, concluding chapter, 'The Emancipation of Thought from Myth'; also found in H. and H. A. Frankfort, et al., *Before Philosophy* (Pelican Books A 198), chap. viii, pp. 241-248.

[3] *Origin and Meaning of Hasidism, op. cit.,* 'Christ, Hasidism, Gnosis.'

This attitude toward the relation between history and myth is developed by Buber in his books of biblical commentary, *Königtum Gottes*, *Moses*, and *The Prophetic Faith*, and it is this which constitutes one of the most significant contributions of these remarkable works. Emil Brunner has written of the first of these, *Königtum Gottes*, that it is 'a book which shows what history is better than any philosophy of history.' [1] In these studies Buber leads us on a narrow ridge between the traditionalist's insistence on the literal truth of the biblical narrative and the modern critic's tendency to regard this narrative as of merely literary or symbolic significance. The former tend to regard the events of the Bible as supernatural miracles and the quest for any reality comparable to our own experiences as illicit. The latter see them as impressive fantasies or fictions, interesting from a purely immanent and human point of view. Between these two approaches Buber sets down a third:

> We must adopt the critical approach and seek reality, here as well, by asking ourselves what human relation to real events this could have been which led gradually, along many bypaths and by way of many metamorphoses, from mouth to ear, from one memory to another, and from dream to dream, until it grew into the written account we have read.[2]

This third way is one which refuses the alternatives of factual history or universal and timeless myth and proclaims the history which gives rise to myth, the myth which remembers history:

> What is preserved for us here is to be regarded not as the 'historization' of a myth or a cult drama, nor is it to be explained as the transposition of something originally beyond time into historical time: a great history-faith does not come into the world through interpretation of the extra-historical as historical, but by receiving an occurrence experienced as a 'wonder,' that is as an event which cannot be grasped except as an act of God.[3]

The saga is the direct and unique expression of the reporter's 'knowledge' of an event. Rather, this knowledge is itself a legendary one, representing through the organic work of mythicizing memory the believed-in action of God on His people. It is not fantasy which is active here but memory, that believing memory of the souls and generations of early times which works unarbitrarily out of the impulse of an extraordinary event. Even the myth which seems most fantastic of all is

---

[1] Emil Brunner, *Man in Revolt* (Philadelphia: Westminster Press, 1947, London: Lutterworth, 1948), p. 448, n. 2.
[2] *Israel and the World*, 'The Man of Today and the Jewish Bible,' pp. 97-100; *Moses*, p. 61 f.
[3] *The Prophetic Faith*, p. 46.

creation around the kernel of the organically shaping memory. 'Here, unlike the concept familiar in the science of religion, myth means nothing other than the report by ardent enthusiasts of that which has befallen them.'

Here history cannot be dissevered from the historical wonder; but the experience which has been transmitted to us, the experience of event as wonder, is itself great history and must be understood out of the element of history.[1]

Buber's third way does not mean a dismissal of the comparative aspects of the history of religions but it guards against the blurring of the historical figure which is caused by the now widespread shifting into the primitive. It recognizes the connections of historical celebrations with ancient nature rites but also points out the essential transformation of those rites which took place when they were given a historical character.[2] Moreover, in addition to understanding an event comparatively and in terms of the stages of religious development, it leaves room for the criterion of *uniqueness*.

There are in the history of religion events, situations, figures, expressions, deeds, the uniqueness of which cannot be regarded as the fruit of thought or song, or as a mere fabrication, but simply and solely as a matter of fact. . . .[3]

This criterion of uniqueness must be used with 'scientific intuition,' and it cannot be applied to all events but only to unusual ones. One such unusual event is that which Buber calls a 'historical mystery.' 'A historical mystery always means a relation between a super-personal fate and a person, and particularly that which is atypical in a person; that by which the person does not belong to his type.' Buber's criterion of the uniqueness of the fact is of especial importance because, as in the concept of the historical mystery, it goes beyond the phenomenological approach which at present dominates the study of the history of religions. 'Irrespective of the importance of the typological view of phenomena in the history of the spirit, the latter, just because it is history, also contains the atypical, the unique in the most precise sense.' This concern with uniqueness is a natural corollary of Buber's belief that the absolute is bound to the concrete and not to the universal and his corresponding valuation of the particular over the general. This valuation of the particular provides Buber with another criterion, that of the

---

[1] *Moses*, pp. 14-17; *Israel and the World*, 'Biblical Leadership,' p. 119 ff.; *Königtum Gottes, op. cit.*, p. 9 f.
[2] *Königtum Gottes*, p. 120 ff.; *Moses*, pp. 56 f., 81, 128, 158.
[3] *The Prophetic Faith*, p. 6.

'historically possible' which leaves room for the unique: 'It is a basic law of methodology not to permit the "firm letter" to be broken down by any general hypothesis based on the comparative history of culture; as long as what is said in that text is historically possible.' By the 'historically possible' Buber does not mean that which is merely not impossible but rather that which accords with the historical conditions of the epoch.[1]

Buber calls his treatment of Biblical history 'tradition criticism' as distinct from 'source criticism.' This tradition criticism seeks to penetrate beneath the layers of different redactions of tradition to a central unity already present in the first redaction and developed, restored, or distorted in the later ones. It is important in this connection to distinguish very clearly within each tradition between its fundamental unity and the unity of harmonization, fruit of the 'Biblical' spirit, 'between saga produced near the historical occurrences, the character of which is enthusiastic report, and saga which is further away from the historical event, and which derives from the tendency to complete and round off what is already given.' Even in the work of harmonization, however, there may be found the influence of a primitive unity, preserved in the memory of generations in spite of different editorial tendencies.[2]

> Tradition is by its nature an uninterrupted change in form; change and preservation function in the identical current. Even while the hand makes its alterations, the ear hearkens to the deeps of the past; not only for the reader but also for the writer himself does the old serve to legitimize the new.[3]

The mythical element may, of course, become so strong that the kernel of historical memory tends to be obscured. Where event and memory cease to rule, myth replaces them by a timeless image. This weakening of the bond with history tends, in particular, to be the case with eschatology, which misses the special, concrete, historical core. This retreat from the historical itself tends to be expressed in myth. 'In so far as faith expresses more and other than its actual relation to the divine, in so far as it wishes to report and describe and not merely call and address, to that extent it must mythicize its object.'[4]

The Bible as 'literal truth' and the Bible as 'living literature' are thus supplanted in Buber's thought by the Bible as a record of the concrete meetings in the course of history between a group of people and the divine. The Bible is not primarily devotional literature, nor is it a

---

[1] *Moses*, pp. 35, 64, 136, 158; *Königtum Gottes*, p. 11.
[2] *The Prophetic Faith*, p. 6 f.; *Moses*, p. 18 f.
[3] *Moses*, p. 18.
[4] *Königtum Gottes*, p. 120 ff. (my translations). Cf. *The Prophetic Faith*, pp. 142, 153; *Moses*, p. 109.

symbolic theology which tells us of the nature of God as He is in Him-self. It is 'anthropogeny,' the historical account of God's relation to man seen through man's eyes.[1]

Buber does not regard his concept of history as applying only to Biblical history but merely as most clearly in evidence there.

What we are accustomed to call history is from the Biblical stand-point only the façade of reality. It is the great failure, the refusal to enter into the dialogue, not the failure in the dialogue, as exempli-fied by Biblical man.[2]

Outer history sees only success. Inner history knows that 'the way, the real way, from the Creation to the Kingdom is trod not on the surface of success but in the deep of failure.' It is the unrecorded and anony-mous work of the secret leadership, the work which leads to the final, Messianic overcoming of history in which outer history and inner history will fuse. Since world history is the advance of the peoples toward the goal of making real the kingship of God, it is essentially holy history. Every great civilization is founded on an original relational event, writes Buber, a concrete religious and normative relation with the Absolute. Man rebels against this relation: 'he wills and wills not to translate the heavenly truth into earthly reality.' It is here in this struggle of man with the spirit that great civilizations rise, and it is this which determines all their wisdom and their art.[3]

History is customarily understood as an interrelation of events none of which are significant in themselves but only in terms of their connec-tion with the past from which they spring and the future to which they give rise. Even when a great emphasis is placed upon the richness of historical fact, these facts are usually felt to be significant only as expressions of historical trends or of periods of culture. As a result 'meaning' in history tends to be associated with the universal and the general to the exclusion of the particular and the unique. The modern historian, as Friedrich Gogarten has pointed out, sees history as a linear process of evolution, comparable to the flow of experience reflected in the consciousness of the unrelated I. This historical evolutionism is a

---

[1] *Israel and the World,* 'The Man of Today and the Jewish Bible,' pp. 89, 92 f.; *The Prophetic Faith,* p. 89.

[2] *Ibid.,* 'Biblical Leadership,' p. 133; cf. *ibid.,* 'The Man of Today and the Jewish Bible,' p. 94 f., 'False Prophets,' p. 114.

[3] *Ibid.,* 'Biblical Leadership,' pp. 124-133, 'In the Midst of History,' p. 78 ff.; *At the Turning, op. cit.,* 'Judaism and Civilization,' p. 11 f., 'The Dialogue between Heaven and Earth,' p. 51. Cf. *Eclipse of God,* 'Religion and Ethics.' The American theologian H. Richard Niebuhr takes an attitude toward history closely similar to that of Buber, and he identifies his distinction between 'objective, external his-tory' and the personal, or 'internal,' history of revelation with Buber's distinc-tion between I-It and I-Thou. H. Richard Niebuhr, *The Meaning of Revelation* (New York: The Macmillan Co., 1941), pp. 59, 64 f., 145 ff.

distortion of reality whether it leans toward the idealist side and emphasizes the suprahistorical meaning which is revealed in history or toward
the empirical side and emphasizes the never-ceasing flow and relativity
of all events. In both cases it takes no account of the prior reality of the
I-Thou relation—the dialogue between man and man and between man
and God. Hence it can never know the event in its uniqueness and
particularity, nor can it really know the extent to which the future is
determined by man's genuine response and his failure to respond to
what meets him.[1]

Subject-object history cannot adequately understand events because
the I of the historian is that of the disinterested spectator while the
persons whom he describes are usually treated as Its rather than as
Thous. I-It history, moreover, takes only the human, immanent side
of events into consideration. No room is left for the 'wonder' which
arises when the encounter with the Thou in the world is perceived to
be not only an event within a causal nexus but a meeting with God. The
worship of historical process, the identification of history with success,
is a part of that shell of impersonality which enables men to remain
unaware of 'the signs' which address them through history as well as
through the other parts of their lives. True history, in contrast, can only
be understood through our participation in it—through its becoming
alive for us as Thou. 'If history is a dialogue between Deity and mankind,' writes Buber, 'we can understand its meaning only when we are
the ones who are addressed, and only to the degree to which we render
ourselves receptive.'

> We are, then, flatly denied the capacity to judge current history
> and arrive at the conclusion that 'This or that is its true meaning'
> ... What we are permitted to know of history comes to this: 'This,
> in one way or another, is history's challenge to me; this is its claim
> on me; and so this is its meaning as far as I am concerned.' This
> meaning, however, is not 'subjective.' ... It is the meaning I
> perceive, experience, and hear in reality. ... It is only with my
> personal life that I am able to catch the meaning of history, for it
> is a dialogical meaning.[2]

---

[1] Gogarten, *Ich glaube an den dreieinigen Gott*, pp. 5, 9, 19-38. In his 'Nachwort'
to *Die Schriften über das dialogische Prinzip* Buber points out that although Gogarten
understands history as 'the meeting of Thou and I,' he holds at the same time the
undialectical thesis, 'History is God's work,' and thus must ultimately fail to grasp
the character of history as meeting.

[2] *Israel and the World*, 'In the Midst of History,' pp. 78-82.

CHAPTER TWENTY-FIVE

THE FAITH OF THE BIBLE

B UBER'S philosophy of dialogue has been of particular importance
in the Biblical interpretation with which he has been mainly concerned in his later years. One of the most significant of his Biblical
works is his translation of the Hebrew Bible into German with the aid
of his friend Franz Rosenzweig. The Buber-Rosenzweig translation of
the Bible, according to Solomon Liptzin, 'has been universally ac-
claimed as a miracle of fidelity and beauty.' Ernest M. Wolf has
explained this translation as an attempt to reproduce in the German
some of the basic linguistic features of Hebrew. 'The result of their
endeavour was the creation of a new Biblical idiom in German which
followed the original meaning of the Hebrew more faithfully than any
other German translation—or any translation in any other language—
had ever done.' The translation is set in the form of cola (*Atemzüge*)—
rhythmic units based on natural breathing pauses. These serve the
purpose of recapturing the original spoken quality of the Bible.[1]

   This translation was accompanied by a volume in which Buber and
Rosenzweig explained the new principles of translation that they used.[2]
Both the translation and the new methods helped to produce a renais-
sance of Bible study among German-speaking Jews.

   Had the generation of young Jews that went through the Buber-
Rosenzweig school of Bible reading and Bible interpreting been

---

[1] Solomon Liptzin, *Germany's Stepchildren* (Philadelphia: The Jewish Publication
Society, 1944), p. 256; Ernest M. Wolf, 'Martin Buber and German Jewry, Prophet
and Teacher to a Generation in Catastrophe,' *Judaism*, Vol. I, No. 4 (October
1952), p. 349; Walter Nigg, *Martin Bubers Weg in unserer Zeit*, first issue of *Religiöse
Gegenwartsfragen, Bausteine zu einem kommenden Protestantismus*, ed. by Josef
Boni and Walter Nigg (Bern: Verlag Paul Haupt, 1940), pp. 21-25; Franz
Rosenzweig, 'Die Schrift und das Wort,' in Martin Buber and Franz Rosenzweig,
Die Schrift und ihrer Verdeutschung (Berlin: Schocken Verlag, 1936), pp. 76-87.
For an unfavourable criticism of the Buber-Rosenzweig translation see Emanuel
bin Gorion (Emanuel Berdyczwesky), *Ceterum Recenseo. Kritische Aufsätze und
Reden* (Tübingen: Alexander Fischer Verlag, 1939), pp. 21-38.
[2] *Die Schrift und ihrer Verdeutschung, op. cit.*

permitted to grow up and to remain together, they would probably have become the most Bible-conscious Jews since the days before the ghetto-walls had fallen in Europe.[1]

Despite the pressing demands on his time, Buber has succeeded in carrying out his original plan of tracing the development of the Messianic idea from the earliest periods of the Hebrew Bible through Jesus and Paul. The volumes of Biblical interpretation in which he has traced this development—*Königtum Gottes, Moses, The Prophetic Faith, Two Types of Faith, Right and Wrong*, and the first section of *Israel and Palestine*—constitute an extremely significant and creative contribution to the field of Biblical scholarship. Commenting on Buber's translation of the Bible and on his Biblical criticism in *Königtum Gottes*, the Old Testament scholar Ludwig Feuchtwanger writes:

> The new total viewpoint of Buber's science of Biblical study has without question created a new situation in Old Testament scholarship. For the first time there has arisen a real Jewish critical study of the Bible—Jewish and critical at once—which does not allow its way to be dictated to it by foreign tendencies.[2]

CREATION

God created man through love, says Buber, as a Thou for His I, an I for His Thou. He created man as a free being because He wished to be freely known, willed, and loved. The action of creation goes on incessantly, for God incessantly calls man and the world into being. Every person in the world represents something original, unique, and unrepeatable. Despite all analysis into elements and all attempts to explain the origin of personality, every man must in the end recognize in his personality an untouched residue, underived and underivable. To seek the origin of this residue means in the final analysis to discover oneself as created. Though man's personality becomes a reality through the relation of the I to the human Thou, it is already potential in his created uniqueness, his relation to the eternal Thou. This uniqueness is

[1] Wolf, 'Martin Buber and German Jewry,' *op. cit.*, p. 350.
[2] Ludwig Feuchtwanger, 'Bibelforschung aus jüdischem Geist, Martin Bubers Erneuerung der Bibel aus Geist des Judentums,' *Der Morgen*, Vol. VIII, No. 3 (August 1932), p. 222 (my translation). See Karl Thieme, 'Martin Buber als Interpret der Bibel,' *Zeitschrift für Religions- und Geistesgeschichte* (Köln), Vol. VI, No. 1 (1954), pp. 1-9, and Hans-Joachim Kraus, 'Gespräch mit Martin Buber. Zur jüdischen und christlichen Auslegung des Alten Testaments,' *Evangelische Theologie* (Munich), Vol. XII, No. 1/2 (July-August 1952), pp. 59-77, for two recent evaluations of Buber's interpretation of the Bible by Catholic and Protestant theologians respectively.

not given to man for mere existence but for the fulfilment of a purpose that only he can fulfil.[1]

Not only is there in everybody a divine particle, but there is in everybody one peculiar to him, to be found nowhere else. . . . Everyone has in the eyes of God a specific importance in the fulfilment of which none can compete with him.[2]

The mystery of our existence, the superhuman chance of mankind is that God places Himself in man's hands: He wants to come into the world through man. Man is the completor of God's creation and the initiator of His redemption.[3] He has, accordingly, real freedom—the freedom of a separate person to go the way of his own personality, to do good and to do evil.

Man, while created by God, was established by Him in an independence which has since remained undiminished. In this independence he stands over against God. So man takes part with full freedom and spontaneity in the dialogue between the two which forms the essence of existence. That this is so despite God's unlimited power and knowledge is just that which constitutes the mystery of man's creation.[4]

If man's redemptive movement toward God is to be real, so also must his fall away from God be real. But this does not mean that an inherited 'original sin' is able to remove immediacy between God and man. Man sins *as* Adam sinned and not *because* he sinned. Although he is increasingly burdened by history, he is always capable of proving true before God.[5]

Man's freedom properly understood is not freedom from external limitations but freedom, despite these limitations, to enter into dialogue with God. This dialogue is implicit, as we have seen, in God's very creation of man. 'The creation itself already means communication between Creator and creature.' [6] In contrast to the customary view that it is monotheism which is the contribution of Judaism to the religions

---

[1] *Hasidism, op. cit.*, 'Spirit and Body of the Hasidic Movement,' pp. 64-68, 'God and the Soul,' pp. 155-158; *The Prophetic Faith, op. cit.*, p. 195; *The Way of Man, op. cit.*, p. 17; *Israel and the World, op. cit.*, 'The Man of Today and the Jewish Bible,' p. 100; *Images of Good and Evil, op. cit.*, p. 82 f.

[2] *Hasidism*, 'Love of God and Love of One's Neighbour,' p. 178 f.

[3] *Ibid.*, 'God and the Soul,' p. 158; *I and Thou*, p. 82; *Eclipse of God, op. cit.*, 'Religion and Modern Thinking,' p. 100 f.; *Images of Good and Evil*, p. 82 f.; *The Way of Man*, p. 44 f.

[4] *Eclipse of God*, 'Religion and Ethics,' p. 138.

[5] *Images of Good and Evil*, pp. 36-40; *Hasidism*, 'Spinoza,' p. 109; *The Prophetic Faith*, p. 210; *Two Types of Faith*, pp. 136 f., 158.

[6] *The Prophetic Faith*, p. 195.

of the world, Buber regards the dialogue with God as the centre and significance of the Jewish religion.

> The great achievement of Israel is not so much that it has told man of the one, real God, the origin and goal of all that exists, but rather that it has taught men that they can address this God in very reality, that men can say Thou to Him, that we human beings can stand face to face with Him, that there is communion between God and man.[1]

This communion between God and man implies partnership and nearness, 'but in everything which grows out of it an ultimate distance persists which is not to be overcome.' This absolute distance between God and man establishes the unconditional in man's relation with God and at the same time discloses the place of redemption. Man remains utterly inferior and God utterly superior; yet if only man truly speaks to God, there is nothing he may not say.[2]

> Again and again God addresses man and is addressed by him. ... To God's sovereign address, man gives his autonomous answer; if he remains silent, his silence is an answer, too. ... The basic doctrine which fills the Hebrew Bible is that our life is a dialogue between the above and the below.[3]

Man must enter into this dialogue with his whole being: it must be 'an exclusive relationship which shapes all other relations and therefore the whole order of life.' This exclusiveness demands a 'religious realism,' a will to realization of one's belief in the whole of one's existence, that cannot be present in a polytheism which sees a different God in each phenomenon of life. 'The man in the Israelite world who has faith is not distinguished from the "heathen" by a more spiritual view of the Godhead, but by the exclusiveness of his relationship to God and by his reference of all things to Him.' [4] This exclusiveness makes it impossible to allow any part of one's life to remain a sphere separate from God, and it makes it necessary to recognize God as He is, and that is as not limited to any one form, image, or manifestation. The exclusive Thou of prayer and devotion is the imageless God, who cannot be confined to any outward form.[5] This reality of faith and life is restricted, says Buber, by those Christians who leave God open to human address only in conjunction with Christ. Although imageless in religious idea, the

---

[1] *Hasidism*, 'Spinoza,' p. 96.
[2] *Two Types of Faith*, p. 9; *Images of Good and Evil*, p. 20; *Between Man and Man*, 'The Question to the Single One,' p. 77; *The Prophetic Faith*, p. 164 f.
[3] *At the Turning*, op. cit., p. 47 f.
[4] *Königtum Gottes*, op. cit., p. 91 f.; *Two Types of Faith*, p. 39.
[5] *Moses*, op. cit., p. 7 f.; *Two Types of Faith*, p. 130 f.

God of the Christian is imaged in actual experience. We have, indeed, the power to glance up to God with our being's eye, writes Buber; but this glance yields no images though it first makes all images possible. To identify God with one of the images that is thus produced is to allow the image to conceal the imageless One, and this means a limitation by man of the fullness of his dialogue with God.[1]

REVELATION

The Holy is not a separate and secluded sphere of being, writes Buber. It is open to all spheres of being and is that through which they find their fulfilment.

> The genuine life of faith develops on the spiritual heights, but it springs from the depths of the distress of the earth-bound body.... Wherever the action of nature as well as spirit is perceived as a gift, Revelation takes place.

God may not be limited to the spiritual and the supersensual. Not only does His imagelessness not prevent Him from manifesting Himself in the visible world, but it is just this imagelessness which makes His manifestation possible: 'He is the history God which He is, only when He is not localized in Nature; and precisely because He makes use of everything potentially visible in Nature, every kind of natural existence, for His manifestation.' [2] God pushes through nature and history to that earthly consummation in which spirit and nature will be unified, the profane sanctified, the kingdom of God established out of the kingdom of man, and *all* of time and creation drawn back into eternity.

> There is not one realm of the spirit and another of nature; there is only the growing realm of God. God is not spirit, but what we call spirit and what we call nature hail equally from the God who is beyond and equally conditioned by both, and whose kingdom reaches its fulness in the complete unity of spirit and nature.[3]

The corollary of this unity of spirit and nature is the belief that there is no essential difference between natural events and 'miracles.' Any natural event may be revelation for him who understands the event as really addressing him and is able to read its meaning for his personal life. In the same way, 'miracle' to Buber is neither an objective event which suspends the laws of nature and history nor a subjective act of

---

[1] *Two Types of Faith*, p. 131 f.; *Hasidism*, 'Spinoza,' p. 96 f.

[2] *Israel and Palestine*, *op. cit.*, pp. 149, 26, 40; *Eclipse of God*, 'Religion and Reality,' p. 32; *Two Types of Faith*, p. 39; *Moses*, pp. 194, 127.

[3] *Israel and the World*, 'Biblical Leadership,' p. 131, 'The Two Foci of the Jewish Soul,' p. 34.

the imagination. It is an event which is experienced by an individual or a group of people as an abiding astonishment which no knowledge of causes can weaken, as wonder at something which intervenes fatefully in the life of this individual and this group. The current system of cause and effect becomes transparent so that one is allowed a glimpse of the sphere in which a sole power, not restricted by any other, is at work. 'To recognize this power on every given occasion as the effecting one ... is religion generally as far as it is reality.' [1]

The God of spirit and nature is also the God of history. The promise of the land to the people of Israel is the promise of a work of community which land and people must undertake in common, and as such it is at once a work of history and nature. History, however, is predominant, for history includes nature. 'In the biblical, which is a history religion ... there is no Nature in the Greek, the Chinese or the modern Occidental sense. What is shown us of Nature is stamped by History.' During the period of the Kings, the magnification of God into the Cosmic King made a symbolical allegiance to God seem satisfactory in the place of the allegiance in every sphere of life which is demanded by the Lord of history. God should indeed be recognized as Lord of the world, writes Buber, but not as removed to the far heavens, for the God of the universe is the God of history who walks with His creatures along the hard way of history.[2]

Although in the biblical view nature ultimately bears the stamp of history, it is necessary to distinguish between the way in which God reveals Himself in these two spheres. The self-communication of God through nature is indirect, impersonal, and continuous, while that through history is direct, personal, and discontinuous. It is the creating God who uninterruptedly speaks in nature, but in history it is the revealing God who speaks, and His revelation 'breaks in again and again upon the course of events and irradiates it.' Following the Maggid of Mesritch, Buber distinguishes between the original Godhead, which desires to impart Itself directly, and Elohim, the impersonal spirit of God working through creation. God's imparting of Himself to man starts as indirect through nature and becomes more and more direct until man is led to meet YHVH Himself, who is at one and the same time the complete unity and the limitless person. It is this limitless original Godhead, and not the self-limited God, that speaks the I of revelation.[3]

It is this second, 'gracious and unforeseeable,' form of spirit through

---

[1] *Israel and the World*, 'The Man of Today and the Jewish Bible,' p. 97 f.; *Moses*, p. 75 ff. Cf. *For the Sake of Heaven, op. cit.*, p. 112.

[2] *Israel and Palestine*, pp. x-xii, 9 f., 14, 19; *Königtum Gottes*, p. 85; *Moses*, pp. 78 f., 158; *The Prophetic Faith*, pp. 85 f., 94.

[3] *At the Turning*, p. 57 f.; *Hasidism*, 'God and the Soul,' pp. 153-156.

which God reveals Himself to man in history. Here we come to know God not only as a revealing God but also as 'a God who hides Himself,' for there are times when God's revelation in history seems clear and unmistakable and others when He seems absent altogether. Just as God's imagelessness is necessary that He may manifest Himself in any form, so His hiding is necessary that He may reveal Himself.

God ever gives Himself to be seen in the phenomena of nature and history and remains invisible. That He reveals Himself and that He 'hides Himself' (Isa. xlv, 15) belong indivisibly together; but for His concealment His revelation would not be real and temporal. Therefore He is imageless; an image means fixing to one manifestation, its aim is to prevent God from hiding Himself, He may not be allowed any longer to be present as the One Who is there as He is there (Exod. iii, 14).

Christianity aims, in effect, to prevent God from hiding Himself, says Buber, in so far as it fixes Him in the image of Christ.[1]

In his concept of revelation Buber combines the meeting of I and Thou with the idea of 'momentary Gods' which Usener has presented as characteristic of the most primitive stage of mythical thinking. God does not arise for us out of inherited tradition, writes Buber, but out of the fusion of a number of 'moment Gods.' If we are addressed by the signs of life, we cannot say that he who speaks is God if we do not reply 'out of that decisive hour of personal existence when we had to forget everything we imagined we knew of God, when we dared to keep nothing handed down or learned or self-contrived, no shred of knowledge, and were plunged into the night.' What we can know of God in such an experience is only what we experience from the signs themselves, so that the speaker of the speech 'is always the God of a moment, a moment God.' But as one comes to know the poet through the separate experience of a number of poems, so 'out of the givers of the signs, the speakers of the words in lived life, out of the moment Gods there arises for us with a single identity the Lord of the voice, the One.' [2] Not only does our world of It experience ever new creation through the flaming forth of the Thou, but each new Thou renews in all presentness the past experiences of Thou. It is this which is the essence of faith: not the past deadening the present, but the present recalling the past to life so that the moments of the past and the moment of the present become simultaneously present and joined in living unity.

In *I and Thou* Buber wrote of revelation as not imparting any specific 'content' but a Presence as power. 'The Word of revelation is *I am that I am.*' In *Königtum Gottes* and in *Moses* Buber rejects 'I am that I am'

---

[1] *At the Turning*, p. 58; *Two Types of Faith*, p. 130 f.
[2] *Between Man and Man*, op. cit., p. 14 f.

for 'I shall be there as I shall be there.' When Moses at the burning bush asks God His name, he is told: *'Ehyeh asher ehyeh.'* 'This is usually understood to mean "I am that I am" in the sense that YHVH describes himself as the Being One or even the Everlasting One, the one unalterably persisting in his being.' The Biblical verb does not include this shade of meaning of pure being. 'It means happening, coming into being, being there, being present . . . but not being in an abstract sense.' [1] God promises that He will always be present, but not in any known or expected form. He identifies Himself only as the Presence which comes and departs, as the imageless God who hides and reveals Himself.

The true meaning of YHVH, the inherited divine name, is unfolded in the *ehyeh asher ehyeh*: YHVH is He who is present in every now and in every here. And in order to make clear that the direct verb explains the indirect name, Moses is first instructed to tell the people *'Ehyeh,* I shall be present, or I am present, sends me to you,' and immediately afterwards: 'YHVH the God of your fathers sends me to you.' [2] Thus Moses at the burning bush clearly experiences the identity of the God whom he meets in the full and timeless present with the God of tradition revealed in time. He recognizes the God of the fathers as the eternal Thou, and he understands the present revelation of God as the assurance of His future presence.

Revelation is thus man's encounter with God's presence rather than information about His essence. Buber rejects the either-or of revelation as objective or subjective in favour of the understanding of revelation as dialogical. To be revelation and not just literature it must come from outside man, but that does not mean that man has no part in the form which it takes.

> My own belief in revelation . . . does not mean that I believe that finished statements about God were handed down from heaven to earth. Rather it means that the human substance is melted by the spiritual fire which visits it, and there now breaks forth from it a word, a statement, which is human in its meaning and form, human conception and human speech, and yet witnesses to Him who stimulated it and to His will. We are revealed to ourselves—and cannot express it otherwise than as something revealed.[3]

Before the word is spoken to man in human language, it is spoken to him in another language, from which he has to translate it into human language. He does not convey a finished speech but shapes to sound a

---

[1] *I and Thou, op. cit.,* p. 110 ff.; *Moses, op. cit.,* pp. 51 f., 160; *Königtum Gottes, op. cit.,* p. 83 ff.

[2] *Moses, op. cit.,* pp. 49-53.

[3] *Eclipse of God, op. cit.,* 'Supplement: Reply to C. G. Jung,' trans. by Maurice S. Friedman, p. 173.

hidden, soundless speech. But this does not mean that he translates subjective emotions into objective speech and then pretends to have the word of God. The word is spoken to him as between person and person, and he must be in the full sense of the word a *person* before God can speak to him.[1]

The anthropomorphism of the Hebrew Bible serves a valid purpose in preserving the concrete quality of the encounter with the divine. In the encounter itself 'we are confronted by something compellingly anthropomorphic, something demanding reciprocity, a primary Thou.' We owe to anthropomorphism the two great concepts of YHVH's divine love for Israel and of His fatherhood. In the Hebrew Bible God is not seen in Himself but in His relation to man, and His revelation changes according to the historical situation. In the pre-exilic period God addressed individuals as members of the people into which they were incorporated and from which they were undetachable. The Ten Commandments were addressed to a single Thou rather than a collective You, yet to every individual as a part of the nation in which he was embedded. Only later in history when the individual discovers and becomes aware of himself does God speak to him as such.[2]

The differences between the prophets, similarly, arise from the fact that each prophet discovered the divine demand meant by his particular historic situation. What is essential in prophecy is that it be based on the reality of history as it is happening and that its tie with this situation reach to the secret ground of creation in which existence is rooted. Jeremiah attacks the dogmatics of a guardian deity during a situation of false security, and Deutero-Isaiah opposes the dogmatics of a punishing deity during a situation of adversity. 'Both prophesy so for the sake of the covenant between godhead and manhood, for the sake of the kingdom of God.'[3]

The prophets sought God to 'know' Him, to be in direct contact with Him, and not in order to hear future things. Even their predictions of the future were for the sake of the present, that the people might turn again to the way of God. The pure prophets are distinguished from the apocalyptic ones, as from the seers and diviners of other religions, by the fact that they did not wish to peep into an already certain and immutable future but were concerned only with the full grasping of the present, actual and potential. Their prophecy was altogether bound up with the situation of the historical hour and with God's direct speaking

[1] *The Prophetic Faith, op. cit.*, p. 164 f.; *Hasidism, op. cit.*, 'Symbolical Existence in Judaism,' pp. 119-129; *The Prophetic Faith, op. cit.*, pp. 110-113.

[2] *Eclipse of God, op. cit.*, 'Religion and Reality,' p. 22 f.; *Moses, op. cit.*, pp. 160, 194; *The Prophetic Faith, op. cit.*, p. 89; *At the Turning, op. cit.*, 'The Silent Question,' p. 37 f.

[3] *Ibid., op. cit.*, pp. 43 f., 49, 178, 182 f.; *Königtum Gottes, op. cit.*, pp. 150-153; *Moses, op. cit.*, p. 131.

in it. They recognized the importance of man's decision in determining the future and therefore rejected any attempts to treat the future as if it were simply a fixed past which had not yet unfolded. Their attitude corresponds to the basic Biblical view that man is set in real freedom in order that he may enter the dialogue with God and through this dialogue take part in the redemption of the world.[1]

Even when the prophet announced an unconditional disaster, this announcement contained a hidden alternative. By the announcement the people were driven into despair, and it was just this despair which touched their innermost soul and evoked the turning to God by which they were saved. The false prophets tell the people what they wish to hear. They set up 'over against the hard divine word of demand and judgment the easy word of a pseudo-deity . . . who is ready to help unconditionally.' The true prophets, in contrast, present the hard demand of God in this historic situation without weakening or compromise. And God does not lighten the choice between the hard truth and the easy fraud. He speaks to the people only in the language of history and in such a way that they can explain what happened as the coincidence of adverse circumstances. 'This God makes it burdensome for the believer and light for the unbeliever; and His revelation is nothing but a different form of hiding His face.'[2]

'Our path in the history of faith is not a path from one kind of deity to another, but in fact a path from the "God Who hides Himself" (Isa. xlv, 15) to the One that reveals Himself.' Amos's 'righteousness,' Hosea's *hesed*, or 'lovingkindness,' and Isaiah's 'holiness' represent three important developments of the meaning of the divine kingship for the life of the community. All three are ways of imitating God for the sake of His work.

> In one generation Israel's faith developed these three basic concepts of the relationship to God, and only all together could express what is meant by the being present of the One Who is present to Israel, Who is 'with it.' The name YHVH was unravelled at the revelation to Moses in the thorn bush; in the revelation to three prophets it has been unfolded.[3]

This unfolding does not eliminate the periods of terror when God seems to withdraw from the world or the periods of insecurity when inherited conceptions of God are tested and found inadequate. The faith relationship has to stand the test of an utterly changed situation, and it must be renewed in a modified form. The force of extreme despair results in a new pondering of dogmatic conceptions which will either result in the

---

[1] *The Prophetic Faith*, pp. 103 f., 116, 175 f.; *At the Turning*, p. 54.
[2] *Ibid.*, pp. 104, 175-179; *At the Turning*, p. 54 f.
[3] *Ibid.*, pp. 44, 101 f., 114 f., 128 f.

sapping of the last will to live or the renewal of the soul. *Emunah*, the faith of the Hebrew Bible, is a trust in the faithfulness of God despite His different manifestations in different historic situations.[1]

The midpoint between creation and redemption is not the revelation at Sinai or at the burning bush but the present perceiving of revelation, and such perception is possible at any time. What is given to an individual in this present moment leads to the understanding of the great revelations, but the vital fact is one's own personal receiving and not what was received in former times. 'At all times,' writes Buber, 'only those persons really grasped the Decalogue who literally felt it as having been addressed to themselves.' We must feel creation, revelation, and redemption as happening to ourselves before we can understand them in the Bible. In our meeting with God in the daily events of life we experience all three: knowledge of our origin, awareness of His presence, and the touch of His saving hand in our darkest hour.[2]

The Bible has, in the form of a glorified memory, given vivid, decisive expression to an ever-recurrent happening. In the infinite language of events and situations, eternally changing, but plain to the truly attentive, transcendence speaks to our hearts at the essential moments of personal life. . . . This fundamental interpretation of our existence we owe to the Hebrew Bible; and whenever we truly read it, our self-understanding is renewed and deepened.[3]

THE KINGSHIP OF GOD

The Biblical dialogue between God and man finds its most significant expression in the concept of the kingship of God. Buber's work of Biblical interpretation, accordingly, is principally devoted to tracing the development of this idea from its earliest expression in the tribal God, or *Melekh*, to its sublimest development in 'the God of the Sufferers.'

The Israelite *Melekh*, the God who led Abraham in his wanderings, differs from other gods of the way in that He does not serve the purposes of the people by leading them to a place that they know and wish to go to. Instead He drives them to do the uncustomary, the untraditional—to overcome enmity of clan and tribe and unite into one people, to take the unbeaten path into the land He has chosen for them.[4] The people of Israel recognize YHVH as their *Melekh*, their King, and they recognize themselves as chosen by Him. This does not mean that He is *their*

[1] *The Prophetic Faith, op. cit.,* pp. 44, 183; *Two Types of Faith, op. cit.,* p. 34.
[2] *Moses, op. cit.,* p. 130; *Israel and the World, op. cit.,* 'The Man of Today and the Jewish Bible,' pp. 94 f., 98-102.
[3] *At the Turning, op. cit.,* 'The Dialogue between Heaven and Earth,' p. 49 f.
[4] *Ibid.,* p. 68; *Moses, op. cit.,* p. 125 f.; *Israel und Palästina,* p. 38. Cf. *Israel and Palestine,* p. 21.

God in the sense that He belongs to them or they in any way possess Him. He whom heaven itself cannot contain (I Kings viii, 27) belongs to no people or place. Yet at the very time when it becomes necessary to destroy Israel's illusion that it has a monopoly on its God, at the time when it becomes unmistakably clear that YHVH is not the God of a tribe, even then and just then He is proclaimed as God of the tribe for ever and ever, as the God who liberated the people from Egypt and brought them forth to the land.[1] The one God, the God of heaven and earth, is the king whose kingship the people must make real through themselves becoming a holy people, a people who bring all spheres of life under His rule.

The time when this recognition of God's kingship takes place is that of the Covenant at Mount Sinai. This covenant between God and the people of Israel is not a contract, as is sometimes thought. It 'means no legal agreement, but a surrender to the divine grace and power.' Not only is it unique among all religions, says Buber, but even in the Old Testament itself there is no analogy to it: 'Only in the Sinai Covenant . . . does an action take place which *sacramentally founds a reciprocity between an Above and a Below.*' This reciprocity is a free action, a 'choice' by both YHVH and the people. Israel cannot be understood as merely YHVH's congregation of faith nor YHVH simply as Israel's protector God. This reciprocal choice entails an active 'over-againstness' of the two partners such as is impossible in the magical view in which the divine side remains passive and in the ordinary sacramental view in which the human remains passive.[2]

The Sinai Covenant is not to be understood as a limitation in the essence of God, as if He were somehow less absolute for having entered into it. Like His revelation to Moses, it says only that He, the hiding and revealing God, will be present with the people in the future, that He will be there as He will be there. It does not mean that Israel is in some way dearer to God than other peoples. Israel is chosen only to fulfil a charge, to become a 'holy people.' Until this charge is fulfilled the choice exists only negatively. When the people are unfaithful, God says to them through His prophet, 'You are not my people and I am not *ehyeh* ("I am present") for you.'[3] God's demand that Israel become 'a holy people' means the spontaneous and ever-renewed act whereby the people dedicate themselves to YHVH with their corporeal national existence, their legal forms and institutions, their internal and external relationships, the whole factuality of worldly life. The 'religious' and the

---

[1] *Königtum Gottes, op. cit.*, pp. 73, 81 (my translation).
[2] *The Prophetic Faith, op. cit.*, p. 51; *Königtum Gottes, op. cit.*, pp. 111-119; *Eclipse of God, op. cit.*, 'Religion and Ethics,' p. 136.
[3] *Königtum Gottes, op. cit.*, p. 115 f.; *At the Turning, op. cit.*, 'Judaism and Civilization,' p. 14; *Moses, op. cit.*, pp. 103, 105, 53 f.

'social' are here closely connected, for Israel cannot become the people of YHVH without just faith between men. The direct relation of each of the children of Israel to YHVH makes them equal to one another and makes their duties to each other duties to YHVH as well.[1] After Moses, the most serious attempt to realize the kingship of God was in the period of the judges. The judge judged not as an appointed official but as one who remained in direct relation to the spirit as an open receiver. There is no security of power here, only the streams of a fullness of power which presents itself and withdraws. In the absence of any means for succession other than the recognition of someone possessing charisma, there comes to the front what Buber calls the 'paradox of all original and direct theocracy.' The very absence of restraint and compulsion which enables the men of faith to wait for the grace which they wish to follow enables those without faith not to follow anyone. The highest binding cannot by its very nature make use of any compulsion; it calls for a perfected community based on spontaneity. But this trust in spontaneity may lead in the end to an anarchy passionately sanctioned in the name of the freedom of God. This paradox is that of the kingship of God itself: it stands in the historical conflict between those who bear the message and those who resist it. It is the visible manifestation of the historical dialogue between the divinity that asks and mankind that refuses an answer yet also seeks one.[2] This tragedy of the contradiction confronted not only Moses but also the judges, the prophets, the 'suffering servant,' and Jesus.

The unity of spirit and law in the judge is succeeded by the king, who had security of power without spirit, and the prophet, who had spirit without power. The kings were commissioned by God and responsible to Him, but they tended to sublimate their responsibility into a divine right granted without obligation and to regard their anointing as demanding of them a merely cultic acknowledgment of YHVH's kingship. It is this failure of the kings in the dialogue with YHVH which resulted in the mission of the prophets. The 'theopolitical' realism of the prophets led them to reject any merely symbolic fulfilment of the divine commission, to fight the division of community life into a 'religious' realm of myth and cult and a 'political' realm of civic and economic laws. YHVH passes judgment on the nations not for their inquity against Him but for their iniquity against each other. He demands 'righteousness' and 'justice' of the people for the sake of the completion of his work (Amos). He seeks not 'religion' but community.[3]

[1] *Königtum Gottes*, p. 106 f.; *Moses*, pp. 106 ff., 144; *The Prophetic Faith*, p. 55.
[2] *Ibid., op. cit.*, pp. 3 f., 11 f., 31 f., 60, 106 f., 139 f., 143-146, 179-182; 2nd enlarged edition (Berlin: Schocken Verlag, 1936), p. xxvii; *Moses*, pp. 184-190.
[3] *Ibid., op. cit.*, pp. 144, 175; *Israel and the World, op. cit.*, 'Biblical Leadership,' 129 f.; *The Prophetic Faith*, pp. 66 ff., 85 f., 97, 101 f., 152 f., 172.

The God of Isaiah whom one knows to be Lord of all is not more spiritual or real than the God of the Covenant of whom one knows only that 'He is King in Jeshurun,' for already He makes the unconditional demand of the genuine kingship. The way of the kingship is the way from failure to failure in the dialogue between the people and God. As the failure of the judge leads to the king and the failure of the king to the prophet, so the failure of the prophet in his opposition to the king leads to the conception of two new types of leader who will set the dialogue aright—the Messiah of YHVH and the 'suffering servant of the Lord.' [1]

Isaiah's Messiah, or 'Immanuel,' is the anti-king, but he is not a spiritual anti-king, as many see it. He is the king of the *remnant*, from which the people will renew itself, and his Messianic kingship is a real theopolitical kingship endowed with political power for the realization of God's will for the peoples. 'Immanuel' is not simply a leader of the people of Israel nor is there any question of the sovereignty of Israel in the world. God leads all peoples to peace and freedom and demands that 'in freedom they shall serve him, as peoples, each in its own way and according to its own character.' The Messiah of Isaiah is the vice-regent who is to make God's leadership of the people real. 'He is anointed to set up with human forces and human responsibility the divine order of human community.' He is in no way divine or more than man; he is godlike as is the man in whom the likeness to the divine has unfolded. 'He is not nearer to God than what is appointed to man as man; . . . he too stands before God in indestructible dialogue.' He does not take the place of man's turning or bring about a redemption which man has merely to accept and enter into. The 'Messianic'prophecy is no prediction of an already certain future: it too conceals an alternative, for there is something essential that must come from man. The belief in the coming of a Messianic leader is in essence the belief that at last man shall speak with his whole being the word that answers God's word. God awaits an earthly consummation, a consummation in and with mankind. The Messianic belief is 'the belief in the real leader, in the setting right of the dialogue, in God's disappointment being at an end.' [2]

THE GOD OF THE SUFFERERS

Although YHVH's sovereignty in every field of life was proclaimed at the time of the Covenant, it was only by a long and slow process that men came to recognize God and His activity in the spheres which seemed

---

[1] *Königtum Gottes, op. cit.*, 89 f., 181 f.; *Israel and the World, op. cit.*, 'Biblical Leadership,' pp. 124-133.
[2] *The Prophetic Faith, op. cit.*, pp. 140-144, 151, 153 f.; *Israel and the World, op. cit.*, 'Biblical Leadership,' p. 131.

necessarily foreign to Him. This difficulty is particularly strong in connection with those unusual events where men feel the presence of the demonic and the irrational, events that arouse terror, threaten security, and disturb faith. The Biblical concept of holiness is that of a power capable of exerting both a destructive and a hallowing effect. The encounter with this holiness is, therefore, a source of danger to man. As in the story of Jacob's wrestle with the angel, it is the perilous test that the wanderer must pass before he enjoys the final grace of God.[1]

> The early stage of Israelite religion knows no Satan; if a power attacks a man and threatens him, it is proper to recognize YHVH in it or behind it, no matter how nocturnally dread and cruel it may be; and it is proper to withstand Him, since after all He does not require anything else of me than myself.

In 'events of the night,' such as that in which the Lord met Moses and tried to kill him (Exod. iv, 24-26), Buber finds one of the deepest roots of Deutero-Isaiah's words (Isa. xlv, 7): 'Who makes peace and creates evil, I YHVH do all this.' [2]

The danger is turned into a grace for those like Jacob and Moses who stand the test. This is the experience of Abraham too when God commands him to sacrifice Isaac. Like the despair which draws forth the 'turning,' the extremest demand here draws forth the innermost readiness to sacrifice out of the depths of Abraham's being. God thus allows Abraham's relation to Him to become wholly real. 'But then, when no further hindrance stood between the intention and the deed, He contented Himself with Abraham's fulfilled readiness and prevented the action.' This is what is called 'temptation' by the faith of the Old Testament, a faith which takes the over-againstness of God and man more seriously than does any other.[3]

Job's trial can also be understood as a 'temptation,' for God's apparent absence occasions a despair in Job which causes his innermost nature to become manifest. Through the intensity of his 'turning,' through his demand that God speak to him, he receives a revelation of God such as could not otherwise be his. It is 'just at the height of Job's trial . . . just in the midst of the terror of the other, the incomprehensible, ununderstandable works, just from out of the secret,' that God's ways of working are revealed. Job accuses God of injustice and tries in vain to penetrate to Him through the divine remoteness. Now God draws near Job and Job 'sees' Him. It is this nearness to God, following His

---

[1] *The Prophetic Faith, op. cit.,* pp. 71, 52; *Moses, op. cit.,* pp. 106, 118.
[2] *Moses,* p. 57 ff.
[3] *Ibid.,* pp. 83, 118; *The Prophetic Faith, op. cit.,* pp. 83, 91 f.; *Königtum Gottes, op. cit.,* pp. 99-104; *Eclipse of God, op. cit.,* 'On the Suspension of the Ethical,' trans. by Maurice S. Friedman, p. 153.

apparent hiddenness, which is God's answer to the suffering Job as to why he suffers—an answer which is understandable only in terms of the relationship itself.[1]

Job remained faithful even when God seemed to hide His face from him. He could not renounce his claim that his faith in God and his faith in justice should once again be united.[2]

At all times in Israel people spoke much about evil powers, but not about one which, for longer than the purpose of temptation, was allowed to rule in God's stead; never, not even in the most deadly act of requital by God, is the bond of immediacy broken.[3]

God sets creation free and at the same time holds it. He does not put an end to man's freedom despite his misuse of it, but neither does He abandon him. Even God's hiding His face is only an apparent hiding which does not contradict the statement in *I and Thou* that only we, and not God, are absent. God does not actually withdraw His presence; He only seems to do so. Yet this must not be understood as a purely immanent event. It does not take place *in* man but *between* man and God. 'To those who do not want to be near to Him God replies by not giving to them any more the experience of nearness' (cf. Ps. x, 1; Jer. xxxi, 3). He lets the resisting experience his fate in history, the fate resulting from his own deeds.[4]

God's anger and His seeming withdrawal are a part of His love for man—a love which wishes man to enter the dialogue with Him but will not compel him to do so. Hence there is no real division between God's mercy and His justice. God's wrath in the Old Testament is always a fatherly anger toward a disobedient child from whom He still does not withdraw His love. Although He may at times harden, He also forgives. Thus Amos knew that God would stay with the people in the midst of the desolation which was the work of His own judgment, and Hosea wrote of God's mercy, 'I will heal their turnings away, I will love them freely.' [5]

Jeremiah, like Amos and Hosea, recognized that both YHVH's blessing and His curse flow from His love. He also recognized that because of His love for man, God takes part in man's suffering. Whoever helps the suffering creature comes close to the Creator, writes Jeremiah.

---

[1] The first sentence of this paragraph is based on a letter from Professor Buber to me of June 18, 1952; *Israel and the World, op. cit.*, 'Imitatio Dei,' p. 76; *The Prophetic Faith, op. cit.*, pp. 192-196.

[2] *The Prophetic Faith*, p. 192.

[3] *Two Types of Faith, op. cit.*, p. 140.

[4] *Ibid.*, p. 151 f.; *I and Thou, op. cit.*, p. 99; *The Prophetic Faith, op. cit.*, p. 94. The quotation and the sentence preceding it are from two letters from Professor Buber to me, both of June 18, 1952.

[5] *Ibid.*, pp. 90, 139, 164; *The Prophetic Faith*, pp. 109-113.

God shares in the trouble and suffering of His creature and even suffers by His own actions at the hour when He comes near to destroying the work of His hands. This 'God of the sufferers' is also acknowledged by Deutero-Isaiah, who writes not only of the God of heaven and earth, who perceives and is above all, but also of the God who remains near the outcast, who dwells 'with the contrite and lowly of spirit.' [1]

It is from among the 'lowly of spirit' that God finds His special servant in whom He is glorified. This is Deutero-Isaiah's 'suffering servant of the Lord,' the righteous man who suffers for the sake of God. Deutero-Isaiah's 'servant' stands in the succession of men whom God has designated as His servant—Abraham, Moses, David, Isaiah, and Job. Of these he is especially linked through his sufferings with Job, the 'faithful rebel.' Like Job he experiences God's nearness in his suffering, and like Job, too, his suffering has a super-personal meaning. The 'servant' differs from Job, however, in that he voluntarily takes on himself all the griefs and sicknesses of the people's iniquities in order to bring them back to YHVH.[2] In suffering for the sake of God he comes to discover the meaning of his own suffering: he recognizes that God suffers with him and that he is working together with God for the redemption of the world. In the figure of the servant the meaning of God's answer to Job becomes clear.

> Man penetrates step by step into the dark which hangs over the meaning of events, until the mystery is disclosed in the flash of light: the *zaddik*, the man justified by God, suffers for the sake of God and of His work of salvation, and God is with him in his suffering.[3]

The 'servant' is bowed down by sorrow, disfigured by disease, despised and shunned by the people. Yet it is just he who experiences God's nearness and receives God's promise that he will be preserved for the task of ushering in God's kingdom.

Deutero-Isaiah's 'servant' cannot be identified either with Israel or with Christ. He is not a corporate but a personal being, yet he is more than a single person. 'This person takes shape in many likenesses and life-ways, the bearers of which are identical in their innermost essence.' But no supernatural event or resurrection of the dead leads from one of these figures to the next. The servant is 'preserved' for the day in which God's salvation shall be to the end of the earth, but it is only the 'servant' who is preserved and not the person who embodies him at any particular time.

There are three stages on the servant's way. The first is the prophetic stage of the futile labour of the prophet to bring Israel back to YHVH,

---

[1] *The Prophetic Faith*, pp. 161 ff., 167, 182 f.
[2] *Ibid.*, pp. 181, 189, 196, 227, 232; *Two Types of Faith*, p. 143 f.
[3] *Two Types of Faith*, p. 144.

the stage in which he sees himself as an arrow which is fated to remain in the quiver, hidden and unused (Isa. xlix, 2). He is promised a great future work reaching all nations and, sustained by this promise, is willing to bear an immense affliction for God's sake. The second stage is the *acting* of the affliction. He not only endures it but also, as it were, accomplishes it: it becomes his act. The third stage is that of the 'success' of the work born out of affliction, the liberation of the subject peoples, and the establishment of the covenant of the people with God, the human centre of which is the servant. Only now is the arrow taken from the quiver and hurled forth. It is laid on the servant to inaugurate God's new order of peace and justice for the world.

The servant thus completes the work of the judges and the prophets, the work of making real God's kingship over the people. Though a prophet, he is no longer a powerless opposition to the powerful, but a real leader like the Israelite *nabi* of early times. Here, in contrast to the Messianic promise of Isaiah, it is not the king but the *nabi* who is appointed to be deputy of God's kingdom. This kingdom now signifies in reality all the human world. Yet there remains a special tie between the personal servant and the servant Israel. Through the nucleus that does not betray the election, the living connection between God and the people is upheld, and from their midst will arise 'the perfected one.' Through his word and life, Israel will turn to God and become God's people. When the suffering servant is allowed to go up and be a light for the nations, the servant Israel, redeemed and cleansed, will establish God's sovereignty upon itself and serve as the beginning of His kingdom.

The unity between the personal servant and the servant Israel passes over to their unity in suffering. In so far as Israel's great suffering in the dispersion was willingly and actively borne, it is interpreted in the image of the servant. 'The great scattering which followed the splitting-up of the state . . . is endowed with the mystery of suffering as with the promise of the God of sufferers.' This is the mystery of history, the mystery of the arrow which is still concealed in the quiver.[1]

> The way, the real way, from the Creation to the Kingdom is trod not on the surface of success, but in the deep of failure. The real work, from the Biblical point of view, is the late-recorded, the unrecorded, the anonymous work. The real work is done in the shadow, in the quiver.[2]

'Whosoever accomplishes in Israel the active suffering of Israel, he is the servant, and he is Israel, in whom YHVH "glorifies Himself."' Thus the ancient God of the way, the God who caused Abraham to 'stray'

---

[1] *The Prophetic Faith*, pp. 224-234.
[2] *Israel and the World*, 'Biblical Leadership,' p. 133.

from his father's house and went before him in his wanderings, is acknowledged by suffering generations as their Shepherd in the way of exile.[1]

When one has given serious consideration to Buber's Biblical exegesis, one is no longer tempted to fall into the easy assumption that Buber has read his dialogical philosophy into his interpretation of Biblical Judaism. It becomes clear instead that it is precisely in the Bible itself that Buber's dialogical philosophy finds its most solid base. Indeed, the full working out of this philosophy would not have been possible without the years that Buber spent in the translation and interpretation of the Bible. 'Only a viewpoint that is Biblical in a very profound sense,' writes the Old Testament scholar J. Coert Rylaarsdam in a discussion of Buber's *The Prophetic Faith*, 'could so consistently illuminate every part of the Bible it touches.'[2] This does not exclude the obvious fact that there has been a fruitful dialectic in Buber's thought between his interpretations and the development of his personal philosophy. 'There are things in the Jewish tradition that I cannot accept at all,' Buber has said, 'and things I hold true that are not expressed in Judaism. But what I hold essential has been expressed more in Biblical Judaism than anywhere else—in the Biblical dialogue between man and God.'[3]

[1] *Hasidism*, 'Spinoza,' p. 112 f.; *The Prophetic Faith*, p. 234 f.

[2] J. Coert Rylaarsdam, 'The Prophetic Faith,' *Theology Today*, Vol. VII (October 1950), p. 399 ff. At the same time, Rylaarsdam accuses Buber of undue subjectivity: 'Basically his interpretation of the Old Testament is a documentation of his own views. . . . Buber's work would have been more generally acceptable if he had more fully permitted objective historical reconstruction to perform an adequate critical function. Questions of literary criticism and history are frequently settled by a too easy reliance on the writer's *a priori* assumptions. . . . Buber's profound insights will be scorned by many on the ground that he is "uncritical" and "too philosophical".' That Rylaarsdam's criticism is in part, at least, based on a misunderstanding of Buber's position and a difference in Rylaarsdam's own *a priori* assumptions is shown by his further statements that 'Because of his individual and personal emphasis the notion of an objective revelation of God in nature and history involving the *whole* community of Israel in the real event of the Exodus does not fit well for him,' that Buber's view of revelation is 'essentially mystical and nonhistorical,' and that 'the realistic disclosure of Yahweh as the Lord of nature and of history recedes into the background because of an overconcern with the experience of personal relation'—criticisms which are all far wide of the mark, as is shown by the present chapter.

[3] From a statement made by Professor Buber at a small discussion group in New York City, December 1951.

CHAPTER TWENTY-SIX

BUBER AND JUDAISM

LUDWIG LEWISOHN, writing in 1935, said of Martin Buber:

> Dr. Buber is the most distinguished and influential of living
> Jewish thinkers. . . . We are all his pupils. The contemporary re-
> integration of modern Western Jewish writers, thinkers, scientists,
> with their people, is unthinkable without the work and voice of
> Martin Buber.[1]

No Jewish thinker has had a greater cultural, intellectual, and religious
influence than has Buber in the last four decades. He is of significance
for Judaism not only as religious philosopher, translator of the Bible,
and translator and re-creator of Hasidic legends and thought, but also
as a religious personality who has provided leadership of a rare quality
during the time of his people's greatest trial and suffering since the
beginning of the diaspora. Since the death of Hermann Cohen, Buber
has been generally acknowledged as the representative figure of Western
European Jewry. He wielded a tremendous influence not only upon the
youth won over to Zionism but also upon the Liberals, and even,
despite his non-adherence to the Jewish Law, upon the Orthodox. 'It
was Buber,' writes Alfred Werner, 'to whom I (like thousands of
Central European men and women devoid of any Jewish background)
owe my initiation into the realm of Jewish culture.' [2]

Today, in the third generation of his writing, speaking, and teaching,
Martin Buber is without question not only the representative figure of
Western European Jewry but of world Jewry as well. No one has done
more than he to bring about a rebirth of Judaism, and his works
promise to affect generations of thinking religious Jews of the future

---

[1] Ludwig Lewisohn, *Rebirth, A Book of Modern Jewish Thought* (New York:
Harper & Brothers, 1935), p. 87; cf. p. 88 f. and Ludwig Lewisohn, *Cities and Men*
(New York: Harper & Brothers, 1927), pp. 200-212.

[2] Franz Rosenzweig, 'Martin Buber,' *Jüdisches Lexikon* (Berlin: Jüdischer
Verlag, 1927), Vol. I, col. 1190 f. Cf. Franz Rosenzweig, *Kleinere Schriften* (Berlin:
Schocken Verlag, 1937), p. 106. Alfred Werner, 'Buber at Seventy,' *Congress Weekly*,
Vol. XV (February 13, 1948), p. 10; Liptzin, *Germany's Stepchildren, op. cit.*, p. 263 f.

The steady spread of his influence from Europe to England and from Israel to America makes it clear that this is no temporary phenomenon but a deep-seated force in the life and destiny of the Jewish people. In his early twenties Buber associated himself with the great Zionist leader, Theodore Herzl, and in 1901 he became the editor of the Zionist journal, *Der Welt*. He broke shortly with Herzl, however, because of the latter's purely political Zionism, and he became the leader of those Zionists (including Chaim Weizmann) who demanded that the movement be founded on the basis of a Jewish cultural renaissance. In 1902 this group founded the Jüdischer Verlag, which later became the publishing house for the most important Zionist literature, and in 1916 Buber founded the journal *Der Jude*, which became the central point for the higher spiritual strivings of the Zionist movement. As a result of its high level, moreover, *Der Jude* became the leading organ of German-speaking Jewry.[1]

Although Buber gave up active leadership in the Zionist movement in favour of his broader religious, philosophical, and social interests, he continued to exert a strong influence on the Zionist movement through his speeches and writings. Through his emphasis on the building of a real Jewish community, he became a co-creator of the idea of the *Chaluzim*, or pioneers. For the furtherance of this goal, his circle joined forces in 1919 with the Palestinian 'Hapoel Hazair,' led by A. D. Gordon. Adolf Böhm lists Buber, Nathan Birnbaum, and A. D. Gordon as the three most influential leaders of Zionism after Herzl. The new perspective which Buber gave to Zionism was not understood outside of a narrow circle, and it evoked the most intense enmity of all the nationalistic-political Zionists. Yet, according to Böhm, whoever was able to follow Buber was freed by his point of view from torturing doubts and inspired to more intensive work. In the whole sphere of Zionist activity, even that of political organization, it was Buber's disciples who accomplished what was essential.[2]

Buber's attitude toward Zionism is integrally related to his conviction that in the work of redemption Israel is called on to play the special part of beginning the kingdom of God through itself becoming a holy people. This election is not an occasion for particularist pride but a commission which must be carried out in all humility. It is not to be understood as an objective fact or a subjective feeling but as an uncompleted dialogical reality, the awareness of an address from God. In it the Biblical covenant to make real the kingship of God through partnership with the land is combined with the Deutero-Isaianic concept

[1] Robert Weltsch, 'Martin Buber,' *Jüdische Lexikon, op. cit.*, Vol. I, col. 1191; Adolf Böhm, *Die zionistische Bewegung bis zum Ende des Weltkrieges*, 2nd enlarged edition (Tel Aviv: Hozaah Ivrith Co., 1935), Vol. I, pp. 203 f., 297 ff., 535.
[2] Böhm, *Die zionistische Bewegung*, Vol. I, pp. 521-540.

of the 'servant' under whose leadership Israel will initiate God's kingdom.[1]

Israel's special vocation is not just another nationalism which makes the nation an end in itself. The people need the land and freedom to organize their own life in order to realize the goal of community. But the state as such is at best only a means to the goal of Zion, and it may even be an obstacle to it if the true nature of Zion as commission and task is not held uppermost.[2]

> Zion means a destiny of mutual perfecting. It is not a calculation but a command; not an idea but a hidden figure waiting to be revealed. Israel would lose its own self if it replaced Palestine by another land and it would lose its own self if it replaced Zion by Palestine.[3]

If Israel reduces Zionism to 'a Jewish community in Palestine' or tries to build a small nation just like other small nations, it will end by attaining neither.[4]

One of the means by which Buber exerted the greatest influence on the Zionist movement was through his discovery and re-creation of Hasidism. According to Robert Weltsch, 'Buber's discovery of Hasidism was epochal for the West: Buber made his thesis believable that no renewal of Judaism would be possible which did not bear in itself elements of Hasidism.'[5] Through this discovery Buber opened up important new aspects of Jewish experience to the Jews of Western Europe and at the same time helped bridge the growing gap between them and the Jews of Eastern Europe.

> Buber proved conclusively that the despised 'poor relations' in the East possessed inner treasures of great power and depth which it was impossible any longer to ignore. . . . Thus he came to embody the ultimate synthesis of the two cultural traditions and to become its living symbol as well as its finest flower.[6]

In his earlier writings Buber regarded Hasidism as the real, though subterranean Judaism, as opposed to official Rabbinism which was only the outer husk. He has since come to feel that in Hasidism the essence of Jewish faith and religiosity was visible in the structure of the

---

[1] *Israel and Palestine, op. cit.*, pp. 34 f., 49 ff., 54; *The Prophetic Faith*, p. 232 ff.

[2] *Israel and the World*, 'On National Education,' p. 159; 'Der Chaluz und seine Welt,' *op. cit.*, p. 90 ff.; *Israel and Palestine*, pp. 70 f., 74, 76 f., 117 ff., 121, 125, 144, 147 f.; *Two Letters to Gandhi, op. cit.*, p. 10 f.

[3] *Israel and Palestine*, p. 142.

[4] *Ibid.*, p. 144 f.

[5] *Jüdisches Lexikon*, Vol. I, col. 1191 (my translation).

[6] Wolf, 'Martin Buber and German Jewry,' *op. cit.*, p. 348.

community but that this essence has also been present 'in a less condensed form everywhere in Judaism,' in the 'inaccessible structure of the personal life.' Buber differs from other thinkers in regarding the life of the Hasidim as the core of Hasidism and the philosophical texts as a gloss on the life as it is depicted in the legends. In his first Hasidic books Buber exercised a great deal of freedom in the retelling of the Hasidic legends in the belief that this was the best way to get at the essence of the Hasidic spirit.[1] In 1921 he rejected this method of translating on the grounds that it was 'too free.' His later tales, accordingly, are closely faithful to the simple and rough originals. They are often fragmentary sayings and anecdotes rather than complete stories.[2] Technical criticism of Buber's retelling of the Hasidic legends is beside the point, writes Ludwig Lewisohn.

, These legends will remain a permanent possession of mankind in the form he has given them by virtue of that form which has itself become a part of their message and meaning. Thus, too, his reinterpretation of the Jewish past is beyond the arbitrament of factual scholarship; it has the permanence of great artistic *vision*; it has created that past in the soul of the present and is *itself* an enduring part of Jewish reality.[3]

No one who has read carefully Buber's later Hasidic tales and Biblical interpretations could now accuse him of undue freedom, no matter how much they might disagree with his methods or with the conclusions that he reaches. A much more serious and frequent criticism is the fact that Buber does not regard the Jewish law as essential to the Jewish tradition. To understand this attitude we must go back to the last of his 'Talks on Judaism' in which he contrasts the false desire for security of the dogmatists of the law with the 'holy insecurity' of the truly religious man who does not divorce his action from his intention. Religious truth is obstructed, writes Buber, by those who demand obedience to all the commandments of the Jewish law without actually believing that law to be directly revealed by God. To obey the *Mizwot* without this basic feeling means to abandon both them and oneself to

---

[1] *Israel and the World*, 'The Faith of Judaism,' p. 13; *Hasidism*, 'The Beginnings of Hasidism,' p. 4 f.; *Die Legende des Baalschem*, *op. cit.*, 'Einleitung.' Lazar Gulkowitsch writes of Buber's early poetic recreations of Hasidism: 'Since Martin Buber is a poet who himself inclines to mysticism, Hasidism in his representation takes on an all too mysterious colouring while its natural childlike quality and its sheer naïveté do not receive adequate emphasis.' Gulkowitsch, *Der Hasidismus*, *op. cit.*, p. 66 (my translation).

[2] *Tales of the Hasidim, The Early Masters*, *op. cit.*, p. xi. Cf. pp. v-xii and Martin Buber, *Der grosse Maggid und seine Nachfolge* (Frankfurt am Main: Rütten & Loenig, 1922), Vorwort, pp. v-ix.

[3] Lewisohn, *Rebirth*, *op. cit.*, p. 87.

an autonomous ethic. The relation to the Absolute is a relation of the whole man, undivided in mind and soul. To cut off the actions that express this relation from the affirmation of the whole human mind means to profane them. The image of man toward which we strive is one in which conviction and will, personality and its deed are one and indivisible.[1]

The dogmatists of the law reply to Buber that spirit remains a shadow and command an empty shell if one does not lend them life and consciousness from the fountain of Jewish tradition. Otherwise, they say, your direction will be self-will and arbitrariness rather than what is necessary. How can you decide between that part of God's word which appears to you fresh and applicable and that which appears to you old and worn out? Buber answers this challenge in terms of the 'holy insecurity' which makes one willing to risk oneself ever again without hoping to find once for all a secure truth.

> O you secure and safe ones who hide yourselves behind the defence-works of the law so that you will not have to look into God's abyss! Yes, you have secure ground under your feet while we hang suspended, looking out over the endless deeps. But we would not exchange our dizzy insecurity and our poverty for your security and abundance. For to you God is one who created once and not again; but to us God is he who 'renews the work of creation every day.' To you God is one who revealed himself once and no more; but to us he speaks out of the burning thorn-bush of the present . . . in the revelations of our innermost hearts— greater than words.
>
> We know of his will only the eternal; the temporal we must command for ourselves, ourselves imprint his wordless bidding ever anew in the stuff of reality. . . . In genuine life between men the new word will reveal itself to us. First we must act, then we shall receive: from out of our own deed.[2]

There is a significant continuity between Buber's present attitude and that of these early essays. To Buber Zionism represents the opportunity of the people to continue its ancient existence on the land which has been interrupted by the generations of exile. This implies that Jewish existence in the diaspora from the time of the exile to the present cannot be understood as Judaism in the full sense of the term. The religious observances developed in the exile have the character, in Buber's opinion, of conserving what was realized in the Jewish state before the exile. Following Moses Hess, he holds that the spirit of the old Jewish

[1] *Reden über das Judentum, op. cit.,* 'Cheruth' (1919), pp. 202-209, 217-224.
[2] *Ibid.,* 'Der heilige Weg' (1919), pp. 65, 71 (my translation).

institutions which is preserved by these observances will have the power to create new laws in accordance with the needs of the time and the people once it is able to develop freely again on the soil of Palestine.[1]

Buber's position on the law has been interpreted by many, such as the Orthodox leader Jacob Rosenheim, as a dangerous glorification of subjective feeling at the expense of the objective content of actions.[2] This criticism reveals a total misunderstanding of Buber's philosophy of dialogue which is, as we have seen, a narrow ridge between the abysses of objectivism on the one side and subjectivism on the other. Even some critics who accept the fundamental reality of the I-Thou relation as 'the centre of any genuine religious experience' treat 'revelation' as the objective—'the act of God whereby He has disclosed the way and destiny of Israel'—and meeting, or the I-Thou relation, as the subjective—'the act of man whereby that destiny and its divine source are drawn into the inner life of the individual.' Man's response to God thus becomes subjective 'apprehension' of an objective truth, and the objectified law becomes more important than the relation with God itself.[3]

Another not infrequent misunderstanding of Buber's attitude toward the law is that it is in reality a form of antinomianism. Here as elsewhere those who think exclusively in terms of either-or find it very difficult to follow Buber's thought. What Buber is really stressing is the danger of 'anticipated objectification'—the danger of preventing the personal renewal of the instruction when it becomes objectified and rigid as it inevitably must.[4] Personal responsibility is as far from lawlessness on the one side as it is from rigidified formal law on the other. The history of antinomian sects and movements, Buber writes, shows clearly that the isolated divine freedom abolishes itself when it rebels against divine law. 'Without law, that is, without any clear-cut and transmissible line of demarcation between that which is pleasing to God and that which is displeasing to Him, there can be no historical continuity of divine rule upon earth.' The reciprocity between man and God implies, however, that the divine law must be freely apprehended by one's own act.[5] This

[1] *Israel and Palestine*, p. 122.
[2] Jacob Rosenheim, *Beiträge zur Orientierung im jüdischen Geistesleben der Gegenwart* (Zürich: Verlag 'Arzenu,' 5680, 1920), pp. 10, 19-23, 27 ff.
[3] Arthur A. Cohen, 'Revelation and Law, Reflections on Martin Buber's Views on Halakah,' *Judaism*, Vol. I, No. 3 (July 1952), pp. 250-256. For a fuller criticism of Cohen see my article, 'Revelation and Law in the Thought of Martin Buber,' *Judaism*, Vol. III, No. 1 (Winter 1954), p. 16. For an attitude similar to Cohen's see Will Herberg's treatment of the law in *Judaism and Modern Man* (New York: Farrar, Straus & Young, 1951).
[4] From a statement made by Professor Buber at a small discussion group in New York City, December 1951.
[5] *Moses, op. cit.*, p. 187 f.; *Eclipse of God*, 'Religion and Ethics,' p. 129 f.

in no way implies the position of the antinomians who claim that the law as such displaces freedom and the spirit and therefore ought to be replaced by them.

The true argument of the rebellion is that in the world of the law what has been inspired always becomes emptied of the spirit, but that in this state it continues to maintain its claim of full inspiration; or, in other words, that the living element always dies off but that thereafter what is left continues to rule over living men. And the *true* conclusion is that the law must again and again immerse itself in the consuming and purifying fire of the spirit, in order to renew itself and anew refine the genuine substance out of the dross of what has become false.[1]

Franz Rosenzweig has written the best-known and most persuasive criticism of Buber's position on the law. In 'Die Bauleute' Rosenzweig makes clear that his support of the law is based upon the covenant that God has made, not with our fathers, 'but with us, us, these here today, us all, the living.' The content of the teaching must be transformed into the power of our actions; general law must become personal command. The selection of that part of the law which the individual shall perform is an entirely individual one since it depends not upon the will but upon what one is able to do. This selection cannot err for it is based upon obedience of the whole person rather than arbitrary choice.[2]

In his reply to 'Die Bauleute' Buber makes a distinction between revelation and the giving of the law which Rosenzweig has failed to make: 'I do not believe that revelation is ever lawgiving, and in the fact that lawgiving always comes out of it, I see the fact of human opposition, the fact of man.' Rosenzweig recognizes the importance of making the law one's own, but he affirms the whole of the law to be divine prior to this personal appropriation, while Buber cannot. Rosenzweig accepts the command as from God and leaves open the question of whether the individual *can* fulfil it, whereas Buber remains close to the dialogue and makes the real question whether it really is a command of God to oneself. To Buber the law cannot be accepted unless it is believed in, and it cannot be believed in as something general or universal but only as an embodiment of a real address by God to particular individuals. 'Is that said to me, really to me?' Buber asks. On this basis he can at times join himself to the Israel to whom a particular law is addressed and many times not. 'And if I could with undivided heart name anything *mitzwa* [3]

---

[1] *Moses*, p. 188.

[2] Franz Rosenzweig, 'Die Bauleute. "Über das Gesetz." An Martin Buber.' *Kleinere Schriften, op. cit.*, pp. 109-117, 120.

[3] Divine command or prescription.

in my own life, it is just this, that I thus do and thus leave undone.'[1]

Rosenzweig wished to induce Buber to accept the law as a universal. This, to Buber, would be 'faith in a proposition' (*pistis*) as opposed to that trust (*emunah*) which he feels to be the essence of Judaism.

The Torah of God is understood as God's instruction in His way and therefore not as a separate *objectivum*. It includes laws, and laws are indeed its most vigorous objectivizations, but the Torah itself is essentially not law. A vestige of the actual speaking always adheres to the commanding word, the directing voice is always present or at least its sound is heard fading away.[2]

This dialogical quality of the Torah is endangered by the hardening process which brought Torah near the conception of law as an objective possession of Israel and which thereafter tends to supplant the vital contact with the ever-living revelation and instruction. The struggle against this tendency to make the keeping of rules independent of the surrender to the divine will runs through the whole history of Israelite-Jewish faith—from the prophet's protest against sacrifice without intention and the Pharisees' protest against the 'tinged-ones' whose inwardness is a pretence up till its peculiarly modern form in Hasidism, in which every action gains validity only by a specific devotion of the whole man turning immediately to God. Thus though the tendency toward the objectivizing of the Torah gained ground in Israel from the beginning, the actuality of faith again and again liberated the living idea. 'This inner dialectic of Having and Being is . . . the main moving force in the spiritual history of Israel.'[3]

Today, however, 'Israel and the principle of its being have come apart.' Despite a national home and freedom to realize itself, the rift between the people and the faith is wider than ever.[4] In this breaking-up of the nation and faith the purpose of becoming a holy nation is repudiated. Reform Judaism tends to look on Judaism as religious creed, Orthodox Judaism tends to look on it as religious laws, both without the real existence of a people as a people. Zionists tend to look on it as a national destiny and perhaps also a culture but not as a people embodying an essential relationship to God in the life of the community.

---

[1] Martin Buber, 'Offenbarung und Gesetz' (from letters to Franz Rosenzweig), *Almanach des Schocken Verlags auf das Jahr 5697 (1936-37)*, pp. 149-153 (my translation). (The dates of the letters are 1/10/22; 1/7/24; 5/7/24.) Cf. Franz Rosenzweig, *Briefe*, ed. by Edith Rosenzweig with the co-operation of Ernst Simon (Berlin: Schocken Verlag, 1935), # 399 To Martin Buber (16/7/24), p. 504 f.; # 398 To Martin Buber (29/6/24), p. 503 f.; and # 400 To Martin Buber (July 1924), p. 505.
[2] *Two Types of Faith, op. cit.*, p. 57.
[3] *Ibid.*, p. 58 f.
[4] *At the Turning, op. cit.*, p. 24.

The only remedy for this splitting-apart of nation and faith is a great renewal of the national faith.

> The dialectic of Israel between those giving up themselves to guidance and those 'letting themselves go' must come to a decision in the souls themselves, so that the task of becoming a holy nation may set itself in a new situation and a new form suitable to it. The individuals, regenerated in the crisis, who maintain themselves in Emunah, would have fulfilled the function . . . of sustaining the living substance of faith through the darkness.[1]

What it means to sustain the living substance of faith through the eclipse is perhaps best shown by Buber's own leadership of the German Jews in their spiritual war against Naziism. After the rise of Hitler, Buber was appointed as director of the Central Office for Jewish Adult Education in Germany, where 'he was responsible for the training of teachers for the new schools which had to be established as a result of the exclusion of Jewish students from all German educational institutions.' He also helped guide the teaching, learning, and training activities of the numerous Jewish youth organizations, and he headed the Frankfurter Jüdische Lehrhaus, a free college for Jewish adult education.[2]

> From these central and strategic positions, Buber directed his spiritual energies to the remotest corners of the Jewish community. To the thousands who were reached and electrified by his words it meant the difference between the suffering of a meaningless fate and the liberating insight into the ultimate triumph of Jewish spirit which knows no defeat. . . . He was able to save many from spiritual despair.[3]

Martin Buber led a whole community of Jews to a deeper affirmation of their Jewishness, Ernest Wolf concludes. And Jacob Minkin writes:

> He counselled, comforted, raised their dejected spirits. . . . Perhaps not many of those who listened to him survived the fiendish slaughter, but if they perished, they died with a firmer faith in their hearts and a deeper conviction in their minds of their people's spiritual destiny. Martin Buber had taught them to die as Jews had always died—sanctifying the Name.[4]

In the spring of 1952 Buber was awarded the Goethe Prize by the University of Hamburg for his 'activity in the spirit of a genuine

---

[1] *Two Types of Faith*, p. 171 f.
[2] Wolf, 'Martin Buber and German Jewry,' p. 351.
[3] *Ibid.*, p. 351 f.
[4] Jacob S. Minkin, 'The Amazing Martin Buber,' *Congress Weekly*, Vol. XVI (January 17, 1949), p. 10 ff.

humanity' and for 'an exemplary cultural activity which serves the mutual understanding of men and the preservation and continuation of a high spiritual tradition.' In accepting this award Buber recalled the number of Germans whom he knew during the time of Hitler who risked punishment and death in order to help the German Jews. 'I see this as a more than personal manifestation and a symbolic confession,' he wrote, 'and accept it as such.' This award was indeed a more than personal symbol, but it was of great personal significance as well: Martin Buber is the only person who stands in such a relation to the Germans, the Jews, and the people of the world that he might receive such a confession for his people.

CHAPTER TWENTY-SEVEN

BUBER AND CHRISTIANITY

I

MARTIN BUBER'S influence on religious thought has steadily grown and spread for more than three generations and has been equally great among Christian thinkers as among Jews. Among the prominent Christian religious thinkers whom Buber has significantly influenced are John Baillie, Karl Barth, Nicholas Berdyaev, Emil Brunner, Father M. C. D'Arcy, Herbert H. Farmer, J. E. Fison, Friedrich Gogarten, Karl Heim, Reuel Howe, Hermann von Keyserling, Ernst Michel, Reinhold Niebuhr, H. Richard Niebuhr, J. H. Oldham, Theodore Steinbüchel, and Paul Tillich. Mention should also be made of a number of Christian thinkers whose religious thought has significantly paralleled Buber's without either influencing or being influenced by him. Of these the most important are Ferdinand Ebner, John Macmurray, Gabriel Marcel, and Eugene Rosenstock-Huessy.

The first of a series of Swiss pamphlets subtitled 'Building Stones of a Coming Protestantism' is devoted to 'Martin Buber's Way in Our Time.' In this pamphlet, written in 1940, Walter Nigg says that Martin Buber 'possesses a paradigmatic significance' for the religious situation of modern man:

> If he was not able to change the face of the present in a decisive way, his groping toward the mainsprings of human existence enables one not only to grasp more deeply the religious situation of our time but also to foresee the direction in which a new breakthrough must be sought.[1]

In 1947 J. H. Oldham, a leader of the ecumenical movement in the Christian Church, made a similar but even more forceful appraisal of Buber's significance for Christianity:

> I am convinced that it is by opening its mind, and conforming its practice, to the truth which Buber has perceived and so power-

---

[1] Nigg, 'Martin Bubers Weg in unserer Zeit,' *op. cit.*, p. 5 (my translation).

fully set forth that the Church can recover a fresh understanding of its own faith, and regain a real connection with the actual life of our time.[1]

In 1948 Paul Tillich, who has himself been greatly influenced by Buber, wrote of his significance for Protestant theology as lying in three main directions: his 'existential interpretation of prophetic religion, his rediscovery of mysticism as an element within prophetic religion, and his understanding of the relation between prophetic religion and culture, especially in the social and political realms.'

> Buber's existential 'I-Thou' philosophy . . . should be a powerful help in reversing the victory of the 'It' over the 'Thou' *and* the 'I' in present civilization. . . . The 'I-Thou' philosophy . . . challenging both orthodox and liberal theology, points a way beyond their alternatives.[2]

'Professor Buber,' writes J. Coert Rylaarsdam, 'is in a unique way the agent through whom, in our day, Judaism and Christianity have met and enriched one another.' The German Catholic theologian Karl Thieme sees Buber's impact as coming principally through his position of 'an outspoken "between,"' the position that we have called 'the narrow ridge.' Although deeply identifying himself with Judaism, Buber cannot be classified as either Orthodox, Reform, or political Zionist, writes Thieme. At the same time, he has gone as far as a Jew could go in honouring Jesus of Nazareth. His insistence that God needs man's help to complete creation brings him close to Catholicism but removes him from Protestant Christianity, while his enmity toward any fixed laws and rules brings him close to radical Protestantism while setting him apart from Catholicism. Such a 'between-existence' poses a question to Buber's contemporaries—whether they will make use of it as a bridge of understanding between camp and camp or lay it aside as indifferent to all camps because it can be exploited by none. The answer to this question, in Thieme's opinion, does not depend so much on the influence of Buber's Hasidic teaching or his existentialist philosophy as on whether Christian theologians will allow themselves in earnest to be fructified by Buber's interpretation of the Bible.[3]

It is *I and Thou* which has in particular received great attention, and

---

[1] Joseph Houldsworth Oldham, *Real Life Is Meeting* (London: The Sheldon Press; New York: The Macmillan Co., 1947), pp. 13-16.

[2] Paul Tillich, 'Martin Buber and Christian Thought,' *Commentary*, Vol. V, No. 6 (June 1948), p. 397. For a further evaluation of Buber's significance as an alternative to orthodox and liberal Protestantism see Tillich, 'Jewish Influences on Contemporary Christian Theology,' *Cross Currents*, Vol. II (1952), pp. 38-42.

[3] Rylaarsdam, 'The Prophetic Faith,' *op. cit.*, p. 399; Thieme, 'Martin Buber als Interpret der Bibel,' *op. cit.*, p. 8 f.

many recent Continental and English works give evidence that it is already recognized as a classic. Walter Marshall Horton points it out as the most explicit example of the new sense of depth in Continental theology since 1914. J. H. Oldham says of it: 'I question whether any book has been published in the present century the message of which, if it were understood and heeded, would have such far-reaching consequences for the life of our time.'[1] Oldham expands this statement in another place:

> The realization of the crucial significance of relations between persons, and of the fundamentally *social* nature of reality is the necessary, saving corrective of the dominance of our age by the scientific way of thinking, the results of which, as we know, may involve us in universal destruction, and by the technical mastery of things, which threatens man with the no less serious fate of dehumanization.[2]

Herbert H. Farmer speaks of the central concept of *I and Thou* as the most important contribution given to us of recent years toward the reflective grasp of our faith. 'It has already entered deeply into the theological thought of our time, and is, I believe, destined to enter still more deeply.'[3]

I and Thou occupies an important place in the Episcopal Church's re-education of its clergy for its new wholesale, long-range education programme, and it has had a decisive influence on the 'relational theology' in terms of which this programme has been oriented.[4] One Anglo-Catholic theologian, J. E. Fison, uses Buber's philosophy as the central element in his plea for a greater emphasis on the blessing of the Holy Spirit. 'The whole conception of spirit,' writes Fison, 'as much in St. John 3 and in St. Augustine as in the Old Testament, points to that between-ness in which Buber sees the essential meaning of life.'[5]

---

[1] Oldham, *op. cit.*, p. 27 f.

[2] J. H. Oldham, 'Life as Dialogue,' *The Christian News-Letter*, Supplement to No. 281 (March 19, 1947), p. 7 f.

[3] H. H. Farmer, *The Servant of the Word* (New York: Charles Scribner's Sons, 1942), p. 25 f.

[4] According to the Rev. James Pike, Dean of the Cathedral of St. John the Divine, the Episcopal Church is now engaged in the development of a programme of education from the cradle to the grave, as a part of which its clergy is being systematically trained, at the College of Preachers in Washington, in 'relational theology,' an application of the I-Thou relation to sacrament, grace, and redemption, conceived in relational terms, primarily in the family. For one such application, and a particularly successful one, see R. L. Howe, *Man's Need and God's Answer* (Greenwich, Conn.: Seabury Press, 1952).

[5] J. E. Fison, *The Blessing of the Holy Spirit* (London: Longmans, Green & Co., 1950), pp. 28, 65, 126 f., 139, 143 f.

II

The widespread influence of *I and Thou* on Christian thought does not mean, unfortunately, an equally widespread understanding of Buber's I-Thou philosophy. Many have not followed Oldham's warning that *I and Thou* is a book which must be reread again and again and allowed slowly to remould one's thought. Not only has Buber's I-Thou philosophy been applied in the most diverse ways, but it has also, at times, been seriously distorted in the application. Melville Channing-Pearce, for example, speaks of *I and Thou* as a 'manifest justification of Christianity as . . . a "cosmic mystery play" of the fall, the redemption and resurrection of being.' [1] This statement is incompatible both with Buber's Jewishness and with the concreteness of the meeting with the Thou. Nicholas Berdyaev has taken over Buber's I-Thou philosophy in *Society and Solitude*, but he has never really understood the ontological significance of the sphere of the 'between.' Though he recognizes that no I exists without a Thou, his real emphasis is on subjectivity and inwardness. At the same time, he criticizes Buber in a way that no careful reader of *I and Thou* could possibly do, suggesting that for Buber the I-Thou relation is uniquely between man and God and not between man and man and within the larger human community.[2]

The German theologian Karl Heim and the Swedish theologian John Cullberg have both systematized the I-Thou philosophy to the point where it bears unmistakable traces of that reliance on the reality of abstraction which characterizes I-It. This is particularly true of Heim's recasting of the distinction between the I-Thou and the I-It relations in terms of a mathematical analogy of dimensions.[3] The greatest danger of this type of overconceptualization is that it may lead one to remain content with dialogical philosophizing in place of lived dialogue. The German Benedictine monk, Fr. Caesarius Lauer, has pointed to this danger with uncommon effectiveness in a letter written to Buber in 1951:

> The 'dialogue' about dialogue is growing on all sides. That should make one glad, but it disquiets me. For—if all the signs do not deceive—the talk about dialogue takes from men the living experience of dialogical life. . . . In dialogic it is the realization

---

[1] Nicodemus (pseud.), *Renascence, An Essay in Faith* (London: Faber and Faber Ltd., 1943), p. 73 ff.

[2] Berdyaev, *Solitude and Society, op. cit.*, p. 79 ff. For a further illustration of Berdyaev's misinterpretation of Buber, mixed with a strong appreciation, cf. Berdyaev's review of *Die chassidischen Bücher, Ich und Du, Zwiesprache*, and *Königtum Gottes* in an article in the Russian religious journal *Put'*, *Organ russkoi religioznoi mysli* (Paris), No. 38 (May 1933), pp. 87-91.

[3] Heim, *Glaube und Denken, op. cit.*, and *God Transcendent, op. cit.*; Cullberg, *Das Du und die Wirklichkeit, op. cit.*, Systematic Part.

271

that is decisive, since it is working reality, that means—Life. Now, the word certainly belongs to this realization, as Ebner has well shown. But just the word, not words, not talk, logicizing dialectic. . . . It is just the 'spiritual' man of today who suffers in a frightful fashion the old temptation of the human spirit, that is to say, that of objectifying the living accomplishment. . . . These 'dialogical' dialecticians do not seem to notice that the dialogic is essentially a way. However, 'the way is there that one may walk on it,' as you once said.[1]

Many of the Christian thinkers and theologians who have adopted the I-Thou philosophy have recast it in the form of a radical dualism between the I-Thou and the I-It relations entirely incompatible with Buber's own thought. Writers like Friedrich Gogarten, Melville Channing-Pearce, Emil Brunner, and Karl Barth in varying degrees equate I-It with man's sinful nature, and I-Thou with the grace and divine love which are only present in their purity in Christ. Even though Brunner and Barth both recognize that man's existence as man is made possible only through the I-Thou relation, they both emphasize the limitations that man's sinfulness places upon his ability to enter into this relationship. Karl Heim, in contrast, writes that both the movement of sacrifice for the other and that of closing oneself against him are possible within the I-Thou relation. By thus divorcing this relation from the clear ethical implications which both Buber and Ferdinand Ebner have given it, Heim makes possible a dualism on the basis of which he characterizes man's relation with the eternal Thou as taking place in an altogether different dimension from his relation with his human Thou. Father M. C. D'Arcy mistakenly assumes that Heim is developing what was implicit in Buber and, as a result, ascribes to Buber the dualism which is present in Heim.[2]

The ultimate ethical consequence of this radical split between I-Thou and I-It is a de-emphasis on the possibility and significance of ethical action and a tendency to reduce man to the role of passive recipient of grace. Thus Gogarten says that the I never initiates ethical action but only fulfils or denies the claim of the Thou.[3] Another result is the tendency to place the ethical choice in terms of the choice between one's

[1] Quoted with the permission of the author (my translation). The quotation in Fr. Caesarius' letter is from Buber's Preface to his book *Das verborgene Licht* (Frankfurt am Main: Rütten & Loening, 1924).

[2] Gogarten, *Ich Glaube an den dreieinigen Gott, op. cit.*, pp. 103-116, 142-152, 182-188; Brunner, *Wahrheit als Begegnung, op. cit.*, pp 66 f., 77 f., *Man in Revolt, op. cit.*, chap. vi; Heim, *Glaube und Denken*, pp. 258-261, 328 ff., 342-349, 370-374; *God Transcendent*, chap. vii; M. C. D'Arcy, *The Mind and Heart of Love, Lion and Unicorn, A Study in Eros and Agape* (New York: Henry Holt & Co., 1947), p. 204, cf. pp. 114-123, 218, 318-321.

[3] Gogarten, *op. cit.*, pp. 110-116.

own interest and that of others. This second result is seen most clearly in Gogarten's reworking of Buber's philosophy of I *and* Thou into a philosophy of I *or* Thou. One must choose *between* the I and the Thou, says Gogarten, and in this he is followed by John Cullberg and to a lesser degree by Heim. This same emphasis is found in the thought of Will Herberg, the modern Jewish thinker who, under the influence of Reinhold Niebuhr, has given a strongly Protestant coloration to the I-Thou philosophy which he has taken over from Buber.[1] This position is unrealistic, for it forgets the participation of the I even in so-called 'altruistic' actions. It also shows that neither Gogarten nor Cullberg have understood the true basis of the I-Thou philosophy which they have adopted, for reality is not *within* each of the two individuals in a relationship, as they seem to think, but *between* them.

Karl Barth has rejected the dualism between *eros* and *agape* in his own Christianizing of the I-Thou relation. He has also followed Buber in emphasizing the quality of spontaneity and reciprocity in the I-Thou relation which must rule out any confusion of this relation with dominance or submission.[2] Writing in 1948, Barth very possibly had in mind the effects that followed in Germany from a confusion of real relationship with what Erich Fromm would call authoritarian or sado-masochistic relationship. Two earlier German theologians who took over Buber's I-Thou philosophy—Friedrich Gogarten and Karl Heim— both distorted it by reconciling it with an authoritarian attitude. In Gogarten's case this means submission to the state and, in Heim's, submission to another person.[3] Thus Heim writes:

I may submit to you as my authority or my guide. You may submit to me and recognize mine as the higher will. We may arrive at a voluntary agreement of comradeship and co-operation. But that this obedience and this fellowship always have the character of a 'Thou' relation, and can never be reduced to an 'It' relation, may be seen from the fact that the tension inherent in the 'Thou' relation cannot be happily resolved except by submission or fellowship.[4]

---

[1] *Ibid.*, pp. 109-149; Cullberg, *op. cit.*, pp. 201 ff., 222-226; Heim, *Glaube und Denken*, pp. 342-349; Will Herberg, *Judaism and Modern Man* (New York: Farrar, Straus & Young, 1951), pp. 63-66, 72-79, 96, 101 f. Herberg writes: 'The dominion of sin can only be broken by a power not our own, the power of divine grace' (p. 77), and 'In the last analysis, the choice is only between love of God and love of self, between a *God*-centred and *self*-centred existence' (p. 96). I have devoted a whole section of my article, 'Martin Buber and Christian Thought,' to this aspect of Herberg's thought (*The Review of Religion*, Vol. XVIII, No. 1/2 (November 1953), p. 41 f. (sec. iv).

[2] Karl Barth, *Kirchliche Dogmatik*, Vol. III, Part 2: *Die Lehre von Schöpfung* (Zurich: Evangelischer Verlag, A. G. Zollikon, 1948), pp. 318-329, 337-340.

[3] For Buber's criticism of Gogarten's *Political Ethics* see *Between Man and Man*, 'The Question to the Single One,' p. 76 f.

[4] *God Transcendent*, pp. 163-167.

In the light of Buber's clear and consistent emphasis on the independence and full freedom of the two partners to the I-Thou relationship, it is ironical to find Karl Barth suggesting that the main difference between his I-Thou philosophy and that of Buber is that he (Barth) makes 'freedom of the heart between man and man the root and crown of the concept of humanity.' This freedom implies for Barth just that rejection of the attempt to remove the distance between the I and the Thou through dominance or submission which has always been the simplest pre-supposition of Buber's I-Thou relationship.[1] Buber's emphasis on spontaneity is much stronger, in fact, than that of Barth himself and the other Christian theologians using the I-Thou terminology—a difference probably caused by the Christian tendency to emphasize the gap between man's fallen nature and Christian love. The Christian tendency from Augustine to the Reformation to see faith as a gift of God has tended, in Buber's opinion, to obscure man's spontaneity:

> This sublime conception, with all that goes with it, resulted in the retreating into obscurity of the Israelite mystery of man as an independent partner of God. The dogma of original sin was not, indeed, adapted to further that especial connection of the ethical with the religious that true theonomy seeks to realize through the faithful autonomy of man.[2]

III

It is not surprising that Christian theologians should have given a more dualistic cast to the I-Thou philosophy than Buber has. It is important that we be aware that this difference exists, however, for Buber's attitude toward evil is an integral part of his philosophy of dialogue and cannot be divorced from that philosophy without radically transforming it. There are many Christian interpretations of the I-Thou philosophy. For Fison it implies that the significance of the sacrifice on the cross lies in a two-way and reciprocal action in which God on the

---

[1] Barth, *op. cit.*, p. 333 ff. That Barth should thus misinterpret Buber is indeed strange in the light of the clearly great influence, both direct and indirect, of Buber's dialogical thought on Barth's revision of his theology in the direction of the I-Thou relationship. Although Barth was undoubtedly also influenced by Ferdinand Ebner and Karl Löwith, most of his terminology (*Ich und Du, Begegnung, Dialog, Monolog*) is Buber's. Testifying to this influence, Tillich writes: 'Through the great Swiss theologians, Barth and Brunner, Buber's basic idea has become a common good of Protestant theology.' 'Jewish Influences on Contemporary Theology,' *op. cit.*, p. 38. In his 'Nachwort' to *Die Schriften über das dialogische Prinzip* (p. 303 ff.) Buber replies at length to Barth's statements concerning him. For Hasidism, Buber writes, freedom of the heart between man and man is 'the innermost presupposition, the ground of grounds.'

[2] *Eclipse of God*, 'Religion and Ethics,' p. 140 f.

cross gave and received all. For Friedrich Gogarten it implies that God must be worshipped in the form of Christ, for only this form makes God sufficiently real as a Thou. For Romano Guardini it implies that Christ, through his perfect I-Thou relation with God, shows us the way to God, and for Barth it implies that Christ, as the son of God, has a perfect I-Thou relation with men, while men, being sinners against God, unfold their existence in opposition and closedness to the Thou.[1]

For Buber, in contrast, the I-Thou philosophy implies that God becomes an absolute person—an imageless and sometimes hiding God who cannot be limited to any one manifestation and, hence, cannot be understood as having become incarnate in Christ.[2] On the other hand, Buber has, recognized and pointed to the tremendous religious significance of Jesus as possibly no Jew has heretofore done while remaining firmly planted on the soil of Judaism. Buber wrote of Jesus in 1950:

> From my youth onwards I have found in Jesus my great brother. That Christianity has regarded and does regard him as God and Saviour has always appeared to me a fact of the highest importance which, for his sake and my own, I must endeavour to understand. . . . My own fraternally open relationship to him has grown ever stronger and clearer, and today I see him more strongly and clearly than ever before. I am more than ever certain that a great place belongs to him in Israel's history of faith and that this place cannot be described by any of the usual categories.[3]

Buber's forty years of concern with Jesus and Jesus' significance for Jewish Messianism have culminated in a study of Jesus and Paul, in *Two Types of Faith*, which cannot fail to be of great significance in both furthering and clarifying the relation between Judaism and Christianity. In this book he identifies faith as trust (*emunah*) with biblical and Pharisaic Judaism and with the teachings of Jesus; faith in the truth of a proposition (*pistis*) he identifies with Greek thought and Paulinism.[4]

'The life-history of Jesus cannot be understood, in my opinion,' writes Buber, 'if one does not recognize that he . . . stood in the shadow of the Deutero-Isaianic servant of the Lord.' Reproached for altering the figure of the 'holy Yehudi' in *For the Sake of Heaven* according to a conscious or unconscious Christian tendency, Buber answers that there is not one single trait of this figure which is not already to be found in the tradition of the suffering servant. But Jesus stepped out of the concealment of the 'quiver' (Isa. xlix, 2) while the 'holy Yehudi'

---

[1] Fison, *op. cit.*, pp. 196-202; Gogarten, *op. cit.*, pp. 142-188; Guardini, *Welt und Person*, *op. cit.*, pp. 114-126; Barth, *op. cit.*, pp. 265-272.

[2] *Two Types of Faith*, p. 38 f.

[3] *Ibid.*, p. 12 f.

[4] *Ibid.*, pp. 7-12.

remained therein.[1] The Messianic mystery is based on a real hiddenness which penetrates to the innermost existence and is essential to the servant's work of suffering. Although each successive servant may be the Promised One, in his consciousness of himself he dare not be anything other than a servant of the Lord. 'The arrow in the quiver is not its own master; the moment at which it shall be drawn out is not for it to determine.' If the servant should tear apart his hiddenness, not only would his work itself be destroyed but a counter-work would set in. It is in this light that we must understand the attitude of Judaism to the appearance of Jesus. The meaning of this appearance for the Gentiles 'remains for me the real seriousness of western history,' writes Buber. But from the point of view of Judaism, Jesus is the first of the series of men who acknowledged their Messiahship to themselves and the world. 'That this first one . . . in the series was incomparably the purest, the most legitimate of them all, the one most endowed with real Messianic power, does not alter the fact of his firstness.' [2]

Jesus's Messianic consciousness was probably influenced by the apocalyptic Book of Enoch, in which the form, but not the person, of the servant has pre-existence, and by the events of the end which may have led Jesus to step out of the concealment of the 'quiver' and imagine himself, after the vision of Daniel, as in his own person the one who will be removed and afterwards sent again to the office of fulfilment. Before the events of the end, Jesus undoubtedly did not see himself as anything other than the hidden servant. And even in the end, he did not hold himself divine in the sense in which he was later held. His Messianic consciousness may have been used by Paul and John as the beginning of the process of deification, but this process was only completed by the substitution of the resurrection for the removal of the servant and personal pre-existence for the pre-existence in form of the Jewish Apocalypses. It was only then that 'the fundamental and persistent character of the Messiah, as of one rising from humanity and clothed with power, was displaced by . . . a heavenly being, who came down to the world, sojourned in it, left it, ascended to heaven and now enters upon the dominion of the world which originally belonged to him.'

Furthermore, whatever was the case with his 'Messianic consciousness,' Jesus, in so far as we know him from the Synoptic tradition, did not summon his disciples to have faith in Christ. The faith which he preached was not the Greek *pistis*—faith in a proposition—but the

---

[1] *For the Sake of Heaven*, 2nd Edition (New York: Harpers & Brothers, 1953), Foreword, p. xii f. (In *Gog und Magog*, the German original, this is a postlude.)

[2] *Hasidism*, 'Spinoza,' p. 113 f. The second and last quotations are my own translation from the original, *Die chassidische Botschaft* (Heidelberg: Verlag Lambert Schneider, 1952), p. 29. *Two Types of Faith*, p. 107.

Jewish *emunah*—'that unconditional trust in the grace which makes a person no longer afraid even of death because death is also of grace.' Paul and John, in contrast, made faith in Christ (*pistis*) the one door to salvation. This meant the abolition of the immediacy between God and man which had been the essence of the Covenant and the kingship of God. '"I am the door" it now runs (John x, 9); it avails nothing, as Jesus thought, to knock where one stands (before the "narrow door"); it avails nothing, as the Pharisees thought, to step into the open door; entrance is only for those who believe in "the door."' [1]

The Jewish position regards the fulfilment of the divine command as valid when it takes place in conformity with the full capacity of the person, whereas Jesus demands that the person go beyond what would ordinarily be his full capacity in order to be ready to enter the kingdom of God which draws near.[2] Apart from this difference, Jesus' attitude toward the fulfilment of the commandments is essentially the same as the Jewish position. Both agree that the heart of man is by nature without direction and that 'there is no true direction except to God.' They also agree in the belief that God has given man the Torah as instruction to teach him to direct his heart to Him. The Torah is not an objective law independent of man's actual relationship to God: it bestows life only on those who receive it in association with its Giver, and for His sake.

For the actuality of the faith of Biblical and post-Biblical Judaism and also for the Jesus of the Sermon on the Mount, fulfilment of the Torah means to extend the hearing of the Word to the whole dimension of human existence.[3]

Paul, in contrast to Jesus, represents a decided turning away from the Biblical conception of the kingship of God and the immediacy between God and man. He posits a dualism between faith and action based on a belief in the impossibility of the fulfilment of the law. Law as he here conceives it is necessarily external; it derives from the Greek conception of an *objectivum* and is foreign to the Jewish understanding of Torah as instruction. This external law makes all men sinners before God, but man can be saved from this dilemma by faith in Christ. This faith, however, is essentially the Greek *pistis, faith in* the truth of a proposition—faith with a knowledge content.[4]

Trust in the immediacy between man and God is further destroyed through Paul's strong tendency to split off God's wrath and His mercy into two separate powers. He regards the world as given over to the

---

[1] *Two Types of Faith*, pp. 96 f., 102-113, 160.
[2] *Ibid.*, pp. 22 f., 56, 60 f., 79, 94.
[3] *Ibid.*, pp. 56 ff., 63 ff., 136 f.
[4] *Ibid.*, pp. 7 f., 11 f., 36-57, 79 f.

power of judgment until the crucifixion and resurrection of Christ brings mercy and redemption, and he regards man as by nature vile and as incapable of receiving pardon from God until the advent of Christ. For Paul, God's will to harden is no longer a part of His direct relation with a particular person or generation. 'For the sake of His plan of salvation God hardens all the generations of Israel, from that assembled on Sinai to that around Golgotha, with the exception of His chosen "Election" (Rom. xi, 7).' Paul's God has no regard for the people to whom He speaks but 'uses them up for higher ends.' [1]

Paul answers the problem of evil by creating, in effect, two separate Gods, one good and one bad. In Paul's view it is God alone who makes man unfree and deserving of wrath while in the work of deliverance God almost disappears behind Christ. 'The Highest Beings stand out from one another as dark omnipotence and shining goodness, not as later with Marcion in dogma and creed, but in the actual experience of the poor soul of man.' Although the Christian Paulinism of our time softens the demonocracy of the world, it too sees existence as divided into 'an unrestricted rule of wrath' and 'a sphere of reconciliation.' It raises energetically the claim for the establishment of a Christian order of life, 'but *de facto* the redeemed Christian soul stands over against an unredeemed world of men in lofty impotence.' This dualistic conception of God and his relation to the world is utterly unacceptable to Buber: 'In the immediacy we experience His anger and His tenderness in one,' he writes. 'No assertion can detach one from the other and make Him into a God of wrath Who requires a mediator.' In this connection Buber contrasts the modern Paulinism of Emil Brunner with Franz Kafka's 'Paulinism of the unredeemed.' Kafka knows God's hiddenness, and he describes most exactly from inner awareness 'the rule of the foul devilry which fills the foreground.' But Kafka, the Jew, also knows that God's hiding Himself does not diminish the immediacy: 'In the immediacy He remains the Saviour and the contradiction of existence becomes for us a theophany.' [2]

IV

Our awareness of the differences between Buber's thought and that of the Christian thinkers who have adopted the I-Thou philosophy need in no way imply a minimization of the very great similarities that exist between these religious leaders of different faiths. On the contrary, we presuppose this similarity, and we begin with the situation in which the resemblances are so great that the differences are often overlooked or obscured. Even where there are important differences, moreover, they

[1] *Two Types of Faith*, pp. 47, 81 ff., 85-90, 131-134, 137-142, 146-150.
[2] *Ibid.*, pp. 138-142, 162 ff., 168 f.

have contributed much to the fruitfulness of Buber's dialogue and friendship with such eminent Christian thinkers as Paul Tillich, Rudolf Bultmann, Albert Schweitzer, Rudolph Otto, and Leonhard Ragaz. The spirit in which Buber has carried on this dialogue is made clear in his reply to Rudolph Pannwitz's criticism that Buber's contrast between Judaism and Christianity has been unfavourable toward the latter: 'Religions,' writes Buber, 'are receptacles into which the spirit of man is fitted. Each of them has its origin in a separate revelation and its goal in the suspension of all separateness. Each represents the universality of its mystery in myth and rite and thus reserves it for those who live in it.' To compare one religion with another, valuing the one which is seen from within and devaluing the one which is seen from without, is always, therefore, a senseless undertaking. One can only compare the corresponding parts of the buildings according to structure, function, and connection with one another.[1] In an address in Jerusalem commemorating his great Christian socialist friend Ragaz, Buber made perhaps his most concise and impassioned statement on the place of Jesus in the Jewish community, a statement which shows at once the sympathy and the 'otherness' which have marked his dialogue with his Christian friends:

> I firmly believe that the Jewish community, in the course of its renaissance, will recognize Jesus; and not merely as a great figure in its religious history, but also in the organic context of a Messianic development extending over millennia, whose final goal is the Redemption of Israel and of the world. But I believe equally firmly that we will never recognize Jesus as the Messiah Come, for this would contradict the deepest meaning of our Messianic passion. . . . There are no knots in the mighty cable of our Messianic belief, which, fastened to a rock on Sinai, stretches to a still invisible peg anchored in the foundations of the world. In our view, redemption occurs forever, and none has yet occurred. Standing, bound and shackled, in the pillory of mankind, we demonstrate with the bloody body of our people the unredeemedness of the world. For us there is no cause of Jesus; only the cause of God exists for us.[2]

The faith of Judaism and that of Christianity will remain separate until the coming of the Kingdom, writes Buber. The Christian sees the Jew as the incomprehensibly obdurate man who declines to see what has happened, and the Jew sees the Christian as the incomprehensibly daring man who affirms redemption in an unredeemed world. Nevertheless, each can acknowledge the other's relation to truth when each cares

[1] *Origin and Meaning of Hasidism, op. cit.,* 'Christ, Hasidism, Gnosis.'
[2] Quoted in Ernst Simon, 'Martin Buber: His Way between Thought and Deed' (on Buber's 70th anniversary), *Jewish Frontier,* XV (February 1948), p. 26.

more for God than for his image of God. 'An Israel striving after the renewal of its faith through the rebirth of the person and a Christianity striving for the renewal of its faith through the rebirth of nations would have something as yet unsaid to say to each other and a help to give to one another hardly to be conceived at the present time.' [1]

[1] *Israel and the World*, 'The Two Foci of the Jewish Soul,' p. 39 f.; *Two Types of Faith*, p. 173 f.

CONCLUSION

I N his combination of spiritual tension, breadth of scope, and central unity Martin Buber is similar to three of his most important intellectual and spiritual masters, Kierkegaard, Dostoievsky, and Nietzsche. He has gone beyond them, however, in his unwillingness to emphasize intensity for its own sake or to sacrifice one element of thought for the dramatization of another. He has held in tension and brought toward unity the various elements that they tended to isolate or to convert into irreconcilable antinomies. He has sacrificed the simpler intensity of the 'Single One,' the 'God-man,' and the 'Superman' for the tremendous spiritual tension of the 'narrow ridge.' He has not, like Kierkegaard, devalued man's relation to man and to culture in favour of his individual relation with God; nor has he, like Nietzsche, stressed the dynamic realization of culture and value in individual life at the expense of the relation to God and fellow-man in all their independent 'otherness.' Like Dostoievsky, he has embraced rather than chosen between the opposites of self-affirmation and turning to God, of the individual and society, but he has gone beyond Dostoievsky in his ability to bring these opposites into true unity.

Buber's philosophy of dialogue has made possible a new understanding of the problem of evil because it has reaffirmed the basic significance of the personal relation between the Absolute, the world, and man as against the tendency to submerge man in a mechanistic universe or to reduce God to an impersonal and indirect first cause, an abstract monistic absolute, or an immanent vital force. The answer which Buber finds in the Book of Job, as in the I-Thou relationship, is not an answer which solves or removes the problem. Wrong does not become right, yet God is near to Job once again, and in this nearness Job finds meaning in what has happened to him, a meaning which cannot be stated in any other terms than those of the relationship itself. This answer is not implied in the statement of the question, as it might seem to be, for God's relation to man as the eternal Thou which never becomes an It does not make any the less real the 'silence' or 'eclipse' of God when He appears to hide Himself and we cut ourselves off from relation with Him. If He comes near to us again, this must be experienced as a real happening and not as a logical deduction from a set of basic assumptions.

Buber has demanded, as no other modern thinker, the hallowing of the everyday—the redemption of evil through the creation of human community in relation with God. Does this attitude toward evil meet the challenge of Sartre's existentialism, which sees evil as radical and unredeemable? Those who understand Buber's philosophy will not hesitate to answer yes, for that philosophy is essentially concrete, close to experience, and realistic as only a life open to the reality of evil in the profoundest sense could produce.

It is the inclusion of tragedy within the redemption of evil which marks Buber's deepest realism. Tragedy for Buber, as we have seen, is the conflict between two men through the fact that each of them is as he is. It is the tragedy of the contradiction, which arises from the fact that men cannot and do not respond to the address that comes to them from that which is over against them. They thereby crystallize this over-againstness into simple opposition and prevent the realization of its possibilities of relationship. This concept of tragedy is not an alternative to a religious view of life but an integral part of it. Not only Moses, but the prophets, the 'suffering servant,' Jesus and the Yehudi are to be understood in its light. Tragedy is not simply an event that should be removed, but in its deepest meaning an integral part of life. 'We cannot leave the soil of tragedy,' Buber has said, 'but in real meeting we can reach the soil of salvation after the tragedy has been completed.' For Buber the real distinction is not between a naïve acceptance of the world and the experiencing of its tragedy, but between the Gnostic belief in a contradiction that cuts the world off from God and the Jewish belief that 'tragedy' can be experienced in the dialogical situation, that the contradiction can become a theophany.

There is a movement from I-Thou to I-It even as from I-It to I-Thou, and one is sometimes tempted to believe that these movements are of equal force. To believe in the redemption of evil, however, means to believe that the movement from I-It to I-Thou, the penetration of I-It by I-Thou, is the fundamental one. This is a faith born out of the I-Thou relationship itself: it is trust in our relation with the Eternal Thou, in the ultimate oneness of the world with God. But redemption does not depend on God alone. Each man helps bring about the unity of God and the world through genuine dialogue with the created beings among whom he lives. Each man lets God into the world through hallowing the everyday.

BIBLIOGRAPHY

WORKS BY BUBER

'Abraham the Seer,' trans. Sophie Meyer, *Judaism*, Vol. 5, No. 4 (Fall).

'Abstrakt und Konkret,' additional note to 'Hoffnung für diese Stunde' (see below). *Merkur: Deutsche Zeitschrift für europaisches Denken*, Vol. 7, No. 1 (January 1953).

'Adult Education.' *Torah* (Magazine of Natl. Federation of Jewish Men's Clubs of United Synagogue of America), June 1952.

'Advice to Frequenters of Libraries,' 'Books for Your Vacation.' *Branch Library Book News*, New York Public Library, Vol. 21, No. 5 (May).

An der Wende: Reden über das Judentum. Köln and Olten: Jacob Hegner Verlag, 1952.

Arab-Jewish Unity. Testimony before the Anglo-American Inquiry Commission for the Ihud (Union) Association by Judah Magnes and Martin Buber. London: Victor Gollancz, 1947.

'Asketismus und Libertinismus,' *Jüdische Rundschau*, Vol. 22, No. 42 (October 19, 1917).

At the Turning; Three Addresses on Judaism. New York: Farrar, Straus, & Young, 1952.

'Die Aufgabe.' *Das werdende Zeitalter*, Vol. 1, No. 2 (April 1922).

'Aus dem Werk: Ueber den Zionismus, Wiedergeburt des Dialogs, Eine Bekehrung, Versöhnung, Gott.' In Hans Schwerte and Wilhelm Spengler, *Denker und Deuter im heutigen Europa: England, Frankreich, Spanien und Portugal, Italien, Osteuropa* (Martin Buber by Hans Joachim Schoeps). Oldenburg: G. Stalling, 1954. (*Gestalten unserer Zeit*, Vol. 2.)

'Aus der Uebersetzung der Bibel' (Neviim, Tehillim). In Rudolf Jockel, *Die Lebenden Religionen*. Berlin and Darmstadt: Deutsche Buch-Gemeinschaft, C. A. Koch's Verlag Nach., 1958.

'Aus einem Rundschreiben vom Ostern 1914.' *Almanach der neuen Jugend auf das Jahr 1917*. Berlin: Verlag der neuen Jugend, 1917.

'Aus erster Hand, ein Gespräch mit Thilo Koch.' Nord- und Westdeutscher Rundfunkverband-Fernsehen-Hamburg-Lokstedt (May, 1959).

Aus Tiefen rufe ich Dich: Dreiundzwanzig Psalmen in der Urschrift mit der Verdeutschung von Martin Bubers. Berlin: Schocken Verlag, 1936.

[Auswahl deutscher Verse.] In Georg Gerster, *Trunken von Gedichten: Eine Anthologie geliebter deutscher Verse, ausgewählt und kommentiert von . . . Martin Buber* (u.a.) Zurich: Verlag der Arche, 1953. (Goethe, Hölderlin, Hoffmannsthal).

'Autobiographical Fragments,' trans. Maurice Friedman. In Paul Arthur Schilpp and Maurice Friedman, *The Philosophy of Martin Buber*. La Salle, Illinois: Open Court; Cambridge: Cambridge University Press,

Bibliography

1967. Also in Buber, *Meetings*.

'Autobiographische Fragmente' and 'Antwort.' In Paul Arthur Schilpp and Maurice Friedman (eds.). *Martin Buber: Philosophen des Zwanzigen Jahrhunderts*. Stuttgart: W. Kohlhammer Verlag, 1963.

Des Baal-Schem-Tow Unterweisung im Umgang mit Gott. Hellerau: Jacob Hegner Verlag, 1927.

Begegnung: Autobiographische Fragmente, ed. Paul Arthur Schilpp and Maurice Friedman. Stuttgart: W. Kohlhammer Verlag, 1960.

'The Beginning of the National Idea.' *Review of Religion*, Vol 10 (1945-46), pp. 254-65.

'Bekenntnis des Schriftstellers.' *Neue Schweizer Rundschau* N. F. Vol. 20, No. 3 (July) (Zum 75. Geburtstag von Hermann Hesse, July 2).

A Believing Humanism: Gleanings, trans. with an Introduction and Explanatory Comments by Maurice Friedman. New York: Simon & Schuster, 1967; Clarion Books-Touchstones, 1969.

'Bemerkungen zur Gemeinschaftsidee.' *Kommende Gemeinde*, Vol. 3, No. 2 (July, 1931).

'Bemerkungen zu Jesaja.' *Monatsschrift für Geschichte und Wissenschaft des Judentums*, Vol. 74, Nos. 5/6, 9/10 (May/June, September/October, 1930).

Between Man and Man, trans. Ronald Gregor Smith. London: Kegan Paul, 1947; Collins-Fontana Books, 1961, 1973; new edition with an Introduction by Maurice Friedman and an Afterword by the Author ('The History of the Dialogical Principle'), trans. Maurice Friedman. New York: Macmillan Paperbacks, 1965.

'Bewegung: Aus einem Brief an einen Höllander' (Frederik van Eeden). *Der Neue Merkur* (Munich), January-February, 1915.

'Die Bibel als Erzähler: Leitwortstil in der Pentateuch-Erzählung,' *Morgen*, Vol. 11, Nos. 11, 12 (February, March 1936).

Biblical Humanism: Eighteen Studies, ed. Nahum N. Glatzer (London: Mac-Donald & Co., 1968. Originally published as *On the Bible* (New York: Schocken Books, 1968).

Bilder von Gut und Böse. Köln und Olten: Jakob Hegner Verlag, 1952.

'Born of Envy.' *Chelsea Review*, Summer 1958.

'Brief an Florens Christian Rang.' In Florens Christian Rang, *Deutsche Bauhütte*. Sannerz: Gemeinschaftsverlag Eberhard Arnold, 1924.

'Brief.' In *Erziehung zur Humanität: Paul Geheeb zum 90. Geburstag*.

Briefwechsel aus sieben Jahrzehnten. Mit einem Geleitwort von Ernst Simon und einem biographischen Abriss als Einleitung von Grete Schaeder. Heidelberg: Verlag Lambert Schneider. Vol. 1, *1897-1918*, 1972; Vol. 2, *1918-1938*, 1973; Vol. 3, *1938-1965*, 1975.

'Ein Briefwechsel' (by Karl Thieme) with M. B. In *Rundbrief zur Förderung der Freundschaft zwischen dem alten und dem neuen Gottesvolk—im Geiste der beiden Testamente*, Vol. 2, No. 5/6 (December), 1949.

Buberheft: Neue Blätter, Vol. 3, No. 1/2. Hellerau/Berlin: Verlag der Neuen Blätter, 1913. Includes 'Das Reden des Ekstatikers,' 'Von der Lehre,' 'Das verborgene Leben,' 'Das Judentum und die Menschheit,' 'Der Sinn der chassidischen Lehre,' 'Kultur und Religiosität,' 'Buddha,' 'Drei Legenden vom Baalschem,' and Gustav Landauer, 'Martin Buber.'

Bibliography

'Bücher die jetzt und immer zu lesen sind' (Antwort auf eine Rundfrage). *Wiener kunst- und Buchschau,* Vienna: December, 1914.

Bücher und Menschen. A four-page booklet privately printed and not sold to the public. St. Gallen: Tschudy-Verlag, 1951.

'Der Chaluz und seine Welt' (Aus einer Rede). *Almanach des Schocken Verlag auf das Jahr* 5697 (1936–37), pp. 87–92. Berlin: Schocken Verlag.

'Character Change and Social Experiment, in Israel,' ed. Maurice Friedman. In Moshe Davis, *Israel: Its Role in Civilization.* New York: Seminary Israel Institute, 1956.

Die chassidische Botschaft. Heidelberg: Lambert Schneider Verlag, 1952.

Die chassidischen Bücher: Gesamtausgabe. Hellerau: Jakob Hegner Verlag, 1928.

'Chassidismus'; 'Dienst an Israel'; 'An das gleichzeitig'; 'Die Biberlarbeit.' In *Martin Buber und sein Werk: Zu seinem sechzigsten Geburtstag im Februar 1938 überreicht vom Schocken Verlag–Jüdischer Buchverlag.* Berlin: Schocken, 1938.

Cheruth: Ein Rede über Jugend und Religion. Vienna and Berlin: R. Löwit Verlag, 1919.

Chinesische Geister- und Liebesgeschichten. Frankfort am Main: Rütten & Loening, 1911. Reissued as a volume in the Manesse Bibliothek der Weltiliteratur (Zurich: Manesse Verlag, 1948).

'Christus, Chassidismus, Gnosis. Einige Bemerkungen' (reply to an article by Rudolph Pannwitz in *Merkur* [1954]). *Merkur* (Berlin), Vol. 8 (1954).

'Church, State, Nation, Jewry,' trans. William Hallo with an Introductory Note by Maurice Friedman. In *Christianity: Some Non-Christian Appraisals,* ed. David W. McKain with an Introduction by Robert Lawson Slater, pp. 174–88. New York: McGraw-Hill Paperbacks, 1964.

'The Crisis and the Truth: A Message.' *Australian Jewish Review,* Vol. 6, No. 7 (September), 1945.

'The Cultural Role of the Hebrew University,' trans. David Sidorsky. *The Reconstructionist,* Vol. 19, No. 10 (June 26), 1953.

Daniel: Dialogues on Realization, ed. and trans. with an Introductory Essay by Maurice Friedman. New York: Holt, Rinehart and Winston, 1964; New York: McGraw-Hill Paperbacks, 1965.

Daniel: Gespräche von der Verwirklichung. Leipzig: Insel Verlag, 1913.

'Dankesrede zum Münchener Kulturpreis.' In *München ehrt Martin Buber.* Munich: Ner-Tamid Verlag, 1961.

Deutung des Chassidismus. Berlin: Schocken Verlag, 1935.

Dialogisches Leben: Gesammelte philosophische und pädagogische Schriften (including *Ich und Du, Zwiesprache, Die Frage an den Einzelnen, Ueber das Erzieherische,* 'Ueber Charaktererziehung,' *Das Problem des Menschen*). Zurich: Gregor Müller Verlag, 1947.

Das dialogische Prinzip, with an index of names added. Heidelberg: Lambert Schneider, 1973.

'Drama und Theater.' *Masken: Zeitschrift für deutsche Theaterkultur* (Düsseldorfer Schauspielhaus), Vol. 18, No. 1 (1922), pp. 5 ff. (Later included in *Hinweise* [1953].)

'Drei Predigten. 1. Das Weinen.' In *Gabe, Herrn Rabbiner Nobel zum 50. Geburtstag dargebracht.* Frankfurt am Main, 1921. (The second and third are included in *Die* chassidischen Bücher [1928].)

Drei Reden über das Judentum. Frankfurt am Main: Rütten & Loening, 1911.

'Drei Rollen Novellis.' *Die Schaubuhne*, Vol. 2, No. 2 (January 11), 1906.

'Drei Sätze eines religiösen Sozialismus.' *Die Neue Wege*, Vol. 22 (1928), pp. 327 ff.

'Die Duse in Florenz.' *Die Schaubuhne*, Vol. 1, No. 15 (December 14, 1905).

Das echte Gespräch und die Möglichkeiten des Friedens. Speech made by Buber on occasion of receiving the Friedenspreis des Deutschen Buchhandels, Frankfurt am Main, Paulskirche, September 27, 1953. Heidelberg: Lambert Schneider Verlag, 1953. Also found as part of *Martin Buber, Friedenspreis,* pp. 33–41.

Eclipse of God: Studies in the Relation between Religion and Philosophy, trans. Maurice S. Friedman et al. New York: Harper & Brothers, 1952; Harper Torchbook, 1957. For contents see Bibliography for 1952 in Martin Buber, *Meetings* or in Paul Arthur Schilpp and Maurice Friedman (eds.), *The Philosophy of Martin Buber.*

'The Education of Character' (an address to the National Conference of Palestinian teachers at Tel Aviv in May 1939), trans. from the German by Ronald Gregor Smith. In *The Mint: A miscellany*, ed. Geoffrey Grigson. London: Routledge, 1945.

'Einführung' (Introduction) to *Die Gesellschaft Sammlung sozial-psychologischer Monographien*, ed. Martin Buber. In Werner Sombart, *Das Proletariat,* Vol. 1. Frankfurt am Main: Rütten & Loening, 1906.

Einsichten: Aus den Schriften gesammelt. Wiesbaden: Insel Verlag, 1953.

Ekstatische Konfessionen. Jena: Eugen Diedrichs Verlag, 1909.

'Elements of the Interhuman.' In John Stewart (ed.), *Bridges Not Walls: A Book about Interpersonal Communication* (Chap. 11). Menlo Park, Calif.: Addison-Wesley Publishing Co., 1973.

Elija: Ein Mysterienspiel. Heidelberg: Lambert Schneider Verlag, 1963.

Elijah: A Mystery Play. Selections from Scenes 1, 3, 4, 6, 8, 10, 11, 16, 18, 20, 22, 23, trans. Maurice Friedman. *Judaism*, Vol. 14, No. 3 (Summer), 1965, pp. 260–66. 'Elijah' is published in full in Maurice Friedman (ed.), *Martin Buber and the Theater.*

'Das Ende der deutsch-jüdischen Symbiose.' *Jüdische Welt-Rundschau*, Vol. 1, No. 1 (March 10), 1939.

'Der Engel und die Weltherrschaft. Ein altjüdisches Märchen.' *Jüdische Rundschau* (Berlin), November 26, 1914.

Ereignisse und Begegnungen. Leipzig: Insel Verlag, 1917.

'Erinnerung.' In *Im Zeichen der Hoffnung,* ed. Erwin de Haar. Munich: Max Huber Verlag, 1961.

'Erkenntnis tut not.' In *Almanach des Schocken Verlags auf das Jahr 5696 (1935/36)*, pp. 11–14. Berlin: Schocken Verlag.

'Die Erwählung Israels: Eine Befragung der Bibel.' In *Almanach des Schocken Verlags auf das Jahr 5699.* Berlin: Schocken, 1938.

'Eine Erwiderung.' *Neue Wege*, Vol. 43, No. 9 (November), 1949.

'Erwiderung auf C. G. Jung.' *Merkur: Deutsche Zeitschrift für europäisches Denken*, Vol. 6, No. 5 (May 1952).

Die Erzählungen der Chassidim. Manesse-Bibliothek der Weltliteratur. Zurich: Manesse-Verlag, 1950.

Bibliography

Erzählungen von Engeln, Geistern und Dämonen. Berlin: Schocken Verlag.

'Eternal truths.' *The Zionist Record,* November, 1945. (New Year annual.)

'Ewige Feindschaft?' Hans Klee and M. B. über das Verhältnis zwischen Juden und Deutschen.' *Freiburger Rundbrief,* Vol. 7, No. 25/28 (September), 1954.

Die Forderung des Geistes und die geschichtliche Wirklichkeit: Antrittsvorlesung gehalten am 25. April 1938 in der Hebraischen Universität, Jerusalem. Leipzig: Schocken Verlag, 1938.

'Foreword.' In Erick Gutkind, *Community and Environment.* London: Watts, 1953.

For the Sake of Heaven, trans. from the German by Ludwig Lewisohn. Philadelphia: Jewish Publication Society, 1945. Second edition with new Foreword, trans. Ludwig Lewisohn, New York: Harper & Brothers, 1953; Meridian Books and Jewish Publication Society (paperback), 1958; reprinted by Atheneum without Foreword.

Fourth William Alanson White Memorial Lectures, with Introduction by Leslie H. Farber. 'Distance and Relation,' 'Elements of the Interhuman,' 'Guilt and Guilt-Feelings.' Reprints from *Psychiatry,* 1610 New Hampshire Avenue, N.W., Washington, D.C. 20009, 1957.

Die Frage an den Einzelnen. Berlin: Schocken Verlag, 1936.

'Freiheit und Verantwortung.' *Die Brücke* (Untermassfeld), December 24, 1928.

From the Treasurehouse of Hassidism: A selection from 'Or hagunuz' by Martin Buber, trans. Haim Shachter, ed. David Harden with Introduction by Aaron Appelfeld. Illustrations by David Rakia. Jerusalem: Cultural Division, Organizacion Sionista Mundial, 1969.

'Geheimnis einer Einheit.' In *Hermann Stehr, sein Werk und seine Welt,* ed. Wilhelm Meridies. Habelschwerdt: Franke Buchhandlung, 1924.

'Geleitwort.' In Ludwig Strauss, *Wintersaat: Ein Buch aus Sätzen.* Zürich: Manesse, 1953.

'Geltung und Grenze des politischen Prinzips.' *Frankfurter Hefte,* September 1953; also included in *Hinweise,* pp. 330–46, and in *Hansischer Goethe-Preis,* 1951, pp. 9–20.

Gemeinschaft, Vol. 2 of *Worte an die Zeit.* Munich: Dreiländer Verlag, 1919.

Die Geschichten des Rabbi Nachman. Frankfurt am Main: Rütten & Loening, 1906. Rev. ed. Köln: Jacob Hegner Verlag, 1955; Frankfurt am Main and Hamburg: Fischer Bücherei, 1955.

Die Gesellschaft: Sammlung sozialpsychologischer Monographien, ed. in 40 vols. by Martin Buber. Frankfurt am Main: Rütten & Loening, 1906-12. Buber's Introduction to the series in 1st ed. of 1st vol., Werner Sombart, *Das Proletariat,* 1906.

Der Glaube der Propheten. Zurich: Manesse Verlag, 1950.

'God and the Soul.' In Dagobert D. Runes, *Treasury of Philosophy.* New York: Philosophical Library, 1955.

Gog und Magog (in Hebrew). *Davar,* serially October 23, 1940–January 10, 1941.

Gog und Magog: Eine Chronik, Heidelberg: Verlag Lambert Schneider, 1949; Frankfurt am Main: Fischer, Fischer Bücherei, 1957.

Good and Evil: Two Interpretations (includes *Right and Wrong* and *Images of*

Bibliography

Good and Evil). New York: Charles Scribner's Sons, 1953. Scribner's paperback.

Gottesfinsternis. Zürich: Manesse Verlag, 1953.

'Greetings to Dr. Mordecai M. Kaplan.' *The Reconstructionist,* Vol. 22, No. 6 (May 4), 1956.

Der grosse Maggid und seine Nachfolge. Frankfurt am Main: Rütten & Loening, 1922.

Grundsätze, Vol. 1 of *Worte an die Zeit.* Munich: Dreiländerverlag, 1919.

'Gruss und Willkommen (Begrüssung Theodore Heuss von der Hebraischen Universität).' In *Staat und Volk im Werden,* ed. Theodor Heuss. Munich: Ner-Tamid Verlag, 1960.

'Gustav Landauer.' *Die Zeit* (Vienna), Vol. 39, No. 506 (June 11), 1904.

Gustav Landauer: Sein Lebensgang in Briefen, ed. Martin Buber in cooperation with Ina Britschgi-Schimmer. 2 vols. Frankfurt am Main: Rütten & Loening, 1929.

Hasidism and Modern Man, ed. and trans. Maurice Friedman. (Vol. 1 of *Hasidism and the Way of Man.*) New York: Horizon Press, 1958.

'Hebrew Humanism.' In Adrienne Koch, *Philosophy for a Time of Crisis.* New York: E. P. Dutton & Co., 1959. For contents see Bibliography for 1958 in Martin Buber, *Meetings* or in Paul Arthur Schilpp & Maurice Friedman (eds.), *The Philosophy of Martin Buber.*

Der Heilige Weg. Frankfurt am Main: Rütten & Loening, 1919.

'Heilung aus der Begegnung.' Preface to Hans Trüb, *Heilung aus der Begegnung: Eine Auseinandersetzung mit der Psychologie C. G. Jungs.* Edited by Ernst Michel and Arie Sborowitz. Stuttgart: Ernst Klett Verlag, 1952. Also published separately in *Neue Schweizer Rundschau,* Vol. 19, No. 6 (October 1951), pp. 382–86.

'Der heimliche Führer (Ansprache über Landauer).' *Die Arbeit* (Berlin), (June), 1920.

Hinweise: Gesammelte Essays (1910–53). Zurich: Manesse Verlag, 1953. For contents see Bibliography for 1953 in *Meetings* or in *The Philosophy of Martin Buber.*

'Hoffnung für diese Stunde.' *Merkur,* Vol. 6, No. 8 (August 1952); *Neue Schweizer Rundschau,* Vol. 20, No. 5 (September 1952), pp. 270–78. *Reden, die die Welt bewegten,* ed. Karl Heinrich Peter. Stuttgart: Cotta-Verlag, 1959. *Wo stehen wir heute?,* ed. H. Walter Bähr. Gütersloh: Bertelsmann Verlag, 1960.

Hundert chassidische Geschichten. Berlin: Schocken Verlag, 1930.

I and Thou. 2d ed. with Postscript by Author added, trans. Ronald Gregor Smith. New York: Scribner & Sons, 1958; Edinburgh: T. & T. Clark, 1959; Scribner (paperback), 1960.

I and Thou. A new translation with introduction and notes by Walter Kaufmann. New York: Scribner (paperback), 1970.

'I and Thou.' In Yervant H. Krikorian and Abraham Edel (eds.), *Contemporary Philosophic Problems: Selected Readings.* New York: Macmillan Co., 1959.

Ich und Du. Nachworterweiterte. Heidelberg: Lambert Schneider Verlag, 1958; 8th ed., Lambert Schneider Verlag, 1974.

'Ich und Du.' In *Sinn und Sein,* ed. Richard Wisser. Tübingen: Max Niemeyer

Bibliography

Verlag, 1960. (The Postscript of the 1958 edition).

Images of Good and Evil. Translated by Michael Bullock. London: Routledge & Kegan Paul, 1952.

'Individual and Society.' In Stanley R. Brav, *Marriage and the Jewish Tradition: Toward a Modern Philosophy of Family Living.* New York, Philosophical Library, 1951.

'In jüngeren Jahren.' In Harald Braun, *Dichterglaube: Stimmen religiösen Erlebens.* Berlin-Steglitz: Echart, 1931.

'Introduction.' In *Chinese Ghost and Love Stories* (a selection from the Liao Chai stories by P'u Sung-ling, trans. Rose Quong). New York: Pantheon, 1945.

Israel and Palestine: The History of an Idea, trans. from the German by Stanley Godman. London: East and West Library; New York: Farrar, Straus and Young, 1952. Reprinted as *On Zion.*

'Israel and the Command of the Spirit,' trans. Maurice Friedman. *Congress Weekly,* Vol. 25, No. 14 (September 8), 1958, pp. 10 ff.

Israel and the World: Essays in a Time of Crisis. New York: Schocken Books, 1948; Schocken Paperbacks, 1963. For contents see Bibliography for 1948 and 1963 in *Meetings* or in *The Philosophy of Martin Buber.*

'Israel's Mission and Zion.' *Forum for the Problems of Zionism, Jewry, and the State of Israel,* Vol. 4 (Spring), 'Proceedings of the Jerusalem Idealogical Conference.' Ed. Nathan Rotenstreich, Sulamith Schwartz Nardi, Zalman Shazar. Jerusalem: Publishing Department of the Jewish Agency, 1959, pp. 145 ff.

Israel und Palästina: Zur Geschichte einer Idee. Erasmus Bibliothek, ed. Walter Rüegg. Zurich: Artemis-Verlag, 1950; Munich: Deutscher Taschenbuch-Verlag, 1968.

Je et Tu. Avant-propos de Gabriel Marcel, Pref. de Gaston Bachelard, trans. G. Bianquis (Coll. la Philosophie en poche). Paris: Editions Montaigne, 1970.

'Jesus und der Knecht.' In *Pro regno, pro sanctuario. Eer bundel studies en bijdragen van vrienden en vereerders bij de zestigste verjaardag van Prof. Dr. G. van der Leeuw ... onder redactie van W. J. Kooiman en J. M. van Veen.* Nijkerk: G. F. Callenbach, 1950.

'Jiskor: Einleitung zu einem Gedenkbuch.' In *Jisrael Volk und Land: Jüdische Anthologie.* Berlin: Hechaluz, Deutscher Landesverband, 1934.

Der Jude: Eine Monatsschrift. Edited by Martin Buber. Vols. 1–8. Berlin: R. Löwit (Jüdischer Verlag), 1916–1924.

With Mahatma Gandhi. *Juden, Palästina und Araben.* Munich: Ner-Tamid Verlag, 1961.

With Nahum Goldmann. *Die Juden in der UdSSR,* trans. from English by Wilfried Freiherr von Bredon. Munich and Frankfurt am Main: Ner-Tamid Verlag, 1961.

Der Jude und sein Judentum: Gesammelte Aufsätze und Reden, with an Introduction by Robert Weltsch. Köln: Joseph Melzer Verlag, 1963.

'J. L. Perez.' In *Jüdischer National-Kalendar 5676.* Vienna: Verlag R. Löwit, 1915.

Die jüdische Bewegung: Gesammelte Aufsätze und Ansprachen. Vol. 1, 1900–1914. Berlin: Jüdischer Verlag, 1916. Vol. 2, 1916–1920. Berlin: Jüdischer

Bibliography

Verlag, 1921. For contents see Bibliography for 1916 and 1921 in *Meetings*, or *The Philosophy of Martin Buber.*

Jüdische Künstler, ed. Martin Buber. Berlin: Jüdischer Verlag, 1903.

Kalewala. Munich: Georg Müller, 1914.

Kampf um Israel: Reden und Schriften (1921–1932). Berlin: Schocken Verlag, 1933. For contents see Bibliography for 1933 in *Meetings* or *The Philosophy of Martin Buber.*

'Keep Faith.' *The Palestine Post*, July 18, 1938.

Kingship of God, trans. Richard Scheimann. New York: Harper & Row, 1967; paperback, Harper Torchbooks.

Der Knecht Gottes; Schicksal, Aufgabe, Trost. The songs of the servant of the Lord from Jeremiah and Isaiah in the Buber-Rosenzweig translation with introduction and commentary by Henri Friedlaender. The Hague: Pulvis Viarum, 1947.

The Knowledge of Man, ed. with an introductory essay (Chap. 1) by Maurice Friedman, trans. Maurice Friedman and Ronald Gregor Smith. London: George Allen & Unwin, 1965; New York: Harper & Row (clothbound and paperback), 1966. For contents see Bibliography for 1965 in *Meetings* or *The Philosophy of Martin Buber.*

Königtum Gottes. Vol. 1 of *Das Kommende: Untersuchungen der Entstehungsgeschichte des messianischen Glaubens.* Berlin: Schocken Verlag, 1932; 2d enlarged ed., 1936. 3d rev. ed., Heidelberg: Lambert Schneider Verlag, 1956.

'Kraft und Richtung, Klugheit und Weisheit.' In *Das werdende Zeitalter* (Kohlgrabe bei Vacha), Röhn, April 1928.

Die Kreatur, a quarterly. Edited by Martin Buber, Joseph Wittig, and Viktor von Weizsäcker. Vols. 1–3. Berlin: Lambert Schneider Verlag, 1926–1930. Reprinted by Kraus Reprint, Nendeln/Liechtenstein, 1969.

'Landauer und die Revolution.' *Masken: Halbmonatschrift des Düsseldorfer Schauspielhauses*, Vol. 14, No. 18/19 (1918/1919), pp. 282–86.

The Legend of the Baal-Shem, trans. Maurice S. Friedman. New York: Harper & Brothers; London: East and West Library, 1955.

Die Legende des Baalschem. Frankfurt am Main: Rütten & Loening, 1908. Rev. new ed., Manesse Bibliothek der Weltliteratur, Zurich: Manesse, 1955.

'Lesser Ury.' In *Jüdische Kunstler*, ed. Martin Buber, pp. 45–71. Berlin: Jüdischer Verlag, 1903.

'Letters to Franz Rosenzweig on the Law.' In Franz Rosenzweig, *On Jewish Education*, ed. Nahum N. Glatzer. New York: Noonday Press, 1954.

'Let Us Make an End to Falsities.' *Freeland*, Vol. 5, No. 1 (January/February) 1949.

Logos: Zwei Reden. Heidelberg: Lambert Schneider Verlag, 1962.

Mamre: Essays in Religion, trans. Greta Hort. Melbourne and London: Melbourne University Press & Oxford University Press, 1946.

Martin Buber and the Theater, ed. and trans. Maurice Friedman. New York: Funk & Wagnalls, 1969. Includes three essays on the theater by Buber, three chapters of introduction and commentary by Maurice Friedman, and the only English publication of the whole of Buber's 'mystery play,' *Elijah.*

Bibliography

'The Meaning,' 'Of Oneness,' 'Ultimate Aims,' 'The True Foundation,' 'The Central Myth,' 'The Only Way,' 'The Primal Powers.' In Ludwig Lewisohn, *Rebirth: A Book of Modern Jewish Thought.* New York: Harper, 1935.

Meetings, ed. and trans. with an Introduction and Bibliography by Maurice Friedman. La Salle, Illinois: Open Court Publishing Company, 1973.

Mein Weg zum Chassidismus: Erinnerungen. Frankfurt am Main: Rütten & Loening, 1918.

Der Mensch und sein Gebild. Heidelberg: Lambert Schneider Verlag, 1955.

Moses: The Revelation and the Covenant. Oxford: East West Library, 1946; Harper Torchbook, 1958.

Moses. Heidelberg: Lambert Schneider Verlag, 1952.

'Mystik als religiöser Solipsismus: Bemerkungen zu einem Vortrag Ernst Troeltschs.' In *Verhandlungen des ersten deutschen Soziologentages 1910,* pp. 206 ff. Tübingen: I. C. B. Mohr Verlag, 1911.

'Myth in Judaism,' trans. Ralph Manheim. *Commentary,* Vol. 9 (June) 1950, pp. 562–66.

'Nach dem Tod.' *Münchener Neuesten Nachrichten,* February 8, 1928.

Nachlese. Heidelberg: Lambert Schneider Verlag, 1965. For contents see Bibliography for 1965 in *Meetings* or in *The Philosophy of Martin Buber.*

'A New Venture in Adult Education.' In *The Hebrew University of Jerusalem.* Semi-jubilee volume published by the Hebrew University, Jerusalem, April 1950, pp. 116–20.

'Offenbarung und Gesetz' (from letters to Franz Rosenzweig). *Almanach des Schocken Verlags auf das Jahr 5697 (1936–37).* Berlin: Schocken Verlag, 147–54.

On Judaism, ed. Nahum N. Glatzer. New York: Schocken, 1968; paperback, 1972. Includes the early addresses from *Reden über das Judentum,* trans. Eva Jospe, the three later addresses from *At the Turning,* and 'The Spirit of Israel and the World of Today.'

'On Responsibility' and seven other essays. In E. William Rollins and Harry Zohn (eds.), *Men of Dialogue: Martin Buber and Albrecht Goes,* with Preface by Maurice Friedman. New York: Funk & Wagnalls, 1969.

'On the Suspension of the Ethical,' trans. Maurice S. Friedman. *Moral Principles of Action,* ed. Ruth Nanda Anshen, Vol. 6 of Science of Culture Series. New York: Harper & Brothers, 1952. (Also in *Eclipse of God*).

The Origin and Meaning of Hasidism, ed. and trans. with an Introduction by Maurice Friedman. New York: Horizon Press, 1960; Harper Torchbooks, 1966; Horizon Press (paperback), 1972. For contents see Bibliography for 1960 in *Meetings* or in *The Philosophy of Martin Buber.*

'Der Ort des Chassidismus in der Religionsgeschichte.' *Theologische Zeitschrift,* Vol. 2, No. 6 (November/December), 1946.

'Our Reply.' In *Towards Union in Palestine: Essays on Zionism and Jewish-Arab Cooperation,* ed. Martin Buber, Judah L. Magnes, and Ernst Simon, pp. 33–36. Jerusalem: Ihud Association, 1945.

Palestine, a Bi-national State (M. B., Judah L. Magnes, Moses Smilansky). New York: Ihud, 1946. Public hearings before the Anglo-American Committee of Inquiry. Jerusalem (Palestine), March 14, 1946.

Paths in Utopia. Translated by R. F. C. Hull. London: Routledge & Kegan

Bibliography

Paul, 1949; Boston: Beacon Paperback, 1958.

Pfade in Utopie. Heidelberg: Lambert Schneider Verlag, 1950.

'The Philosophical Anthropology of Max Scheler,' trans. Ronald Gregor Smith.
Philosophy and Phenomenological Research, Vol. 6, No. 2 (December), 1945.

'Philosophie und Religiöse Weltanschauung in der Erwachsenenbildung.' In *Tagungsbericht des Hohenrodter Bundes,* Vol. 2, Berlin, 1929.

Pointing the Way: Collected Essays. Translated and edited by Maurice Friedman. New York: Harper & Brothers; London: Routledge & Kegan Paul, 1957. Reissued with an Introduction by Maurice Friedman, New York: Harper Torchbooks, 1963; Schocken (paperback), 1974. For contents see Bibliography for 1957 in *Meetings* or in *The Philosophy of Martin Buber.*

Das Problem des Menschen. Heidelberg: Lambert Schneider Verlag, 1961. Reissued with an index of names, 1971.

'Productivity and Existence' (from *Pointing the Way,* trans. Maurice Friedman). In Maurice A. Stein, Arthur J. Vidick, David M. White (eds.), *Identity and Anxiety: Survival of the Person in a Mass Society,* pp. 628–32. Glencoe, Illinois: The Free Press, 1960.

The Prophetic Faith, trans. from Hebrew by Carlyle Witton-Davies. New York: Macmillan Co., 1949; London: H. Hamilton, 1960; Harper Torchbooks, 1966.

'Ragaz und "Israel" ' (address at a memorial for Ragaz in the synagogue Emet Ve-Emuna, Jerusalem). *Neue Wege,* Vol. 41, No. 11 (November), 1947.

'A Realist of the Spirit,' trans. Maurice Friedman. In *To Dr. Albert Schweitzer: A Festschrift Commemorating His 80th Birthday from a Few of His Friends,* January 14, 1955. Edited by Homer Jack. Evanston (Ill.), Friends of Albert Schweitzer.

Die Rede, die Lehre, und das Lied. Leipzig: Insel Verlag, 1920. Includes Buber's introductory essays to *Ekstatische Konfessionen, Reden und Gleichnisse des Tschuang-Tse,* and *Kalewala.*

'Rede über das Erzieherische.' In Wilhelm Flitner, *Die Erziehung: Pädagogen und Philosophen über die Erziehung und ihre Probleme.* Wiesbaden: Dieterich, 1953.

'Reden auf der sozialistischen Tagung in Heppenheim: Die Begründung des Sozialismus. Sozialismus und persönliche Lebensgestaltung.' In *Sozialismus aus dem Glauben: Verhandlungen der sozialistischen Tagung in Heppenheim,* Pfingstwoche, 1928, pp. 90 ff., 121 ff., 217 ff. Zürich: Rotapfel-Verlag, 1929.

Reden über das Judentum. Frankfurt am Main: Rütten & Loening, 1923. Reissued by Schocken Verlag, Berlin: 1932.

Reden über Erziehung. Heidelberg: Lambert Schneider Verlag, 1953. 8 Aufl., Heidelberg: Lambert Schneider, 1964.

Reden und Gleichnisse des Tschuang-Tse. Leipzig: Insel Verlag, 1914.

'Referat über jüdische Erziehung auf dem Deutschen Zionistichem Delegiertentag, December 1916.' *Jüdische Rundschau* (Berlin), January 5, 1917. See also 'Eine Erklärung,' *Jüdische Rundschau,* March 16, 1917.

'Religion und Philosophie,' *Europäische Revue,* August 1929, pp. 325–35.

'Remarks on Goethe's Concept of Humanity.' *Goethe and the Modern Age,*

Bibliography

ed. Arnold Bergstraesser, pp. 227–33. Chicago: Henry Regnery, 1950.

'Replies to my Critics,' trans. Maurice Friedman. In Paul Arthur Schilpp and Maurice Friedman (eds.), *The Philosophy of Martin Buber*. La Salle, Illinois: Open Court, 1967; Cambridge University Press, 1967. The first three sections of this reply constitute Buber's 'Philosophical Accounting.'

'Responsa.' In 'Martin Buber' section, conducted, edited, and translated by Maurice Friedman, of *Philosophical Interrogations*, ed. Sidney and Beatrice Rome. New York: Holt, Rinehart & Winston, 1964.

'Richtung soll kommen.' *Masken*, Vol. 10, No. 11, 1915.

Right and Wrong: An Interpretation of Some Psalms, trans. Ronald Gregor Smith. London: S.C.M. Press, 1952.

'Robert Weltsch zum 70. Geburtstag.' *Mitteilungsblatt*, June 16, 1961.

'Rosenzweig und die Existenz.' *Mitteilungsblatt*, Vol. 24, No. 52 (December 28), 1956.

'Samuel und die Lade.' In *Essays Presented to Leo Baeck on His Eightieth Birthday*. London: East and West Library, 1954. (A chapter from *Der Gesalbte*, the unfinished sequel to *Konigtum Gottes*, 1936.)

'Schlichtung.' *Frankfurter Zeitung*, 1. Mörgenblatt, October 18, 1924. Reprinted in *Berliner Tageblatt*, Abendausgabe February 26, 1927. (On Buddha-translation.)

'Schlussbemerkungen.' In *'Die Schrift'—Zum Abschluss ihrer Verdeutschung*, pp. 8 ff. Sonderdruck überreicht vom 'Mitteilungsblatt' (MB) des Irgun Olej Merkas Europa. Tel Aviv: Biaton Publishing Co., 1961.

Die Schrift. Translation of the Bible from Hebrew into German by Martin Buber in co-operation with Franz Rosenzweig. Berlin: Schocken Verlag, 14 vols. Rev. ed., 4 vols.: *Die fünf Bücher der Weisung* (1954), *Bücher der Geschichte*, *Bücher der Kundung* (1958), *Die Schriftwerke* (1961). Köln and Olten: Jakob Hegner Verlag.

With Franz Rosenzweig. *Die Schrift und ihrer Verdeutschung*. Berlin: Schocken Verlag, 1936.

Die Schriften über das dialogische Prinzip. Heidelberg: Lambert Schneider Verlag, 1954. Includes *Ich und Du*, *Zwiesprache*, *Die Frage an den Einzelnen*, 'Elemente des Zwischennmenschlichen,' and 'Nachwort,' the last two not previously published in book form, the last an important historical survey published here for the first time.

Schuld und Schuldgefühle. Heidelberg: Verlag Lambert Schneider, 1958. Also in *Der leidende Mensch*, Vol. 1: *Wege der Forschung*. Darmstadt: Wissenschaftliche Buchgesellschaft, 1959.

Das Sehertum: Anfang und Ausgang. Köln: Jakob Hegner Verlag, 1955.

'Seit ein Gespräch wir sind, Ludwig Strauss zum Gedächtnis.' In *Holderlin-Jahrbuch*, 1958–1960, Vol. 11. Tubingen: J. C. G. Mohr (Paul Siebeck), 1960.

Selections from eighteen of Buber's works in *The Worlds of Existentialism: A Critical Reader*. Edited with Introductions and a Conclusion by Maurice Friedman. New York: Random House, 1964; paperback, University of Chicago Press Phoenix Books. For contents see Bibliography for 1964 in *Meetings* or in *The Philosophy of Martin Buber*.

'Sieben Geschichten vom Baalschem.' In *Judischer National-Kalender 5678*. Vienna: Verlag 'Jüdische Zeitung,' 1917. (The sixth story, 'Die Sabbatseele' was not included in *Die chassidischen Bücher* [1928].)

'Social experiments in Jewish Palestine.' *The New Palestine*, Vol. 35, No. 1 (October 13), 1944.

Stationen des Glaubens. Aus dem Schriften gesammelten. Wiesbaden: Insel, 1960.

Die Stunde und die Erkenntnis: Reden und Aufsätze, 1933–35. Berlin: Schocken Verlag, 1936.

'Symbolic and Sacramental Existence in Judaism,' trans. Ralph Manheim. In *Spiritual Disciplines*, Vol. 4 of *Papers from the Eranos Yearbooks*, pp. 168–85. Bollingen Series No. 30. New York: Pantheon Books, 1959.

Tales of Angels, Spirits and Demons, trans. David Antin and Jerome Rothenberg. New York: Hawk's Well Press, 1958.

Tales of Rabbi Nachman, trans. Maurice Friedman. New York: Horizon Press, 1968; Souvenir Press, 1974.

Tales of the Hasidim, trans. Olga Marx. 2 vols.: *The Early Masters, The Later Masters*. New York: Schocken, 1948; paperback, 1961.

Ten Rungs: Hasidic Savings, trans. Olga Marx. New York: Schocken Books, 1947; paperback, 1962.

'To Chaim Weizmann.' In *Chaim Weizmann: A Tribute on His Seventieth Birthday*, ed. Paul Goodman. London: V. Gollancz, 1945.

To Hallow This Life, ed. Jacob Trapp. New York: Harper and Brothers, 1958. Reprint of 1958 edition, Greenwood.

Die Tröstung Israels. Aus Jeschajahu, Kapitel 40 bis 55. Translated into German by M. B. and Franz Rosenzweig. Berlin: Schocken-Bücherei des Schocken-Verlags, Vol. 1, 1933.

'Die Tugend der Propaganda.' *Jüdische Rundschau*, Vol. 39, No. 43 (May 29, 1934).

Two Letters to Gandhi. With Judah Magnes and including public letters by Buber and Magnes and the original text of Gandhi's statement about the Jews in *Harijan*, November 26, 1938. Pamphlets of *The Bond.* Jerusalem: Rubin Mass, April 1939.

Two Types of Faith, trans. Norman P. Goldhawk. London: Routledge & Kegan Paul, 1951; New York: Macmillan Co., 1952; Harper Torchbook (subtitled *The Interpretation of Judaism and Christianity*), 1961.

'Ueber Stefan George.' *Literarische Welt* (Berlin), July 13, 1928.

'Ueber Agnon.' In *Treue: Eine jüdische Sammelschrift*, ed. Leo Hermann. Berlin: Jüdischer Verlag, 1916.

'Ueber Asien und Europa.' In *Chinesisch-deutscher Almanach für das Jahr 1929/1930*. Frankfurt am Main: China-Institute, 1929.

'Ueber den deutschen Aufsatz.' In *Wilhelm Schneider: Meister des Stils über Sprache und Stillehre*. Leipzig: B. G. Teubner, 1922.

'Ueber den Kontakt.' Aus Jerusalemer pädagogischen Radio-Reden. In *Die Idee einer Schule im Spiegel der Zeit: Festschrift für Paul Geheeb zum 80. Geburtstag und zum 40 jährigen Bestehen der Odenwaldschule*. Heidelberg: Lambert Schneider Verlag, 1950.

'Ueber die Todesstrafe.' In E. M. Mungenast, *Der Mörder und der Staat*, p. 65. Stuttgart: Walter Hädecke Verlag, 1928.

'Ueber Jakob Böhme.' *Wiener Rundschau*, Vol. 5, No. 12 (June 15, 1901), pp. 251–53.

Bibliography

'Ueber Rathenau (Briefliche Mitteilung).' In Harry Graf Kesler, *Walther Rathenau, sein Leben und sein Werk*, pp. 89 ff. Berlin-Brünewald: Verlag Hermann Klemm, 1928.

'Ueber Selbstmord: Antwort auf eine Rundfrage.' In Karl Baumann, *Selbst-Mord und Freitod in sprachlicher und geistesgeschichtlicher Beleuchtung* (Diss. Giessen, 1933). Würzburg-Aumühle: K. Trilsch, 1934.

Urdistanz und Beziehung. Heidelberg: Verlag Lambert Schneider, 1951.

Der utopische Sozialismus. Neuaufl. Köln: Jakob Hegner Verlag, 1967. First edition published 1950 as *Pfade in Utopia* (Heidelberg: Lambert Schneider Verlag).

Das verborgene Licht. Frankfurt am Main: Rütten & Loening, 1924.

'Versuch einer Auskunft.' In *Wegweiser in der Zeitwende*, ed. Elga Kern, pp. 264 ff. Munich and Basle: Ernst Reinhardt Verlag, 1955.

'Vier Gleichnisse des Ferid-ed-din-Attar.' In *Inselalmanach auf das Jahr 1922. Die vier Zweige des Mabinogi*, ed. Martin Buber. Leipzig: Insel Verlag, 1914.

Völker, Staaten und Zion. (A letter to Hermann Cohen and comments on his reply.) Vienna: R. Löwit Verlag, 1917. Later included in *Die Jüdische Bewegung*, Vol. 2 (1921).

Vom Geist des Judentums. Leipzig: Kurt Wolff Verlag, 1916.

'Von jüdischen Dichtern und Erzählern.' In *Jüdischer National-Kalender, 5677.* Vienna: Verlag der Jüdischen Zeitung, 1916.

'Vorbemerkung' to Hermann Cohen, *Der Nächste.* Berlin: Schocken Verlag, 1935.

'Die Wanderschaft des Kinderlosen,' by Martin Buber and H. H. Cohn. In Ch. Z. Klotzel, *Drei Legenden*, Berlin: Jüdischer Verlag, 1920.

The Way of Man, according to the Teachings of Hasidism, with Foreword by Maurice Friedman. Wallingford, Pennsylvania: Pendle Hill Pamphlet No. 106, 1959. Reprinted without Foreword: London: Vincent Stuart, 1963; London: Collins Books, 1964; Secaucus, New Jersey: Citadel Press (paperback), 1966. Also in Walter Kaufmann, *Religion from Tolstoy to Camus* (New York: Harper Torchbooks, 1964).

The Way of Response: Martin Buber, Selections from His Writings, ed. Nahum N. Glatzer. New York: Schoken, 1966; paperback, 1971.

'We Need the Arabs, They Need Us! Interview with M. B.' *Frontpage*, Vol. 2, No. 3 (January 20, 1955).

Der Weg des Menschen: Nach der chassidischen Lehre. Jerusalem: copyright by Martin Buber, 1948, printed in the Netherlands by 'Pulvis Viarum' Press; Heidelberg: Lambert Schneider Verlag, 1960.

Werke. Munich: Kösel Verlag; Heidelberg: Lambert Schneider Verlag, 1962–1964. Vol. 1, *Schriften zur Philosophie* (1962). Vol. 2, *Schriften zur Bibel* (1964). Vol. 3, *Schriften zum Chassidismus* (1963). For contents see Bibliography for respective years in *Meetings* or *The Philosophy of Martin Buber*.

Worte an die Jugend. Berlin: Schocken Verlag, 1938.

'Ein Wort über den Chassidismus.' *Theologische Blätter* (Marburg), Vol. 3, Sp. 161 (1924).

'Ein Wort über Nietzsche und die Lebenswerte.' *Kunst und Leben* (Berlin), December 1900.

Bibliography

Zion als Ziel und Aufgabe. Berlin: Schocken Verlag, 1936.

'Zuchthaus für männliche Prostitution (Antwort auf eine Rundfrage).' *Das Forum* (Berlin), December 1928.

Zu einer neuen Verdeutschung der Schrift: Beilage zu dem Werk. 'Die fünf Bücher der Weisung, translated into German by M. B. in cooperation with Franz Rosenzweig.' Olten (Switzerland): Jakob Hegner, 1954.

'Zum Einheitscharakter des Jesajabuches.' *Der Morgen,* Vol. 12, No. 8 (November, 1936).

'Zur Erzählung von Abraham.' *Monatsschrift für Geschichte und Wissenschaft des Judentums,* Vol. 83 (January/December 1939).

'Zur Situation der Philosophie.' *Library of the 10th International Congress of Philosophy* (Amsterdam, August 11–18, 1948), Vol. 1: *Proceedings of the Congress,* pp. 317 f.

Zwei Glaubensweisen. Zurich: Manesse Verlag, 1950.

'Zwei Tagebuchstellen. 1. Pescara an einem Augustmorgen (1914). 2. Nach der Heimkehr.' *Zeit Echo: Ein Kriegstagebuch der Künstler* (Munich), No. 3 (1919).

'Zwiegespräch (Kleine legendäre Anekdote nach dem Japanischen).' *Insel-Almanach auf das Jahr 1926* (1926).

Zwiesprache. Berlin: Schocken Verlag, 1932.

Zwischen Gesellschaft und Staat. Heidelberg: Verlag Lambert Schneider, 1952.

'Zwischen Religion und Philosophie' (answer to Hugo Bergmann's criticism of *Eclipse of God). Neue Wege,* Vol. 47, No. 11/12 (November/December 1953), pp. 436–39.

Zwischen Zeit und Ewigkeit Gog und Magog: Eine Chronik. 2d ed. Heidelberg: Lambert Schneider Verlag, 1969. (Originally published in 1949 by Lambert Schneider as *Gog und Magog.)*

For works by Buber not included here, including works in Hebrew and works translated into other languages, see also the Bibliography in *Meetings* or *The Philosophy of Martin Buber,* as well as Moche Catanè, *Bibliographia shel Cheteveii Mordecai Martin Buber* (in Hebrew).

WORKS ABOUT BUBER

Agus, Jacob. *Modern Philosophies of Judaism.* New York: Behrman's Jewish Book House, 1941.

Anzenbacher, Arno. *Die Philosophie Martin Bubers.* Vienna: A. Schendl, 1965.

Babolin, Alkino. *Essere e alterità in Martin Buber.* Padua: Gregoriana, 1965.

Baillie, John. *Our Knowledge of God,* pp. 161, 201–39. New York: Charles Scribner's Sons, 1939.

Balogh, Zoltan Imre. *Martin Buber und die Welt des Es.* Meisenheim am Glan: Hain, 1969. (Originally presented as the author's thesis, Munich, under the title *Die Welt des Es,* 1968.)

Beek, Martinus Adrianus, and Weiland, J. Sperna. *Martin Buber.* 2d ed. Baain: Het Wereldvenster, 1967.

———. *Martin Buber: Personalist and Prophet.* Westminster, Md.: Newman Press, 1968.

Bibliography

Ben-Chorin, Schalom. *Zwiesprache mit Martin Buber: Ein Erinnerungsbuch.* Munich: List, 1966.

Berdyaev, Nicholas. 'Martin Buber. Die chassidischen Buecher; Ich und Du; Zwiesprache; Koenigtum Gottes I.' *Put': Organ russkoi religioznoi mysli* (also under French title *Voie*) (Paris). No. 38 (May 1933), pp. 87-91.

Berdyczwesky, Emanual (Emanuel bin Gorion). *Ceterum Recenseo: Kritische Aufsätze und Reden.* Tübingen: Alexander Fischer Verlag, 1929. 'Eine neue Verdeutschung der Bibel,' pp. 21-38.

Bergmann, Hugo. 'Begriff und Wirklichkeit: Ein Beitrag zur Philosophie Martin Bubers und J. G. Fichtes.' *Der Jude,* Vol. 10, No. 5 (March 1928), 'Sonderheft zu Martin Bubers fünfzigstem Geburtstag,' pp. 89-101.

———. *Hoge Haddor (Thinkers of the Epoch)* (in Hebrew), pp. 179-93. Tel-Aviv: Hoza'ath 'Mizpeh,' 5695 (1934-35).

———. 'Der Physiker Whitehead.' *Die Kreatur,* Vol. 2 (1927-28), pp. 356-63.

Berkovitz, Eliezer. *A Jewish Critique of the Philosophy of Martin Buber.* New York: Yeshivah University, 1962.

Berl, Heinrich. *Martin Buber und die Wiedergeburt des Judentums aus dem Geiste der Mystik.* Heidelberg: 1924.

Blumenfeld, Walter. *La antropologia filosófica de Martin Buber y la filosofia antropologica: Un ensayo.* Sociedad Peruana de Filosofia, Colleccion 'Plena Luz, Pleno Ser,' No. 6. Lima: Tipografia Santa Rosa, 1951.

Böhm, Adolf. *Die Zionistische Bewegung bis zum Ende des Weltkrieges.* 2d enlarged ed., Vol 1, pp. 297 ff., 521-40, 544 f., 572 f. Tel-Aviv: Hozaah Ivrith, 1935.

Borowitz, Eugene B. *A Layman's Introduction to Religious Existentialism,* Chap. 7. Philadelphia: Westminster Press, 1965.

———. *A New Jewish Theology in the Making.* Philadelphia: Westminster Press, 1968. Chapter 6: 'Martin Buber: The Lure of Religious Existentialism.'

Brod, Max. 'Zur Problematik des Bösen und des Rituals.' *Der Jude,* Vol. 10, No. 5 (March 1928), 'Sonderheft zu Martin Bubers fünfzigstem Geburtstag,' p. 109 f.

Casper, Bernhard. *Das dialogische Denken: Eine Untersuchung der religionsphilosophischen Bedeutung F. Rosenzweigs, Ferdinand Ebners, und Martin Bubers.* Freiburg, Basel, and Vienna: Herder, 1967.

Catanè, Moche. *Bibliografia shel Cethavi Mordecai Martin Buber* (in Hebrew). Jerusalem: Mosad Bialik, 1961.

Chestov, Leon. 'Martin Buber: Un mystique juif de langue allemande,' trans. from Russian into French by B. de Schloezer. *Revue Philosophique de la France et de l'Etrangère,* Vol. 116 (1933), pp. 430-42.

Clarke, Sir Fred. *Freedom in the Educative Society: Educational Issues of Today,* ed. W. R. Niblett, pp. 56-68. London: University of London Press., 1948.

Coates, J. B. *The Crisis of the Human Person: Some Personalist Interpretations,* pp. 23 f., 32-35, 65-81, 158, 240-48. London: Longmans, Green, 1949.

Cohen, Arthur A. *Martin Buber.* Studies in Modern European Literature and Thought. New York: Hillary House, 1957; London: Bowes & Bowes, 1957.

———. *The Natural and the Supernatural Jew: An Historical Introduction,*

Bibliography

Chap. 2, Sec. 5. New York: Pantheon Books, 1962.

Dejung, Berta. *Dialogische Erziehung. Martin Bubers Rede über das Erzieherische: Eine Interpretation.* Zürich: Juris-Verlag, 1971.

Diamond, Malcolm. *Martin Buber, Jewish Existentialist.* New York and London: Oxford University Press, 1960; New York: Harper Torchbooks, 1968; Gannon, 1970.

Duesberg, Hans. *Person und Gemeinschaft: Philosophisch-systematische Untersuchungen des Sinnzusammenhangs von personaler Selbständigkeit und interpersonaler Beziehung an Texten von J. G. Fichte und Martin Buber.* Bonn: H. Bouvier, 1970.

Doujoune, Leon. *Martin Buber: Sus ideas religiosas, filosóficas y sociales.* Buenos Aires: Bibliográfica Omeba, 1965.

Edwards, Paul. *Buber and Buberism: A Critical Evaluation.* Lawrence: Department of Philosophy, University of Kansas, 1971.

Emmet, Dorothy M. *The Nature of Metaphysical Thinking*, pp. 207-14. London: Macmillan and Co., 1949. See also Chapters 3, 5, and 10.

Faber, Werner, of Aachen. *Das dialogische Prinzip Martin Buber und das erzieherische Verhältnis.* Ratingen bei Düsseldorf: A. Henn, 1962 and 1967.

Fackenheim, Emil L. *Quest for Past and Future: Essays in Jewish Theology*, Chaps. 11-16. Bloomington and London: Indiana University Press, 1968.

Farber, Leslie H. 'Martin Buber and Psychiatry.' *Psychiatry*, Vol. 19, No. 2 (May) 1956), pp. 109-20.

———. 'Martin Buber and Psychoanalysis.' In *The Ways of the Will: Essays in the Psychology and Psychopathology of the Will.* New York: Basic Books, 1966.

Farber, Leslie H.; Friedman, Maurice S.; and Howe, Reuel L. 'Martin Buber and Psychotherapy.' *Pastoral Psychology*, Vol. 7, No. 69 (December 1956).

Feuchtwanger, Ludwig. 'Bibelforschung aus jüdischem Geist. Martin Bubers Erneuerung der Bibel aus Geist des Judentums.' *Der Morgen*, Vol. 8, No. 3 (August 1932), pp. 209-24.

Fox, Everett. 'In the Beginning: An English Rendition of the Book of Genesis.' Based on the German Version of Martin Buber and Franz Rosenzweig, with an Introduction by Nahum N. Glatzer. *Response: A Contemporary Jewish Review*, Volume 6, No. 2 (Summer) 1972.

———. 'Toward a New Translation of the Bible.' *Response: A Contemporary Jewish Review*, Volume 5, No. 3 (Winter 1971-72), pp. 29-42.

Friedman, Maurice. 'Le basi dell'etica nella filosofia di Martin Buber.' Lead essay in *De Homine, 19-20*. Rome: Centro di Ricerca per le Scienze Morali e Sociali, Instituto di Filosofia della Universita Roma, 1966.

———. 'Contemporary Christian Theology, Jewish Influences on.' *Encyclopaedia Judaica.*

———. Dialectical Faith versus Dialogical Trust.' *The Eastern Buddhist*, New Series, Vol. 4, No. 1 (May 1971).

———. 'Dialogue and the "Essential We": The Bases of Values in the Philosophy of Martin Buber.' *American Journal of Psychoanalysis*, Vol. 20, No. 1 (1960). Also in *Group Psychotherapy and Group Function*, ed. Max Rosenbaum and Milton Berger. New York and London: Basic Books, 1963.

Bibliography

————. 'Existential Man: Buber.' In Paul Nash, Andreas M. Kazamias, and Henry J. Perkinson, eds., *The Educated Man: Studies in the History of Educational Thought*. New York and London: John Wiley & Sons, 1965.

————. 'Healing through Meeting: Martin Buber and Psychotherapy.' *Cross Currents*, Vol. 5, No. 4 (Fall 1955).

————. '*I and Thou*—How A Book Came into Being.' *Sh'ma: A Journal of Jewish Responsibility*, Vol. 4, No. 65 (January 11, 1974).

————. 'I-Thou and I-It.' In Marvin Halverson and Arthur A. Cohen, eds., *A Handbook of Christian Theology*. New York: Living Age Books, Meridian Books, 1958.

————. 'Martin Buber.' Translated from English into French by Jenny Thieberger. *Allemagne d'Aujourd'hui, Réalités Allemandes*, pp. 816–22.

————. 'Martin Buber.' *Encyclopaedia Britannica*.

————. 'Martin Buber.' *Funk & Wagnalls Universal Encyclopedia*.

————. 'Martin Buber.' *The New Catholic Encyclopedia*.

————. 'Martin Buber.' *Encyclopaedia Judaica*.

————. 'Martin Buber.' In Simon Noveck, ed., *Great Jewish Thinkers of the Twentieth Century*, Vol. 2 of B'nai B'rith Great Books Series. Washington, D.C.: B'nai B'rith Department of Adult Jewish Education, 1963.

————. 'Martin Buber' section (edited with an Introduction). *Philosophical Interrogations*, ed. Sydney and Beatrice Rome. New York: Holt, Rinehart, & Winston, 1964; Harper Torchbooks, 1970.

————. 'Martin Buber—A Modern Bridge between Judaism and Christianity.' In *Search for Identity in a Changing World*. Woman's Division, Board of Missions, the Methodist Church, 1967.

————. 'Martin Buber and the Covenant of Peace.' *Hadassah Newsletter*, September 1959. Revised version in *Fellowship*, January 1961.

————. 'Martin Buber and Judaism.' *Central Conference of American Rabbis Journal*, October 1955.

————. 'Martin Buber and Pacifism.' *Shalom*, December 1968.

————. 'Martin Buber and Peace.' *Jewish Peace Fellowship Tidings*, April 1955.

————. 'Martin Buber and Psychiatry.' *Pastoral Psychology*, December 1956.

————. 'Martin Buber and the Social Problems of Our Time.' *Yivo Annual*, 1959.

————. 'Martin Buber and the Theater,' 'Drama and the Theater: Buber and Hofmannsthal,' and 'Martin Buber's *Elijah*.' Chapters 1, 2, and 7 of *Martin Buber and the Theatre*. New York: Funk & Wagnalls, 1969.

————. 'Martin Buber at Seventy-Five.' *Religion in Life*, Vol. 23, No. 3 (Summer 1954), pp. 405–17.

————. *Martin Buber: Mystic, Existentialist, Social Prophet—A Study in the Redemption of Evil*. Doctoral dissertation for the University of Chicago, June 1950. The University of Chicago Library, Microfilm No. T 809.

————. 'Martin Buber, Prophet and Philosopher.' *Faith Today*, Vol. 1, No. 5 (December-January, 1954–55).

————. 'Martin Buber's Biblical Judaism.' *CCAR Journal*, No. 24, (January 1959).

————. 'Martin Buber's Biblical Judaism.' *The Bible Today*, April 1967.

————. 'Martin Buber's Challenge to Jewish Philosophy.' *Judaism*, July

1965.

———. 'Martin Buber's Concept of Education: A New Approach to College Teaching.' *Christian Scholar*, Vol. 45, No. 2 (June 1957).

———. 'Martin Buber's Encounter with Mysticism' (monograph). *Human Inquiries: Review of Existential Psychology and Psychiatry*, Vol. 11 (1970).

———. 'Martin Buber's Final Legacy: *The Knowledge of Man.' Journal for the Scientific Study of Religion*, Winter 1966.

———. 'Martin Buber's Hasidic Books: A Contemporary Image of Man.' In *Jewish Book Annual*, Vol. 23 (1965/66). New York: Jewish Book Council of America, 1965.

———. 'Martin Buber's Life and Thought' (Vol. 3, *Modern Jewish Thinkers*) and 'Martin Buber Anthology' (Vol. 4, *Modern Jewish Thought*). B'nai B'rith Great Books Series, ed. Simon Noveck. New York: Farrar Straus & Cudahy, 1960.

———'Martin Buber's New View of Evil.' In *Faith and Reason: Essays in Judaism*, ed. Robert Gordis & Ruth B. Waxman. New York: KTAV Publishing, 1973.

———. 'Martin Buber's Ontology.' *Review of Existential Psychology and Psychiatry*, Vol. 11, No. 3 (1972).

———. 'Revelation and Reason in Martin Buber's Philosophy of Religion.' *Bucknell Review*, Winter 1971.

———. 'Martin Buber's "Theology" and Religious Education.' *Religious Education*, Vol. 54, No.1 (January-February, 1959).

———. 'Martin Buber's Theory of Education.' *Educational Theory*, January 1956.

———. 'Martin Buber's Theory of Knowledge.' *Review of Metaphysics*, December 1954.

———. 'Sex in Sartre and Buber.' *Review of Existential Psychology and Psychiatry*, Fall 1963. Also in Henrik M. Ruitenbeek, ed., *Sexuality and Identity* (New York: Delta Books, 1970).

———. *To Deny Our Nothingness: Contemporary Images of Man*. New York: Delacorte Press; London: Victor Gollancz, 1967; New York: Delta Books (paperback), 1968.

———. *The Worlds of Existentialism: A Critical Reader* (edited with Introduction and a Conclusion). New York: Random House, 1964; University of Chicago Press, Phoenix Books (paperback), 1973.

Goes, Albrecht. 'Martin Buber, Der Beistand.' In *Martin Buber: Friedenspreis des Deutschen Buchhandels*, 1953, pp. 21-29.

———. 'Martin Buber: Our Support.' In Ernest Wm. Rollins, and Harry Zohn, eds., *Men of Dialogue: Martin Buber and Albrecht Goes*. Preface by Maurice Friedman. New York: Funk & Wagnalls, 1969.

Goldschmidt, Hermann Levin. *Hermann Cohen und Martin Buber: Ein Jahrhundert Ringen um jüdische Wirklichkeit*. Geneva: Editions Migdal, 1946.

Goldstein, Walter. *Begegnung mit Martin Buber*. Jerusalem: Edition Dr. Peter Freund, 1943.

———. *Die Botschaft Martin Bubers*. Vol. 1, *Die vordialogische Epoch*. Vol. 2, *Der Dialogik universaler Teil*. Vol. 3, *Von der Bibel*. Jerusalem: Edition Dr. Peter Freund, 1952-56.

Bibliography

————. *Der Glaube Martin Buber*. Jerusalem: Reuben Mass, 1969.

————. *Jean-Paul Sartre und Martin Buber: Eine vergleichende Betrachtung von Existentialismus und Dialogik*. Jerusalem: Reuben Mass, 1965.

————. *Martin Buber: Gespräche, Briefe, Worte*. Jerusalem: Reuben Mass, 1967

Grünfeld, Werner. *Der Begegnungscherakter der Wirklichkeit in Philosophie und Pädagogik Martin Bubers*. Ratingen and Düsseldorf: Henn, 1965.

Hammerstein, Franz, Freiherr von. *Das Messias Problem bei Martin Buber*. Published as Vol. 1 of *Studia Delitzschiana*. Stuttgart: W. Kohlhammer, 1958.

Hansischer Goethe-Preis, 1951, Stiftung F.V.S. Hamburg, presented on June 24, 1953. Includes 'Ansprache des Rektors Prof. Dr. Bruno Snell' and Buber's 'Geltung und Grenze.' Hamburg: Gebrüder Hoesch, 1953.

Hartshorne, Charles, and Reese, William L. *Philosophers Speak of God*. pp. 302-6. Chicago: University of Chicago Press, 1953.

Herberg, Will. *Four Existentialist Theologians*, pp. 169-253. New York: Doubleday Anchor Books, 1958.

————. *The Writings of Martin Buber* (edited with an Introduction). New York: Meridian Books, 1956; Cleveland: World Publishing Co., 1961; New American Library.

Hermann, Leo. 'Aus Tagebuchblättern. I. Erinnerungen an Bubers "Drei Reden" in Prag.' *Der Jude*, Vol. 10, No. 5 (March 1928), 'Sonderheft zu Martin Bubers funfzigstem Geburtstag.'

Hesse, Herman. *Briefe*. Vol. 8 of *Gesammelte Werke*, pp. 122, 130 ff., 159 f., 289 f., 302 f., 324 ff. Berlin: Suhrkamp Verlag, 1951.

Heydorn, Heinz-Joachim. 'Martin Buber und der Sozialismus.' *Gewerkschaftliche Monatshefte*, Vol. 4, No. 12 (December 1953), pp. 705-9.

Höltershinken, Dieter. *Anthropologische Grundlager personalistische Erziehungslehren Martin Buber, Romano Guardini, P. Peterson: Eine vergleichende Untersuchung*. Weinheim, Berlin, Basel, and Beltz, 1971.

Honigsheim, Paul. 'Besprechung von "Ich und Du." ' *Kölner Vierteljahrhefte für Soziologie*, Vol. 3 (1923-24), p. 77 f.

Horwitz, Rivka. *Martin Buber und Franz Rosenzweig: Studien zur Entstehungsgeschichte von 'Ich und Du'*, with first printing of Buber's lecture, 'Religion as Presence' (1922). Heidelberg: Lambert Schneider Verlag, 1976.

Huber, Gerhard. *Menschenbild und Erziehung bei Martin Buber*. Vertrag gehalten am 13 November 1959 in der Vereinigung demokratisch sozialistischer Erzieher, Basel. Zürich: Polygraphischer Verlag, 1960.

International Martin Buber Institute and Peace Fund. *I & Thou: The Magazine for Existential Thought and Dialogue*. London, 1969.

Jahrsetz, Heinz. *Martin Buber: Ein Gelegenheitsverzeichnis*. 1964.

Kaplan, Mordecai M. 'Martin Buber: Theologian, Philosopher and Prophet.' *The Reconstructionist*, May 2, 1952.

Kerényi, Karl. 'Martin Buber als Klassiker.' *Neue Schweizer Rundschau*, Vol. 20, No. 2 (June 1952), pp. 89-99.

Klein, Abraham. 'Three Chapters in Martin Buber's Philosophy' (in Hebrew), *Iyyun: A Hebrew Philosophical Quarterly*, Vol. 3, No. 3 (July 1952), pp. 136-50.

Bibliography

Kogon, Eugene and Thieme, Karl. 'Das Porträt: Martin Buber.' *Frankfurter Hefte: Zeitschrift für Kultur und Politik*, Vol. 6, No. 3 (March 1951), pp. 195–200.

Kohanski, Alexander. *An Analytical Interpretation of Martin Buber's I & Thou*. Cornell University Press, 1973 (paperback).

Kohn, Hans. *Martin Buber, sein Werk und seine Zeit: Ein Versuch über Religion und Politik*. Hellerau: Jakob Hegner Verlag, 1930.

———. *Martin Buber, sein Werk und seine Zeit: Ein Beitrag zur Geistesgeschichte Mitteleuropas 1880–1930*. Supplement 1930–1960 by Robert Weltsch. (2d ed. enlarged by a Foreword and an Afterword.) Köln: J. Melzer Verlag, 1961.

Kraft, Werner. *Gespräche mit Martin Buber*. Munich: Kösel Verlag, 1966.

Kraus, Hans-Joachim. 'Gespräch mit Martin Buber.' *Evangelische Theologie* (Munich), July–August, 1952, pp. 59–77.

Lang, Bernhard. *Martin Buber und das dialogische Leben*. Bern: H. Lang, 1963.

Levin-Goldschmidt, Hermann. *Abschied von Martin Buber*. Köln and Olten: Jakob Hegner Verlag, 1966.

Levinson, Nathan Peter. *Martin Buber: Ein jüdischer Denker und Humanist*. Frankfurt am Main: Europäische Verlagsanstalt, 1966.

Lewisohn, Ludwig. *Cities and Men*. New York: Harper & Brothers, 1927. 'Martin Buber,' pp. 200–212.

———. *Rebirth: A Book of Modern Jewish Thought*, p. 87 ff. New York: Harper & Brothers, 1935.

Liptzin, Solomon. *Germany's Stepchildren*. Philadelphia: The Jewish Publication Society of America, 5074/1944. Chapter 17, 'Martin Buber,' pp. 255–69.

Manheim, Werner. *Martin Buber*. New York: Twayne, 1974.

Maringer, Simon. *Martin Bubers Metaphysik der Dialogik im Zusammenhang neuerer philosophischer und theologischer Stroemungen—Darstellung und Kritik*. Köln: Buchdruckerei Steiner, 1936.

Martin, Bernard. *Great Twentieth-Century Jewish Philosophers: Chestov, Rosenzweig, Buber*. With selections from their writings. (Edited with an Introduction.) New York: Macmillan, 1969, 1970.

Martin Buber: An Appreciation of His Life and Thought. New York: American Friends of the Hebrew University, 1965. (Contributors: Judah Nadich, Maurice Friedman, Seymour Siegel, Paul Tillich, Henry Sonneborn.)

Martin Buber: Fünf Ansprachen: Anlässlich der Verleihung des Friedenspreises des Deutschen Buchhandels. Frankfurt am Main: Börsenverein Deutscher Verleger- und Buchhändler-Verbände, 1953.

Martin Buber: L'homme et le philosophe. Introduction by Robert Weltsch (Centre national des hautes études juives, Bruxelles). Brussels: Inst. de Sociologie Solvay, 1968. Contents: 'L'anthropologie philosophique de Martin Buber' by Gabriel Marcel; 'La pensée de Martin Buber et le judaïsme contemporaine' by Emmanuel Levinas; 'Martin Buber: De l'individu à la personne' by André Lacocque.

Martin Buber: Reden und Aufsätze zum 80 Geburtstag. Düsseldorf: Zentralrat den Juden in Deutschland, 1958.

Martin Buber und sein Werk: Zu seinem sechzigsten Geburtstag im Februar

Bibliography

1938 überreicht vom Schocken Verlag-Jüdischer Buchverlag. Berlin: Schocken, 1938.

Mente, A. *Das Gepenstands—Verständnis personale—Pedagogik: Systematische erörtert min Anschluss an M.B. und Romano Guardini als Beitrag zu Diskussion vom der Begriff der Bildungsguts.* 1964.

Michel, Wilhelm. *Das Leiden am Ich.* ('Martin Bubers Gang in die Wirklichkeit,' pp. 267-93.) Bremen: Carl Schünemann Verlag, 1930.

———. *Martin Buber: Sein Gang in die Wirklichkeit.* Frankfurt am Main: Rütten & Loening, 1926.

Misrahi, R. *Martin Buber, philosophe de la relation.* Présentation, choix de textes, bibliographie (Coll. Phil. de tous les temps). Paris: Seghers, 1968.

Moore, Donald J. *Martin Buber, Prophet of Religious Secularism: The Criticism of Institutional Religion in the Writings of Martin Buber.* Philadelphia: Jewish Publication Society of America, 1974.

München ehrt Martin Buber. Munich: Ner-Tamid Verlag, 1961.

Neuenschwander, Ulrich. *Denker des Glaubens.* Gütersloh: Gütersloher Verlagshaus Mohn, 1974.

Nicodemus (Melville Channing-Pearce). *Renascence: An Essay in Faith*, pp. 67-75, 161 f. London: Faber and Faber, 1943.

Nieler, Josef Maria. *Begegnungen, Carl Sonnenschein, Peter Lippert, Theador Steinbüchel, Johannes Pinsk, Ernst Beutler, Ernst Michel, Martin Buber.* 1966.

Nigg, Walter. *Martin Bubers Weg in unserer Zeit.* First issue of *Religiöse Gegenwartsfragen, Bausteine zu einem kommenden Protestantismus*, ed. Josef Böni and Walter Nigg. Bern: Verlag Paul Haupt, 1940.

Noveck, Simon (ed.). *Contemporary Jewish Thought: A Reader.* (Sections 48-54, pp. 243-87.) B'nai B'rith Great Books Series: Volume 4. Washington, D.C.: B'nai B'rith Department of Adult Jewish Education, 1963.

Oesterreicher, John M. (ed.). *The Bridge: A Yearbook of Judaeo-Christian Studies*, Vol. 3. (John M. Oesterreicher, 'The Hasidic Movement'; John McDermott, 'Martin Buber's I-Thou Philosophy'; Gerard S. Sloyan, 'Buber and the Significance of Jesus.') New York: Pantheon Books, 1958.

Oldham, Joseph Houldsworth. 'Life as Dialogue.' *The Christian News-Letters.* Supplement to No. 281 (March 19, 1974), pp. 7-16.

———. *Real Life Is Meeting.* London: The Sheldon Press; New York: Macmillan Co., 1947.

Oliver, Roy. *The Wanderer and the Way: The Hebrew Tradition in the Writings of Martin Buber.* Ithaca, New York: Cornell University Press, 1968; London: East & West Library, 1968.

Pannwitz, Rudolph. 'Der Chassidismus' (a discussion of Buber's *Hasidism, Tales of the Hasidim,* and *For the Sake of Heaven*). *Merkur* (Munich), Vol. 8 (1954), pp. 810-30.

Paul, Leslie Allen. *The Meaning of Human Existence*, pp. 24, 90 f., 110, 129 ff., 136-40, 148-53, 158, 182 f., 192 ff., 197 f., 227-32. Philadelphia and New York: J. P. Lippincott, 1950.

Pfeiffer, Johannes. 'Zwiesprache mit Martin Buber.' *Eckart* (Berlin), Vol. 21 (February-March 1952), 219-28.

Pfuetze, Paul E. 'Martin Buber and Jewish Mysticism.' *Religion in Life*, Vol. 16 (1947), 553-67.

Bibliography

————. *Self, Society, Existence: Human Nature and Dialogue in the Thought of G. H. Mead and Martin Buber.* Foreword by H. Richard Niebuhr. Westport, Conn.: Greenwood Press, 1973. (Published 1954 under title *The Social Self.*)

Przywara, Erich, S. J. 'Judentum und Christentum.' *Stimme der Zeit*, Vol. 110 (1925–26), pp. 81–99. Reprinted in Przywara's *Das Ringen der Zeit.*

Read, Herbert. *Education Through Art.* (2d ed., pp. 137 f., 279–89.) New York: Pantheon Books, 1945.

Reeves, Marjorie. *Growing Up in a Modern Society*, pp. 9–12, 34–38. London: University of London Press, 1946.

Rollins, Ernest Wm. and Zohn, Harry (eds.). *Men of Dialogue: Martin Buber and Albrecht Goes.* Preface by Maurice Friedman. New York: Funk & Wagnalls, 1969.

Rosenblüth, Pinchas Erich. *Martin Buber: Sein Denken und Wirken.* Hannover: Niedersächsischen Landeszentrale für Politische Bildung, 1968.

Rosenheim, Jacob. *Beiträge zur Orientierung im jüdischen Geistesleben der Gegenwart.* (Chapter 2, 'Martin Buber und sein Kreis,' pp. 6–32.) Zurich: Verlag 'Arzenu,' 5680/1920.

Rosenzweig, Franz. 'Aus Bubers Dissertation.' In *Aus unbekannten Schriften: Festgabe für Martin Buber,* ed. Karl Joel, pp. 240–44. Berlin: Lambert Schneider Verlag, 1928.

————. 'The Builders: Concerning the Law' and 'Revelation and Law (Martin Buber and Franz Rosenzweig).' In *On Jewish Learning,* ed. Nahum N. Glatzer. New York: Schocken Books, 1955 (clothbound and paperback).

————. 'Die Bauleute. Ueber das Gesetz. An Martin Buber.' In *Kleinere Schriften,* pp. 106–20. Berlin: Schocken Verlag, 1937.

————. *Briefe,* selected and edited by Edith Rosenzweig in cooperation with Ernst Simon. (Pp. 371, 437, 443 f., 502 ff., 542, 546, 553, 561 f., 608 ff., 613, 630, 633. Cf. also letter No. 508.) Berlin: Schocken Verlag, 1935.

————. 'Martin Buber.' *Jüdisches Lexikon.* Berlin: Jüdischer Verlag, 1927.

Rosenzweig, Franz, and Strauss, Ludwig (eds.). *Aus unbekannten Schriften: Festgabe für Martin Buber.* Berlin: Lambert Schneider Verlag, 1928.

Rotten, Elizabeth. 'Aus den Offenbarungen der Schwester Mechtild von Magdeburg.' In *Aus unbekannten Schriften: Festgabe für Martin Buber,* p. 654. Berlin: Lambert Schneider Verlag, 1928.

Sainio, Matti A. *Pädagogisches Denken bei Martin Buber.* Jyväskylä: Verlag von Jyväskylän Ylipistoyhdistys, 1955.

Sborowitz, Arie. 'Beziehung und Bestimmung: Die Lehren von Martin Buber und C. G. Jung in ihrem Verhältnis zueinander.' *Psyche.* (Heidelberg), Vol. 2 (1948), pp. 9–56.

Schaeder, Grete. 'Einem biographischen Abriss.' In *Martin Buber: Briefwechsel aus sieben Jahrzehnten.* Heidelberg: Lambert Schneider Verlag, 1972.

————. *Martin Buber: Hebräischer Humanismus.* Göttingen: Vandenhoeck und Ruprecht, 1966.

————. *The Hebrew Humanism of Martin Buber,* trans. Noah J. Jacobs. Detroit: Wayne State University Press, 1973.

Schilpp, Paul Arthur, and Friedman, Maurice (eds.). *Martin Buber.* Stuttgart: W. Kohlhammer Verlag, 1963. (The German edition of *The Philosophy of Martin Buber,* Vol. 12 in *The Library of Living Philosophers.*)

Bibliography

————. *The Philosophy of Martin Buber.* La Salle, Illinois: Open Court, 1967; Cambridge University Press, 1967.

'Die Schrift'—Zum Abschluss ihrer Verdeutschung. Special issue published by 'Mitteilungsblatt' (MB) des Irgun Olej Merkas Europa. Tel Aviv: Biaton Publishing Co., 1961.

Schraeder, Janet E. *Dialogue with Martin Buber: Martin Buber and the Quaker Experience.* Wallingford, Pennsylvania: Pendle Hill Publications, 1973.

Simon, Charlie M. *Martin Buber: Wisdom in Our Time.* New York: E. P. Dutton, 1969.

Simon, Ernst. 'Jewish Adult Education in Nazi Germany as Spiritual Resistance.' In *Leo Baeck Institute Year Book,* pp. 68–104. London: East and West Library, 1956.

————. 'Martin Buber and the Faith of Israel.' *Iyyun* (Hebrew), Philosophical Quarterly (Jerusalem), Vol. 9, No. 1 (1958), pp. 13–50.

————. 'Martin Buber and German Jewry.' In *Leo Baeck Institute Year Book,* pp. 3–39. London: East and West Library, 1958.

————. 'Martin Buber: His Way between Thought and Deed' (on his 70th Anniversary). *Jewish Frontier,* Vol. 15, No. 2 (February 1948), pp. 25–28.

————. 'Martin Buber und das deutsche Jüdentum.' In *Deutsches Jüdentum: Aufstieg und Krise: Gestalten, Ideen, Werke.* Fourteen monographs edited by Robert Weltsch. Stuttgart: Deutsche Verlags-Anstalt, 1963.

————. 'Religious Humanism.' In *Goethe and the Modern Age,* ed. Arnold Bergstraesser, pp. 304–25. Chicago: Henry Regnery, 1950.

Smith, Ronald Gregor. *Martin Buber: Exposition and Criticism.* London: Carey Kingsgate Press, 1966; and Richmond: John Knox Press, 1967.

————. *Martin Buber.* Makers of Contemporary Theology Series. Richmond: John Knox Press, 1967 (also paperback).

Stahmer, Harold. *'Speak That I May See Thee!': The Religious Significance of Language.* (Chapter 5.) New York: Macmillan Co., 1968.

Streiker, Lowell D. *The Promise of Buber: Desultory Philippics and Ironic Affirmations.* Promise of Theology series, ed. Martin Marty. Philadelphia: Lippincott, 1969.

Susman, Margaret. 'Die Botschaft der chassidischen Mystik an unsere Zeit.' *Der Jude,* Vol. 10, No. 5 (March 1928), 'Sonderheft zu Martin Bubers fünfzigstem Geburtstag.'

Sutter, Gerda. *Wirklichkeit als Verhältnis: Der dialogische Aufstieg bei Martin Buber.* Munich: A. Pustet, 1972.

Tepfer, John J. 'Martin Buber's Neo-Mysticism.' In *Yearbook of the Central Conference of American Rabbis,* Vol. 44 (1934).

Thieme, Karl. 'Martin Buber als Interpret der Bibel.' *Zeitschrift für Religions- und Geistesgeschichte* (Köln), Vol. 6, No. 1 (1954), pp. 1–9.

Tillich, Paul. 'Jewish Influences on Contemporary Christian Theology.' *Cross Currents,* Vol. 2, No. 3 (Spring 1952), pp. 38–42.

————. 'Martin Buber and Christian Thought.' *Commentary,* Vol. 5, No. 6 (June 1948), pp. 515–21.

Trüb, Hans. *Heilung aus der Begegnung: Eine Auseinandersetzung mit der Psychologie C. G. Jungs,* ed. Ernst Michel and Arie Sborowitz. Stuttgart: Ernst Klett Verlag, 1952.

305

Bibliography

————. 'Individuation, Schuld und Entscheidung: Ueber die Grenzen der Psychologie.' In *Die kulturelle Bedeutung der komplexen Psychologie*, edited by Psychologischen Club Zurich, pp. 529–55. Berlin: Julius Springer Verlag, 1935.

————. 'Vom Selbst zur Welt: Der zwiefache Auftrag des Psychotherapeuten,' *Psyche* (Heidelberg), Vol. 1 (1947), 41–67. Also separately, Zurich: R. Römer, Speer-Verlag, 1947.

Urs von Balthasar, Hans. *Einsame Zwiesprache: Martin Buber und das Christentum.* Köln and Olten: Jakob Hegner Verlag, 1958.

————. *Martin Buber and Christianity: A Dialogue between Israel and the Church*, trans. Alexander Dru. London: Harvill Press, 1961; New York: Macmillan.

Van der Hoop, J. H. 'Religion as a Psychic Necessity.' *Psyche* (London), Vol. 7, No. 4 (April 1927), pp. 102–119.

Wachinger, Lorenz. *Der Glaubensbegriff Martin Bubers.* Munich: M. Hueber, 1974.

Wasmuth, Ewald. 'Martin Buber: Prophet in verdunkelter Zeit,' *Die Neue Rundschau*, No. 4 (1957).

Wehr, Gerhard. *Martin Buber in Selbstzeugnissen und Bilddokumenten.* 2d ed. Reinbek bei Hamburg: Rowohlt, 1971.

Weiser, Richard. *Verantwortung im Wandel der Zeit: Einübung in geistiges Handeln: Jaspers, Buber, C. F. von Weizsächer, Guardini, Heidegger.* Mainz: U. Hase and Koehler, 1967.

Weltsch, Felix. 'Freiheit un Bindung in Nationalismus und Religiostät,' *Der Jude*, Vol. 10, No. 5 (March 1928), 'Sonderheft zu Martin Bubers fünfzigstem Geburtstag,' pp. 86–89.

Weltsch, Robert. 'Martin Buber.' In *Jüdisches Lexikon.* Berlin: Jüdischer Verlag, 1927.

————. 'Nachwort: 1930–1960.' In Hans Kohn, *Martin Buber, sein Werk und sein Zeit: Ein Beitrag zur Geistesgeschichte Mitteleuropas 1880–1930.* Köln: Joseph Melzer Verlag, 1961.

————. 'Sonderheft zu Martin Bubers fünfzigstem Geburtstag' (*Der Jude*, Vol. 10, No. 5 [March 1928]), ed. Robert Weltsch.

Wodehouse, Helen. 'Martin Buber's "I and Thou."' *Philosophy*, Vol. 20 (1945), pp. 17–30.

Wolf, Ernst M. 'Martin Buber and German Jewry: Prophet and Teacher to a Generation in Catastrophe.' *Judaism*, Vol. 1, No. 4 (October 1952), 346–52.

Wood, Robert E. *Martin Buber's Ontology: An Analysis of I and Thou.* Evanston: Northwestern University Press, 1969.

For other articles on Buber, 1930 and before, see Hans Kohn, *Martin Buber.*

WORKS OTHER THAN BUBER'S ON DIALOGUE AND THE I-THOU RELATION

Barth, Karl. *Die kirchliche Dogmatik.* Vol. 3: *Die Lehre von der Schöpfung*, Second Part (published separately), 'Die Grundform der Menschlichkeit,'

Bibliography

pp. 265–340. Zurich: Evangelischer Verlag, A. G. Zollikon, 1948.

Berdyaev, Nicholas. *Solitude and Society*, Third and Fifth Meditations. (See previous section for facts of publication.)

Binswanger, Ludwig. *Grundformen und Erkenntnis menschlichen Daseins.* Zurich: Max Niehans Verlag, 1942.

Brunner, Emil. *Man in Revolt: A Christian Anthropology.* Translated by Olive Wyon. Philadelphia: Westminster Press, 1947.

———. *Warheit als Begegnung: Sechs Vorlesungen über das christliche Wahrheitsverständnis.* Berlin: Furche-Verlag, 1938. Translated as *The Divine Human Encounter* (Philadelphia: Westminster Press, 1943; London: S.C.M. Press, 1944).

Camus, Albert. 'Neither Victims nor Executioners.' In Paul Goodman (ed.). *Seeds of Liberation.* New York: George Braziller, 1964.

———. *The Rebel: An Essay on Man in Revolt.* New York: Alfred A. Knopf, Vintage Books, 1956.

———. *Resistance, Rebellion, and Death.* New York: Modern Library, 1960.

Cullberg, John. *Das Du und die Wirklichkeit.* (See Works about Buber, above.)

Ebner, Ferdinand. *Das Wort und die geistigen Realitäten: Pneumatologische Fragmente.* Innsbruck: Brenner-Verlag, 1921.

Farber, Leslie H. *The Ways of the Will: Essays in the Psychology and Psychopathology of the Will.* New York: Basic Books, 1966.

Farmer, Herbert H. *The Servant of the Word.* (Chapter 2, 'The I-Thou Relationship.') New York: Charles Scribner's Sons, 1942.

———. *The World and God: A Study of Prayers, Providence, and Miracle in Christian Experience.* London: Nisbet & Co., 1935.

Feuerbach, Ludwig. *Grundsätze der Philosophie der Zukunft* (1843).

Fison, J. E. *The Blessing of the Holy Spirit.* London: Longmans, Green, 1950.

Frankfort, H., and Frankfort, H. A. 'Myth and Reality.' In *The Intellectual Adventure of Ancient Man: An Essay on Speculative Thought in the Ancient Near East,* by H. and H. A. Frankfort, John A. Wilson, Thorkild Jacobsen, and William A. Irwin. Chicago: University of Chicago Press, 1946.

Friedman, Maurice. *Touchstones of Reality: Existential Trust and the Community of Peace.* New York: E. P. Dutton, 1972; paperback, 1974.

Goes, Albrecht. *Von Mensch zu Mensch: Bemühungen.* Berlin: S. Fischer Verlag, 1953.

Gogarten, Friedrich. *Glaube und Wirklichkeit.* Jena: Eugen Diedrichs Verlag, 1928.

———. *Ich glaube an den dreienigen Gott: Eine Untersuchung über Glauben und Geschichte.* Jena: Eugen Diedrichs Verlag, 1926.

Grisebach, Eberhard. *Gegenwart: Eine kritsche Ethik,* 1928.

Guardini, Romano. *Welt und Person: Versuche zur christlichen Lehre vom Menschen.* Würzburg: Werkbund-Verlag, 1950.

Heim, Karl. *Glaube und Denken,* Vol. I of *Der evangelische Glaube und das Denken der Gegenwart: Grundzüge einer christlichen Lebensanschauung.* Berlin: Furche-Verlag, 1931.

———. *God Transcendent: Foundation for a Christian Metaphysic.* Translated from the third revised and shortened edition of *Glaube und Denken*

by Edgar Primrose Dickie. New York: Charles Scribner's Sons, 1936.
Herberg, Will. *Judaism and Modern Man.* (See works about Buber, above.)
Howe, Reuel L. *Man's Need and God's Answer.* Greenwich, Conn.: Seabury Press, 1952.
Hutchins, Robert Maynard. 'Goethe and the Unity of Mankind.' In *Goethe and the Modern Age,* ed. Arnold Bergstraesser, pp. 385–402. Chicago: Henry Regnery, 1950.
Jaspers, Karl. *Philosophy,* Vol. 2. Chicago: University of Chicago Press, 1970.
Keyserling, Graf Hermann. 'Das Zwischenreich,' 'Instinkt und Intuition,' 'Gleichgültigkeit und Liebe.' In *Das Buch vom Ursprung.* Baden-Baden: Verlag Hans Bühler Junior, 1947 (special edition for Internationalen Keyserling-Gesellschaft).
Die Kreatur. 'Das Zwischenreich,' 'Instinkt und Intuition,' 'Gleichgültigkeit und Liebe.' A Periodical devoted primarily to religion and education. Edited by Martin Buber, Viktor von Weizsäcker, and Joseph Wittig. Berlin: Verlag Lambert Schneider, 1926–30.
Goldschmidt, Hermann Levin. *Philosophie als Dialogik.* Affoltern a. A.: Aehren Verlag, 1948.
Litt, Theodor. *Individuum und Gemeinschaft: Grundlegung der Kulturphilosophie.* 2d ed., 1923.
Löwith, Karl. *Das Individuum in der Rolle des Mitmenschen: Ein Beitrag zur anthropologischen Grundlegung der ethischen Probleme.* Munich: Drei Masken Verlag, 1928.
Macmurray, John. *The Self as Agent: The Gifford Lectures delivered in the University of Glasgow.* New York: Harper & Brothers, 1957.
———. 'The Self in Religious Reflection.' In *The Structure of Religious Experience* (chap. 2). Terry Lectures. New Haven: Yale University Press, 1936.
Marcel, Gabriel. *Being and Having.* Translated from *Etre et Avoir* by Katherine Farrer. Westminster: Dacre Press, 1949.
———. *Journal Métaphysique* (pt. 2, pp. 135–303). Paris: Librairie Gallimard, 1927.
Mayeroff, Milton. *On Caring: World Perspectives,* ed. Ruth Nanda Anshen. Vol. 43. New York and London: Harper & Row, 1971 (paperback, 1972).
Michel, Ernst. *Der Partner Gottes.* Stuttgart: 1948.
Nédoncelle, Maurice. *La réciprocité des consciences.* Paris: Aubier, Éditions Montaigne, 1942.
Niebuhr, Reinhold. *The Self and the Dramas of History.* New York: Charles Scribner's Sons, 1955.
Ricoeur, Paul. *Gabriel Marcel et Karl Jaspers: Philosophie du Mystère et Philosophie du Paradoxe.* Paris: Éditions du Temps Present, 1947. See especially Part 2, Chapter 2—'Le "toi" et la "communication." '
Riezler, Kurt. 'What is Public Opinion?' *Social Research,* Vol. 11 (1944), pp. 397–427.
Rosenstock-Huessey, Eugen. *Angewandte Seelenkunde.* Darmstadt: Roethenverlag, 1924.
———. *Der Atem des Geistes.* Frankfurt am Main: Verlag der Frankfurter Hefte, 1951.
Rosenzweig, Franz. 'Das neue Denken.' In *Kleine Schriften,* by Franz Rosen-

Bibliography

zweig. Berlin: Schocken Verlag, 1935.

————. *Der Stern der Erlösung*, 3d ed. Heidelberg: Verlag Lambert Schneider, 1954.

Scheler, Max. *Wesen und Formen der Sympathie*. 2d. ed., 1923. English translation, *Nature of Sympathy* (London: Routledge & Kegan Paul; New Haven: Yale University Press, 1954).

Stahmer, Harold. *'Speak That I May See Thee!'*: *The Religious Significance of Language*. New York: Macmillan Co., 1968.

Steinbüchel, Theodor. *Christliche Lebenshaltungen in der Krisis der Zeit und des Menschen*. Frankfurt am Main: Verlag Joseph Knecht, 1949.

Stewart, John (ed.). *Bridges Not Walls: A Book about Interpersonal Communication*. Menlo Park, Calif.: Addison-Wesley Publishing Co., 1973.

Strasser, Stephen. *The Idea of Dialogal Phenomenology*. Duquesne Studies, Philosophical Series 25. Pittsburgh: Duquesne University Press, 1969.

Tillich, Paul. *Biblical Religion and the Search for Ultimate Reality*. Chicago: University of Chicago Press, 1955.

Tournier, Paul. *The Meaning of Persons*. New York: Harper & Row, 1957.

Weizsäcker, Viktor von. 'Stücke einer medizinischen Anthropologie.' In *Arzt und Kranker*, Vol. 1, pp. 79–179. Stuttgart: K. F. Koehler Verlag, 1949.

Wust, Peter. *Naivität und Pietät*. Tübingen: Verlag von J. C. B. Mohr (Paul Siebeck), 1925.

See also the bibliographies in Cullberg, *Das Du und die Wirklichkeit*, in Goldschmidt, *Philosophie als Dialogik*, and in Rosenstock Huessy, *Der Atem des Geistes*.

INDEX